THE NEW YORK
OLD-TIME RADIO
SCHEDULE BOOK

VOLUME 3
1946·1954

KEITH D. LEE

The New York Old-Time Radio Schedule Book — Volume 3, 1946-1954
© 2011 Keith D. Lee. All Rights Reserved.

No part of this book may be reproduced in any form or by any means, electronic, mechanical, digital, photocopying or recording, except for the inclusion in a review, without permission in writing from the publisher.

Published in the USA by:
BearManor Media
PO Box 1129
Duncan, Oklahoma 73534-1129
www.bearmanormedia.com

ISBN 978-1-59393-670-9

Printed in the United States of America.
Book design by Brian Pearce | Red Jacket Press.

TABLE OF CONTENTS

Introduction 5

Listings for 1946 9

Listings for 1947 67

Listings for 1948 125

Listings for 1949 183

Listings for 1950 241

Listings for 1951 299

Listings for 1952 357

Listings for 1953 415

Listings for 1954 473

INTRODUCTION

The purpose of this series of books is not to be the ultimate source of OTR information; rather, it is to be used alongside the sources listed below. This book is meant to be used not only by OTR fans who want to research the history of OTR; but, to also remind the older generation of the superior quality of entertainment they once had and to introduce to future generations the wonderful imagination and creativity that was once OTR.

These books are a list of national and local New York-based OTR shows from Fall, 1929 through Summer, 1954, in an easy-to-read grid format. Each section lists the OTR shows that were playing during that particular calendar season in that particular OTR year. The shows that are listed were on the four major OTR networks (Blue/ABC, CBS, MBS, and NBC) and their local New York affiliates from 9am to 11pm, Monday through Sunday.

In reading any of the sample chapters, please note the following:

Each cell in the grid represents a fifteen minute block of time.

Each blank cell means that the preceding show is still on. I deferred from using quotation marks because it looked too unreadable.

A slash between the names of two or more daily shows either in the same cell or adjoining cells signifies that those shows shared that timeslot on intermittant days for each week during that particular calendar season. In the case of weekly shows, a slash signifies that the shows shared the same timeslot for part of that particular calendar season.

Such generic show titles as "Concert Orchestra," "Dance Orchestra," "Health Talk," "Music," "News," "Public Affairs," "Sports," "Symphony Orchestra," and "Talk," and any combination thereof, are used. In the case of a daily show, such a generic title signifies the type of show on during the week. In the case of a weekly show, the networks or their affiliated stations couldn't find a sponsor for that timeslot and filled it with a generic show of music, talk, etc.

The information has been thoroughly checked for absolute correctness based on the OTR sources that still exist, contradictions and errors in them notwithstanding. Every effort has been made to correct errors introduced in the process of typesetting these books, but corrections are welcome and can be sent to the publisher.

This series of books are the summation of two and one half years of research using the following sources:

New York Times (1929-1954).

Summers, Harrison B. *A Thirty Year History of Radio Programs 1926-1956.* Ayer Company, NH, 1958.

Dunning, John. *The Encyclopedia of Old-Time Radio.* Oxford University Press, NY, 1998.

Hickerson, Jay. *The New, Revised Ultimate History of Network Radio Programming and Guide to All Circulating Shows.* Self Published, CT, 1996.

Since there aren't too many OTR sources left anymore and many of them contradict one another, many thanks are necessary to the fellow OTR fans who helped me gather the correct schedule information for this book. Thanks to Elizabeth McLeod and Jay Hickerson for allowing me access to their voluminous expertise. Thanks to Tom Van Der Voort for sending me copies of his many OTR magazines. Thanks to Charlie Summers for allowing me to advertise on his OTR list and digest. Thanks to Lou Genco for advertising my book on his OTR website. A final thank you to the many OTR fans who sent me their information and remembrances. All have been very helpful in figuring out what shows went where and when. Hopefully, this will inspire the next generations to research even more into the history of OTR.

LISTINGS FOR 1946

EVENING — WINTER, 1946

Sunday

	ABC	CBS	MBS	NBC
6pm	The Radio Hall of Fame	The Adventures of Ozzie and Harriet	The Return of Nick Carter	The Catholic Hour
6:15				
6:30	Phil Davis' Sunday Party	The Baby Snooks Show	Cedric Foster, news	The Great Gildersleeve
6:45			Forest Lewis Jr., news	
7pm	Drew Pearson, news	The Adventures of the Thin Man	The Operatic Revue	The Lucky Strike Program, Jack Benny
7:15	Don Gardiner, news			
7:30	The Quiz Kids	Blondie	Melvin Elliott, news	The Fitch Bandwagon
7:45			Max Lerner, news	
8pm	The Ford Sunday Evening Hour	The Marlin Hurt and Beulah Show	A. L. Alexander's Mediation Board	The Charlie McCarthy Show
8:15				
8:30		Crime Doctor	Don't Be a Sucker	The Fred Allen Show
8:45		Ned Calmer, news (8:55pm)	Gabriel Heatter, news	
9pm	Walter Winchell's Jergens Journal	Request Performance	Exploring the Unknown	The Manhattan Merry-Go-Round
9:15	Louella Parsons, gossip			
9:30	Listen to La Guardia	The Texaco Star Theater, James Melton	Double or Nothing	The American Album of Familiar Music
9:45	Jimmy Fidler, gossip			
10pm	The Theater Guild on the Air	Take It or Leave It	Freedom of Opportunity	The Hour of Charm
10:15				
10:30		We, the People	The Hollywood Theater	Meet Me at Parky's
10:45				

EVENING — WINTER, 1946

Monday

ABC	CBS	MBS	NBC	
Walter Kiernan, news	Quincy Howe, news	Paul Schubert, news	Lyle Van, news	6pm
Here's Morgan	James Carroll, songs	The Man on the Street	Serenade to America	6:15
Harry Wismer, sports	The Voice of Eileen Farrell	Fred Vandeventer, news		6:30
Cal Tinney, news	The World Today	Stan Lomax, sports	Lowell Thomas, news	6:45
Taylor Grant, news	The Jack Kirkwood Show	Fulton Lewis Jr., news	The Chesterfield Supper Club	7pm
Raymond Gram Swing, news	The Jack Smith Show	The Answer Man	John W. Vandercook, news	7:15
The Lone Ranger	The Bob Hawk Show	Frank Singiser, news	Red Barber's Star Review	7:30
		Bill Brandt, sports sports	H. V. Kaltenborn, news	7:45
Lum and Abner	Vox Pop	Bulldog Drummond	The Cavalcade of America	8pm
Hedda Hopper, gossip				8:15
The Fat Man	Joanie's Tea Room	Sherlock Holmes	The Voice of Firestone	8:30
	Bill Henry, news (8:55pm)			8:45
I Deal in Crime	The Lux Radio Theater	Gabriel Heatter, news	The Bell Telephone Hour	9pm
		Real Stories from Real Life		9:15
Forever Tops		Spotlight Bands	Information, Please	9:30
				9:45
Jimmy Gleason's Diner	The Lady Esther Screen Guild Theater	Henry J. Taylor, news	The Carnation Contented Hour	10pm
		The John Gart Trio		10:15
Hoosier Hop	Crime Photographer	Detect A Tune	Dr. I. Q., The Mental Banker	10:30
				10:45

EVENING — WINTER, 1946

Tuesday

	ABC	CBS	MBS	NBC
6pm	Walter Kiernan, news	Quincy Howe, news	Paul Schubert, news	Lyle Van, news
6:15	Here's Morgan	Patti Clayton, songs	The Man on the Street	Serenade to America
6:30	Harry Wismer, sports	Evelyn Pasen, songs	Fred Vandeventer, news	
6:45	Cal Tinney, news	The World Today	Stan Lomax, sports	Lowell Thomas, news
7pm	Taylor Grant, news	The Jack Kirkwood Show	Fulton Lewis Jr., news	The Chesterfield Supper Club
7:15	Raymond Gram Swing, news	The Jack Smith Show	The Answer Man	John W. Vandercook, news
7:30	Boston Blackie	The American Melody Hour	Arthur Hale, news	His Honor, the Barber
7:45			Bill Brandt, sports sports	
8pm	Lum and Abner	Big Town	Leave It to Mike	The Johnny Desmond Follies
8:15	Elmer Davis, news			
8:30	The Alan Young Show	Theater of Romance	The Falcon	A Date with Judy
8:45		Bill Henry, news (8:55pm)		
9pm	Guy Lombardo Orchestra	Inner Sanctum Mysteries	Gabriel Heatter, news	Amos 'n' Andy
9:15			Real Stories from Real Life	
9:30	The Doctors Talk It Over	This is My Best	The American Forum of the Air	Fibber Magee and Molly
9:45	Hank D'Amico Orchestra			
10pm	Concert Time	Bob Crosby Orchestra		The Pepsodent Show, Bob Hope
10:15			I Was a Convict	
10:30	The Green Hornet	Congress Speaks	The Longines Symphonette	The Raleigh Cigarette Program, Red Skelton
10:45		Behind the Scenes at CBS		

EVENING — WINTER, 1946

Wednesday

ABC	CBS	MBS	NBC	
Walter Kiernan, news	Quincy Howe, news	Paul Schubert, news	Lyle Van, news	6pm
Here's Morgan	James Carroll, songs	The Man on the Street	Serenade to America	6:15
Harry Wismer, sports	The Voice of Eileen Farrell	Fred Vandeventer, news		6:30
Cal Tinney, news	The World Today	Stan Lomax, sports	Lowell Thomas, news	6:45
Taylor Grant, news	The Jack Kirkwood Show	Fulton Lewis Jr., news	The Chesterfield Supper Club	7pm
Raymond Gram Swing, news	The Jack Smith Show	The Answer Man	John W. Vandercook, news	7:15
The Lone Ranger	The Adventures of Ellery Queen	Frank Singiser, news	Red Barber's Star Review	7:30
		Bill Brandt, sports sports	H. V. Kaltenborn, news	7:45
Lum and Abner	The Jack Carson Show	Can You Top This	Mr. and Mrs. North	8pm
Elmer Davis, news				8:15
The Fishing and Hunting Club	Dr. Christian	The Fresh Up Show, Bert Lahr	The Raleigh Room, Hildegarde	8:30
	Bill Henry, news (8:55pm)			8:45
Edgar Hayes Orchestra	Songs By Sinatra	Gabriel Heatter, news	Time to Smile, Eddie Cantor	9pm
		Real Stories from Real Life		9:15
So You Want to Lead a Band	Maisie	Spotlight Bands	Mr. District Attorney	9:30
				9:45
Ralph Norman Orchestra	Great Moments in Music	Radio Auction	Kay Kyser's College of Musical Knowledge	10pm
				10:15
Betty and Buddy, songs	The N-K Musical Showroom, Andrew Sisters	The Longines Symphonette		10:30
The Galli Sisters, songs				10:45

EVENING — WINTER, 1946

Thursday

	ABC	CBS	MBS	NBC
6pm	Walter Kiernan, news	Quincy Howe, news	Paul Schubert, news	Lyle Van, news
6:15	Here's Morgan	Patti Clayton, songs	The Man on the Street	Serenade to America
6:30	Harry Wismer, sports	Encore Appearance	Fred Vandeventer, news	
6:45	Cal Tinney, news	The World Today	Stan Lomax, sports	Lowell Thomas, news
7pm	Taylor Grant, news	The Jack Kirkwood Show	Fulton Lewis Jr., news	The Chesterfield Supper Club
7:15	Raymond Gram Swing, news	The Jack Smith Show	The Answer Man	John W. Vandercook, news
7:30	Professor Quiz	Mr. Keen, Tracer of Lost Persons	Arthur Hale, news	The Bob Burns Show
7:45			Bill Brandt, sports sports	
8pm	Lum and Abner	Suspense	One Night Stand	Maxwell House Coffee Time, Burns and Allen
8:15	Earl Godwin, news			
8:30	America's Town Meeting of the Air	The FBI in Peace and War	Rogue's Gallery	The Birdseye Open House, Dinah Shore
8:45		Bill Henry, news (8:55pm)		
9pm		Music Millions Love	Gabriel Heatter, news	The Kraft Music Hall, Bing Crosby
9:15			Real Stories from Real Life	
9:30	Detect and Collect	Hobby Lobby	The Treasure Hour of Song	The Sealtest Village Store, Arden and Haley
9:45				
10pm	Curtain Time	Island Venture	You Make the News	Abbott and Costello
10:15				
10:30	Bob Grant Orchestra	The Powder Box Theater	The Longines Symphonette	The Rudy Vallee Show
10:45	Janet Flanner, news			

EVENING — WINTER, 1946

Friday

ABC	CBS	MBS	NBC	
Walter Kiernan, news	Quincy Howe, news	Paul Schubert, news	Lyle Van, news	6pm
Here's Morgan	James Carroll, songs	The Man on the Street	Serenade to America	6:15
Harry Wismer, sports	The Voice of Eileen Farrell	Fred Vandeventer, news		6:30
Cal Tinney, news	The World Today	Stan Lomax, sports	Lowell Thomas, news	6:45
Taylor Grant, news	The Jack Kirkwood Show	Fulton Lewis Jr., news	The Chesterfield Supper Club	7pm
Raymond Gram Swing, news	The Jack Smith Show	The Answer Man	John W. Vandercook, news	7:15
The Lone Ranger	The Ginny Simms Show	Frank Singiser, news	Red Barber's Star Review	7:30
		Bill Brandt, sports sports	H. V. Kaltenborn, news	7:45
Blind Date	The Aldrich Family	Ray Bloch Orchestra	Highways in Melody	8pm
				8:15
This is Your FBI	Kate Smith Sings	So You Think You Know Music	Duffy's Tavern	8:30
	Bill Henry, news (8:55pm)			8:45
Famous Jury Trials	It Pays to Be Ignorant	Gabriel Heatter, news	People Are Funny	9pm
		Real Stories from Real Life		9:15
The Sheriff	Those Websters	Spotlight Bands	Waltz Time	9:30
				9:45
Madison Square Garden Boxing	The Jimmy Durante Show	Henry J. Taylor, news	The Molle' Mystery Theater	10pm
		The John Gart Trio		10:15
	Pabst Blue Ribbon Town, Danny Kaye	The Longines Symphonette	The Colgate Sports Newsreel, Bill Stern	10:30
			Public Affairs	10:45

EVENING — WINTER, 1946

Saturday

	ABC	CBS	MBS	NBC
6pm	William Fleisher, news	Quincy Howe, news	Paul Schubert, news	Lyle Van, news
6:15	Edwin D. Canham, news	The People's Platform	Strictly Personal	Music of Manhattan
6:30	Harry Wismer, sports		Fred Vandeventer, news	
6:45	Labor USA	The World Today	Stan Lomax, sports	Religion in the News
7pm	It's Your Business	The Textron Theater	Guess Who	Our Foreign Policy
7:15	Correspondents Abroad			
7:30	Dick Tracy	The First Nighter Program	Arthur Hale, news	Easy Money
7:45			The Answer Man	
8pm	Woody Herman Orchestra	The Dick Haymes Show	The Whisper Men	The Life of Riley
8:15				
8:30	The Man from G-2	The Mayor of the Town	Rhapsody for Strings	Truth or Consequences
8:45		Ned Calmer, news (8:55pm)		
9pm	Gangbusters	Your Hit Parade	Leave It to the Girls	The National Barn Dance
9:15				
9:30	Boston Symphony Orchestra		Break the Bank	Can You Top This
9:45		Saturday Night Serenade		
10pm			The Chicago Theater of the Air	The Judy Canova Show
10:15		The Continental Celebrity Club, Jackie Kelk		
10:30	The Garden of Song			Grand Ole Opry
10:45	Hayloft Hoedown	Public Affairs		

DAYTIME — WINTER, 1946

Sunday

	ABC	CBS	MBS	NBC
9am	News	News	Uncle Don Reads the Comics	News
9:15	Coast-to-Coast on a Bus	From the Organ Loft		Story to Order
9:30			The Mutual Radio Chapel	Songs for Strings
9:45		New Voices in Song		Music
10am	Message of Israel	The CBS Church of the Air	Leo Egan, news	The National Radio Pulpit
10:15			Frank Kingdon, news	
10:30	The Southernaires Quartet	Wings Over Jordan	Chaplain Jim, USA	The Horn and Hardart Children's Hour
10:45				
11am	Brunch with the Fitzgeralds	The Blue Jacket Choir	Snow Village Sketches	
11:15				
11:30	The Hour of Faith	Invitation to Learning	Brunch with Dorothy and Dick	Charles F. McCarthy, news
11:45				Solitaire Time
12pm	Fiorello H. La Guardia, talk	The Salt Lake Tabernacle Choir	The Show Shop	The Eternal Light
12:15				
12:30	The Piano Playhouse	Transatlantic Call	Keeping Up with Wigglesworth	The Robert Merrill Show
12:45			Melvin Elliott, news	
1pm	John B. Kennedy, news	The CBS Church of the Air	The Canary Pet Shop	Ed Herlihy, news
1:15	Orson Welles, talk		Ilka Chase, talk	America United
1:30	Sammy Kaye's Sunday Serenade	Problems of Peace	Sweetheart Time	The University of Chicago Round Table
1:45		Edward R. Murrow, news		

DAYTIME — WINTER, 1946

Monday-Friday

ABC	CBS	MBS	NBC	
The Breakfast Club	Joe King, news	Frazier Hunt, news	Honeymoon in New York	*9am*
	Arthur Godfrey Time	Aunt Mary		*9:15*
		Alfred W. McCann, food	Adelaide Hawley, talk	*9:30*
			Around Town / Daytime Classics	*9:45*
My True Story	Valiant Lady	Henry Gladstone, news	Robert St. John, news	*10am*
	The Light of the World	Bessy Beatty, talk	Lora Lawton	*10:15*
Hymns of All Churches	The Strange Romance of Evelyn Winters		The Road of Life	*10:30*
Listening Post / Lisa Sergio, talk	Bachelor's Children		Joyce Jordan, MD	*10:45*
Breakfast with Breneman	Amanda of Honeymoon Hill	Prescott Robinson, news	Fred Waring Orchestra	*11am*
	Second Husband	Tello-Test Quiz		*11:15*
Home Edition	A Woman's Life	Morning Matinee / Take It Easy Time	Barry Cameron	*11:30*
Between the Bookends	Aunt Jenny's True Life Stories	Victor Lindlahr, health	David Harum	*11:45*
Glamour Manor, Cliff Arquette	Kate Smith Speaks	William Lang, news	Don Goddard, news	*12pm*
	Big Sister	Hymns You Love, Richard Maxwell	Maggie McNellis, talk	*12:15*
The Women's Exchange	The Romance of Helen Trent	Henry Gladstone, news	The Art Van Damme Quartet	*12:30*
	Our Gal Sunday	The Answer Man		*12:45*
H. R. Baukhage, news	Life Can Be Beautiful	Musical Appetizer	Mary Margaret McBride, talk	*1pm*
Constance Bennett, talk	Ma Perkins	Jack Bundy's Album		*1:15*
Galen Drake, talk	Young Dr. Malone	Vincent Lopez Orchestra		*1:30*
	The Road of Life	The John J. Anthony Program	Morgan Beatty, news	*1:45*

DAYTIME — WINTER, 1946

Sunday

	ABC	CBS	MBS	NBC
2pm	Dorothy Claire, songs	The Radio Reader's Digest	Judy Lang, songs	Harvest of Stars
2:15			The Stan Lomax Album	
2:30	National Vespers	Hollywood Star Time	Melvin Elliott, news	The Westinghouse Program, John C. Thomas
2:45			Symphonic Strings	
3pm	Elmer Davis, news	New York Philharmonic Orchestra	The Quiz of Two Cities	The Sheaffer Parade
3:15	Galen Drake, talk			
3:30	Johnny Thompson and Ilene Woods, songs		The Longines Symphonette	One Man's Family
3:45				
4pm	Here's Morgan		Murder is My Hobby	The National Hour
4:15	News			
4:30	Mary Small's Revue	The Electric Hour, Nelson Eddy	True Detective Mysteries	The RCA Victor Show
4:45				
5pm	Jones and I	The Prudential Family Hour	The Shadow	NBC Symphony Orchestra
5:15				
5:30	Counterspy	Gene Autry's Melody Ranch	Quick as a Flash	
5:45		Quincy Howe, news		

DAYTIME — WINTER, 1946

Monday-Friday

ABC	CBS	MBS	NBC	
John B. Kennedy, news	The Second Mrs. Burton	Cedric Foster, news	The Guiding Light	2pm
Ethel and Albert	Perry Mason	Music	Today's Children	2:15
Bride and Groom	Rosemary	Queen for a Day	The Woman in White	2:30
	Tena and Tim		Masquerade	2:45
Al Pearce and His Gang	Time to Remember	Martha Deane, talk	A Woman of America	3pm
	This is New York, Danny O'Neill		Ma Perkins	3:15
Ladies Be Seated		Rambling with Gambling	Pepper Young's Family	3:30
	The Landt Trio and Curley		The Right of Happiness	3:45
The Jack Berch Show	House Party	The Better Half	Mary Noble, Backstage Wife	4pm
The Fitzgeralds, talk			Stella Dallas	4:15
Time for Women	Gordon MacRae, songs	Dr. Eddy's Food Forum	Lorenzo Jones	4:30
Hop Harrigan	Feature Story		Young Widder Brown	4:45
Terry and the Pirates	The American School of the Air	Uncle Don	When a Girl Marries	5pm
Dick Tracy		The Adventures of Superman	Portia Faces Life	5:15
Jack Armstrong, the All-American Boy	Cimarron Tavern	Captain Midnight	Just Plain Bill	5:30
Tennessee Jed	Sparrow and the Hawk	The Tom Mix Ralston Straight Shooters	Front Page Farrell	5:45

DAYTIME — WINTER, 1946

Saturday

	ABC	CBS	MBS	NBC
9am	Wake Up and Smile	Joe King, news	California Melodies	Home is What You Make It
9:15		The Garden Gate		
9:30		Columbia's Country Journal	Meet the Press	Adelaide Hawley, talk
9:45				Jeanne McKenna, songs
10am	Galen Drake, talk	Give and Take	Henry Gladstone, news	The Eileen Barton Show
10:15	Club Time		We've Got Your Number	
10:30	Vera Massey and Bob Johnson, songs	Mary Lee Taylor, cooking	Rainbow House	Archie Andrews
10:45				
11am	Tell Me Doctor	Let's Pretend	Prescott Robinson, news	The Teentimer's Club
11:15	Bible Message		Tex Fletcher, songs	
11:30	Chester Bowles, news	The Billie Burke Show	The Land of the Lost	Smilin' Ed's Buster Brown Gang
11:45	Chet Gaylord, songs			
12pm	The Piano Playhouse	The Armstrong Theater of Today	The House of Mystery	John McVane, news
12:15	Elizabeth Woodward, songs			Consumer Time
12:30	The American Farmer	Stars Over Hollywood	Henry Gladstone, news	Atlantic Spotlight
12:45			The Answer Man	
1pm	Symphonies for Youth	Grand Central Station	The Man on the Farm	The National Farm and Home Hour
1:15				
1:30		County Fair	Opry House Matinee, Eddy Arnold	The Veterans Advisor
1:45	John B. Kennedy, news			Edward Tomlinson, news

DAYTIME — WINTER, 1946

Saturday

	ABC	CBS	MBS	NBC
2pm	The Metropolitan Opera	Of Men and Books	The Louis Kaufman Show	Harry Slick Orchestra
2:15		Adventures in Science		Your Radio Reporter
2:30		Treasury Bandstand	Courtney's Record Carnival	The Baxters
2:45				The Camp Meetin' Choir
3pm		Assignment Home		Orchestras of the Nation
3:15			It's Up to You	
3:30		Public Affairs		
3:45		Cross-Section USA		
4pm		Monaghan, the Record Man	The Better Half	Doctors at Home
4:15				
4:30			One Man's Destiny	The First Piano Quartet
4:45			Horse Racing	
5pm	A Date with the Duke	Philadelphia Symphony Orchestra	The Musical Grab Bag	Music of the Moment
5:15				
5:30			Uncle Don	John W. Vandercook, news
5:45	Pleasure Parade, Paula Kelly		Lanny and Ginger, songs	Tin Pan Alley of the Air

EVENING — SPRING, 1946

Sunday

	ABC	CBS	MBS	NBC
6pm	The Radio Hall of Fame	The Adventures of Ozzie and Harriet	Those Websters	The Catholic Hour
6:15				
6:30	Phil Davis' Sunday Party	The Baby Snooks Show	Cedric Foster, news	The Great Gildersleeve
6:45			Quenton Reynolds, news	
7pm	Drew Pearson, news	The Adventures of the Thin Man	The Operatic Revue	The Lucky Strike Program, Jack Benny
7:15	Don Gardiner, news			
7:30	The Quiz Kids	Blondie	Melvin Elliott, news	The Fitch Bandwagon
7:45			Max Lerner, news	
8pm	The Ford Sunday Evening Hour	Calamity Jane /	A. L. Alexander's Mediation Board	The Charlie McCarthy Show
8:15		The Amazing Mrs. Danberry		
8:30		Crime Doctor	Don't Be a Sucker	The Fred Allen Show
8:45		Ned Calmer, news (8:55pm)	Gabriel Heatter, news	
9pm	Walter Winchell's Jergens Journal	Request Performance	Exploring the Unknown	The Manhattan Merry-Go-Round
9:15	Louella Parsons, gossip			
9:30	Listen to La Guardia	The Texaco Star Theater, James Melton	Double or Nothing	The American Album of Familiar Music
9:45	Jimmy Fidler, gossip			
10pm	The Theater Guild on the Air	Take It or Leave It	Freedom of Opportunity	The Hour of Charm
10:15				
10:30		We, the People	The Hollywood Theater	Meet Me at Parky's
10:45				

EVENING — SPRING, 1946

Monday

ABC	CBS	MBS	NBC	
Walter Kiernan, news	Harry Marble, news	Easy Aces	Lyle Van, news	6pm
Ethel and Albert	Patti Clayton, songs	Bob Elson Interviews	Serenade to America	6:15
Harry Wismer, sports	Skyline Roof, Gordon MacRae	Fred Vandeventer, news		6:30
Here's Morgan	The World Today	Stan Lomax, sports	Lowell Thomas, news	6:45
Taylor Grant, news	The Lanny Ross Show	Fulton Lewis Jr., news	The Chesterfield Supper Club	7pm
Raymond Gram Swing, news	The Jack Smith Show	The Answer Man	John W. Vandercook, news	7:15
The Lone Ranger	The Bob Hawk Show	Henry J. Taylor, news	Claude Hopkins Orchestra	7:30
		Bill Brandt, sports sports	H. V. Kaltenborn, news	7:45
Lum and Abner	Forever Ernest	Bulldog Drummond	The Cavalcade of America	8pm
Hedda Hopper, gossip				8:15
The Fat Man	Joanie's Tea Room	Sherlock Holmes	The Voice of Firestone	8:30
	Bill Henry, news (8:55pm)			8:45
I Deal in Crime	The Lux Radio Theater	Gabriel Heatter, news	The Bell Telephone Hour	9pm
		Real Stories from Real Life		9:15
Forever Tops		Spotlight Bands	Information, Please	9:30
				9:45
The Bill Thompson Show	The Lady Esther Screen Guild Theater	The Monday Night Fights	The Carnation Contented Hour	10pm
				10:15
Question for America	Lefty		Dr. I. Q., The Mental Banker	10:30
				10:45

EVENTING — SPRING, 1946

Tuesday

	ABC	CBS	MBS	NBC
6pm	Walter Kiernan, news	Quincy Howe, news	Easy Aces	Lyle Van, news
6:15	Ethel and Albert	Patti Clayton, songs	Bob Elson Interviews	Serenade to America
6:30	Harry Wismer, sports	Skyline Roof, Gordon MacRae	Fred Vandeventer, news	
6:45	Here's Morgan	The World Today	Stan Lomax, sports	Lowell Thomas, news
7pm	Taylor Grant, news	The Lanny Ross Show	Fulton Lewis Jr., news	The Chesterfield Supper Club
7:15	Raymond Gram Swing, news	The Jack Smith Show	The Answer Man	John W. Vandercook, news
7:30	Boston Blackie	The American Melody Hour	Arthur Hale, news	Warde Donovan, songs
7:45			Bill Brandt, sports sports	H. V. Kaltenborn, news
8pm	Lum and Abner	Big Town	The Return of Nick Carter	The Johnny Desmond Follies
8:15	Don Hollenbeck, news			
8:30	Dark Venture	Theater of Romance	The Falcon	A Date with Judy
8:45		Bill Henry, news (8:55pm)		
9pm	Ed Sullivan's Pipelines	Inner Sanctum Mysteries	Gabriel Heatter, news	Amos 'n' Andy
9:15	The Eugenia Baird Show		Real Stories from Real Life	
9:30	The Doctors Talk It Over	This is My Best	The American Forum of the Air	Fibber Magee and Molly
9:45	George Hicks, news			
10pm	Concert Time	Crime Photographer		The Pepsodent Show, Bob Hope
10:15			Take These Notes	
10:30	Hoosier Hop	Open Hearing	The Longines Symphonette	The Raleigh Cigarette Program, Red Skelton
10:45				

EVENING — SPRING, 1946

Wednesday

ABC	CBS	MBS	NBC	
Walter Kiernan, news	Harry Marble, news	Easy Aces	Lyle Van, news	6pm
Ethel and Albert	Patti Clayton, songs	Bob Elson Interviews	Serenade to America	6:15
Harry Wismer, sports	Skyline Roof, Gordon MacRae	Fred Vandeventer, news		6:30
Here's Morgan	The World Today	Stan Lomax, sports	Lowell Thomas, news	6:45
Taylor Grant, news	The Lanny Ross Show	Fulton Lewis Jr., news	The Chesterfield Supper Club	7pm
Raymond Gram Swing, news	The Jack Smith Show	The Answer Man	John W. Vandercook, news	7:15
The Lone Ranger	The Adventures of Ellery Queen	Frank Singiser, news	Claude Hopkins Orchestra	7:30
		Bill Brandt, sports sports	H. V. Kaltenborn, news	7:45
Lum and Abner	The Jack Carson Show	Can You Top This	Mr. and Mrs. North	8pm
Don Hollenbeck, news				8:15
The Fishing and Hunting Club	Dr. Christian	The Fresh Up Show, Bert Lahr	The Penguin Room, Hildegarde	8:30
	Bill Henry, news (8:55pm)			8:45
Jones and I	Songs By Sinatra	Gabriel Heatter, news	Time to Smile, Eddie Cantor	9pm
		Real Stories from Real Life		9:15
So You Want to Lead a Band	Bob Crosby Orchestra	Spotlight Bands	Mr. District Attorney	9:30
				9:45
Ralph Norman Orchestra	Great Moments in Music	Endorsed By Dorsey	Kay Kyser's College of Musical Knowledge	10pm
				10:15
Betty and Buddy, songs	Holiday for Music, Curt Massey	The Longines Symphonette		10:30
Fantasy in Melody				10:45

EVENING — SPRING, 1946

Thursday

	ABC	CBS	MBS	NBC
6pm	Walter Kiernan, news	Harry Marble, news	Easy Aces	Lyle Van, news
6:15	Ethel and Albert	Patti Clayton, songs	Bob Elson Interviews	Serenade to America
6:30	Harry Wismer, sports	Skyline Roof, Gordon MacRae	Fred Vandeventer, news	
6:45	Here's Morgan	The World Today	Stan Lomax, sports	Lowell Thomas, news
7pm	Taylor Grant, news	The Lanny Ross Show	Fulton Lewis Jr., news	The Chesterfield Supper Club
7:15	Raymond Gram Swing, news	The Jack Smith Show	The Answer Man	John W. Vandercook, news
7:30	Professor Quiz	Mr. Keen, Tracer of Lost Persons	Arthur Hale, news	The Bob Burns Show
7:45			Bill Brandt, sports sports	
8pm	Lum and Abner	Suspense	The Carrington Playhouse	Maxwell House Coffee Time, Burns and Allen
8:15	Earl Godwin, news			
8:30	America's Town Meeting of the Air	The FBI in Peace and War	Rogue's Gallery	The Birdseye Open House, Dinah Shore
8:45		Bill Henry, news (8:55pm)		
9pm		Music Millions Love	Gabriel Heatter, news	The Kraft Music Hall, Bing Crosby
9:15			Real Stories from Real Life	
9:30	Detect and Collect	Hobby Lobby	The Treasure Hour of Song	The Sealtest Village Store, Arden and Haley
9:45				
10pm	Curtain Time	Island Venture	You Make the News	Abbott and Costello
10:15				
10:30	Fantasy in Melody	The Year One	The Longines Symphonette	The Rudy Vallee Show
10:45	Janet Flanner, news			

EVENING — SPRING, 1946

Friday

ABC	CBS	MBS	NBC	
Walter Kiernan, news	Harry Marble, news	Easy Aces	Lyle Van, news	6pm
Ethel and Albert	Patti Clayton, songs	Bob Elson Interviews	Serenade to America	6:15
Harry Wismer, sports	Skyline Roof, Gordon MacRae	Fred Vandeventer, news		6:30
Here's Morgan	The World Today	Stan Lomax, sports	Lowell Thomas, news	6:45
Taylor Grant, news	The Lanny Ross Show	Fulton Lewis Jr., news	The Chesterfield Supper Club	7pm
Raymond Gram Swing, news	The Jack Smith Show	The Answer Man	John W. Vandercook, news	7:15
The Lone Ranger	The Ginny Simms Show	Henry J. Taylor, news	Claude Hopkins Orchestra	7:30
		Bill Brandt, sports sports	H. V. Kaltenborn, news	7:45
Woody Herman Orchestra	The Aldrich Family	Passport to Romance	Highways in Melody	8pm
				8:15
This is Your FBI	Kate Smith Sings	So You Think You Know Music	Duffy's Tavern	8:30
	Bill Henry, news (8:55pm)			8:45
The Alan Young Show	Holiday and Company	Gabriel Heatter, news	People Are Funny	9pm
		Real Stories from Real Life		9:15
The Sheriff	The Jimmy Durante Show	Spotlight Bands	Waltz Time	9:30
				9:45
Madison Square Garden Boxing	Pabst Blue Ribbon Town, Danny Kaye	Public Affairs	The Molle' Mystery Theater	10pm
				10:15
	Maisie	The Longines Symphonette	The Colgate Sports Newsreel, Bill Stern	10:30
			Public Affairs	10:45

EVENING — SPRING, 1946

Saturday

	ABC	CBS	MBS	NBC
6pm	Jack Beall, news	Harry Marble, news	Paul Schubert, news	Kenneth Banghart, news
6:15	Edwin D. Canham, news	American Portrait	Strictly Personal	Around Town
6:30	Harry Wismer, sports		Fred Vandeventer, news	
6:45	Labor USA	The World Today	Stan Lomax, sports	Religion in the News
7pm	The Voice of Business	The Academy Award Theater	Guess Who	Our Foreign Policy
7:15	Correspondents Abroad			
7:30	The Green Hornet	Listen to a Love Song, Tony Martin	Arthur Hale, news	The Jimmy Edmondson Show
7:45			The Answer Man	
8pm	Dick Tracy	The Dick Haymes Show	The Three Hundred Party	The Life of Riley
8:15				
8:30	Famous Jury Trials	The Mayor of the Town		Truth or Consequences
8:45		Ned Calmer, news (8:55pm)		
9pm	Gangbusters	Your Hit Parade		The National Barn Dance
9:15				
9:30	Boston Symphony Orchestra			Can You Top This
9:45		Saturday Night Serenade		
10pm			The Chicago Theater of the Air	The Judy Canova Show
10:15		The Continental Celebrity Club, Jackie Kelk		
10:30	Gloria Galbo, songs			Grand Ole Opry
10:45	Hayloft Hoedown	Public Affairs		

DAYTIME — SPRING, 1946

Sunday

	ABC	CBS	MBS	NBC
9am	Bert Bacharach, talk	News	Uncle Don Reads the Comics	News
9:15		From the Organ Loft		Story to Order
9:30	Coast-to-Coast on a Bus		The Mutual Radio Chapel	Songs for Strings
9:45		St. Paul's Trinity Choir		Music
10am	Message of Israel	The CBS Church of the Air	Leo Egan, news	The National Radio Pulpit
10:15			Frank Kingdon, news	
10:30	The Southernaires Quartet		Chaplain Jim, USA	The Horn and Hardart Children's Hour
10:45				
11am	Brunch with the Fitzgeralds	Wings Over Jordan	Snow Village Sketches	
11:15				
11:30	The Hour of Faith	The Salt Lake Tabernacle Choir	Brunch with Dorothy and Dick	Charles F. McCarthy, news
11:45				Solitaire Time
12pm	Fiorello H. La Guardia, talk	Invitation to Learning	The Show Shop	The Eternal Light
12:15				
12:30	Stradivari Orchestra	Transatlantic Call	Keeping Up with Wigglesworth	Packham Inn
12:45			Melvin Elliott, news	
1pm	Cliff Edwards, songs	The People's Platform	The Canary Pet Shop	Ed Herlihy, news
1:15	Orson Welles, talk		Ilka Chase, talk	America United
1:30	Sammy Kaye's Sunday Serenade	Problems of Peace	Sweetheart Time	The University of Chicago Round Table
1:45		Edward R. Murrow, news		

DAYTIME — SPRING, 1946

Monday-Friday

ABC	CBS	MBS	NBC	
The Breakfast Club	Joe King, news	The Story of Myrt and Marge	Honeymoon in New York	9am
	Arthur Godfrey Time	Aunt Mary		9:15
		Alfred W. McCann, food	This Business of Living	9:30
			Robert St. John, news	9:45
My True Story	Valiant Lady	Henry Gladstone, news	Lone Journey	10am
	The Light of the World	Bessy Beatty, talk	Lora Lawton	10:15
Hymns of All Churches	The Strange Romance of Evelyn Winters		The Road of Life	10:30
Listening Post / Lisa Sergio, talk	Bachelor's Children		Joyce Jordan, MD	10:45
Breakfast with Breneman	Amanda of Honeymoon Hill	Prescott Robinson, news	Fred Waring Orchestra	11am
	Second Husband	Tello-Test Quiz		11:15
Home Edition	Time to Remember	Morning Matinee / Take It Easy Time	Barry Cameron	11:30
Between the Bookends	Aunt Jenny's True Life Stories	Victor Lindlahr, health	David Harum	11:45
Glamour Manor, Cliff Arquette	Kate Smith Speaks	Lyle Van, news	Joe Heinline, news	12pm
	Big Sister	Hymns You Love, Richard Maxwell	Maggie McNellis, talk	12:15
The Women's Exchange	The Romance of Helen Trent	Henry Gladstone, news	The Eddie Newman Show	12:30
	Our Gal Sunday	The Answer Man	Music of Manhattan	12:45
H. R. Baukhage, news	Life Can Be Beautiful	Musical Appetizer	Mary Margaret McBride, talk	1pm
The Powers Charm School	Ma Perkins	Jack Bundy's Album		1:15
Galen Drake, talk	Young Dr. Malone	Vincent Lopez Orchestra		1:30
	The Road of Life	The John J. Anthony Program	Morgan Beatty, news	1:45

DAYTIME — SPRING, 1946

Sunday

	ABC	CBS	MBS	NBC
2pm	Warriors of Peace	The Radio Reader's Digest	Hawaii Calls	Harvest of Stars
2:15			The Stan Lomax Album	
2:30	National Vespers	Hollywood Star Time	Melvin Elliott, news	The Westinghouse Program, John C. Thomas
2:45			The Kenny Baker Program	
3pm	Elmer Davis, news	New York Philharmonic Orchestra	The Quiz of Two Cities	The Sheaffer Parade
3:15	Galen Drake, talk			
3:30	A Present from Hollywood		The World's Most Honored Flights	One Man's Family
3:45	Johnny Thompson, songs			
4pm	Fantasy in Melody	The Columbia Workshop	Murder is My Hobby	The National Hour
4:15				
4:30	Right Down Your Alley	The Electric Hour, Nelson Eddy	True Detective Mysteries	The RCA Victor Show
4:45				
5pm	The Court of Missing Heirs	The Prudential Family Hour	The Shadow	NBC Symphony Orchestra
5:15				
5:30	Counterspy	Gene Autry's Melody Ranch	Quick as a Flash	
5:45		Quincy Howe, news		

DAYTIME — SPRING, 1946

Monday-Friday

ABC	CBS	MBS	NBC	
John B. Kennedy, news	The Second Mrs. Burton	Daily Dilemmas	The Guiding Light	2pm
Pat Barnes, talk	Perry Mason		Today's Children	2:15
Bride and Groom	Rosemary	Queen for a Day	The Woman in White	2:30
	Tena and Tim		Masquerade	2:45
Al Pearce and His Gang	You're in the Act	Martha Deane, talk	A Woman of America	3pm
			Ma Perkins	3:15
Ladies Be Seated	Cinderella, Inc.	Rambling with Gambling	Pepper Young's Family	3:30
			The Right of Happiness	3:45
The Jack Berch Show	House Party	The Better Half	Mary Noble, Backstage Wife	4pm
The Allen Prescott Show			Stella Dallas	4:15
Time for Women	The Landt Trio and Curley	Dr. Eddy's Food Forum	Lorenzo Jones	4:30
Hop Harrigan			Young Widder Brown	4:45
Terry and the Pirates	The American School of the Air	Uncle Don	When a Girl Marries	5pm
Dick Tracy		The Adventures of Superman	Portia Faces Life	5:15
Jack Armstrong, the All-American Boy	Cimarron Tavern	Captain Midnight	Just Plain Bill	5:30
Tennessee Jed	Sparrow and the Hawk	The Tom Mix Ralston Straight Shooters	Front Page Farrell	5:45

DAYTIME — SPRING, 1946

Saturday

	ABC	CBS	MBS	NBC
9am	Wake Up and Smile	Joe King, news	Vera Holly, songs	Home is What You Make It
9:15		The Garden Gate		
9:30		Carolina Calling	Married for Life	This Business of Living
9:45				A Miss and a Male
10am	Galen Drake, talk	Give and Take	Henry Gladstone, news	The Eileen Barton Show
10:15	Club Time		Lorenzo Fuller, piano	
10:30	Teen Town	Mary Lee Taylor, cooking	Rainbow House	Archie Andrews
10:45				
11am	Tell Me Doctor	Let's Pretend	Prescott Robinson, news	The Teentimer's Club
11:15	Bible Message		Tex Fletcher, songs	
11:30	Betty Moore, talk	The Billie Burke Show	The Land of the Lost	Smilin' Ed's Buster Brown Gang
11:45	Chet Gaylord, songs			
12pm	Chester Bowles, talk	The Armstrong Theater of Today	The House of Mystery	John McVane, news
12:15	Elizabeth Woodward, songs			Consumer Time
12:30	The American Farmer	Stars Over Hollywood	Henry Gladstone, news	Music for Saturday
12:45			The Answer Man	
1pm	To Live in Peace	Grand Central Station	The Man on the Farm	The National Farm and Home Hour
1:15				
1:30	The Museum of Modern Music	County Fair	Opry House Matinee, Eddy Arnold	The Veterans Advisor
1:45				The American World

DAYTIME — SPRING, 1946

Saturday

	ABC	CBS	MBS	NBC
2pm	Chicago Serenade	Of Men and Books	Meet the Press	The Name Speaks
2:15		Adventures in Science		Your Radio Reporter
2:30	Hilltoppers Music	Treasury Bandstand	Courtney's Record Carnival	The Baxters
2:45				Stories By Olmstead
3pm	The Piano Playhouse	Assignment Home		Orchestras of the Nation
3:15	Roundup Time		It's Up to Youth	
3:30		Public Affairs		
3:45		Cross-Section USA		
4pm	Saturday Date with the Duke	Monaghan, the Record Man	The Better Half	Doctors at Home
4:15				
4:30			Horse Racing	World of Melody
4:45			Waples Orchestra	
5pm	The Saturday Concert	Philadelphia Symphony Orchestra	What's the Name of That Song	Phone Again Finnegan
5:15				
5:30			The Man on the Street	John W. Vandercook, news
5:45			Lanny and Ginger, songs	Tin Pan Alley of the Air

EVENING — SUMMER, 1946

Sunday

	ABC	CBS	MBS	NBC
6pm	Phil Davis' Sunday Party	The Silver Theater	Those Websters	The Catholic Hour
6:15				
6:30	The Eugenia Baird Show	Viva America	Cedric Foster, news	Ask Me Another
6:45			Stan Lomax, sports	
7pm	Drew Pearson, news	Gene Autry's Melody Ranch	Let's Go to the Opera	The Fabulous Dr. Tweedy
7:15	Don Gardiner, news			
7:30	The Quiz Kids	Blondie	Melvin Elliott, news	Rogue's Gallery
7:45			Max Lerner, news	
8pm	The Ford Festival of American Music	Richard Lawless	A. L. Alexander's Mediation Board	Alec Templeton Time
8:15				
8:30		Crime Doctor	Special Investigator	Tommy Dorsey Orchestra
8:45		Ned Calmer, news (8:55pm)	George Putnam, news	
9pm	Quentin Reynolds, news	Request Performance	Exploring the Unknown	The Manhattan Merry-Go-Round
9:15	Louella Parsons, gossip			
9:30	Harry Von Zell, gossip	The Texaco Star Theater, James Melton	Double or Nothing	The American Album of Familiar Music
9:45	Police Woman			
10pm	The Hour of Mystery	Take It or Leave It	Mystery is My Hobby	The Hour of Charm
10:15				
10:30		We, the People	Meet the Press	Rhapsody in Rhythm
10:45				

EVENING — SUMMER, 1946

Monday

ABC	CBS	MBS	NBC	
Walter Kiernan, news	Harry Marble, news	Frank Kingdon, news	Lyle Van, news	6pm
Ethel and Albert	In My Opinion	Bob Elson Interviews	Serenade to America	6:15
New York Tonight, Allen Prescott	The Larry Carr Show	Fred Vandeventer, news		6:30
The Leslie Scott Show	The World Today	Stan Lomax, sports	Lowell Thomas, news	6:45
Taylor Grant, news	Patti Clayton, songs	Fulton Lewis Jr., news	The Chesterfield Supper Club	7pm
Carey Longmire, news	Skyline Roof, Gordon MacRae	The Answer Man	John W. Vandercook, news	7:15
The Lone Ranger	The Bob Hawk Show	Henry J. Taylor, news	Claim Agent	7:30
		Bill Brandt, sports sports	H. V. Kaltenborn, news	7:45
Lum and Abner	Forever Ernest	Bulldog Drummond	Travelin' Man	8pm
Ed Sullivan's Pipelines				8:15
The Fat Man	Fighting Senator	The Casebook of Gregory Hood	The Voice of Firestone	8:30
	Bill Henry, news (8:55pm)			8:45
I Deal in Crime	Kiss and Make Up, Milton Berle	Gabriel Heatter, news	The Bell Telephone Hour	9pm
		Real Stories from Real Life		9:15
Forever Tops	The Jack Kirkwood Show	Spotlight Bands	The Music Festival	9:30
				9:45
Question for America	The Lady Esther Screen Guild Theater	The Summer Playhouse	The Carnation Contented Hour	10pm
				10:15
Earl Godwin, news	Tonight on Broadway	The Longines Symphonette	Dr. I. Q., The Mental Banker	10:30
Ralph Norman Orchestra				10:45

EVENING — SUMMER, 1946

Tuesday

	ABC	CBS	MBS	NBC
6pm	Walter Kiernan, news	Harry Marble, news	Frank Kingdon, news	Lyle Van, news
6:15	Ethel and Albert	Frontiers of Science	Bob Elson Interviews	Serenade to America
6:30	New York Tonight, Allen Prescott	The Larry Carr Show	Fred Vandeventer, news	
6:45	The Leslie Scott Show	The World Today	Stan Lomax, sports	Lowell Thomas, news
7pm	Taylor Grant, news	Patti Clayton, songs	Fulton Lewis Jr., news	The Chesterfield Supper Club
7:15	Carey Longmire, news	Skyline Roof, Gordon MacRae	The Answer Man	John W. Vandercook, news
7:30	Boston Blackie	The American Melody Hour	Arthur Hale, news	The Hollywood Theater
7:45			Bill Brandt, sports sports	
8pm	Lum and Abner	Big Town	The Return of Nick Carter	The Johnny Desmond Follies
8:15	The O'Neills			
8:30	So You Want to Lead a Band	Theater of Romance	The Falcon	A Date with Judy
8:45		Bill Henry, news (8:55pm)		
9pm	The Society of Amateur Chefs	Arthur Godfrey Talent Scouts	Gabriel Heatter, news	Grand Marquee
9:15			Real Stories from Real Life	
9:30	The Doctors Talk It Over	Encore Theater	The American Forum of the Air	Fred Waring Orchestra
9:45	Bella Spewack Reports			
10pm	Concert Time	Night Life		The Man Called X
10:15			Alan Scott, talk	
10:30	Public Affairs	Open Hearing	The Longines Symphonette	An Evening with Romberg
10:45				

EVENING — SUMMER, 1946

Wednesday

ABC	CBS	MBS	NBC	
Walter Kiernan, news	Harry Marble, news	Frank Kingdon, news	Lyle Van, news	6pm
Ethel and Albert	Patti Clayton, songs	Bob Elson Interviews	Serenade to America	6:15
New York Tonight, Allen Prescott	The Larry Carr Show	Fred Vandeventer, news		6:30
The Leslie Scott Show	The World Today	Stan Lomax, sports	Lowell Thomas, news	6:45
Taylor Grant, news	Patti Clayton, songs	Fulton Lewis Jr., news	The Chesterfield Supper Club	7pm
Raymond Gram Swing, news	Skyline Roof, Gordon MacRae	The Answer Man	John W. Vandercook, news	7:15
The Lone Ranger	The Adventures of Ellery Queen	Cecil Brown, news	Claim Agent	7:30
		Bill Brandt, sports sports	H. V. Kaltenborn, news	7:45
Lum and Abner	The Whistler	Can You Top This	Mr. and Mrs. North	8pm
Listen to La Guardia				8:15
The Fishing and Hunting Club	Dr. Christian	The Beatrice Kay Show	The Penguin Room, Hildegarde	8:30
	Bill Henry, news (8:55pm)			8:45
The Court of Missing Heirs	The Sad Sack	Gabriel Heatter, news	McGarry and the Mouse	9pm
		Real Stories from Real Life		9:15
Frankie Carle Orchestra	Intrigue	Spotlight Bands	Mr. District Attorney	9:30
				9:45
Sports Review	The Academy Award Theater	Endorsed By Dorsey	Kay Kyser's College of Musical Knowledge	10pm
				10:15
Earl Godwin, news	Holiday for Music, Curt Massey	Author Meets the Critics		10:30
Hoosier Hop				10:45

EVENTS — SUMMER, 1946

Thursday

	ABC	CBS	MBS	NBC
6pm	Walter Kiernan, news	Harry Marble, news	Frank Kingdon, news	Lyle Van, news
6:15	Ethel and Albert	In My Opinion	Bob Elson Interviews	Serenade to America
6:30	New York Tonight, Allen Prescott	The Larry Carr Show	Fred Vandeventer, news	
6:45	The Leslie Scott Show	The World Today	Stan Lomax, sports	Lowell Thomas, news
7pm	Taylor Grant, news	Patti Clayton, songs	Fulton Lewis Jr., news	The Chesterfield Supper Club
7:15	Raymond Gram Swing, news	Skyline Roof, Gordon MacRae	The Answer Man	John W. Vandercook, news
7:30	Professor Quiz	Mr. Keen, Tracer of Lost Persons	Arthur Hale, news	The Johnny Morgan Show
7:45			Bill Brandt, sports sports	
8pm	Lum and Abner	Suspense	The Carrington Playhouse	The Nelson Olmstead Playhouse
8:15	The O'Neills			
8:30	America's Town Meeting of the Air	Sound Off	Vic and Sade	Meredith Willson Orchestra
8:45		Bill Henry, news (8:55pm)		
9pm		The Dick Haymes Show	Gabriel Heatter, news	The Kraft Music Hall, Edward Horton
9:15			Real Stories from Real Life	
9:30	Take It from There	Crime Photographer	By Popular Demand	The Sealtest Village Store, Arden and Haley
9:45				
10pm	Harry Kogen Orchestra	That's Life	California Melodies	The Camel Caravan, Vaughn Monroe
10:15				
10:30	Fantasy in Melody	Phone Again Finnegan	The Longines Symphonette	The Fifth Horsemen
10:45				

EVENING — SUMMER, 1946

Friday

ABC	CBS	MBS	NBC	
Walter Kiernan, news	Harry Marble, news	Frank Kingdon, news	Lyle Van, news	6pm
Ethel and Albert	Patti Clayton, songs	Bob Elson Interviews	Serenade to America	6:15
New York Tonight, Allen Prescott	The Larry Carr Show	Fred Vandeventer, news		6:30
The Leslie Scott Show	The World Today	Stan Lomax, sports	Lowell Thomas, news	6:45
Taylor Grant, news	Patti Clayton, songs	Fulton Lewis Jr., news	The Chesterfield Supper Club	7pm
Raymond Gram Swing, news	Skyline Roof, Gordon MacRae	The Answer Man	John W. Vandercook, news	7:15
The Lone Ranger	Tommy Riggs and Betty Lou	Henry J. Taylor, news	Claim Agent	7:30
		Bill Brandt, sports sports	H. V. Kaltenborn, news	7:45
The Adventures of Sam Spade	The Aldrich Family	Passport to Romance	Highways in Melody	8pm
				8:15
This is Your FBI	The Adventures of the Thin Man	A Voice in the Night	Easy Money	8:30
	Bill Henry, news (8:55pm)			8:45
Break the Bank	It Pays to Be Ignorant	Gabriel Heatter, news	Vacation with Music	9pm
		Real Stories from Real Life		9:15
The Sheriff	Wayne King Orchestra	Spotlight Bands	Waltz Time	9:30
				9:45
Madison Square Garden Boxing	The Mercury Summer Theater	Spotlight on America	The Molle' Mystery Theater	10pm
				10:15
	Hawk Durango	The Longines Symphonette	The Colgate Sports Newsreel, Bill Stern	10:30
			Public Affairs	10:45

EVENING — SUMMER, 1946

Saturday

	ABC	CBS	MBS	NBC
6pm	Jack Beall, news	Harry Marble, news	Paul Schubert, news	Kenneth Banghart, news
6:15	Jimmy Blair, songs	American Portrait	Lorenzo Fuller, songs	Horse Racing
6:30	Harry Wismer, sports		Fred Vandeventer, news	
6:45	Labor USA	The World Today	Stan Lomax, sports	The Art of Living
7pm	The Voice of Business	St. Louis Municipal Opera	Guess Who	Our Foreign Policy
7:15	Correspondents Abroad			
7:30	The Green Hornet	Listen to a Love Song, Tony Martin	Arthur Hale, news	Curtain Time
7:45			The Answer Man	
8pm	Dark Venture	Hollywood Star Time	Twenty Questions	Carnival with Bernie West
8:15				
8:30	Famous Jury Trials	The Danny O'Neil Show	Juvenile Jury	Honeymoon in New York
8:45		Ned Calmer, news (8:55pm)		
9pm	Gangbusters	Your Hit Parade	Leave It to the Girls	The National Barn Dance
9:15				
9:30	Detect and Collect		Jonathan Trimble, Esquire	Can You Top This
9:45		Saturday Night Serenade		
10pm	American Melodies		The Chicago Theater of the Air	Lights Out
10:15		Oklahoma Roundup		
10:30	Hayloft Hoedown			Grand Ole Opry
10:45		Public Affairs		

DAYTIME — SUMMER, 1946

Sunday

	ABC	CBS	MBS	NBC
9am	Bert Bacharach, talk	News	Uncle Don Reads the Comics	News
9:15		From the Organ Loft		Story to Order
9:30	Coast-to-Coast on a Bus		The Mutual Radio Chapel	Songs for Strings
9:45		St. Paul's Trinity Choir		Music
10am	Message of Israel	The CBS Church of the Air	George Putnam, news	Highlights of the Bible
10:15			Frank Kingdon, news	
10:30	The Southernaires Quartet		Hawaii Calls	The Horn and Hardart Children's Hour
10:45				
11am	Brunch with the Fitzgeralds	Wings Over Jordan	George Putnam, news	
11:15			Brunch with Dorothy and Dick	
11:30	The Hour of Faith	The Salt Lake Tabernacle Choir		Charles F. McCarthy, news
11:45				Solitaire Time
12pm	Hugo E. Rogers, talk	Invitation to Learning	The Show Shop	The Eternal Light
12:15				
12:30	Sunday Strings	Yours, Sincerely	Special Assignment	Packham Inn
12:45			Melvin Elliott, news	
1pm	Cliff Edwards, songs	The People's Platform	Keeping Up with Wigglesworth	Ed Herlihy, news
1:15	Orson Welles, talk		Ilka Chase, talk	America United
1:30	Sammy Kaye's Sunday Serenade	Problems of Peace	Sweetheart Time	The University of Chicago Round Table
1:45		Howard K. Smith, news	Jimmy Farrell, songs	

DAYTIME — SUMMER, 1946

Monday-Friday

ABC	CBS	MBS	NBC	
The Breakfast Club	Bob Hite, news	The Story of Myrt and Marge	Honeymoon in New York	9am
	This is New York, Danny O'Neill	Aunt Mary		9:15
		Alfred W. McCann, food	Daytime Classics	9:30
			Robert St. John, news	9:45
My True Story	Valiant Lady	Henry Gladstone, news	Lone Journey	10am
	The Light of the World	Bessy Beatty, talk	Lora Lawton	10:15
Hymns of All Churches	The Strange Romance of Evelyn Winters		The Road of Life	10:30
Music / Listening Post	Bachelor's Children		Joyce Jordan, MD	10:45
Breakfast with Breneman	Arthur Godfrey Time	Prescott Robinson, news	Fred Waring Orchestra	11am
		Tello-Test Quiz		11:15
Home Edition	Time to Remember	Music	Barry Cameron	11:30
Between the Bookends	Rosemary	Victor Lindlahr, health	David Harum	11:45
Glamour Manor, Kenny Baker	Kate Smith Speaks	George Putnam, news	Joe Heinline, news	12pm
	Aunt Jenny's True Life Stories	The Coke Club, Morton Downey	Maggie McNellis, talk	12:15
The Powers Charm School	The Romance of Helen Trent	Henry Gladstone, news	Music / Here's to Veterans	12:30
	Our Gal Sunday	The Answer Man	Music of Manhattan	12:45
H. R. Baukhage, news	Big Sister	Musical Appetizer	Mary Margaret McBride, talk	1pm
The Women's Exchange	Ma Perkins	Jack Bundy's Album		1:15
Galen Drake, talk	Young Dr. Malone	Vincent Lopez Orchestra		1:30
	The Road of Life	The John J. Anthony Program	Robert McCormick, news	1:45

DAYTIME — SUMMER, 1946

Sunday

	ABC	CBS	MBS	NBC
2pm	Warriors of Peace	Assignment Home	Private Showing	The RCA Victor Show
2:15				
2:30	National Vespers	The Weekly News Review	George Putnam, news	Harvest of Stars
2:45			What Veterans Want to Know	
3pm	Carey Longmire, news	Columbia Symphony Orchestra	The Quiz of Two Cities	The Sheaffer Parade
3:15	The Vagabonds Quartet			
3:30	A Present from Hollywood		Vera Holly, songs	One Man's Family
3:45	Samuel Pettengell, news			
4pm	Stump the Authors	The Columbia Workshop	The Mysterious Traveler	The National Hour
4:15				
4:30	Right Down Your Alley	The Electric Summer Hour	True Detective Mysteries	America United
4:45				
5pm	Allen Prescott's Party	The Prudential Family Hour	Under Arrest	NBC Symphony Orchestra
5:15				
5:30	Counterspy	John Henry Faulk, talk	The Abbott Mysteries	
5:45		William L. Shirer, news		

DAYTIME — SUMMER, 1946

Monday-Friday

ABC	CBS	MBS	NBC	
John B. Kennedy, news	The Second Mrs. Burton	Daily Dilemmas	The Guiding Light	*2pm*
Pat Barnes, talk	Perry Mason		Today's Children	*2:15*
Bride and Groom	The Landt Trio and Curley	Queen for a Day	The Woman in White	*2:30*
			Masquerade	*2:45*
Al Pearce and His Gang	Surprise Party / Winner Take All	Martha Deane, talk	Life Can Be Beautiful	*3pm*
			Ma Perkins	*3:15*
Ladies Be Seated	Cinderella, Inc.	Rambling with Gambling	Pepper Young's Family	*3:30*
			The Right of Happiness	*3:45*
The Jack Berch Show	House Party	The Better Half	Mary Noble, Backstage Wife	*4pm*
Something for the Girls			Stella Dallas	*4:15*
Meet Me in Manhattan	Give and Take	Dr. Eddy's Food Forum	Lorenzo Jones	*4:30*
			Young Widder Brown	*4:45*
Terry and the Pirates	Feature Story	Uncle Don	When a Girl Marries	*5pm*
Dick Tracy	The Woman's Club	The Adventures of Superman	Portia Faces Life	*5:15*
Jack Armstrong, the All-American Boy	Cimarron Tavern	Captain Midnight	Just Plain Bill	*5:30*
Tennessee Jed	Sparrow and the Hawk	The Tom Mix Ralston Straight Shooters	Front Page Farrell	*5:45*

DAYTIME — SUMMER, 1946

Saturday

	ABC	CBS	MBS	NBC
9am	Wake Up and Smile	Bob Hite, news	Jack and Loretta Clemens, songs	Music as You Like It
9:15		This is New York, Danny O'Neil		
9:30			The Star Show	This Business of Living
9:45		The Garden Gate		Your City and How It Works
10am	The Buddy Weed Trio	Give and Take	Henry Gladstone, news	Percolator Party
10:15	The Brown Dots Quartet		African Trek	
10:30	Junior Junction	Mary Lee Taylor, cooking	Rainbow House	Archie Andrews
10:45				
11am	Elizabeth Woodword, songs	Let's Pretend	Prescott Robinson, news	The Teentimer's Club
11:15	String Ensemble		Songs for You	
11:30	It's Harvel Music Time, Johnny Thompson	The Billie Burke Show	Vacation Symphonies	Home is What You Make It
11:45	Adele Clark, songs			
12pm	Paul Porter, talk	The Armstrong Theater of Today	It's Up to Youth	John McVane, news
12:15	Earl Wilde, piano			Consumer Time
12:30	The American Farmer	Stars Over Hollywood	Henry Gladstone, news	Smilin' Ed's Buster Brown Gang
12:45			The Answer Man	
1pm	To Live in Peace	Grand Central Station	Vincent Lopez Orchestra	The National Farm and Home Hour
1:15				
1:30	Johnny Olsen's Rumpus Room	County Fair	Checkerboard Matinee	The Veterans Advisor
1:45				Elmer Peterson, news

DAYTIME — SUMMER, 1946

Saturday

	ABC	CBS	MBS	NBC
2pm	Chicago Serenade	Columbia's Country Journal	Courtney's Record Carnival	Your Host is Buffalo
2:15				Your Radio Reporter
2:30	Hilltoppers Music	Of Men and Books		The Baxters
2:45		Adventures in Science		Nature Sketches
3pm	The Piano Playhouse	Treasury Bandstand	Double Feature, Les Tremayne	The Saturday Showcase
3:15				
3:30	Roundup Time	Public Affairs		Let's Laugh
3:45		Cross-Section USA		
4pm	Saturday Date with the Duke	Chicagoans Orchestra	The Better Half	Doctors at Home
4:15				
4:30		Harry Cool Orchestra	Herb Fields Orchestra	The Schools Are Yours
4:45				Stories By Olmstead
5pm	The Saturday Concert	Philadelphia Symphony Orchestra	The Sports Parade	No Happy Ending
5:15				
5:30			The Listener Reports	The American World
5:45			Vera Massey and Hal Horton, songs	Tin Pan Alley of the Air

EVENING — FALL, 1946

Sunday

	ABC	CBS	MBS	NBC
6pm	Phil Davis' Sunday Party	The Adventures of Ozzie and Harriet	Those Websters	The Catholic Hour
6:15				
6:30	Tales of Willie Piper	Kate Smith Sings	The Return of Nick Carter	The Bob Burns Show
6:45				
7pm	Drew Pearson, news	Gene Autry's Melody Ranch	Let's Go to the Opera	The Lucky Strike Program, Jack Benny
7:15	Don Gardiner, news			
7:30	Stump the Authors	Blondie	Melvin Elliott, news	The Phil Harris - Alice Faye Show
7:45			Max Lerner, news	
8pm	Paul Whiteman Orchestra	The Adventures of Sam Spade	A. L. Alexander's Mediation Board	The Charlie McCarthy Show
8:15				
8:30	The Clock	Crime Doctor	Special Investigator	The Fred Allen Show
8:45		Bill Henry, news (8:55pm)	George Putnam, news	
9pm	Walter Winchell's Jergens Journal	The Campbell Room, Hildegarde	Exploring the Unknown	The Manhattan Merry-Go-Round
9:15	Louella Parsons, gossip			
9:30	Jimmy Fidler, gossip	The Eddie Bracken Show	Double or Nothing	The American Album of Familiar Music
9:45	Police Woman			
10pm	The Theater Guild on the Air	Take It or Leave It	A Brighter Tomorrow	The Bickersons
10:15				
10:30		We, the People	Meet the Press	Meet Me at Parky's
10:45				

EVENING — FALL, 1946

Monday

ABC	CBS	MBS	NBC	
Walter Kiernan, news	Harry Marble, news	Frank Kingdon, news	Kenneth Banghart, news	6pm
Ethel and Albert	In My Opinion	Bob Elson Interviews	Serenade to America	6:15
New York Tonight, Allen Prescott	Red Barber, sports	Fred Vandeventer, news		6:30
Here's Morgan	The World Today	Stan Lomax, sports	Lowell Thomas, news	6:45
Taylor Grant, news	Mystery of the Week	Fulton Lewis Jr., news	The Chesterfield Supper Club	7pm
Elmer Davis, news	The Jack Smith Show	The Answer Man	John W. Vandercook, news	7:15
The Lone Ranger	The Bob Hawk Show	Henry J. Taylor, news	Barry Wood, songs	7:30
		Bill Brandt, sports sports	H. V. Kaltenborn, news	7:45
Lum and Abner	Inner Sanctum Mysteries	Bulldog Drummond	The Cavalcade of America	8pm
Earl Godwin, news				8:15
The Fat Man	Joanie's Tea Room	The Casebook of Gregory Hood	The Voice of Firestone	8:30
	Bill Henry, news (8:55pm)			8:45
Dark Venture	The Lux Radio Theater	Gabriel Heatter, news	The Bell Telephone Hour	9pm
		Real Stories from Real Life		9:15
Johnny Olsen's Rumpus Room		Guy Lombardo Orchestra	The Victor Borge Show	9:30
				9:45
The Doctors Talk It Over	The Lady Esther Screen Guild Theater	Broadway Talks Back	The Carnation Contented Hour	10pm
Fantasy in Melody				10:15
Murder at Midnight	Tonight on Broadway	The Longines Symphonette	Dr. I. Q., the Mental Banker	10:30
				10:45

EVENING — FALL, 1946

Tuesday

	ABC	CBS	MBS	NBC
6pm	Walter Kiernan, news	Harry Marble, news	Frank Kingdon, news	Kenneth Banghart, news
6:15	Ethel and Albert	Public Affairs	Bob Elson Interviews	Serenade to America
6:30	New York Tonight, Allen Prescott	Red Barber, sports	Fred Vandeventer, news	
6:45	Here's Morgan	The World Today	Stan Lomax, sports	Lowell Thomas, news
7pm	Taylor Grant, news	Mystery of the Week	Fulton Lewis Jr., news	The Chesterfield Supper Club
7:15	Elmer Davis, news	The Jack Smith Show	The Answer Man	John W. Vandercook, news
7:30	Boston Blackie	The American Melody Hour	Arthur Hale, news	The Hollywood Theater
7:45			Bill Brandt, sports sports	H. V. Kaltenborn, news
8pm	Lum and Abner	Big Town	Michael Shayne, Private Detective	The Rudy Vallee Show
8:15	Earl Godwin, news			
8:30	The O'Neills	The Mel Blanc Show	The Falcon	A Date with Judy
8:45		Bill Henry, news (8:55pm)		
9pm	Echoes of New York	Vox Pop	Gabriel Heatter, news	Amos 'n' Andy
9:15			Real Stories from Real Life	
9:30	Boston Symphony Orchestra	Hollywood Players	The American Forum of the Air	Fibber Magee and Molly
9:45				
10pm		Arthur Godfrey Talent Scouts		The Pepsodent Show, Bob Hope
10:15			Upton Close, news	
10:30	Bob Elson, news	Open Hearing	The Longines Symphonette	The Raleigh Cigarette Program, Red Skelton
10:45	Hoosier Hop			

EVENING — FALL, 1946

Wednesday

ABC	CBS	MBS	NBC	
Walter Kiernan, news	Harry Marble, news	Frank Kingdon, news	Kenneth Banghart, news	6pm
Ethel and Albert	Public Affairs	Bob Elson Interviews	Serenade to America	6:15
New York Tonight, Allen Prescott	Red Barber, sports	Fred Vandeventer, news		6:30
Here's Morgan	The World Today	Stan Lomax, sports	Lowell Thomas, news	6:45
Taylor Grant, news	Mystery of the Week	Fulton Lewis Jr., news	The Chesterfield Supper Club	7pm
Raymond Gram Swing, news	The Jack Smith Show	The Answer Man	John W. Vandercook, news	7:15
The Lone Ranger	The Adventures of Ellery Queen	Cecil Brown, news	Barry Wood, songs	7:30
		Bill Brandt, sports sports	H. V. Kaltenborn, news	7:45
Lum and Abner	The Jack Carson Show	Can You Top This	Mr. and Mrs. North	8pm
Listen to La Guardia				8:15
The Fishing and Hunting Club	Dr. Christian	It's Up to Youth	The Great Gildersleeve	8:30
	Bill Henry, news (8:55pm)			8:45
So You Want to Lead a Band	Songs By Sinatra	Gabriel Heatter, news	Duffy's Tavern	9pm
		Real Stories from Real Life		9:15
Pot o' Gold	The Ford Show, Dinah Shore	Xavier Cugat Orchestra	Mr. District Attorney	9:30
				9:45
Philco Radio Time, Bing Crosby	The Academy Award Theater	Emerson Buckley Orchestra	The Fabulous Dr. Tweedy	10pm
				10:15
The Henry Morgan Show	Information, Please	The Longines Symphonette	Kay Kyser's College of Musical Knowledge	10:30
				10:45

EVENING — FALL, 1946

Thursday

	ABC	CBS	MBS	NBC
6pm	Walter Kiernan, news	Harry Marble, news	Frank Kingdon, news	Kenneth Banghart, news
6:15	Ethel and Albert	In My Opinion	Bob Elson Interviews	Serenade to America
6:30	New York Tonight, Allen Prescott	Red Barber, sports	Fred Vandeventer, news	
6:45	Here's Morgan	The World Today	Stan Lomax, sports	Lowell Thomas, news
7pm	Taylor Grant, news	Mystery of the Week	Fulton Lewis Jr., news	The Chesterfield Supper Club
7:15	Raymond Gram Swing, news	The Jack Smith Show	The Answer Man	John W. Vandercook, news
7:30	Professor Quiz	Mr. Keen, Tracer of Lost Persons	Arthur Hale, news	A Day in the Life of Dennis Day
7:45			Bill Brandt, sports sports	
8pm	Lum and Abner	Suspense	Sound Off	The Aldrich Family
8:15	Edwin D. Canham, news			
8:30	America's Town Meeting of the Air	The FBI in Peace and War	Strictly from Dixie	Maxwell House Coffee Time, Burns and Allen
8:45		Bill Henry, news (8:55pm)		
9pm		The Dick Haymes Show	Gabriel Heatter, news	The Kraft Music Hall, Edward Horton
9:15			Real Stories from Real Life	
9:30	Take It from There	Crime Photographer	By Popular Demand	The Sealtest Village Store, Arden and Haley
9:45				
10pm	So You Want to Lead a Band	The Radio Reader's Digest	Eddie Dooley, sports	Abbott and Costello
10:15			Scout About Town	
10:30	Bob Elson, news	Phone Again Finnegan	The Longines Symphonette	Pabst Blue Ribbon Town, Eddie Cantor
10:45	Leggy Holland, songs			

EVENING — FALL, 1946

Friday

ABC	CBS	MBS	NBC	
Walter Kiernan, news	Harry Marble, news	Frank Kingdon, news	Kenneth Banghart, news	*6pm*
Ethel and Albert	Public Affairs	Bob Elson Interviews	Serenade to America	*6:15*
New York Tonight, Allen Prescott	Red Barber, sports	Fred Vandeventer, news		*6:30*
Here's Morgan	The World Today	Stan Lomax, sports	Lowell Thomas, news	*6:45*
Taylor Grant, news	Mystery of the Week	Fulton Lewis Jr., news	The Chesterfield Supper Club	*7pm*
Raymond Gram Swing, news	The Jack Smith Show	The Answer Man	John W. Vandercook, news	*7:15*
The Lone Ranger	Sparkle Time	Henry J. Taylor, news	Barry Wood, songs	*7:30*
		Bill Brandt, sports sports	H. V. Kaltenborn, news	*7:45*
The Court of Missing Heirs	The Baby Snooks Show	The Burl Ives Show	Highways in Melody	*8pm*
		Monica's Music Box		*8:15*
This is Your FBI	The Adventures of the Thin Man	Endorsed By Dorsey	The Alan Young Show	*8:30*
	Bill Henry, news (8:55pm)			*8:45*
Break the Bank	The Ginny Simms Show	Gabriel Heatter, news	People Are Funny	*9pm*
		Real Stories from Real Life		*9:15*
The Sheriff	The Jimmy Durante Show	Harry James Orchestra	Waltz Time	*9:30*
				9:45
Madison Square Garden Boxing	It Pays to Be Ignorant	Spotlight on America	The Molle' Mystery Theater	*10pm*
				10:15
	Maisie	The Longines Symphonette	The Colgate Sports Newsreel, Bill Stern	*10:30*
			Public Affairs	*10:45*

EVENING — FALL, 1946

Saturday

	ABC	CBS	MBS	NBC
6pm	Jimmy Blair, songs	Harry Marble, news	The Sports Question Box	Kenneth Banghart, news
6:15	The Chittison Trio	The Columbia Workshop	Lorenzo Fuller, songs	Marion Hutton, songs
6:30	Harry Wismer, sports		Fred Vandeventer, news	Sports Round-Up
6:45	Labor USA	Larry Lesueur, news	Stan Lomax, sports	Religion in the News
7pm	It's Your Business	Sweeney and March	Guess Who	Our Foreign Policy
7:15	Elmer Davis, news			
7:30	The Curt Massey Show	The Camel Caravan, Vaughn Monroe	Arthur Hale, news	Curtain Time
7:45			The Answer Man	
8pm	Famous Jury Trials	Hollywood Star Time	Twenty Questions	The Life of Riley
8:15				
8:30	I Deal in Crime	The Mayor of the Town	Juvenile Jury	Truth or Consequences
8:45		Ned Calmer, news (8:55pm)		
9pm	Gangbusters	Your Hit Parade	The Gold and Silver Minstrels, Eddie Green	The Roy Rogers Show
9:15				
9:30	Sherlock Holmes		Leave It to the Girls	Can You Top This
9:45		Saturday Night Serenade		
10pm	American Melodies		The Chicago Theater of the Air	The Judy Canova Show
10:15		This is Hollywood		
10:30	Bob Elson, news			Grand Ole Opry
10:45	Hayloft Hoedown	Public Affairs		

DAYTIME — FALL, 1946

Sunday

	ABC	CBS	MBS	NBC
9am	Bert Bacharach, talk	News	Uncle Don Reads the Comics	News
9:15		From the Organ Loft		Story to Order
9:30	Coast-to-Coast on a Bus		The Mutual Radio Chapel	Songs for Strings
9:45		St. Paul's Trinity Choir		Music
10am	Message of Israel	The CBS Church of the Air	George Putnam, news	The National Radio Pulpit
10:15			Frank Kingdon, news	
10:30	The Southernaires Quartet		Hawaii Calls	The Horn and Hardart Children's Hour
10:45				
11am	Brunch with the Fitzgeralds	Wings Over Jordan	George Putnam, news	
11:15			Brunch with Dorothy and Dick	
11:30	The Hour of Faith	The Salt Lake Tabernacle Choir		Charles F. McCarthy, news
11:45				Solitaire Time
12pm	Fiorello H. La Guardia, talk	Invitation to Learning	The Show Shop	Packham Inn
12:15				
12:30	Sunday Strings	Yours, Sincerely	Special Assignment	The Eternal Light
12:45			Melvin Elliott, news	
1pm	Johnny Thompson, songs	The People's Platform	The Canary Pet Shop	Ed Herlihy, news
1:15	Leo Durocher, sports		The Crime Cases of Warden Lawes	Sunday Matinee
1:30	Sammy Kaye's Sunday Serenade	Problems of Peace	Sweetheart Time	The University of Chicago Round Table
1:45		Howard K. Smith, news	Jimmy Farrell, songs	

DAYTIME — FALL, 1946

Monday-Friday

ABC	CBS	MBS	NBC	
The Breakfast Club	Joe King, news	The Green River Revue	Honeymoon in New York	9am
	This is New York, Danny O'Neill	Aunt Mary		9:15
		Alfred W. McCann, food	Daytime Classics	9:30
			The Nelson Olmsted Playhouse	9:45
My True Story	Joe Powers of Oakville	Henry Gladstone, news	Lee Sullivan's Varieties	10am
		Bessy Beatty, talk	Lora Lawton	10:15
Hymns of All Churches	The Strange Romance of Evelyn Winters		The Road of Life	10:30
Music / Listening Post	Time to Remember		Joyce Jordan, MD	10:45
Breakfast with Breneman	Arthur Godfrey Time	Prescott Robinson, news	Fred Waring Orchestra	11am
		Tello-Test Quiz		11:15
Home Edition	Grand Slam	Success Story / The Nooners Club	The Jack Berch Show	11:30
Between the Bookends	Rosemary	Victor Lindlahr, health	David Harum	11:45
Glamour Manor, Kenny Baker	Kate Smith Speaks	The Nooners Club	Rad Hall, news	12pm
	Aunt Jenny's True Life Stories	The Coke Club, Morton Downey	Richard Harkness, news	12:15
Nancy Booth Craig, talk	The Romance of Helen Trent	Henry Gladstone, news	Maggie McNellis, talk	12:30
	Our Gal Sunday	The Answer Man	Post Parade	12:45
H. R. Baukhage, news	Big Sister	The Better Half	Mary Margaret McBride, talk	1pm
The Women's Exchange	Ma Perkins			1:15
Galen Drake, talk	Young Dr. Malone	Jack Bundy's Album		1:30
	The Road of Life	The John J. Anthony Program	Ray Barrett, news	1:45

DAYTIME — FALL, 1946

Sunday

	ABC	CBS	MBS	NBC
2pm	Warriors of Peace	The Weekly News Review	Married for Life	The RCA Victor Show
2:15				
2:30	National Vespers	Stradaveri Orchestra	Sports	Harvest of Stars
2:45				
3pm	Danger, Dr. Danfield	New York Philharmonic Orchestra		The Sheaffer Parade
3:15				
3:30	A Present from Hollywood			One Man's Family
3:45	Samuel Pettengell, news			
4pm	Are These Our Children		The House of Mystery	The Quiz Kids
4:15				
4:30	The Green Hornet	The Hour of Charm	True Detective Mysteries	America United
4:45				
5pm	Quizdom Class	The Prudential Family Hour	The Shadow	NBC Symphony Orchestra
5:15				
5:30	Counterspy	The Hoagy Carmichael Show	Quick as a Flash	
5:45		William L. Shirer, news		

DAYTIME — FALL, 1946

Monday-Friday

ABC	CBS	MBS	NBC	
John B. Kennedy, news	The Second Mrs. Burton	Daily Dilemmas	The Guiding Light	2pm
The Powers Charm School	Perry Mason		Today's Children	2:15
Bride and Groom	Lone Journey	Queen for a Day	The Woman in White	2:30
	The Landt Trio and Curley		Masquerade	2:45
Ladies Be Seated	Surprise Party / Cinderella, Inc.	Martha Deane, talk	Life Can Be Beautiful	3pm
			Ma Perkins	3:15
Pat Barnes, talk	Winner Take All	Rambling with Gambling	Pepper Young's Family	3:30
The George Barnes Octet			The Right to Happiness	3:45
Meet Me in Manhattan	House Party	Dr. Eddy's Food Forum	Mary Noble, Backstage Wife	4pm
			Stella Dallas	4:15
Cliff Edwards, songs	Give and Take /	Uncle Don	Lorenzo Jones	4:30
Dick Tracy	Hollywood Jackpot	Buck Rogers of the 25th Century	Young Widder Brown	4:45
Terry and the Pirates	The American School of the Air	Hop Harrigan	When a Girl Marries	5pm
Sky King		The Adventures of Superman	Portia Faces Life	5:15
Jack Armstrong, the All-American Boy	Music / Theater of Romance /	Captain Midnight	Just Plain Bill	5:30
Tennessee Jed	Hawk Larabee / That's Life	The Tom Mix Ralston Straight Shooters	Front Page Farrell	5:45

DAYTIME — FALL, 1946

Saturday

	ABC	CBS	MBS	NBC
9am	Wake Up and Smile	Joe King, news	Jack and Loretta Clemens, talk	Percolator Party
9:15		This is New York, Danny O'Neill		
9:30			I Was a Convict	Story to Order
9:45		The Garden Gate		Your City and How It Works
10am	The Buddy Weed Trio	The Columbia Record Shop	Henry Gladstone, news	The Adventures of Frank Merriwell
10:15	The Brown Dots Quartet		Mission Sunday	
10:30	Junior Junction	Mary Lee Taylor, cooking	Rainbow House	Archie Andrews
10:45				
11am	Elizabeth Woodward, songs	Let's Pretend	Prescott Robinson, news	The Teentimer's Club
11:15	Johnny Thompson, songs		Musical Curtain Calls	
11:30	Tell Me Doctor	Give and Take	The Man on the Farm	Smilin' Ed's Buster Brown Gang
11:45	The Piano Playhouse			
12pm	Paul Porter, talk	The Armstrong Theater of Today	Judy, Jill and Johnny, songs	Rad Hall, news
12:15	Earl Wild, piano			Consumer Time
12:30	The American Farmer	Stars Over Hollywood	Henry Gladstone, news	Home is What You Make It
12:45			The Answer Man	
1pm	To Live in Peace	Grand Central Station	The Better Half	The National Farm and Home Hour
1:15				
1:30	Joe Hasel, sports	County Fair	Win, Lose or Draw	The Veterans Advisor
1:45	Sports		Sports	Elmer Peterson, news

DAYTIME — FALL, 1946

Saturday

	ABC	CBS	MBS	NBC
2pm		Sports		Your Host is Buffalo
2:15				
2:30				The Baxters
2:45				Sports
3pm				
3:15				
3:30				
3:45				
4pm				
4:15				
4:30	Sports Comments	Chicagoans Orchestra	Checkerboard Jamboree	
4:45	George Paxton Orchestra			
5pm	The Saturday Concert	Philadelphia Symphony Orchestra	What's the Name of That Song	
5:15				
5:30			The Listener Responds	Edward Tomlinson, news
5:45			Vera Massey and Hal Horton, songs	The King Cole Trio

LISTINGS FOR 1947

EVENING — WINTER, 1947

Sunday

	ABC	CBS	MBS	NBC
6pm	The Court of Missing Heirs	The Adventures of Ozzie and Harriet	Those Websters	The Catholic Hour
6:15				
6:30	The Greatest Story Ever Told	Kate Smith Sings	Nick Carter, Master Detective	The Bob Burns Show
6:45				
7pm	Drew Pearson, news	Gene Autry's Melody Ranch	The Mysterious Traveler	The Lucky Strike Program, Jack Benny
7:15	Don Gardiner, news			
7:30	The Clock	Blondie	Melvin Elliott, news	The Phil Harris - Alice Faye Show
7:45			Max Lerner, news	
8pm	Detroit Symphony Orchestra	The Adventures of Sam Spade	A. L. Alexander's Mediation Board	The Charlie McCarthy Show
8:15				
8:30		Crime Doctor	Special Investigator	The Fred Allen Show
8:45		Ned Calmer, news (8:55pm)	George Putnam, news	
9pm	Walter Winchell's Jergens Journal	The Campbell Room, Hildegarde	Exploring the Unknown	The Manhattan Merry-Go-Round
9:15	Louella Parsons, gossip			
9:30	Jimmy Fidler, gossip	The Eddie Bracken Show	Double or Nothing	The American Album of Familiar Music
9:45	Police Woman			
10pm	The Theater Guild on the Air	Take It or Leave It	A Brighter Tomorrow	The Bickersons
10:15				
10:30		We, the People	Meet the Press	Meet Me at Parky's
10:45				

EVENING — WINTER, 1947

Monday

ABC	CBS	MBS	NBC	
Walter Kiernan, news	Harry Marble, news	George Putnam, news	Kenneth Banghart, news	6pm
Ethel and Albert	In My Opinion	Bob Elson Interviews	Serenade to America	6:15
New York Tonight, Allen Prescott	Red Barber, sports	Fred Vandeventer, news		6:30
Dinner with the Fitzgeralds	The World Today	Connie Desmond, sports	Lowell Thomas, news	6:45
Taylor Grant, news	Mystery of the Week	Fulton Lewis Jr., news	The Chesterfield Supper Club	7pm
Elmer Davis, news	The Jack Smith Show	The Answer Man	Morgan Beatty, news	7:15
The Lone Ranger	The Bob Hawk Show	Henry J. Taylor, news	Barry Wood, songs	7:30
		Bill Brandt, sports	H. V. Kaltenborn, news	7:45
Lum and Abner	Inner Sanctum Mysteries	McGarry and the Mouse	The Cavalcade of America	8pm
The Skip Farrell Show				8:15
Sherlock Holmes	Joanie's Tea Room	The Casebook of Gregory Hood	The Voice of Firestone	8:30
	Bill Henry, news (8:55pm)			8:45
Dark Venture	The Lux Radio Theater	Gabriel Heatter, news	The Bell Telephone Hour	9pm
		Real Stories from Real Life		9:15
So You Want to Lead a Band		Guy Lombardo Orchestra	The Victor Borge Show	9:30
				9:45
The Doctors Talk It Over	The Lady Esther Screen Guild Theater	Broadway Talks Back	The Carnation Contented Hour	10pm
The Joe Mooney Quartet				10:15
Murder at Midnight	Sweeney and March	The Longines Symphonette	Dr. I. Q., The Mental Banker	10:30
				10:45

EVENING — WINTER, 1947

Tuesday

	ABC	CBS	MBS	NBC
6pm	Walter Kiernan, news	Harry Marble, news	George Putnam, news	Kenneth Banghart, news
6:15	Ethel and Albert	You and Alcohol	Bob Elson Interviews	Serenade to America
6:30	New York Tonight, Allen Prescott	Red Barber, sports	Fred Vandeventer, news	
6:45	Dinner with the Fitzgeralds	The World Today	Connie Desmond, sports	Lowell Thomas, news
7pm	Taylor Grant, news	Mystery of the Week	Fulton Lewis Jr., news	The Chesterfield Supper Club
7:15	Elmer Davis, news	The Jack Smith Show	The Answer Man	Morgan Beatty, news
7:30	Boston Blackie	The American Melody Hour	Arthur Hale, news	The Hollywood Theater
7:45			Bill Brandt, sports	H. V. Kaltenborn, news
8pm	Lum and Abner	Big Town	Scotland Yard's Inspector Burke	The Rudy Vallee Show
8:15	The Skip Farrell Show			
8:30	Boston Symphony Orchestra	The Mel Blanc Show	The Falcon	A Date with Judy
8:45		Bill Henry, news (8:55pm)		
9pm		Vox Pop	Gabriel Heatter, news	Amos 'n' Andy
9:15			Real Stories from Real Life	
9:30	Rex Maupin Orchestra	Arthur Godfrey's Talent Scouts	The American Forum of the Air	Fibber Magee and Molly
9:45				
10pm	Hank D'Amico Orchestra	One World Flight		The Pepsodent Show, Bob Hope
10:15			Upton Close, news	
10:30	Bob Elson, news	Open Hearing	The Longines Symphonette	The Raleigh Cigarette Program, Red Skelton
10:45	Earl Godwin, news			

EVENING — WINTER, 1947

Wednesday

ABC	CBS	MBS	NBC	
Walter Kiernan, news	Harry Marble, news	George Putnam, news	Kenneth Banghart, news	6pm
Ethel and Albert	Word from the Country	Bob Elson Interviews	Serenade to America	6:15
New York Tonight, Allen Prescott	Red Barber, sports	Fred Vandeventer, news		6:30
Dinner with the Fitzgeralds	The World Today	Connie Desmond, sports	Lowell Thomas, news	6:45
Taylor Grant, news	Mystery of the Week	Fulton Lewis Jr., news	The Chesterfield Supper Club	7pm
Elmer Davis, news	The Jack Smith Show	The Answer Man	Morgan Beatty, news	7:15
The Lone Ranger	The Adventures of Ellery Queen	Henry J. Taylor, news	Barry Wood, songs	7:30
		Bill Brandt, sports	H. V. Kaltenborn, news	7:45
Lum and Abner	The Jack Carson Show	Can You Top This	A Day in the Life of Dennis Day	8pm
The Skip Farrell Show				8:15
Tales of Willie Piper	Dr. Christian	It's Up to Youth	The Great Gildersleeve	8:30
	Bill Henry, news (8:55pm)			8:45
Paul Whiteman Orchestra	Songs By Sinatra	Gabriel Heatter, news	Duffy's Tavern	9pm
		Real Stories from Real Life		9:15
Pot o' Gold	The Ford Show, Dinah Shore	What's the Name of That Song	Mr. District Attorney	9:30
				9:45
Philco Radio Time, Bing Crosby	Hollywood Players	Did Justice Triumph	The Fabulous Dr. Tweedy	10pm
				10:15
The Henry Morgan Show	Information, Please	The Longines Symphonette	Kay Kyser's College of Musical Knowledge	10:30
				10:45

EVENING — WINTER, 1947

Thursday

	ABC	CBS	MBS	NBC
6pm	Walter Kiernan, news	Harry Marble, news	George Putnam, news	Kenneth Banghart, news
6:15	Ethel and Albert	In My Opinion	Bob Elson Interviews	Serenade to America
6:30	New York Tonight, Allen Prescott	Red Barber, sports	Fred Vandeventer, news	
6:45	Dinner with the Fitzgeralds	The World Today	Connie Desmond, sports	Lowell Thomas, news
7pm	Taylor Grant, news	Mystery of the Week	Fulton Lewis Jr., news	The Chesterfield Supper Club
7:15	Elmer Davis, news	The Jack Smith Show	The Answer Man	Morgan Beatty, news
7:30	Professor Quiz	Mr. Keen, Tracer of Lost Persons	Arthur Hale, news	Grand Marquee
7:45			Bill Brandt, sports	
8pm	Lum and Abner	Suspense	Sound Off	The Aldrich Family
8:15	Roscoe Drummond, news			
8:30	America's Town Meeting of the Air	The FBI in Peace and War	The Count of Monte Cristo	Maxwell House Coffee Time, Burns and Allen
8:45		Bill Henry, news (8:55pm)		
9pm		The Dick Haymes Show	Gabriel Heatter, news	The Kraft Music Hall, Eddie Foy
9:15			Real Stories from Real Life	
9:30	Echoes of New York	Crime Photographer	The Treasure Hour of Song	The Sealtest Village Store, Arden and Haley
9:45				
10pm	World Security Workshop	The Radio Reader's Digest	The Crime Club	Abbott and Costello
10:15				
10:30	Bob Elson, news	Phone Again Finnegan	The Longines Symphonette	Pabst Blue Ribbon Town, Eddie Cantor
10:45	Earl Godwin, news			

EVENING — WINTER, 1947

Friday

ABC	CBS	MBS	NBC	
Walter Kiernan, news	Harry Marble, news	George Putnam, news	Kenneth Banghart, news	6pm
Ethel and Albert	Report from Washington	Bob Elson Interviews	Serenade to America	6:15
New York Tonight, Allen Prescott	Red Barber, sports	Fred Vandeventer, news		6:30
Dinner with the Fitzgeralds	The World Today	Connie Desmond, sports	Lowell Thomas, news	6:45
Taylor Grant, news	Mystery of the Week	Fulton Lewis Jr., news	The Chesterfield Supper Club	7pm
Elmer Davis, news	The Jack Smith Show	The Answer Man	Morgan Beatty, news	7:15
The Lone Ranger	Sparkle Time	Henry J. Taylor, news	Barry Wood, songs	7:30
		Bill Brandt, sports	H. V. Kaltenborn, news	7:45
The Fat Man	The Baby Snooks Show	The Burl Ives Show	Highways in Melody	8pm
		Memorable Moments		8:15
This is Your FBI	The Adventures of the Thin Man	Love Story Theater	The Alan Young Show	8:30
	Bill Henry, news (8:55pm)			8:45
Break the Bank	The Ginny Simms Show	Gabriel Heatter, news	People Are Funny	9pm
		Real Stories from Real Life		9:15
The Sheriff	The Jimmy Durante Show	Bulldog Drummond	Waltz Time	9:30
				9:45
Madison Square Garden Boxing	It Pays to Be Ignorant	Spotlight on America	The Molle' Mystery Theater	10pm
				10:15
	Maisie	The Longines Symphonette	The Colgate Sports Newsreel, Bill Stern	10:30
			Public Affairs	10:45

EVENING — WINTER, 1947

Saturday

	ABC	CBS	MBS	NBC
6pm	Jimmy Blair, songs	Harry Marble, news	The Sport Question Box	Kenneth Banghart, news
6:15	The Chittison Trio	Once Upon a Tune	Guest House	Marion Hutton, songs
6:30	Harry Wismer, sports		Fred Vandeventer, news	The Boston Tune Party
6:45	Labor USA	Larry Lesueur, news	Stan Lomax, sports	Religion in the News
7pm	It's Your Business	Patti Clayton, songs	Guess Who	Our Foreign Policy
7:15	The Song Spinners	The Jean Sablon Show		
7:30	Stump the Authors	The Camel Caravan, Vaughn Monroe	Arthur Hale, news	Curtain Time
7:45			The Answer Man	
8pm	Famous Jury Trials	Hollywood Star Time	Twenty Questions	The Life of Riley
8:15				
8:30	I Deal in Crime	The Mayor of the Town	Scramby Amby	Truth or Consequences
8:45		Ned Calmer, news (8:55pm)		
9pm	Gangbusters	Your Hit Parade	The Gold and Silver Minstrels, Eddie Green	The Roy Rogers Show
9:15				
9:30	Murder and Mr. Malone		Leave It to the Girls	Can You Top This
9:45		Saturday Night Serenade		
10pm	American Melodies		The Chicago Theater of the Air	The Judy Canova Show
10:15		This is Hollywood		
10:30	Bob Elson, news			Grand Ole Opry
10:45	Hayloft Hoedown	Public Affairs		

DAYTIME — WINTER, 1947

Sunday

	ABC	CBS	MBS	NBC
9am	Bert Bacharach, talk	News	Your Problems	News
9:15		From the Organ Loft	Uncle Don Reads the Comics	Story to Order
9:30	Coast-to-Coast on a Bus		The Mutual Radio Chapel	Musical Favorites
9:45		Harry Marble, news		Music
10am	Message of Israel	The CBS Church of the Air	George Putnam, news	The National Radio Pulpit
10:15			Frank Kingdon, news	
10:30	The Southernaires Quartet		California Melodies	The Horn and Hardart Children's Hour
10:45				
11am	Brunch with the Fitzgeralds	Wings Over Jordan	George Putnam, news	
11:15			Brunch with Dorothy and Dick	
11:30	The Hour of Faith	The Salt Lake Tabernacle Choir		Charles F. McCarthy, news
11:45				Solitaire Time
12pm	Fiorello H. La Guardia, talk	Invitation to Learning	The Pilgrim Hour	World Front
12:15				
12:30	Sunday Strings	Yours, Sincerely	Special Assignment	The Eternal Light
12:45			Melvin Elliott, news	
1pm	Johnny Thompson, songs	The People's Platform	The Canary Pet Shop	Ed Herlihy, news
1:15	Leo Durocher, sports		Sigmund Spaeth's Music Quiz	Here's to Veterans
1:30	Sammy Kaye's Sunday Serenade	Problems of Peace	Juvenile Jury	The University of Chicago Round Table
1:45		Howard K. Smith, news		

DAYTIME — WINTER, 1947

Monday-Friday

ABC	CBS	MBS	NBC	
The Breakfast Club	Joe King, news	Henry La Crosett, news	Honeymoon in New York	9am
	This is New York, Danny O'Neill	Record Riddles		9:15
		Alfred W. McCann, food	Daytime Classics	9:30
			Jose Bethancourt Orchestra	9:45
My True Story	Hits and Misses	Henry Gladstone, news	Lee Sullivan's Varieties	10am
		Bessy Beatty, talk	The Nelson Olmstead Playhouse	10:15
Hymns of All Churches	The Strange Romance of Evelyn Winters		The Road of Life	10:30
Music / Listening Post	David Harum		Joyce Jordan, MD	10:45
Breakfast with Breneman	Arthur Godfrey Time	Prescott Robinson, news	Fred Waring Orchestra	11am
		Tello-Test Quiz		11:15
Hollywood Story	Grand Slam	Success Story / Easy Does It	The Jack Berch Show	11:30
Between the Bookends	Rosemary	Victor Lindlahr, health	Lora Lawton	11:45
The Kenny Baker Show	Kate Smith Speaks	Checkerboard Jamboree	Rad Hall, news	12pm
	Aunt Jenny's True Life Stories	The Coke Club, Morton Downey	Richard Harkness, news	12:15
Nancy Booth Craig, talk	The Romance of Helen Trent	Henry Gladstone, news	Maggie McNellis, talk	12:30
	Our Gal Sunday	So This is Love	Post Parade	12:45
H. R. Baukhage, news	Big Sister	The Better Half	Mary Margaret McBride, talk	1pm
The Powers Charm School	Ma Perkins			1:15
Galen Drake, talk	Young Dr. Malone	Listen Here Ladies		1:30
	The Road of Life	The Answer Man	Robert McCormick, news	1:45

DAYTIME — WINTER, 1947

Sunday

	ABC	CBS	MBS	NBC
2pm	Warriors of Peace	The Weekly News Review	The Crime Cases of Warden Lawes	The RCA Victor Show
2:15			Official Detective	
2:30	National Vespers	Here's to You	George Putnam, news	Harvest of Stars
2:45			Dr. Parker Presents	
3pm	Danger, Dr. Danfield	New York Philharmonic Orchestra	The Quiz of Two Cities	The Sheaffer Parade
3:15				
3:30	A Present from Hollywood		Crimes of Carelessness	One Man's Family
3:45	Samuel Pettengell, news			
4pm	Are These Our Children		The House of Mystery	The Quiz Kids
4:15				
4:30	The Green Hornet	The Hour of Charm	True Detective Mysteries	America United
4:45				
5pm	Quizdom Class	The Prudential Family Hour	The Shadow	NBC Symphony Orchestra
5:15				
5:30	Counterspy	The Hoagy Carmichael Show	Quick as a Flash	
5:45		William L. Shirer, news		

DAYTIME — WINTER, 1947

Monday-Friday

ABC	CBS	MBS	NBC	
Walter Kiernan, news	The Second Mrs. Burton	Daily Dilemmas	Today's Children	*2pm*
The Women's Exchange	Perry Mason		The Woman in White	*2:15*
Bride and Groom	Lone Journey	Queen for a Day	Masquerade	*2:30*
	Rose of My Dreams		The Light of the World	*2:45*
Ladies Be Seated	Bouquet For You, Patti Clayton	Martha Deane, talk	Life Can Be Beautiful	*3pm*
			Ma Perkins	*3:15*
Pat Barnes, talk	Winner Take All	Rambling with Gambling	Pepper Young's Family	*3:30*
Hollywood Tour			The Right to Happiness	*3:45*
Tommy Bartlett Time	House Party	Dr. Eddy's Food Forum	Mary Noble, Backstage Wife	*4pm*
			Stella Dallas	*4:15*
Cliff Edwards, songs	That's Life /	Uncle Don	Lorenzo Jones	*4:30*
Dick Tracy	Hollywood Jackpot	Buck Rogers of the 25th Century	Young Widder Brown	*4:45*
Terry and the Pirates	The American School of the Air	Hop Harrigan	When a Girl Marries	*5pm*
Sky King		The Adventures of Superman	Portia Faces Life	*5:15*
Jack Armstrong, the All-American Boy	Treasury Bandstand	Captain Midnight	Just Plain Bill	*5:30*
Tennessee Jed		The Tom Mix Ralston Straight Shooters	Front Page Farrell	*5:45*

DAYTIME — WINTER, 1947

Saturday

	ABC	CBS	MBS	NBC
9am	Wake Up and Smile	Joe King, news	Ask Dr. Eddy	The Ted Brown Show
9:15		This is New York, Danny O'Neill		
9:30			Rainbow House	The Camp Meetin' Choir
9:45		The Garden Gate		Your City and How It Works
10am	Johnny Thompson, songs	The Columbia Record Shop	Henry Gladstone, news	The Adventures of Frank Merriwell
10:15	The Buddy Weed Trio		African Trek	
10:30	Junior Junction	Mary Lee Taylor, cooking	The PAL Show	Archie Andrews
10:45				
11am	Elizabeth Woodward, songs	Let's Pretend	Prescott Robinson, news	The Teentimer's Club
11:15	Johnny Thompson, songs		Tello-Test Quiz	
11:30	The Piano Playhouse	The Adventurer's Club	The Man on the Farm	Smilin' Ed's Buster Brown Gang
11:45				
12pm	Texas Jim Robertson, songs	The Armstrong Theater of Today	Shirley Eder Presents	Rad Hall, news
12:15	Tell Me Doctor			Consumer Time
12:30	The American Farmer	Stars Over Hollywood	Henry Gladstone, news	Home is What You Make It
12:45			The Answer Man	
1pm	To Live in Peace	Grand Central Station	The Better Half	The National Farm and Home Hour
1:15				
1:30	Rex Maupin Orchestra	County Fair	Monaghan, the Record Man	The Veterans Advisor
1:45				Elmer Peterson, news

DAYTIME — WINTER, 1947

Saturday

	ABC	CBS	MBS	NBC
2pm	The Metropolitan Opera	Give and Take	Movie Matinee	Your Host is Buffalo
2:15				Your Radio Reporter
2:30		Columbia's Country Journal		The Baxters
2:45				Bob Houston, songs
3pm		Cross-Section USA	Barry Gray, talk	Orchestras of the Nation
3:15				
3:30		Treasury Bandstand		
3:45				
4pm		Elliott Lawrence Orchestra		Doctors, Then and Now
4:15				
4:30		Adventures in Science	Horse Racing	Names of Tomorrow
4:45		Of Men and Books		
5pm	Tea and Crumpets	Philadelphia Symphony Orchestra	For Your Approval	The Nelson Olmsted Playhouse
5:15				Snooky Lanson, songs
5:30			Vera Holly, songs	Edward Tomlinson, news
5:45			Vera Massey and Hal Horton, songs	The King Cole Trio

EVENING — SPRING, 1947

Sunday

	ABC	CBS	MBS	NBC
6pm	Drew Pearson, news	The Adventures of Ozzie and Harriet	Those Websters	The Catholic Hour
6:15	Don Gardiner, news			
6:30	The Greatest Story Ever Told	Kate Smith Sings	Nick Carter, Master Detective	The Bob Burns Show
6:45				
7pm	Tales of Willie Piper	Gene Autry's Melody Ranch	The Mysterious Traveler	The Lucky Strike Program, Jack Benny
7:15				
7:30	The Clock	Blondie	Melvin Elliott, news	The Phil Harris - Alice Faye Show
7:45			Max Lerner, news	
8pm	Detroit Symphony Orchestra	The Adventures of Sam Spade	A. L. Alexander's Mediation Board	The Charlie McCarthy Show
8:15				
8:30		Crime Doctor	Jack Reilly, sports	The Fred Allen Show
8:45		Ned Calmer, news (8:55pm)	George Putnam, news	
9pm	Walter Winchell's Jergens Journal	Meet Corliss Archer	Exploring the Unknown	The Manhattan Merry-Go-Round
9:15	Louella Parsons, gossip			
9:30	Jimmy Fidler, gossip	The Texaco Star Theater, Tony Martin	Double or Nothing	The American Album of Familiar Music
9:45	Police Woman			
10pm	The Theater Guild on the Air	Take It or Leave It	A Brighter Tomorrow	The Bickersons
10:15				
10:30		We, the People	The Family Theater	The First Piano Quartet
10:45				

EVENING — SPRING, 1947

Monday

ABC	CBS	MBS	NBC	
Joe Hasel, sports	Eric Severeid, news	George Putnam, news	Kenneth Banghart, news	6pm
Ethel and Albert	In My Opinion	Bob Elson Interviews	Serenade to America	6:15
New York Tonight, Allen Prescott	Red Barber, sports	Fred Vandeventer, news		6:30
Dinner with the Fitzgeralds	The World Today	Stan Lomax, sports	Lowell Thomas, news	6:45
Taylor Grant, news	Mystery of the Week	Fulton Lewis Jr., news	The Chesterfield Supper Club	7pm
Elmer Davis, news	The Jack Smith Show	The Answer Man	Morgan Beatty, news	7:15
The Lone Ranger	The Bob Hawk Show	Henry J. Taylor, news	Patterns of Melody	7:30
		Bill Brandt, sports	H. V. Kaltenborn, news	7:45
Lum and Abner	Inner Sanctum Mysteries	Scotland Yard's Inspector Burke	The Cavalcade of America	8pm
The Bobby Doyle Show				8:15
Sherlock Holmes	Joanie's Tea Room	The Casebook of Gregory Hood	The Voice of Firestone	8:30
	Bill Henry, news (8:55pm)			8:45
Treasury Agent	The Lux Radio Theater	Gabriel Heatter, news	The Bell Telephone Hour	9pm
		Real Stories from Real Life		9:15
So You Want to Lead a Band		Guy Lombardo Orchestra	The Victor Borge Show	9:30
				9:45
The Doctors Talk It Over	The Lady Esther Screen Guild Theater	The Fishing and Hunting Club	The Carnation Contented Hour	10pm
The Buddy Weed Trio				10:15
Murder at Midnight	Sweeney and March	The Longines Symphonette	Dr. I. Q., The Mental Banker	10:30
				10:45

EVENING — SPRING, 1947

Tuesday

	ABC	CBS	MBS	NBC
6pm	Joe Hasel, sports	Eric Severeid, news	George Putnam, news	Kenneth Banghart, news
6:15	Ethel and Albert	Frontiers of Science	Bob Elson Interviews	Serenade to America
6:30	New York Tonight, Allen Prescott	Red Barber, sports	Fred Vandeventer, news	
6:45	Dinner with the Fitzgeralds	The World Today	Stan Lomax, sports	Lowell Thomas, news
7pm	Taylor Grant, news	Mystery of the Week	Fulton Lewis Jr., news	The Chesterfield Supper Club
7:15	Elmer Davis, news	The Jack Smith Show	The Answer Man	Morgan Beatty, news
7:30	Boston Blackie	The American Melody Hour	Arthur Hale, news	The Hollywood Theater
7:45			Bill Brandt, sports	
8pm	Lum and Abner	Big Town	The Crime Cases of Warden Lawes	At Home with the Berles
8:15	The Bobby Doyle Show		Special Investigator	
8:30	Boston Symphony Orchestra	The Mel Blanc Show	The Falcon	A Date with Judy
8:45		Bill Henry, news (8:55pm)		
9pm		Arthur Godfrey's Talent Scouts	Gabriel Heatter, news	Amos 'n' Andy
9:15			Real Stories from Real Life	
9:30	Rex Maupin Orchestra	Studio One	The American Forum of the Air	Fibber Magee and Molly
9:45				
10pm	Hank D'Amico Orchestra			The Pepsodent Show, Bob Hope
10:15			The Vic Damone Show	
10:30	Hoosier Hop	Open Hearing	The Longines Symphonette	The Raleigh Cigarette Program, Red Skelton
10:45	Earl Godwin, news			

LISTINGS FOR 1947

EVENING — SPRING, 1947

Wednesday

ABC	CBS	MBS	NBC	
Joe Hasel, sports	Eric Severeid, news	George Putnam, news	Kenneth Banghart, news	6pm
Ethel and Albert	Henry A. Wallace, comment	Bob Elson Interviews	Serenade to America	6:15
New York Tonight, Allen Prescott	Red Barber, sports	Fred Vandeventer, news		6:30
Dinner with the Fitzgeralds	The World Today	Stan Lomax, sports	Lowell Thomas, news	6:45
Taylor Grant, news	Mystery of the Week	Fulton Lewis Jr., news	The Chesterfield Supper Club	7pm
Elmer Davis, news	The Jack Smith Show	The Answer Man	Morgan Beatty, news	7:15
The Lone Ranger	Theater of Romance	Strange As It Seems	Manor House Party	7:30
		Bill Brandt, sports	H. V. Kaltenborn, news	7:45
Lum and Abner	The Jack Carson Show	Can You Top This	A Day in the Life of Dennis Day	8pm
The Bobby Doyle Show				8:15
The Court of Missing Heirs	Dr. Christian	Opinionaire	The Great Gildersleeve	8:30
	Bill Henry, news (8:55pm)			8:45
Paul Whiteman Orchestra	Songs By Sinatra	Gabriel Heatter, news	Duffy's Tavern	9pm
		Real Stories from Real Life		9:15
The Beulah Show	The Ford Show, Dinah Shore	Let's Go to the Movies	Mr. District Attorney	9:30
				9:45
Philco Radio Time, Bing Crosby	The Whistler	Did Justice Triumph	The Big Story	10pm
				10:15
The Henry Morgan Show	Information, Please	The Longines Symphonette	Kay Kyser's College of Musical Knowledge	10:30
				10:45

EVENING — SPRING, 1947

Thursday

	ABC	CBS	MBS	NBC
6pm	Joe Hasel, sports	Eric Severeid, news	George Putnam, news	Kenneth Banghart, news
6:15	Ethel and Albert	In My Opinion	Bob Elson Interviews	Serenade to America
6:30	New York Tonight, Allen Prescott	Red Barber, sports	Fred Vandeventer, news	
6:45	Dinner with the Fitzgeralds	The World Today	Stan Lomax, sports	Lowell Thomas, news
7pm	Taylor Grant, news	Mystery of the Week	Fulton Lewis Jr., news	The Chesterfield Supper Club
7:15	Elmer Davis, news	The Jack Smith Show	The Answer Man	Morgan Beatty, news
7:30	The Studs Terkel Show	Mr. Keen, Tracer of Lost Persons	Arthur Hale, news	Grand Marquee
7:45			Bill Brandt, sports	
8pm	Lum and Abner	Suspense	Johnny Modero, Pier 23	The Aldrich Family
8:15	Edwin D. Canham, news			
8:30	America's Town Meeting of the Air	The FBI in Peace and War	The Count of Monte Cristo	Maxwell House Coffee Time, Burns and Allen
8:45		Bill Henry, news (8:55pm)		
9pm		The Dick Haymes Show	Gabriel Heatter, news	The Kraft Music Hall, Eddie Foy
9:15			Real Stories from Real Life	
9:30	Those Sensational Years	Casey, Crime Photographer	The Treasure Hour of Song	The Sealtest Village Store, Arden and Haley
9:45				
10pm	World Security Workshop	The Radio Reader's Digest	The Crime Club	Abbott and Costello
10:15				
10:30	Ralph Norman Orchestra	The Man Called X	The Longines Symphonette	Pabst Blue Ribbon Town, Eddie Cantor
10:45	Earl Godwin, news			

EVENING — SPRING, 1947

Friday

ABC	CBS	MBS	NBC	
Joe Hasel, sports	Eric Severeid, news	George Putnam, news	Kenneth Banghart, news	*6pm*
Ethel and Albert	Report from Washington	Bob Elson Interviews	Serenade to America	*6:15*
New York Tonight, Allen Prescott	Red Barber, sports	Fred Vandeventer, news		*6:30*
Dinner with the Fitzgeralds	The World Today	Stan Lomax, sports	Lowell Thomas, news	*6:45*
Taylor Grant, news	Mystery of the Week	Fulton Lewis Jr., news	The Chesterfield Supper Club	*7pm*
Elmer Davis, news	The Jack Smith Show	The Answer Man	Morgan Beatty, news	*7:15*
The Lone Ranger	Sound Off	Henry J. Taylor, news	Manor House Party	*7:30*
		Bill Brandt, sports	H. V. Kaltenborn, news	*7:45*
The Fat Man	The Baby Snooks Show	The Burl Ives Show	Highways in Melody	*8pm*
		Memorable Moments		*8:15*
This is Your FBI	The Adventures of the Thin Man	Leave It to the Girls	The Alan Young Show	*8:30*
	Bill Henry, news (8:55pm)			*8:45*
Break the Bank	The Ginny Simms Show	Gabriel Heatter, news	People Are Funny	*9pm*
		Real Stories from Real Life		*9:15*
The Sheriff	The Jimmy Durante Show	Bulldog Drummond	Waltz Time	*9:30*
				9:45
Madison Square Garden Boxing	It Pays to Be Ignorant	Meet the Press	The Molle' Mystery Theater	*10pm*
				10:15
	My Friend Irma	The Longines Symphonette	The Colgate Sports Newsreel, Bill Stern	*10:30*
			Public Affairs	*10:45*

EVENING — SPRING, 1947

Saturday

	ABC	CBS	MBS	NBC
6pm	Jimmy Blair, songs	Bob Hite, news	George Putnam, news	Kenneth Banghart, news
6:15	The Chittison Trio	Word from the Country	Bill Berns, songs	The Ballot Box
6:30	Harry Wismer, sports	Red Barber, sports	Fred Vandeventer, news	
6:45	Labor USA	Larry Lesueur, news	Stan Lomax, sports	Religion in the News
7pm	It's Your Business	Patti Clayton, songs	Guess Who	Our Foreign Policy
7:15	The Song Spinners	The Jean Sablon Show		
7:30	The Music Library	The Camel Caravan, Vaughn Monroe	Arthur Hale, news	Curtain Time
7:45			The Answer Man	
8pm	Famous Jury Trials	Once Upon a Tune	Twenty Questions	The Life of Riley
8:15				
8:30	I Deal in Crime	The Mayor of the Town	Scramby Amby	Truth or Consequences
8:45		Ned Calmer, news (8:55pm)		
9pm	Gangbusters	The Bill Goodwin Show	The Mighty Casey	Your Hit Parade
9:15				
9:30	Murder and Mr. Malone	Saturday Night Serenade	High Adventure	Can You Top This
9:45				
10pm	Professor Quiz	This is Hollywood	The Chicago Theater of the Air	The Judy Canova Show
10:15				
10:30	Hayloft Hoedown	Public Affairs		Grand Ole Opry
10:45				

DAYTIME — SPRING, 1947

Sunday

	ABC	CBS	MBS	NBC
9am	Bert Bacharach, talk	News	Your Problems	News
9:15		From the Organ Loft	The Sermon of the Week	Your City and How It Works
9:30	Coast-to-Coast on a Bus		The Mutual Radio Chapel	Kurt Maler, piano
9:45		Harry Marble, news		Music
10am	Message of Israel	The CBS Church of the Air	George Putnam, news	The National Radio Pulpit
10:15			Frank Kingdon, news	
10:30	The Southernaires Quartet		Time for Remembrance	The Horn and Hardart Children's Hour
10:45				
11am	Brunch with the Fitzgeralds	Wings Over Jordan	George Putnam, news	
11:15			Brunch with Dorothy and Dick	
11:30	The Hour of Faith	The Salt Lake Tabernacle Choir		Charles F. McCarthy, news
11:45				Solitaire Time
12pm	Fiorello H. La Guardia, talk	Invitation to Learning	The Show Shop	Hi Jinx
12:15				
12:30	Galen Drake, talk	As Others See It	Special Assignment	The Eternal Light
12:45			Melvin Elliott, news	
1pm	Johnny Thompson, songs	The People's Platform	The Canary Pet Shop	Ed Herlihy, news
1:15			Take These Notes	Frank Parker, songs
1:30	Sammy Kaye's Sunday Serenade	Time for Reason About Radio	Juvenile Jury	The University of Chicago Round Table
1:45		Howard K. Smith, news		

DAYTIME — SPRING, 1947

Monday-Friday

ABC	CBS	MBS	NBC	
The Breakfast Club	Joe King, news	Henry La Crosett, news	Honeymoon in New York	9am
	This is New York, Danny O'Neill	Record Riddles		9:15
		Alfred W. McCann, food	The Jim Fleming Show	9:30
				9:45
My True Story	Hits and Misses	Henry Gladstone, news	Katie's Daughter	10am
		Martha Deane, talk	Jack Kilty, songs	10:15
Betty Crocker, cooking	The Strange Romance of Evelyn Winters		The Road of Life	10:30
Music / Listening Post	David Harum		Joyce Jordan, MD	10:45
Breakfast with Breneman	Arthur Godfrey Time	Prescott Robinson, news	Fred Waring Orchestra	11am
		Tello-Test Quiz		11:15
Hollywood Story	Grand Slam	Heart's Desire	The Jack Berch Show	11:30
Between the Bookends	Rosemary		Lora Lawton	11:45
The Kenny Baker Show	Kate Smith Speaks	Albert Warner, news	Rad Hall, news	12pm
	Aunt Jenny's True Life Stories	Victor Lindlahr, health	Richard Harkness, news	12:15
Nancy Booth Craig, talk	The Romance of Helen Trent	Henry Gladstone, news	Maggie McNellis, talk	12:30
	Our Gal Sunday	So This is Love	The Memory Album	12:45
H. R. Baukhage, news	Big Sister	The Better Half	Mary Margaret McBride, talk	1pm
Nancy Booth Craig, talk	Ma Perkins			1:15
Galen Drake, talk	Young Dr. Malone	Listen Here Ladies		1:30
	The Road of Life	The Answer Man	Robert McCormick, news	1:45

DAYTIME — SPRING, 1947

Sunday

	ABC	CBS	MBS	NBC
2pm	Deadline Mystery	The Weekly News Review	Married for Life	The RCA Victor Show
2:15				
2:30	National Vespers	Here's to You	George Putnam, news	Harvest of Stars
2:45			Word Stories	
3pm	Warriors of Peace	New York Philharmonic Orchestra	Lawyer Q	The Sheaffer Parade
3:15				
3:30	The Vagabonds Quartet		Crimes of Carelessness	One Man's Family
3:45	Samuel Pettengell, news			
4pm	Are These Our Children		The House of Mystery	The Quiz Kids
4:15				
4:30	This Week Around the World	The Hour of Charm	True Detective Mysteries	America United
4:45				
5pm	Quizdom Class	The Prudential Family Hour	The Shadow	NBC Symphony Orchestra
5:15				
5:30	Counterspy	The Hoagy Carmichael Show	Quick as a Flash	
5:45		Joseph C. Harsch, news		

DAYTIME — SPRING, 1947

Monday-Friday

ABC	CBS	MBS	NBC	
Walter Kiernan, news	The Second Mrs. Burton	Queen for a Day	Today's Children	*2pm*
The Women's Exchange	Perry Mason		The Woman in White	*2:15*
Bride and Groom	Lone Journey	Daily Dilemmas	Masquerade	*2:30*
	Rose of My Dreams		The Light of the World	*2:45*
Ladies Be Seated	Bouquet For You, Patti Clayton	Martha Deane, talk	Life Can Be Beautiful	*3pm*
			Ma Perkins	*3:15*
Pat Barnes, talk	Winner Take All	Rambling with Gambling	Pepper Young's Family	*3:30*
Tommy Bartlett Time			The Right to Happiness	*3:45*
	Hint Hunt	Ask Dr. Tobey	Mary Noble, Backstage Wife	*4pm*
Hollywood Tour			Stella Dallas	*4:15*
Cliff Edwards, songs	Give and Take	Barry Gray, talk	Lorenzo Jones	*4:30*
Dick Tracy		Adventure Parade	Young Widder Brown	*4:45*
Terry and the Pirates	House Party	Hop Harrigan	When a Girl Marries	*5pm*
Sky King		The Adventures of Superman	Portia Faces Life	*5:15*
Jack Armstrong, the All-American Boy	Treasury Bandstand	Captain Midnight	Just Plain Bill	*5:30*
Tennessee Jed		The Tom Mix Ralston Straight Shooters	Front Page Farrell	*5:45*

DAYTIME — SPRING, 1947

Saturday

	ABC	CBS	MBS	NBC
9am	Wake Up and Smile	Joe King, news	Record Riddles	The Triple B Ranch
9:15		This is New York, Danny O'Neill	Let's Go	
9:30			Uncle Don's Record Party	All Aboard for Adventure
9:45		The Columbia Record Shop		The NBC Stamp Club
10am	Your Home Beautiful		Henry Gladstone, news	The Adventures of Frank Merriwell
10:15	The Buddy Weed Trio	The Garden Gate	Robin Morgan, songs	
10:30	Junior Junction	Mary Lee Taylor, cooking	The PAL Show	Archie Andrews
10:45				
11am	Elizabeth Woodward, songs	Let's Pretend	Prescott Robinson, news	The Teentimer's Club
11:15	Johnny Thompson, songs		Tello-Test Quiz	
11:30	The Piano Playhouse	The Adventurer's Club	The Man on the Farm	Smilin' Ed's Buster Brown Gang
11:45				
12pm	Your Children and Your Schools	The Armstrong Theater of Today	Shirley Eder Presents	Rad Hall, news
12:15	Tell Me Doctor		New York Soapbox	Consumer Time
12:30	The American Farmer	Stars Over Hollywood	Henry Gladstone, news	Spending for Happiness
12:45			The Answer Man	Let's Ask Mom
1pm	Youth asks the Government	Grand Central Station	Luncheon at Sardi's	The National Farm and Home Hour
1:15				
1:30	Galen Drake, talk	County Fair	What's the Name of That Song	The Veterans Advisor
1:45				Here's to Veterans

DAYTIME — SPRING, 1947

Saturday

	ABC	CBS	MBS	NBC
2pm	Our Town Speaks	Give and Take	On the Swing Side	How's Your Health
2:15				Your Radio Reporter
2:30	Hill Toppers Music	Columbia's Country Journal	This is Jazz	The Baxters
2:45	This is for You			The Camp Meetin' Choir
3pm	Phil Brestoff Orchestra	Cross-Section USA	Barry Gray, talk	Orchestras of the Nation
3:15				
3:30	Sunset Roundup	Treasury Bandstand		
3:45				
4pm	Stars in the Afternoon	Elliott Lawrence Orchestra	Horse Racing	Doctors, Then and Now
4:15			Barry Gray, talk	
4:30	The Treasury Band Show	Adventures in Science		Home is What You Make It
4:45		Of Men and Books		
5pm	Tea and Crumpets	Philadelphia Symphony Orchestra	For Your Approval	The US Treasury Show
5:15				Art Mooney Orchestra
5:30			Jean Tighe, songs	The Three Suns
5:45			Jan August, songs	The King Cole Trio

EVENING — SUMMER, 1947

Sunday

	ABC	CBS	MBS	NBC
6pm	Drew Pearson, news	The Silver Theater	Those Websters	The Catholic Hour
6:15	Don Gardiner, news			
6:30	The Greatest Story Ever Told	The Pause That Refreshes	Nick Carter, Master Detective	The Adventures of Ellery Queen
6:45				
7pm	The Candid Microphone	Gene Autry's Melody Ranch	The Mysterious Traveler	The Jack Paar Show
7:15				
7:30	Those Sensational Years	Blondie	Melvin Elliott, news	Rogue's Gallery
7:45			Mel Allen, sports	
8pm	Detroit Symphony Orchestra	The Adventures of Sam Spade	A. L. Alexander's Mediation Board	Alex Templeton Time
8:15				
8:30		Crime Doctor	A Brighter Tomorrow	Front and Center, Dorothy Lamour
8:45		Ned Calmer, news (8:55pm)		
9pm	Walter Winchell's Jergens Journal	Meet Corliss Archer	Exploring the Unknown	The Manhattan Merry-Go-Round
9:15	Louella Parsons, gossip			
9:30	Jimmy Fidler, gossip	The Texaco Star Theater, Tony Martin	The Jim Backus Show	The American Album of Familiar Music
9:45	Rex Maupin Orchestra			
10pm	The Theater Guild on the Air	Xavier Cugat Orchestra	George Putnam, news	Take It or Leave It
10:15			Max Lerner, news	
10:30		Strike It Rich	The Family Theater	The Big Break
10:45				

EVENING — SUMMER, 1947

Monday

ABC	CBS	MBS	NBC	
Walter Kiernan, news	Eric Severeid, news	George Putnam, news	Kenneth Banghart, news	6pm
Ethel and Albert	In My Opinion	Bob Elson Interviews	Serenade to America	6:15
Joe Hasel, sports	Red Barber, sports	Fred Vandeventer, news		6:30
Dinner with the Fitzgeralds	The World Today	Stan Lomax, sports	Lowell Thomas, news	6:45
Taylor Grant, news	The Robert Q. Lewis Show	Fulton Lewis Jr., news	The Chesterfield Supper Club	7pm
Joseph Alsop, news		The Answer Man	Morgan Beatty, news	7:15
The Lone Ranger	Club Fifteen	Henry J. Taylor, news	Patterns of Melody	7:30
	Robert Trout, news	Bill Brandt, sports	Henry Cassidy, news	7:45
Lum and Abner	Inner Sanctum Mysteries	Scotland Yard's Inspector Burke	Plays by Ear	8pm
The Bobby Doyle Show				8:15
Treasury Agent	Arthur Godfrey's Talent Scouts	The Casebook of Gregory Hood	The Voice of Firestone	8:30
	Ned Calmer, news (8:55pm)			8:45
The Clock	You Are There	Gabriel Heatter, news	The Bell Telephone Hour	9pm
		Real Stories from Real Life		9:15
So You Want to Lead a Band	Escape	Guy Lombardo Orchestra	Dr. I. Q., the Mental Banker	9:30
				9:45
The Doctors Talk It Over	My Friend Irma	Quiet, Please	The Carnation Contented Hour	10pm
The Buddy Weed Trio				10:15
Murder at Midnight	The Bob Hawk Show	The Longines Symphonette	The First Piano Quartet	10:30
				10:45

EVENING — SUMMER, 1947

Tuesday

	ABC	CBS	MBS	NBC
6pm	Walter Kiernan, news	Eric Severeid, news	George Putnam, news	Kenneth Banghart, news
6:15	Ethel and Albert	Frontiers of Science	Bob Elson Interviews	Serenade to America
6:30	Joe Hasel, sports	Red Barber, sports	Fred Vandeventer, news	
6:45	Dinner with the Fitzgeralds	The World Today	Stan Lomax, sports	Lowell Thomas, news
7pm	Taylor Grant, news	The Robert Q. Lewis Show	Fulton Lewis Jr., news	The Chesterfield Supper Club
7:15	Joseph Alsop, news		The Answer Man	Morgan Beatty, news
7:30	The Green Hornet	Club Fifteen	Arthur Hale, news	The Hollywood Theater
7:45		Robert Trout, news	Bill Brandt, sports	
8pm	Lum and Abner	Big Town	The Crime Cases of Warden Lawes	At Home with the Berles
8:15	The Bobby Doyle Show		Official Detective	
8:30	Esplanade Concert Orchestra	Mr. and Mrs. North	The Falcon	A Date with Judy
8:45		Ned Calmer, news (8:55pm)		
9pm		We, the People	Gabriel Heatter, news	Call the Police
9:15			Real Stories from Real Life	
9:30	Summer Serenade	Studio One	The American Forum of the Air	Fred Waring Orchestra
9:45				
10pm	Hank D'Amico Orchestra			The Adventures of Philip Marlowe
10:15			Scout About Town	
10:30	Hoosier Hop	Return Engagement	The Longines Symphonette	An Evening with Romberg
10:45	Earl Godwin, news			

EVENING — SUMMER, 1947

Wednesday

ABC	CBS	MBS	NBC	
Walter Kiernan, news	Eric Severeid, news	George Putnam, news	Kenneth Banghart, news	6pm
Ethel and Albert	Dr. Carlos Lozano, comment	Bob Elson Interviews	Serenade to America	6:15
Joe Hasel, sports	Red Barber, sports	Fred Vandeventer, news		6:30
Dinner with the Fitzgeralds	The World Today	Stan Lomax, sports	Lowell Thomas, news	6:45
Taylor Grant, news	The Robert Q. Lewis Show	Fulton Lewis Jr., news	The Chesterfield Supper Club	7pm
Joseph Alsop, news		The Answer Man	Morgan Beatty, news	7:15
The Lone Ranger	Club Fifteen	Strange As It Seems	Manor House Party	7:30
	Robert Trout, news	Bill Brandt, sports	Henry Cassidy, news	7:45
Lum and Abner	The American Melody Hour	Can You Top This	Gramps	8pm
The Bobby Doyle Show				8:15
Paul Whiteman Orchestra	Dr. Christian	Boston Blackie	Summerfield Bandstand	8:30
	Ned Calmer, news (8:55pm)			8:45
The Beulah Show	Rhapsody in Rhythm	Gabriel Heatter, news	Hi Jinx	9pm
		Real Stories from Real Life		9:15
The Eddie Albert Show	The Ford Showroom	Let's Go to the Movies	Mr. District Attorney	9:30
				9:45
The Phil Silvers Show	The Whistler	Shadows of the Mind	The Big Story	10pm
				10:15
Lights Out	Doorway to Life	The Longines Symphonette	Dan Carson	10:30
				10:45

EVENING — SUMMER, 1947				
Thursday				
	ABC	CBS	MBS	NBC
6pm	Walter Kiernan, news	Eric Severeid, news	George Putnam, news	Kenneth Banghart, news
6:15	Ethel and Albert	In My Opinion	Bob Elson Interviews	Serenade to America
6:30	Joe Hasel, sports	Red Barber, sports	Fred news	
6:45	Dinner with the Fitzgeralds	The World Today	Stan Lomax, sports	Lowell Thomas, news
7pm	Taylor Grant, news	The Robert Q. Lewis Show	Fulton Lewis Jr., news	The Chesterfield Supper Club
7:15	Joseph Alsop, news		The Answer Man	Morgan Beatty, news
7:30	Tales of Willie Piper	Club Fifteen	Arthur Hale, news	Grand Marquee
7:45		Robert Trout, news	Bill Brandt, sports	
8pm	Lum and Abner	Suspense	Johnny Modero, Pier 23	Colonel Humphrey Flack
8:15	Edwin D. Canham, news			
8:30	America's Town Meeting of the Air	Rooftops of the City	The Voyage of the Scarlet Queen	Musical Americana
8:45		Ned Calmer, news (8:55pm)		
9pm		Lawyer Tucker	Gabriel Heatter, news	The Kraft Music Hall, Nelson Eddy
9:15			Real Stories from Real Life	
9:30	Mr. President	Casey, Crime Photographer	Mutual's Block Party	The Sealtest Village Store, Eve Arden
9:45				
10pm	World Security Workshop	The Radio Reader's Digest	The Crime Club	Mystery in the Air
10:15				
10:30	Public Affairs	The Man Called X	The Longines Symphonette	David Rose Orchestra
10:45				

EVENING — SUMMER, 1947

Friday

ABC	CBS	MBS	NBC	
Walter Kiernan, news	Eric Severeid, news	George Putnam, news	Kenneth Banghart, news	6pm
Ethel and Albert	Report from the UN	Bob Elson Interviews	Serenade to America	6:15
Joe Hasel, sports	Red Barber, sports	Fred news		6:30
Dinner with the Fitzgeralds	The World Today	Stan Lomax, sports	Lowell Thomas, news	6:45
Taylor Grant, news	The Robert Q. Lewis Show	Fulton Lewis Jr., news	The Chesterfield Supper Club	7pm
Joseph Alsop, news		The Answer Man	Morgan Beatty, news	7:15
The Lone Ranger	Club Fifteen	Henry J. Taylor, news	Manor House Party	7:30
	Robert Trout, news	Bill Brandt, sports	H. V. Kaltenborn, news	7:45
The Fat Man	The Gordon MacRae Show	The Burl Ives Show	Highways in Melody	8pm
		Memorable Moments		8:15
This is Your FBI	The Adventures of the Thin Man	Leave It to the Girls	Henry Russell Orchestra	8:30
	Ned Calmer, news (8:55pm)			8:45
Break the Bank	Arthur's Place	Gabriel Heatter, news	The Third Horseman	9pm
		Real Stories from Real Life		9:15
The Sheriff	The FBI in Peace and War	Bulldog Drummond	Waltz Time	9:30
				9:45
Madison Square Garden Boxing	It Pays to Be Ignorant	Meet the Press	The Molle' Mystery Theater	10pm
				10:15
	Eileen Farrell, songs	The Longines Symphonette	The Colgate Sports Newsreel, Bill Stern	10:30
			Public Affairs	10:45

EVENING — SUMMER, 1947

Saturday

	ABC	CBS	MBS	NBC
6pm	Jimmy Blair, songs	Bob Hite, news	George Putnam, news	Kenneth Banghart, news
6:15	The Vagabonds Quartet	CBS Views the Press	Bill Berns, songs	Rhapsody of the Rockies
6:30	Harry Wismer, sports	Red Barber, sports	Fred Vandeventer, news	The Boston Tune Party
6:45	Labor USA	Bill Downs, news	Stan Lomax, sports	The Art of Living
7pm	It's Your Business	Hawk Larabee	Guess Who	Our Foreign Policy
7:15	Betty Russell, songs			
7:30	Challenge of the Yukon	Sound Off	The Listener Responds	Curtain Time
7:45			The Answer Man	
8pm	I Deal in Crime	The Robert Q. Lewis Show	Twenty Questions	The Wayne and Shuster Show
8:15				
8:30	Famous Jury Trials	Sweeney and March	The Better Half	The Mad Masters
8:45		Ned Calmer, news (8:55pm)		
9pm	Gangbusters	The Bill Goodwin Show	Listen Carefully	Your Hit Parade
9:15				
9:30	Murder and Mr. Malone	The Camel Caravan, Vaughn Monroe	High Adventure	Can You Top This
9:45				
10pm	Professor Quiz	Saturday Night Serenade	The Chicago Theater of the Air	Mystery Without Murder
10:15				
10:30	Hayloft Hoedown	The Abe Burrows Show		Grand Ole Opry
10:45		Les Brown Orchestra		

DAYTIME — SUMMER, 1947

Sunday

	ABC	CBS	MBS	NBC
9am	Bert Bacharach, talk	News	Red Hook 31	News
9:15		From the Organ Loft	The Sermon of the Week	The Comic Weekly Man
9:30	Coast-to-Coast on a Bus		The Mutual Radio Chapel	Kurt Maler, piano
9:45		Fielden Farrington, news		Music
10am	Message of Israel	The CBS Church of the Air	George Putnam, news	Highlights of the Bible
10:15			Frank Kingdon, news	
10:30	The Southernaires Quartet		Time for Remembrance	The Horn and Hardart Children's Hour
10:45			Erskine Johnson, news	
11am	Brunch with the Fitzgeralds	Wings Over Jordan	George Putnam, news	
11:15			Brunch with Dorothy and Dick	
11:30	The Hour of Faith	The Salt Lake Tabernacle Choir		Charles F. McCarthy, news
11:45				Solitaire Time
12pm	Stanley Issacs, talk	Invitation to Learning	The Show Shop	Hi Jinx
12:15				
12:30	Sunday Strings	As Others See It	Special Assignment	The Eternal Light
12:45	Raymond Gram Swing, news		Melvin Elliott, news	
1pm	Warriors of Peace	The People's Platform	The Mutual Music Box	America United
1:15				
1:30	Sammy Kaye's Sunday Serenade	Time for Reason About Radio		Ed Herlihy, news
1:45		Howard K. Smith, news		Treasury Guest Star

DAYTIME — SUMMER, 1947

Monday-Friday

ABC	CBS	MBS	NBC	
The Breakfast Club	Joe King, news	Robert Gardner, news	Honeymoon in New York	9am
	This is New York, Danny O'Neill	Record Riddles		9:15
		Alfred W. McCann, food	The Jim Fleming Show	9:30
				9:45
My True Story	Missus Goes A Shopping	Henry Gladstone, news	Katie's Daughter	10am
		Martha Deane, talk	Jack Kilty, songs	10:15
Betty Crocker, cooking	The Strange Romance of Evelyn Winters		The Road of Life	10:30
Music / Listening Post	David Harum		Joyce Jordan, MD	10:45
Breakfast with Breneman	Arthur Godfrey Time	Prescott Robinson, news	Fred Waring Orchestra	11am
		Tello-Test Quiz		11:15
Galen Drake, talk	Grand Slam	Heart's Desire	The Jack Berch Show	11:30
Between the Bookends	Rosemary		Lora Lawton	11:45
Welcome, Travelers	Wendy Warren and the News	Kate Smith Speaks	Rad Hall, news	12pm
	Aunt Jenny's True Life Stories	Kate Smith Sings	Richard Harkness, news	12:15
Nancy Booth Craig, talk	The Romance of Helen Trent	Henry Gladstone, news	The Norman Brokenshire Show	12:30
	Our Gal Sunday	The Answer Man		12:45
H. R. Baukhage, news	Big Sister	Luncheon at Sardi's	Mary Margaret McBride, talk	1pm
Nancy Booth Craig, talk	Ma Perkins			1:15
Galen Drake, talk	Young Dr. Malone	The Listener Responds		1:30
	The Guiding Light	Your Time	Believe It or Not	1:45

DAYTIME — SUMMER, 1947

Sunday

	ABC	CBS	MBS	NBC
2pm	Deadline Mystery	The Weekly News Review	The Five Mysteries	The RCA Victor Show
2:15				
2:30	National Vespers	Bob Reid Sings	George Putnam, news	Harvest of Stars
2:45		Here's to You	Word Stories	
3pm	Lassie	New York Philharmonic Orchestra	Reunion	The Sheaffer Parade
3:15	Johnny Thompson, songs			
3:30	This Week Around the World		The Count of Monte Cristo	One Man's Family
3:45				
4pm	Are These Our Children		The House of Mystery	The Quiz Kids
4:15				
4:30	The Lee Sweetland Show	The Electric Summer Hour	True Detective Mysteries	Author Meets the Critics
4:45				
5pm	Crossword Quiz	The Prudential Family Hour	Under Arrest	NBC Symphony Orchestra
5:15				
5:30	Counterspy	The Jean Sablon Show	The Abbott Mysteries	
5:45		Joseph C. Harsch, news		

DAYTIME — SUMMER, 1947

Monday-Friday

ABC	CBS	MBS	NBC	
Maggie McNellis, talk	The Second Mrs. Burton	Queen for a Day	Today's Children	2pm
	Perry Mason		The Woman in White	2:15
Bride and Groom	Lone Journey	Daily Dilemmas	Masquerade	2:30
	Rose of My Dreams		The Light of the World	2:45
Ladies Be Seated	Double or Nothing	Barbera Welles, talk	Life Can Be Beautiful	3pm
			Ma Perkins	3:15
Paul Whiteman's Record Club	Winner Take All	Song of the Stranger	Pepper Young's Family	3:30
		Public Notice	The Right to Happiness	3:45
	Hint Hunt	The Ladies Man	Mary Noble, Backstage Wife	4pm
			Stella Dallas	4:15
Toby Reed's Hollywood Scrapbook	Give and Take	Rambling with Gambling	Lorenzo Jones	4:30
Dick Tracy			Young Widder Brown	4:45
Terry and the Pirates	House Party	Melody Theater	When a Girl Marries	5pm
Sky King		Adventure Parade	Portia Faces Life	5:15
Jack Armstrong, the All-American Boy	Hits and Misses	Hop Harrigan	Just Plain Bill	5:30
Tennessee Jed		The Tom Mix Ralston Straight Shooters	Front Page Farrell	5:45

DAYTIME — SUMMER, 1947

Saturday

	ABC	CBS	MBS	NBC
9am	Al Pearce and His Gang	Joe King, news	Record Riddles	The Triple B Ranch
9:15		This is New York, Danny O'Neill		
9:30			Uncle Don's Record Party	All Aboard for Adventure
9:45		The Columbia Record Shop		The NBC Stamp Club
10am	Tommy Bartlett Time		Henry Gladstone, news	The Adventures of Frank Merriwell
10:15		Les Adams, songs	Robin Morgan, songs	
10:30	Junior Junction	Mary Lee Taylor, cooking	The PAL Show	Archie Andrews
10:45				
11am	The Piano Playhouse	Let's Pretend	Prescott Robinson, news	The Teentimer's Club
11:15			Tello-Test Quiz	
11:30	Junior Junction	The Adventurer's Club	The Man on the Farm	Smilin' Ed's Buster Brown Gang
11:45				
12pm	Texas Jim Robertson, songs	The Armstrong Theater of Today	What Am I Offered	Rad Hall, news
12:15	Melodies to Remember		New York Soapbox	Consumer Time
12:30	The American Farmer	Stars Over Hollywood	Henry Gladstone, news	Spending for Happiness
12:45			The Answer Man	Let's Ask Mom
1pm	Youth Asks the Government	Grand Central Station	Luncheon at Sardi's	Irene and Rene Kuhn, talk
1:15				Your Radio Reporter
1:30	Galen Drake, talk	County Fair	On the Swing Side	The Veterans Advisor
1:45				Here's to Veterans

DAYTIME — SUMMER, 1947

Saturday

	ABC	CBS	MBS	NBC
2pm	Our Town Speaks	Give and Take	The Harlem Hospitality Club	The National Farm and Home Hour
2:15				
2:30	Hill Toppers Music	Columbia's Country Journal	This is Jazz	The Baxters
2:45	This is for You			Story to Order
3pm	Speaking of Songs	Treasury Bandstand	Barry Gray, talk	The Saturday Showcase
3:15				
3:30	Sunset Roundup	The Seth Grainer Show		Your Host is Buffalo
3:45				Nature Sketches
4pm	Stars in the Afternoon	Chicagoans Orchestra		Storehouse of Music
4:15				
4:30	The Treasury Band Show	Adventures in Science		Home is What You Make It
4:45		Of Men and Books		
5pm	ABC Symphony Orchestra	Cross-Section USA	Make Believe Ballroom	Edward Tomlinson, news
5:15				Whitney Berquist Orchestra
5:30		Saturday at the Chase	Jean Tighe, songs	The Mel Torme Show
5:45			Jan August, songs	The King Cole Trio

EVENING — FALL, 1947

Sunday

	ABC	CBS	MBS	NBC
6pm	Drew Pearson, news	The Adventures of Ozzie and Harriet	Those Websters	The Catholic Hour
6:15	Don Gardiner, news			
6:30	The Greatest Story Ever Told	The Pause That Refreshes	Nick Carter, Master Detective	Hollywood Star Preview
6:45				
7pm	Rex Maupin Orchestra	Gene Autry's Melody Ranch	Sherlock Holmes	The Lucky Strike Program, Jack Benny
7:15				
7:30	Exploring the Unknown	Blondie	Behind the Front Page	The Phil Harris - Alice Faye Show
7:45				
8pm	Detroit Symphony Orchestra	The Adventures of Sam Spade	A. L. Alexander's Mediation Board	The Charlie McCarthy Show
8:15				
8:30		Crime Doctor	Jimmy Fidler, gossip	The Fred Allen Show
8:45		Ned Calmer, news (8:55pm)	Hy Gardner, news	
9pm	Walter Winchell's Jergens Journal	Meet Corliss Archer	Meet Me at Parky's	The Manhattan Merry-Go-Round
9:15	Louella Parsons, gossip			
9:30	The Theater Guild on the Air	The Texaco Star Theater, Tony Martin	The Jim Backus Show	The American Album of Familiar Music
9:45				
10pm		The Adventures of Christopher Wells	Voices of Strings	Take It or Leave It
10:15				
10:30	Jimmy Fidler, gossip	Strike It Rich	Edmund Hockridge	The Big Break
10:45	Beryl Davis, songs			

EVENING — FALL, 1947

Monday

ABC	CBS	MBS	NBC	
Walter Kiernan, news	Eric Severeid, news	Lyle Van, news	Kenneth Banghart, news	6pm
Ethel and Albert	In My Opinion	Bob Elson Interviews	Bill Stern, sports	6:15
New York Tonight, Allen Prescott	Red Barber, sports	Fred Vandeventer, news	Sketches in Melody	6:30
	Lowell Thomas, news	Stan Lomax, sports	Three Star Extra	6:45
Taylor Grant, news	Mystery of the Week	Fulton Lewis Jr., news	The Chesterfield Supper Club	7pm
Elmer Davis, news	The Jack Smith Show	The Answer Man	Morgan Beatty, news	7:15
The Lone Ranger	Club Fifteen	Henry J. Taylor, news	Patterns of Melody	7:30
	Edward R. Murrow, news	Bill Brandt, sports	H. V. Kaltenborn, news	7:45
You Bet Your Life	Inner Sanctum Mysteries	Scotland Yard's Inspector Burke	The Cavalcade of America	8pm
				8:15
The Opie Cates Show	Arthur Godfrey's Talent Scouts	Charlie Chan	The Voice of Firestone	8:30
	Bill Henry, news (8:55pm)			8:45
On Stage America	The Lux Radio Theater	Gabriel Heatter, news	The Bell Telephone Hour	9pm
		Real Stories from Real Life		9:15
So You Want to Lead a Band		Guy Lombardo Orchestra	Dr. I. Q., the Mental Banker	9:30
				9:45
The Doctors Talk It Over	My Friend Irma	The Fishing and Hunting Club	The Carnation Contented Hour	10pm
Earl Godwin, news				10:15
Xavier Cugat Orchestra	The Camel Screen Guild Players	The Longines Symphonette	Fred Waring Orchestra	10:30
				10:45

EVENING — FALL, 1947

Tuesday

	ABC	CBS	MBS	NBC
6pm	Walter Kiernan, news	Eric Severeid, news	Lyle Van, news	Kenneth Banghart, news
6:15	Ethel and Albert	Frontiers of Science	Bob Elson Interviews	Bill Stern, sports
6:30	New York Tonight, Allen Prescott	Red Barber, sports	Fred Vandeventer, news	Sketches in Melody
6:45		Lowell Thomas, news	Stan Lomax, sports	Three Star Extra
7pm	Taylor Grant, news	Mystery of the Week	Fulton Lewis Jr., news	The Chesterfield Supper Club
7:15	Elmer Davis, news	The Jack Smith Show	The Answer Man	Morgan Beatty, news
7:30	The Green Hornet	Club Fifteen	Arthur Hale, news	The Hollywood Theater
7:45		Edward R. Murrow, news	Bill Brandt, sports	H. V. Kaltenborn, news
8pm	Youth Asks the Government	Big Town	The Mysterious Traveler	At Home with the Berles
8:15	Christian Science News			
8:30	America's Town Meeting of the Air	Mr. and Mrs. North	Official Detective	A Date with Judy
8:45		Bill Henry, news (8:55pm)		
9pm		We, the People	Gabriel Heatter, news	Amos 'n' Andy
9:15			Real Stories from Real Life	
9:30	Boston Symphony Orchestra	Studio One	The Zane Grey Theater	Fibber Magee and Molly
9:45				
10pm			The American Forum of the Air	The Pepsodent Show, Bob Hope
10:15				
10:30	Labor USA	CBS is There	The Longines Symphonette	The Raleigh Cigarette Program, Red Skelton
10:45	Let Freedom Ring			

EVENING — FALL, 1947

Wednesday

ABC	CBS	MBS	NBC	
Walter Kiernan, news	Eric Severeid, news	Lyle Van, news	Kenneth Banghart, news	*6pm*
Ethel and Albert	George C. McGhee, talk	Bob Elson Interviews	Bill Stern, sports	*6:15*
New York Tonight, Allen Prescott	Red Barber, sports	Fred Vandeventer, news	Sketches in Melody	*6:30*
	Lowell Thomas, news	Stan Lomax, sports	Three Star Extra	*6:45*
Taylor Grant, news	Mystery of the Week	Fulton Lewis Jr., news	The Chesterfield Supper Club	*7pm*
Elmer Davis, news	The Jack Smith Show	The Answer Man	Morgan Beatty, news	*7:15*
The Lone Ranger	Club Fifteen	Strange As It Seems	Manor House Party	*7:30*
	Edward R. Murrow, news	Bill Brandt, sports	H. V. Kaltenborn, news	*7:45*
The Mayor of the Town	The American Melody Hour	Can You Top This	A Day in the Life of Dennis Day	*8pm*
				8:15
Vox Pop	Dr. Christian	Quiet, Please	The Great Gildersleeve	*8:30*
	Bill Henry, news (8:55pm)			*8:45*
Abbott and Costello	The Bickersons	Gabriel Heatter, news	Duffy's Tavern	*9pm*
		Real Stories from Real Life		*9:15*
The Jack Paar Show	Sweeney and March	Let's Go to the Movies	Mr. District Attorney	*9:30*
				9:45
Philco Radio Time, Bing Crosby	The Whistler	Racket Smashers	The Big Story	*10pm*
				10:15
The Henry Morgan Show	Escape	The Longines Symphonette	The Jimmy Durante Show	*10:30*
				10:45

EVENING — FALL, 1947

Thursday

	ABC	CBS	MBS	NBC
6pm	Walter Kiernan, news	Eric Severeid, news	Lyle Van, news	Kenneth Banghart, news
6:15	Ethel and Albert	In My Opinion	Bob Elson Interviews	Bill Stern, sports
6:30	New York Tonight, Allen Prescott	Red Barber, sports	Fred Vandeventer, news	Sketches in Melody
6:45		Lowell Thomas, news	Stan Lomax, sports	Three Star Extra
7pm	Taylor Grant, news	Mystery of the Week	Fulton Lewis Jr., news	The Chesterfield Supper Club
7:15	Elmer Davis, news	The Jack Smith Show	The Answer Man	Morgan Beatty, news
7:30	Challenge of the Yukon	Club Fifteen	Arthur Hale, news	Guy Lombardo Orchestra
7:45		Edward R. Murrow, news	Bill Brandt, sports	
8pm	The Candid Microphone	Suspense	Ted Lewis Orchestra	The Aldrich Family
8:15				
8:30	The Clock	Mr. Keen, Tracer of Lost Persons	The Voyage of the Scarlet Queen	Maxwell House Coffee Time, Burns and Allen
8:45		Bill Henry, news (8:55pm)		
9pm	Tales of Willie Piper	The Dick Haymes Show	Gabriel Heatter, news	The Kraft Music Hall, Al Jolson
9:15			Real Stories from Real Life	
9:30	Darts for Dough	Casey, Crime Photographer	Mutual's Block Party	The Sealtest Village Store, Arden and Carson
9:45				
10pm	Mr. President	The Radio Reader's Digest	The Family Theater	The Bob Hawk Show
10:15				
10:30	The Lennie Herman Quintet	The Man Called X	The Longines Symphonette	Pabst Blue Ribbon Town, Eddie Cantor
10:45	Earl Godwin, news			

EVENING — FALL, 1947

Friday

ABC	CBS	MBS	NBC	
Walter Kiernan, news	Eric Severeid, news	Lyle Van, news	Kenneth Banghart, news	6pm
Ethel and Albert	Report from the UN	Bob Elson Interviews	Bill Stern, sports	6:15
New York Tonight, Allen Prescott	Red Barber, sports	Fred Vandeventer, news	Sketches in Melody	6:30
	Lowell Thomas, news	Stan Lomax, sports	Three Star Extra	6:45
Taylor Grant, news	Mystery of the Week	Fulton Lewis Jr., news	The Chesterfield Supper Club	7pm
Elmer Davis, news	The Jack Smith Show	The Answer Man	Morgan Beatty, news	7:15
The Lone Ranger	Club Fifteen	Henry J. Taylor, news	Manor House Party	7:30
	Edward R. Murrow, news	Bill Brandt, sports	H. V. Kaltenborn, news	7:45
The Fat Man	The Baby Snooks Show	The Burl Ives Show	Highways in Melody	8pm
		Scout About Town		8:15
This is Your FBI	The Adventures of the Thin Man	Leave It to the Girls	Can You Top This	8:30
	Bill Henry, news (8:55pm)			8:45
Break the Bank	Mark Warnow Orchestra	Gabriel Heatter, news	People Are Funny	9pm
		Real Stories from Real Life		9:15
The Sheriff	The FBI in Peace and War	Information, Please	Waltz Time	9:30
				9:45
Madison Square Garden Boxing	It Pays to Be Ignorant	Meet the Press	Mystery Theater	10pm
				10:15
Joe Hasel's Sports Page	Spotlight Revue	The Longines Symphonette	The Colgate Sports Newsreel,	10:30
			Public Affairs	10:45

EVENING — FALL, 1947

Saturday

	ABC	CBS	MBS	NBC
6pm	The Vagabonds Quartet	Robert Hite, news	George Putnam, news	Kenneth Banghart, news
6:15	Betty Russell, songs	CBS Views the Press	Bill Berns, songs	Sports Round-Up
6:30	Harry Wismer, sports	Red Barber, sports	Fred Vandeventer, news	NBC Symphony Orchestra
6:45	Jack Beall, talk	Larry Lesueur, news	Stan Lomax, sports	
7pm	It's Your Business	Hawk Larabee	Guess Who	
7:15	Elmer Davis, news			
7:30	Hank D'Amico Orchestra	Theater of Romance	The Listener Responds	Curtain Time
7:45			The Answer Man	
8pm	I Deal in Crime	The First Nighter Program	Twenty Questions	The Life of Riley
8:15				
8:30	Famous Jury Trials	The Bill Goodwin Show	The Harlem Hospitality Club	Truth or Consequences
8:45		Ned Calmer, news (8:55pm)		
9pm	Gangbusters	Leave It to Joan	Stop Me If You've Heard This One	Your Hit Parade
9:15				
9:30	Murder and Mr. Malone	The Camel Caravan, Vaughn Monroe	The Better Half	The Judy Canova Show
9:45				
10pm	Professor Quiz	Saturday Night Serenade	The Chicago Theater of the Air	Kay Kyser's College of Musical Knowledge
10:15				
10:30	Joe Hasel, sports	The Abe Burrows Show		Grand Ole Opry
10:45	Hayloft Hoedown	Mark Warnow Orchestra		

DAYTIME — FALL, 1947

Sunday

	ABC	CBS	MBS	NBC
9am	Bert Bacharach, talk	News	Red Hook 31	John McVane, news
9:15		From the Organ Loft	The Sermon of the Week	Story to Order
9:30	Coast-to-Coast on a Bus		The Mutual Radio Chapel	Kurt Maler, piano
9:45		Fieden Farrington, news		Music
10am	Message of Israel	The CBS Church of the Air	Henry Gladstone, news	The National Radio Pulpit
10:15			Frank Kingdon, news	
10:30	The Southernaires Quartet		Time for Remembrance	The Horn and Hardart Children's Hour
10:45				
11am	Brunch with the Fitzgeralds	Wings Over Jordan	George Putnam, news	
11:15			Brunch with Dorothy and Dick	
11:30	The Hour of Faith	The Salt Lake Tabernacle Choir		Charles F. McCarthy, news
11:45				Solitaire Time
12pm	Frank Kingdon, news	Invitation to Learning	The Show Shop	Hi Jinx
12:15	Texas Jim Robertson, songs			
12:30	World Security Workshop	As Others See It	Special Assignment	The Eternal Light
12:45			Melvin Elliott, news	
1pm	Stewart Alsop, news	The People's Platform	The Canary Pet Shop	America United
1:15	Raymond Gram Swing, news		Public Affairs	
1:30	Sammy Kaye's Sunday Serenade	Doorway to Life	For Your Approval	The University of Chicago Round Table
1:45				

DAYTIME — FALL, 1946

Monday-Friday

ABC	CBS	MBS	NBC	
The Breakfast Club	Joe King, news	Adelaide Hawley, talk	Honeymoon in New York	9am
	Oklahoma Roundup	Music		9:15
		Alfred W. McCann, food	John McCaffrey, news	9:30
			Stories By Olmsted	9:45
My True Story	Missus Goes A Shopping	Cecil Brown, news	Fred Waring Orchestra	10am
		Martha Deane, talk		10:15
Betty Crocker, cooking	The Strange Romance of Evelyn Winters		The Road of Life	10:30
Music / Listening Post / Dorothy Kilgallen, gossip	David Harum		Joyce Jordan, MD	10:45
Breakfast with Breneman	Arthur Godfrey Time	Prescott Robinson, news	Jack Kilty, songs	11am
		Tello-Test Quiz	Katie's Daughter	11:15
Galen Drake, talk	Grand Slam	Heart's Desire	The Jack Berch Show	11:30
Between the Bookends	Rosemary		Lora Lawton	11:45
Welcome, Travelers	Wendy Warren and the News	Kate Smith Speaks	Rad Hall, news	12pm
	Aunt Jenny's True Life Stories	Kate Smith Sings	Echoes from the Tropics	12:15
Nancy Booth Craig, talk	The Romance of Helen Trent	Henry Gladstone, news	The Norman Brokenshire Show	12:30
	Our Gal Sunday	The Answer Man		12:45
H. R. Baukhage, news	Big Sister	Luncheon at Sardi's	Mary Margaret McBride, talk	1pm
Nancy Booth Craig, talk	Ma Perkins			1:15
Galen Drake, talk	Young Dr. Malone	The Listener Responds		1:30
	The Guiding Light	Victor Lindlahr, health	Believe It or Not	1:45

DAYTIME — FALL, 1947

Sunday

	ABC	CBS	MBS	NBC
2pm	The Lee Sweetland Show	The Robert Q. Lewis Show	The Five Mysteries	The RCA Victor Show
2:15				
2:30	National Vespers	Bob Reid Sings	George Putnam, news	Harvest of Stars
2:45		Here's to You	Word Stories	
3pm	Lassie	New York Philharmonic Orchestra	Melody Theater	The Sheaffer Parade
3:15	Johnny Thompson, songs			
3:30	This Week Around the World		Juvenile Jury	One Man's Family
3:45				
4pm	Are These Our Children		The House of Mystery	The Quiz Kids
4:15				
4:30	The Patti Page Show	The Hour of Charm	True Detective Mysteries	Author Meets the Critics
4:45				
5pm	The Adventures of Bill Lance	The Prudential Family Hour	The Shadow	The Ford Theater
5:15				
5:30	Counterspy	The Jean Sablon Show	Quick as a Flash	
5:45		Joseph C. Harsh, news		

DAYTIME — FALL, 1946

Monday-Friday

ABC	CBS	MBS	NBC	
Maggie McNellis, talk	Second Mrs. Burton	Queen for a Day	Today's Children	*2pm*
	Perry Mason		The Woman in White	*2:15*
Bride and Groom	Look Your Best	Daily Dilemmas	The Story of Holly Sloan	*2:30*
	Rose of My Dreams		The Light of the World	*2:45*
Ladies Be Seated	Double or Nothing	Barbera Welles, talk	Life Can Be Beautiful	*3pm*
			Ma Perkins	*3:15*
Paul Whiteman's Record Club	House Party	Song of the Stranger	Pepper Young's Family	*3:30*
		Bob Reid Sings	The Right to Happiness	*3:45*
	Hint Hunt	The Ladies Man	Mary Noble, Backstage Wife	*4pm*
			Stella Dallas	*4:15*
A Date with Duchin	Winner Take All	Rambling with Gambling	Lorenzo Jones	*4:30*
Dick Tracy			Young Widder Brown	*4:45*
Tennessee Jed	The American School of the Air	Hop Harrigan	When a Girl Marries	*5pm*
Terry and the Pirates		The Adventures of Superman	Portia Faces Life	*5:15*
Sky King /	Hits and Misses	Captain Midnight	Just Plain Bill	*5:30*
Jack Armstrong, the All-American Boy	Lum and Abner	The Tom Mix Ralston Straight Shooters	Front Page Farrell	*5:45*

DAYTIME — FALL, 1947

Saturday

	ABC	CBS	MBS	NBC
9am	Al Pearce and His Gang	Joe King, news	Record Riddles	The Triple B Ranch
9:15		This is New York, Danny O'Neill		
9:30			Uncle Don's Record Party	All Aboard for Adventure
9:45		The Columbia Record Shop		The NBC Stamp Club
10am	Tommy Bartlett Time	The Garden Gate	Henry Gladstone, news	The Adventures of Frank Merriwell
10:15		Lee Adams, talk	Robin Morgan, songs	
10:30		Mary Lee Taylor, cooking	The Shady Valley Folks	Archie Andrews
10:45				
11am	The Piano Playhouse	Let's Pretend	Prescott Robinson, news	Meet the Meeks
11:15			Tello-Test Quiz	
11:30	The Land of the Lost	The Adventurer's Club	The Man on the Farm	Smilin' Ed's Buster Brown Gang
11:45				
12pm	Johnny Thompson, songs	The Armstrong Theater of Today	What Am I Offered	Rad Hall, news
12:15	Facing the Future			Public Affairs
12:30	The American Farmer	Stars Over Hollywood	Henry Gladstone, news	Home is What You Make It
12:45			The Answer Man	
1pm	UN Highlights	Grand Central Station	Luncheon at Sardi's	The National Farm and Home Hour
1:15				
1:30	Galen Drake, talk	County Fair	Win, Lose or Draw	The Veterans Advisor
1:45				

DAYTIME — FALL, 1947

Saturday

	ABC	CBS	MBS	NBC
2pm	Sports	Give and Take	Sports	Sports
2:15				
2:30		Sports		
2:45				
3pm				
3:15				
3:30				
3:45				
4pm				
4:15			Barry Gray, talk	
4:30				
4:45				
5pm				Edward Tomlinson, news
5:15				The Swanee River Boys
5:30		Saturday at the Chase	Jean Tighe, songs	The Mel Torme Show
5:45			Jan August, songs	The King Cole Trio

LISTINGS FOR 1948

EVENING — WINTER, 1948

Sunday

	ABC	CBS	MBS	NBC
6pm	Drew Pearson, news	The Prudential Family Hour	Those Websters	The Catholic Hour
6:15	Don Gardiner, news			
6:30	The Greatest Story Ever Told	The Pause That Refreshes	Nick Carter, Master Detective	Hollywood Star Preview
6:45				
7pm	Child's World	Gene Autry's Melody Ranch	Sherlock Holmes	The Lucky Strike Program, Jack Benny
7:15				
7:30	Exploring the Unknown	Blondie	Melvin Elliott, news	The Phil Harris - Alice Faye Show
7:45			The Periscope	
8pm	Detroit Symphony Orchestra	The Adventures of Sam Spade	A. L. Alexander's Mediation Board	The Charlie McCarthy Show
8:15				
8:30		The Man Called X	Jimmy Fidler, gossip	The Fred Allen Show
8:45		Ned Calmer, news (8:55pm)	Hy Gardner, news	
9pm	Walter Winchell's Jergens Journal	Meet Corliss Archer	Meet Me at Parky's	The Manhattan Merry-Go-Round
9:15	Louella Parsons, gossip			
9:30	The Theater Guild on the Air	The Gordon MacRae Show	The Jim Backus Show	The American Album of Familiar Music
9:45				
10pm		The Adventures of Christopher Wells	Behind the Front Page	Take It or Leave It
10:15				
10:30	Jimmy Fidler, gossip	Strike It Rich	Play at Home	The Youth Opportunity Program
10:45	We CARE			

EVENING — WINTER, 1948

Monday

ABC	CBS	MBS	NBC	
Joe Hasel, sports	Eric Severeid, news	Lyle Van, news	Kenneth Banghart, news	6pm
Ethel and Albert	In My Opinion	Bob Elson Interviews	Bill Stern, sports	6:15
New York Tonight, Allen Prescott	Lum and Abner	Fred Vandeventer, news	Sketches in Melody	6:30
	Lowell Thomas, news	Stan Lomax, sports	Three Star Extra	6:45
Taylor Grant, news	The Beulah Show	Fulton Lewis Jr., news	The Chesterfield Supper Club	7pm
Elmer Davis, news	The Jack Smith Show	The Answer Man	Morgan Beatty, news	7:15
The Lone Ranger	Club Fifteen	Henry J. Taylor, news	Patterns of Melody	7:30
	Edward R. Murrow, news	Bill Brandt, sports	H. V. Kaltenborn, news	7:45
Point Sublime	Inner Sanctum Mysteries	The Falcon	The Cavalcade of America	8pm
				8:15
The Opie Cates Show	Arthur Godfrey's Talent Scouts	Charlie Chan	The Voice of Firestone	8:30
	Bill Henry, news (8:55pm)			8:45
On Stage America	The Lux Radio Theater	Gabriel Heatter, news	The Bell Telephone Hour	9pm
		A. L. Alexander, poetry		9:15
So You Want to Lead a Band		High Adventure	Dr. I. Q., the Mental Banker	9:30
				9:45
This is Adventure	My Friend Irma	Quiet, Please	The Carnation Contented Hour	10pm
				10:15
Arthur Gaeth, news	The Camel Screen Guild Players	The Longines Symphonette	Fred Waring Orchestra	10:30
Earl Godwin, news				10:45

EVENING — WINTER, 1948

Tuesday

	ABC	CBS	MBS	NBC
6pm	Joe Hasel, sports	Eric Severeid, news	Lyle Van, news	Kenneth Banghart, news
6:15	Ethel and Albert	Frontiers of Science	Bob Elson Interviews	Bill Stern, sports
6:30	Pat Barnes, talk	Lum and Abner	Fred Vandeventer, news	World Over Playhouse
6:45		Lowell Thomas, news	Stan Lomax, sports	Three Star Extra
7pm	Taylor Grant, news	The Beulah Show	Fulton Lewis Jr., news	The Chesterfield Supper Club
7:15	Elmer Davis, news	The Jack Smith Show	The Answer Man	Morgan Beatty, news
7:30	The Green Hornet	Club Fifteen	Wendell Noble, news	The Hollywood Theater
7:45		Edward R. Murrow, news	Bill Brandt, sports	
8pm	Youth Asks the Government	Big Town	The Mysterious Traveler	At Home with the Berles
8:15	Edwin D. Canham, news			
8:30	America's Town Meeting of the Air	Mr. and Mrs. North	Official Detective	A Date with Judy
8:45		Bill Henry, news (8:55pm)		
9pm		We, the People	Gabriel Heatter, news	Amos 'n' Andy
9:15			A. L. Alexander, poetry	
9:30	Boston Symphony Orchestra	Studio One	The Zane Grey Theater	Fibber Magee and Molly
9:45				
10pm			The American Forum of the Air	The Pepsodent Show, Bob Hope
10:15				
10:30	It's Your Business	Open Hearing	The Longines Symphonette	The Raleigh Cigarette Program, Red Skelton
10:45	It's in the Family			

EVENING — WINTER, 1948

Wednesday

ABC	CBS	MBS	NBC	
Joe Hasel, sports	Eric Severeid, news	Lyle Van, news	Kenneth Banghart, news	6pm
Ethel and Albert	Report from the UN	Bob Elson Interviews	Bill Stern, sports	6:15
New York Tonight, Allen Prescott	Lum and Abner	Fred Vandeventer, news	Junior Reporter	6:30
	Lowell Thomas, news	Stan Lomax, sports	Three Star Extra	6:45
Taylor Grant, news	The Beulah Show	Fulton Lewis Jr., news	The Chesterfield Supper Club	7pm
Elmer Davis, news	The Jack Smith Show	The Answer Man	Morgan Beatty, news	7:15
The Lone Ranger	Club Fifteen	Carey Longmire, news	Johnny Duffy and Marilyn, songs	7:30
	Edward R. Murrow, news	Bill Brandt, sports	H. V. Kaltenborn, news	7:45
The Mayor of the Town	The American Melody Hour	Can You Top This	A Day in the Life of Dennis Day	8pm
				8:15
Vox Pop	Dr. Christian	Boston Blackie	The Great Gildersleeve	8:30
	Bill Henry, news (8:55pm)			8:45
Abbott and Costello	The New Border Program	Gabriel Heatter, news	Duffy's Tavern	9pm
		A. L. Alexander, poetry		9:15
You Bet Your Life	Sweeney and March	Box 13	Mr. District Attorney	9:30
				9:45
Philco Radio Time, Bing Crosby	The Whistler	Bulldog Drummond	The Big Story	10pm
				10:15
The Texaco Star Theater, Tony Martin	Escape	The Longines Symphonette	The Jimmy Durante Show	10:30
				10:45

EVENING — WINTER, 1948

Thursday

	ABC	CBS	MBS	NBC
6pm	Joe Hasel, sports	Eric Severeid, news	Lyle Van, news	Kenneth Banghart, news
6:15	Ethel and Albert	In My Opinion	Bob Elson Interviews	Bill Stern, sports
6:30	New York Tonight, Allen Prescott	Lum and Abner	Fred Vandeventer, news	Godfrey Schmidt, stories
6:45		Lowell Thomas, news	Stan Lomax, sports	Three Star Extra
7pm	Taylor Grant, news	The Beulah Show	Fulton Lewis Jr., news	Chesterfield Supper Club
7:15	Elmer Davis, news	The Jack Smith Show	The Answer Man	Morgan Beatty, news
7:30	The Henry Morgan Show	Club Fifteen	Wendell Noble, news	Hollywood Open House
7:45		Edward R. Murrow, news	Bill Brandt, sports	
8pm	The Adventures of Ellery Queen	The FBI in Peace and War	Jan August, songs	The Aldrich Family
8:15			Kay Lorraine, songs	
8:30	The Clock	Mr. Keen, Tracer of Lost Persons	Mutual's Block Party	Maxwell House Coffee Time, Burns and Allen
8:45		Bill Henry, news (8:55pm)		
9pm	Tales of Willie Piper	The Dick Haymes Show	Gabriel Heatter, news	The Kraft Music Hall, Al Jolson
9:15			A. L. Alexander, poetry	
9:30	The Candid Microphone	Casey, Crime Photographer	RFD America	The Sealtest Village Store, Arden and Carson
9:45				
10pm	The Lee Sweetland Show	The Radio Reader's Digest	The Family Theater	The Bob Hawk Show
10:15				
10:30	The Lennie Herman Quintet	The First Nighter Program	The Longines Symphonette	Pabst Blue Ribbon Town, Eddie Cantor
10:45	Earl Godwin, news			

EVENING — WINTER, 1948

Friday

ABC	CBS	MBS	NBC	
Joe Hasel, sports	Eric Severeid, news	Lyle Van, news	Kenneth Banghart, news	6pm
Ethel and Albert	Report from the UN	Bob Elson Interviews	Bill Stern, sports	6:15
Pat Barnes, talk	Lum and Abner	Fred Vandeventer, news	Junior Reporter	6:30
	Lowell Thomas, news	Stan Lomax, sports	Three Star Extra	6:45
Taylor Grant, news	The Beulah Show	Fulton Lewis Jr., news	The Chesterfield Supper Club	7pm
Elmer Davis, news	The Jack Smith Show	The Answer Man	Morgan Beatty, news	7:15
The Lone Ranger	Club Fifteen	Henry J. Taylor, news	Mel Allen, sports	7:30
	Edward R. Murrow, news	Bill Brandt, sports	H. V. Kaltenborn, news	7:45
The Fat Man	The Baby Snooks Show	The Burl Ives Show	Highways in Melody	8pm
		Kay Lorraine, songs		8:15
This is Your FBI	The Danny Thomas Show	Leave It to the Girls	Can You Top This	8:30
	Bill Henry, news (8:55pm)			8:45
Break the Bank	The Bickersons	Gabriel Heatter, news	People Are Funny	9pm
		A. L. Alexander, poetry		9:15
The Sheriff	The Adventures of Ozzie and Harriet	Information, Please	Waltz Time	9:30
				9:45
Madison Square Garden Boxing	It Pays to Be Ignorant	Meet the Press	Mystery Theater	10pm
				10:15
Joe Hasel's Sports Page	Spotlight Revue	The Longines Symphonette	The Colgate Sports Newsreel, Bill Stern	10:30
			Pro and Con	10:45

EVENING — WINTER, 1948

Saturday

	ABC	CBS	MBS	NBC
6pm	Here's Harriet	Bob Hite, news	George Putnam, news	Kenneth Banghart, news
6:15	Music By Adlam	CBS Views the Press	Hy Gardner, news	Religion in the News
6:30	Harry Wismer, sports	Red Barber, sports	Fred Vandeventer, news	NBC Symphony Orchestra
6:45	Jack Beall, talk	Larry Lesueur, news	Stan Lomax, sports	
7pm	Quizdom Class	Hawk Larabee	Guess Who	
7:15				
7:30	Challenge of the Yukon	The Abe Burrows Show	Wendell Noble, news	Curtain Time
7:45		The Hoagy Carmichael Show	The Answer Man	
8pm	Red Dolan, Detective	Suspense	Twenty Questions	The Life of Riley
8:15				
8:30	Famous Jury Trials		The Al Schacht Sports Show	Truth or Consequences
8:45		Ned Calmer, news (8:55pm)		
9pm	Gangbusters	Leave It to Joan	Stop Me If You've Heard This One	Your Hit Parade
9:15				
9:30	Murder and Mr. Malone	The Camel Caravan, Vaughn Monroe	Song Writing Machine	The Judy Canova Show
9:45				
10pm	Professor Quiz	Saturday Night Serenade	The Chicago Theater of the Air	Kay Kyser's College of Musical Knowledge
10:15				
10:30	Hayloft Hoedown	Guy Lombardo Orchestra		Grand Ole Opry
10:45				

DAYTIME — WINTER, 1948

Sunday

	ABC	CBS	MBS	NBC
9am	Bert Bacharach, talk	News	Harry Hennessy, news	John McVane, news
9:15		From the Organ Loft	The Sermon of the Week	The Comic Weekly Man
9:30	Coast-to-Coast on a Bus		The Mutual Radio Chapel	
9:45		Fieden Farrington, news		Music
10am	Message of Israel	The CBS Church of the Air	Henry Gladstone, news	The National Radio Pulpit
10:15			Tunes of the Week	
10:30	The Southernaires Quarter		Time for Remembrance	The Horn and Hardart Children's Hour
10:45			The Hymnal	
11am	Brunch with the Fitzgeralds	Wings Over Jordan	Lyle Van, news	
11:15			Brunch with Dorothy and Dick	
11:30	The Hour of Faith	The Salt Lake Tabernacle Choir		Charles F. McCarthy, news
11:45				Solitaire Time
12pm	George Putnam, news	Invitation to Learning	The Show Shop	Hi Jinx
12:15	Foreign Reporters			
12:30	World Security Workshop	The People's Platform	Melvin Elliott, news	The Eternal Light
12:45			Milton Rettenberg, piano	
1pm	Samuel Pettengell, news	Doorway to Life	William L. Shirer, news	America United
1:15	Raymond Gram Swing, news		The Canary Pet Shop	
1:30	Sammy Kaye's Sunday Serenade	Tell It Again	The Mutual Music Box	Charles F. McCarthy, news
1:45				Public Affairs

DAYTIME — WINTER, 1948

Monday-Friday

ABC	CBS	MBS	NBC	
The Breakfast Club	Joe King, news	Harry Hennessy, news	Peter Roberts, news	9am
	This is New York, Danny O'Neill	Record Riddles	John McCaffrey, news	9:15
		Alfred W. McCann, food	The Norman Brokenshire Show	9:30
				9:45
My True Story	Missus Goes A Shopping	Henry Gladstone, news	Fred Waring Orchestra	10am
		Martha Deane, talk		10:15
Betty Crocker	The Strange Romance of Evelyn Winters		The Road of Life	10:30
Music / Listening Post / Dorothy Kilgallen, gossip	David Harum		Joyce Jordan, MD	10:45
Breakfast with Breneman	Arthur Godfrey Time	Prescott Robinson, news	This is Nora Drake	11am
		Tello-Test Quiz	Katie's Daughter	11:15
Galen Drake, talk	Grand Slam	Heart's Desire	The Jack Berch Show	11:30
Between the Bookends	Rosemary		Lora Lawton	11:45
Welcome, Travelers	Wendy Warren and the News	Kate Smith Speaks	Rad Hall, news	12pm
	Aunt Jenny's True Life Stories	Kate Smith Sings	Richard Harkness, news	12:15
Nancy Booth Craig, talk	The Romance of Helen Trent	Henry Gladstone, news	The Norman Brokenshire Show	12:30
	Our Gal Sunday	The Answer Man		12:45
H. R. Baukhage, news	Big Sister	Luncheon at Sardi's	Mary Margaret McBride, talk	1pm
Nancy Booth Craig, talk	Ma Perkins			1:15
Pat Barnes, talk	Young Dr. Malone	The Listener Responds		1:30
	The Guiding Light	Victor Lindlahr, health	Believe It or Not	1:45

DAYTIME — WINTER, 1948

Sunday

	ABC	CBS	MBS	NBC
2pm	Mr. President	The Air Force Hour	The Five Mysteries	The RCA Victor Show
2:15				
2:30	National Vespers	Joseph C. Harsch, news	Lyle Van, news	Harvest of Stars
2:45		Bob Reid Sings	Robert S. Allen, news	
3pm	Lassie	New York Philharmonic Orchestra	The Better Half	The Sheaffer Parade
3:15	Johnny Thompson, songs			
3:30	This Week Around the World		Juvenile Jury	One Man's Family
3:45				
4pm	Sound Off		The House of Mystery	The Quiz Kids
4:15				
4:30	The Metropolitan Opera Auditions	The Earl Wrightson Show	True Detective Mysteries	Author Meets the Critics
4:45				
5pm	Treasury Agent	Janette Davis, songs	The Shadow	The Ford Theater
5:15		Here's to You		
5:30	Counterspy	The Hour of Charm	Quick as a Flash	
5:45				

DAYTIME — WINTER, 1948

Monday-Friday

ABC	CBS	MBS	NBC	
Maggie McNellis, talk	The Second Mrs. Burton	Queen for a Day	Today's Children	*2pm*
	Perry Mason		The Woman in White	*2:15*
Bride and Groom	Look Your Best	Daily Dilemmas	The Story of Holly Sloan	*2:30*
	Rose of My Dreams		The Light of the World	*2:45*
Ladies Be Seated	Double or Nothing	Barbera Welles, talk	Life Can Be Beautiful	*3pm*
			Ma Perkins	*3:15*
Paul Whiteman's Record Club	House Party	Song of the Stranger	Pepper Young's Family	*3:30*
		Bob Reid Sings	The Right to Happiness	*3:45*
	Hint Hunt	The Ladies Man	Mary Noble, Backstage Wife	*4pm*
			Stella Dallas	*4:15*
The Treasury Band Show	Winner Take All	Rambling with Gambling	Lorenzo Jones	*4:30*
			Young Widder Brown	*4:45*
Dick Tracy	The American School of the Air	Hop Harrigan	When a Girl Marries	*5pm*
Terry and the Pirates		The Adventures of Superman	Portia Faces Life	*5:15*
Sky King /	Winner Take All	Captain Midnight	Just Plain Bill	*5:30*
Jack Armstrong, the All-American Boy		The Tom Mix Ralston Straight Shooters	Front Page Farrell	*5:45*

DAYTIME — WINTER, 1948

Saturday

	ABC	CBS	MBS	NBC
9am	Shoppers Special	Joe King, news	Harry Hennessey, news	The Triple B Ranch
9:15		This is New York, Danny O'Neill	Songs of Romance	
9:30			The Voyage of the Scarlet Queen	All Aboard for Adventure
9:45		Galen Drake, talk		The NBC Stamp Club
10am	The US Navy Band		Henry Gladstone, news	The Adventures of Frank Merriwell
10:15		The Garden Gate	All About Stamps	
10:30	The Piano Playhouse	Mary Lee Taylor, cooking	The PAL Show	Archie Andrews
10:45				
11am	The Abbott and Costello Children's Show	Let's Pretend	Prescott Robinson, news	Meet the Meeks
11:15			Tello-Test Quiz	
11:30	The Land of the Lost	Escape	The Man on the Farm	Smilin' Ed's Buster Brown Gang
11:45				
12pm	Junior Junction	The Armstrong Theater of Today	What Am I Offered	Rad Hall, news
12:15				Irene and Rene Kuhn, talk
12:30	The American Farmer	Stars Over Hollywood	Henry Gladstone, news	Home is What You Make It
12:45			The Answer Man	
1pm	Maggie McNellis and Herb Sheldon, talk	Grand Central Station	Luncheon at Sardi's	The National Farm and Home Hour
1:15				
1:30	Our Town Speaks	County Fair	Midnight to Dawn	Your Radio Reporter
1:45				Public Affairs

DAYTIME — WINTER, 1948

Saturday

	ABC	CBS	MBS	NBC
2pm	The Metropolitan Opera	Give and Take	The Penny Parade	Vincent Lopez Orchestra
2:15				
2:30		Columbia's Country Journal		The Veterans Advisor
2:45				
3pm		Report from Overseas		Orchestras of the Nation
3:15		Adventures in Science		
3:30		Cross-Section USA		
3:45				
4pm		Treasury Bandstand		Doctors Today
4:15				
4:30		Saturday at the Chase		The First Piano Quartet
4:45	Tea and Crumpets			
5pm		Philadelphia Symphony Orchestra		Edward Tomlinson, news
5:15				Here's to Veterans
5:30			True or False	The Handy Man
5:45	Dorothy Fuldheim, news		While Berns Roams	The King Cole Trio

EVENING — SPRING, 1948

Sunday

	ABC	CBS	MBS	NBC
6pm	Drew Pearson, news	The Prudential Family Hour	Those Websters	The Catholic Hour
6:15	Don Gardiner, news			
6:30	The Greatest Story Ever Told	The Pause That Refreshes	Nick Carter, Master Detective	Hollywood Star Preview
6:45				
7pm	I Love Adventure	Gene Autry's Melody Ranch	Sherlock Holmes	The Lucky Strike Program, Jack Benny
7:15				
7:30	Exploring the Unknown	Blondie	Melvin Elliott, news	The Phil Harris - Alice Faye Show
7:45			Robert S. Allen, news	
8pm	Stop the Music	The Adventures of Sam Spade	A. L. Alexander's Mediation Board	The Charlie McCarthy Show
8:15				
8:30		The Man Called X	Jimmy Fidler, gossip	The Fred Allen Show
8:45		Ned Calmer, news (8:55pm)	Hy Gardner, news	
9pm	Walter Winchell's Jergens Journal	Meet Corliss Archer	Meet Me at Parky's	The Manhattan Merry-Go-Round
9:15	Louella Parsons, gossip			
9:30	The Theater Guild on the Air	Shorty Bell	The Jim Backus Show	The American Album of Familiar Music
9:45				
10pm		Escape	Behind the Front Page	Take It or Leave It
10:15				
10:30	Jimmy Fidler, gossip	Strike It Rich	The Unexpected	The Youth Opportunity Program
10:45	Sidney Walton, news		Strange As It Seems	

EVENING — SPRING, 1948

Monday

ABC	CBS	MBS	NBC	
Joe Hasel, sports	Eric Severeid, news	Lyle Van, news	Kenneth Banghart, news	6pm
Johnny Olsen's Quiz	In My Opinion	Bob Elson Interviews	Bill Stern, sports	6:15
New York Tonight, Allen Prescott	Lum and Abner	Fred Vandeventer, news	The PAL Show	6:30
Ethel and Albert	Lowell Thomas, news	Stan Lomax, sports	Three Star Extra	6:45
Taylor Grant, news	The Beulah Show	Fulton Lewis Jr., news	The Chesterfield Supper Club	7pm
Elmer Davis, news	The Jack Smith Show	The Answer Man	Morgan Beatty, news	7:15
The Lone Ranger	Club Fifteen	Henry J. Taylor, news	Patterns of Melody	7:30
	Edward R. Murrow, news	Bill Brandt, sports	H. V. Kaltenborn, news	7:45
Point Sublime	Inner Sanctum Mysteries	The Falcon	The Cavalcade of America	8pm
				8:15
Sound Off	Arthur Godfrey's Talent Scouts	Charlie Chan	The Voice of Firestone	8:30
	Bill Henry, news (8:55pm)			8:45
On Stage America	The Lux Radio Theater	Gabriel Heatter, news	The Bell Telephone Hour	9pm
		The Mutual Newsreel		9:15
So You Want to Lead a Band		Quiet, Please	Dr. I. Q., the Mental Banker	9:30
				9:45
Arthur Gaeth, news	My Friend Irma	The Radio Telephone Game	The Carnation Contented Hour	10pm
Earl Godwin, news				10:15
Public Affairs	The Camel Screen Guild Players	The Longines Symphonette	Fred Waring Orchestra	10:30
				10:45

EVENING — SPRING, 1948

Tuesday

	ABC	CBS	MBS	NBC
6pm	Joe Hasel, sports	Eric Severeid, news	Lyle Van, news	Kenneth Banghart, news
6:15	Johnny Olsen's Quiz	Frontiers of Science	Bob Elson Interviews	Bill Stern, sports
6:30	New York Tonight, Allen Prescott	Lum and Abner	Fred Vandeventer, news	World Over Playhouse
6:45	Ethel and Albert	Lowell Thomas, news	Stan Lomax, sports	Three Star Extra
7pm	Taylor Grant, news	The Beulah Show	Fulton Lewis Jr., news	Chesterfield Supper Club
7:15	Elmer Davis, news	The Jack Smith Show	The Answer Man	Morgan Beatty, news
7:30	The Green Hornet	Club Fifteen	Wendell Noble, news	The Hollywood Theater
7:45		Edward R. Murrow, news	Bill Brandt, sports	
8pm	Youth Asks the Government	Big Town	The Mysterious Traveler	At Home with the Berles
8:15	Edwin D. Canham, news			
8:30	America's Town Meeting of the Air	Mr. and Mrs. North	Official Detective	A Date with Judy
8:45		Bill Henry, news (8:55pm)		
9pm		We, the People	Gabriel Heatter, news	Amos 'n' Andy
9:15			The Mutual Newsreel	
9:30	Boston Symphony Orchestra	The Adventures of Christopher Wells	The Casebook of Gregory Hood	Fibber Magee and Molly
9:45				
10pm		Studio One	The American Forum of the Air	The Pepsodent Show, Bob Hope
10:15				
10:30	Let Freedom Ring		Roger Kilgore, Public Defender	The Raleigh Cigarette Program, Red Skelton
10:45	It's in the Family			

EVENING — SPRING, 1948

Wednesday

ABC	CBS	MBS	NBC	
Joe Hasel, sports	Eric Severeid, news	Lyle Van, news	Kenneth Banghart, news	6pm
Johnny Olsen's Quiz	Report from the UN	Bob Elson Interviews	Bill Stern, sports	6:15
New York Tonight, Allen Prescott	Lum and Abner	Fred Vandeventer, news	The PAL Show	6:30
Ethel and Albert	Lowell Thomas, news	Stan Lomax, sports	Three Star Extra	6:45
Taylor Grant, news	The Beulah Show	Fulton Lewis Jr., news	The Chesterfield Supper Club	7pm
Elmer Davis, news	The Jack Smith Show	The Answer Man	Morgan Beatty, news	7:15
The Lone Ranger	Club Fifteen	Carey Longmire, news	Johnny Duffy and Marilyn	7:30
	Edward R. Murrow, news	Bill Brandt, sports	H. V. Kaltenborn, news	7:45
The Mayor of the Town	The American Melody Hour	Can You Top This	A Day in the Life of Dennis Day	8pm
				8:15
Vox Pop	Dr. Christian	Boston Blackie	The Great Gildersleeve	8:30
	Bill Henry, news (8:55pm)			8:45
Abbott and Costello	Your Song and Mine	Gabriel Heatter, news	Duffy's Tavern	9pm
		The Mutual Newsreel		9:15
You Bet Your Life	Harvest of Stars	Box 13	Mr. District Attorney	9:30
				9:45
Philco Radio Time, Bing Crosby	The Whistler	Bulldog Drummond	The Big Story	10pm
				10:15
The Texaco Star Theater, Gordon MacRae	Presidential Timber	The Longines Symphonette	The Jimmy Durante Show	10:30
	Capital Cloak Room			10:45

EVENING — SPRING, 1948

Thursday

	ABC	CBS	MBS	NBC
6pm	Joe Hasel, sports	Eric Severeid, news	Lyle Van, news	Kenneth Banghart, news
6:15	Johnny Olsen's Quiz	In My Opinion	Bob Elson Interviews	Bill Stern, sports
6:30	New York Tonight, Allen Prescott	Lum and Abner	Fred Vandeventer, news	Junior Reporter
6:45	Ethel and Albert	Lowell Thomas, news	Stan Lomax, sports	Three Star Extra
7pm	Taylor Grant, news	The Beulah Show	Fulton Lewis Jr., news	The Chesterfield Supper Club
7:15	Elmer Davis, news	The Jack Smith Show	The Answer Man	Morgan Beatty, news
7:30	The Henry Morgan Show	Club Fifteen	Wendell Noble, news	Hollywood Open House
7:45		Edward R. Murrow, news	Bill Brandt, sports	
8pm	The Candid Microphone	The FBI in Peace and War	The All-Star Revue	The Aldrich Family
8:15			A. L. Alexander, poetry	
8:30	The Adventures of Ellery Queen	Mr. Keen, Tracer of Lost Persons	The Big Talent Hunt	Maxwell House Coffee Time, Burns and Allen
8:45		Bill Henry, news (8:55pm)		
9pm	Tales of Willie Piper	The Dick Haymes Show	Gabriel Heatter, news	The Kraft Music Hall, Al Jolson
9:15			The Mutual Newsreel	
9:30	The Clock	Casey, Crime Photographer	The Smiths of Hollywood	The Sealtest Village Store, Arden and Carson
9:45				
10pm	Child's World	The Radio Reader's Digest	The Family Theater	The Bob Hawk Show
10:15				
10:30	Public Affairs	The First Nighter Program	The Longines Symphonette	Pabst Blue Ribbon Town, Eddie Cantor
10:45	Earl Godwin, news			

EVENING — SPRING, 1948

Friday

ABC	CBS	MBS	NBC	
Joe Hasel, sports	Eric Severeid, news	Lyle Van, news	Kenneth Banghart, news	6pm
Johnny Olsen's Quiz	Of Men and Books	Bob Elson Interviews	Bill Stern, sports	6:15
New York Tonight, Allen Prescott	Lum and Abner	Fred Vandeventer, news	Junior Reporter	6:30
Ethel and Albert	Lowell Thomas, news	Stan Lomax, sports	Three Star Extra	6:45
Taylor Grant, news	The Beulah Show	Fulton Lewis Jr., news	The Chesterfield Supper Club	7pm
Elmer Davis, news	The Jack Smith Show	The Answer Man	Morgan Beatty, news	7:15
The Lone Ranger	Club Fifteen	Henry J. Taylor, news	The Three Suns Trio	7:30
	Edward R. Murrow, news	Bill Brandt, sports	H. V. Kaltenborn, news	7:45
The Fat Man	Call for Music	Background for Stardom	Highways in Melody	8pm
		A. L. Alexander, poetry		8:15
This is Your FBI	The Danny Thomas Show	Leave It to the Girls	Can You Top This	8:30
	Bill Henry, news (8:55pm)			8:45
Break the Bank	The Bickersons	Gabriel Heatter, news	People Are Funny	9pm
		The Mutual Newsreel		9:15
The Sheriff	The Adventures of Ozzie and Harriet	Information, Please	Waltz Time	9:30
				9:45
Madison Square Garden Boxing	Everybody Wins	Meet the Press	Mystery Theater	10pm
				10:15
Joe Hasel's Sports Page	Spotlight Revue	The Longines Symphonette	The Colgate Sports Newsreel, Bill Stern	10:30
			Pro and Con	10:45

EVENING — SPRING, 1948

Saturday

	ABC	CBS	MBS	NBC
6pm	Manhattan Close-Up	Don Pyror, news	Lyle Van, news	Kenneth Banghart, news
6:15	Bible Message	CBS Views the Press	Hy Gardner, news	Religion in the News
6:30	Harry Wismer, sports	Red Barber, sports	Fred Vandeventer, news	NBC Symphony Orchestra
6:45	Jack Beall, talk	Larry Lesueur, news	Stan Lomax, sports	
7pm	Quizdom Class	Mr. ace & JANE	Guess Who	
7:15				
7:30	Challenge of the Yukon	The Abe Burrows Show	Wendell Noble, news	Curtain Time
7:45		The Hoagy Carmichael Show	The Answer Man	
8pm	Red Dolan, Detective	Suspense	Twenty Questions	The Life of Riley
8:15				
8:30	Famous Jury Trials		Stop Me If You've Heard This One	Truth or Consequences
8:45		Ned Calmer, news (8:55pm)		
9pm	Gangbusters	Leave It to Joan	Secret Agent	Your Hit Parade
9:15				
9:30	Murder and Mr. Malone	The Camel Caravan, Vaughn Monroe	High Adventure	The Judy Canova Show
9:45				
10pm	Professor Quiz	Saturday Night Serenade	The Chicago Theater of the Air	Kay Kyser's College of Musical Knowledge
10:15				
10:30	Hayloft Hoedown	It Pays to Be Ignorant		Grand Ole Opry
10:45				

DAYTIME — SPRING, 1948

Sunday

	ABC	CBS	MBS	NBC
9am	Bert Bacharach, talk	News	Harry Hennessy, news	John McVane, news
9:15		From the Organ Loft	The Sermon of the Week	The Comic Weekly Man
9:30	Coast-to-Coast on a Bus		The Mutual Radio Chapel	
9:45		Art Hannes, news		Music
10am	Message of Israel	The CBS Church of the Air	Henry Gladstone, news	The National Radio Pulpit
10:15			Fix It Yourself	
10:30	The Southernaires Quarter		Let's Go	The Horn and Hardart Children's Hour
10:45			The Hymnal	
11am	Brunch with the Fitzgeralds	Howard K. Smith, news	Lyle Van, news	
11:15		As Others See Us	Brunch with Dorothy and Dick	
11:30	The Hour of Faith	The Salt Lake Tabernacle Choir		Charles F. McCarthy, news
11:45				Solitaire Time
12pm	George Putnam, news	Invitation to Learning	The Show Shop	Hi Jinx
12:15	Foreign Reporters			
12:30	On Trial	The People's Platform	Melvin Elliott, news	The Eternal Light
12:45			Milton Rettenberg, piano	
1pm	Samuel Pettengell, news	Doorway to Life	William L. Shirer, news	America United
1:15	Edward Weeks, news		The Canary Pet Shop	
1:30	National Vespers	Tell It Again	The Mutual Music Box	Author Meets the Critics
1:45				

DAYTIME — SPRING, 1948

Monday-Friday

ABC	CBS	MBS	NBC	
The Breakfast Club	Joe King, news	Harry Hennessy, news	Peter Roberts, news	*9am*
	This is New York, Danny O'Neill	The Passing Parade	John McCaffrey, news	*9:15*
		Alfred W. McCann, food	The Norman Brokenshire Show	*9:30*
				9:45
My True Story	Missus Goes A Shopping	Henry Gladstone, news	Fred Waring Orchestra	*10am*
		Martha Deane, talk		*10:15*
Betty Crocker	The Strange Romance of Evelyn Winters		The Road of Life	*10:30*
Music / Listening Post / Dorothy Kilgallen, gossip	David Harum		Joyce Jordan, MD	*10:45*
Breakfast with Breneman	Arthur Godfrey Time	Prescott Robinson, news	This is Nora Drake	*11am*
		Tello-Test Quiz	Katie's Daughter	*11:15*
Galen Drake, talk	Grand Slam	Heart's Desire	The Jack Berch Show	*11:30*
Between the Bookends	Rosemary		Lora Lawton	*11:45*
Welcome, Travelers	Wendy Warren and the News	Kate Smith Speaks	Rad Hall, news	*12pm*
	Aunt Jenny's True Life Stories	Kate Smith Sings	Richard Harkness, news	*12:15*
Nancy Booth Craig, talk	The Romance of Helen Trent	Henry Gladstone, news	The Norman Brokenshire Show	*12:30*
	Our Gal Sunday	The Answer Man		*12:45*
H. R. Baukhage, news	Big Sister	Luncheon at Sardi's	Mary Margaret McBride, talk	*1pm*
Nancy Booth Craig, talk	Ma Perkins			*1:15*
Pat Barnes, talk	Young Dr. Malone	John Gambling Calling		*1:30*
	The Guiding Light	Victor Lindlahr, health	Believe It or Not	*1:45*

DAYTIME — SPRING, 1948

Sunday

	ABC	CBS	MBS	NBC
2pm	This Week Around the World	CBS is There	The Five Mysteries	Norman Cloutier Orchestra
2:15				
2:30	Mr. President	Joseph C. Harsch, news	Lyle Van, news	The RCA Victor Show
2:45		Where the People Stand	The Periscope	
3pm	Lassie	New York Philharmonic Orchestra	The Better Half	The Sheaffer Parade
3:15	American Almanac			
3:30	Sammy Kaye's Sunday Serenade		Juvenile Jury	One Man's Family
3:45				
4pm	Speak Up, America		The House of Mystery	The Quiz Kids
4:15	Cal Tinney, news			
4:30	The Metropolitan Opera Auditions	Public Affairs	True Detective Mysteries	Living 1948
4:45				
5pm	Treasury Agent	Janette Davis, songs	The Shadow	The Ford Theater
5:15		Here's to You		
5:30	Counterspy	The Hour of Charm	Quick as a Flash	
5:45				

DAYTIME — SPRING, 1948

Monday-Friday

ABC	CBS	MBS	NBC	
Maggie McNellis, talk	The Second Mrs. Burton	Queen for a Day	Today's Children	2pm
	Perry Mason		The Woman in White	2:15
Bride and Groom	This is Nora Drake	Here's Hogan	The Story of Holly Sloan	2:30
	Rose of My Dreams		The Light of the World	2:45
Ladies Be Seated	Double or Nothing	Movie Matinee	Life Can Be Beautiful	3pm
			Ma Perkins	3:15
Paul Whiteman's Record Club	House Party	Daily Dilemmas	Pepper Young's Family	3:30
			The Right to Happiness	3:45
	Hint Hunt	Barbara Welles, talk	Mary Noble, Backstage Wife	4pm
			Stella Dallas	4:15
The Treasury Band Show	Galen Drake, talk	The Ladies Man	Lorenzo Jones	4:30
			Young Widder Brown	4:45
Dick Tracy	The American School of the Air	Adventure Parade	When a Girl Marries	5pm
Terry and the Pirates		The Adventures of Superman	Portia Faces Life	5:15
Sky King /	Winner Take All	Captain Midnight	Just Plain Bill	5:30
Jack Armstrong, the All-American Boy		The Tom Mix Ralston Straight Shooters	Front Page Farrell	5:45

DAYTIME — SPRING, 1948

Saturday

	ABC	CBS	MBS	NBC
9am	Shoppers Special	Joe King, news	Harry Hennessey, news	The Triple B Ranch
9:15		This is New York, Danny O'Neill	Songs of Romance	
9:30			Gardening with Gambling	All Aboard for Adventure
9:45		Galen Drake, talk		The NBC Stamp Club
10am	Your Home Beautiful		Henry Gladstone, news	The Adventures of Frank Merriwell
10:15	This is for You	The Garden Gate	All About Stamps	
10:30	Hollywood Headlines	Mary Lee Taylor, cooking	Strange As It Seems	Archie Andrews
10:45	Saturday Strings		Bill Berns' Knitting Circle	
11am	The Abbott and Costello Children's Show	Let's Pretend	Prescott Robinson, news	Meet the Meeks
11:15			Florence Pritchet, talk	
11:30	The Land of the Lost	Junior Miss	Movie Matinee	Smilin' Ed's Buster Brown Gang
11:45				
12pm	Junior Junction	The Armstrong Theater of Today	Keep Up with the Kids	Rad Hall, news
12:15				Irene and Rene Kuhn, talk
12:30	The American Farmer	Stars Over Hollywood	Henry Gladstone, news	Coffee with Congress
12:45			The Answer Man	
1pm	Maggie McNellis and Herb Sheldon, talk	Grand Central Station	Luncheon at Sardi's	The National Farm and Home Hour
1:15				
1:30	Dr. Robert J. Ditolla, children	County Fair	On the Beam	Your Radio Reporter
1:45	Here's to Veterans			Public Affairs

DAYTIME — SPRING, 1948

Saturday

	ABC	CBS	MBS	NBC
2pm	Harry Kogen Orchestra	Give and Take	Music 'Til Five	Vincent Lopez Orchestra
2:15				
2:30	The Hitching Post	Columbia's Country Journal		The Veterans Advisor
2:45				
3pm	The Piano Playhouse	Report from Overseas		Orchestras of the Nation
3:15		Adventures in Science		
3:30	ABC Symphony Orchestra	Cross-Section USA		
3:45				
4pm		Stan Dougherty Presents	Horse Racing	Doctors Today
4:15			Music 'Til Five	
4:30	Horse Racing	Treasury Bandstand		The First Piano Quartet
4:45				
5pm	The Treasury Band Show	Philadelphia Symphony Orchestra	Take a Number	The Swanee River Boys
5:15				The Three Suns
5:30	Melodies to Remember		True or False	Dr. I. Q. Jr.
5:45	Dorothy Fuldheim, news	CBS Views the Press		

EVENING — SUMMER, 1948

Sunday

	ABC	CBS	MBS	NBC
6pm	Drew Person, news	The Prudential Family Hour	Those Websters	The Catholic Hour
6:15	Don Gardiner, news			
6:30	Earl Godwin, news	The Pause That Refreshes	Nick Carter, Master Detective	The Hollywood Star Theater
6:45	Bob Considine, talk			
7pm	Rex Maupin's Musicale	Gene Autry's Melody Ranch	Mystery Playhouse	Let's Talk Hollywood
7:15				
7:30	Johnny Fletcher	Blondie	Gabriel Heatter, news	Dan Carson
7:45			Robert S. Allen, news	
8pm	Stop the Music	The Adventures of Sam Spade	A. L. Alexander's Mediation Board	Robert Shaw Chorale
8:15				
8:30		The Man Called X	Jimmy Fidler, gossip	RFD America
8:45			Melvin Elliott, news	
9pm	Arlene Francis, talk	Winner Take All	Secret Missions	The Manhattan Merry-Go-Round
9:15	Louella Parsons, gossip			
9:30	Superstition on the Air	Strike It Rich	Box 13	The American Album of Familiar Music
9:45				
10pm	The Comedy Writers Show	Hollywood Showcase	Behind the Front Page	Take It or Leave It
10:15				
10:30	Jimmy Fidler, gossip	Escape	Russ Hodges, talk	The Youth Opportunity Program
10:45	We CARE		Fix It Yourself	

EVENING — SUMMER, 1948

Monday

ABC	CBS	MBS	NBC	
Joe Hasel, sports	Eric Severeid, news	Lyle Van, news	Kenneth Banghart, news	6pm
New York Tonight, Allen Prescott	In My Opinion	Bob Elson Interviews	Bill Stern, sports	6:15
	Lum and Abner	Fred Vandeventer, news	Wayne Howell, news	6:30
	Lowell Thomas, news	Stan Lomax, sports	Three Star Extra	6:45
Taylor Grant, news	The Robert Q. Lewis Show	Fulton Lewis Jr., news	The Chesterfield Supper Club	7pm
Elmer Davis, news		The Answer Man	Morgan Beatty, news	7:15
The Lone Ranger	Club Fifteen	Henry J. Taylor, news	Patterns of Melody	7:30
	Edward R. Murrow, news	Bill Brandt, sports	Richard Harkness, news	7:45
Sound Off	Inner Sanctum Mysteries	The Falcon	The First Piano Quartet	8pm
				8:15
Stars in the Night	Cabin B-13	The Casebook of Gregory Hood	The Voice of Firestone	8:30
				8:45
Tomorrow's Tops	Our Miss Brooks	Gabriel Heatter, news	The Bell Telephone Hour	9pm
		The Mutual Newsreel		9:15
Get Rich Quick	The Amazing Mr. Tutt	Quiet, Please	Dr. I. Q., the Mental Banker	9:30
				9:45
Arthur Gaeth, news	My Friend Irma	Philo Vance	The Carnation Contented Hour	10pm
Earl Godwin, news				10:15
The Curt Massey Show	Freddy Martin Orchestra	The Longines Symphonette	Appointment with Music	10:30
				10:45

EVENING — SUMMER, 1948

Tuesday

	ABC	CBS	MBS	NBC
6pm	Joe Hasel, sports	Eric Sevareid, news	Lyle Van, news	Kenneth Banghart, news
6:15	New York Tonight, Allen Prescott	Frontiers of Science	Bob Elson Interviews	Bill Stern, sports
6:30		Lum and Abner	Fred Vandeventer, news	Wayne Howell, news
6:45		Lowell Thomas, news	Stan Lomax, sports	Three Star Extra
7pm	Taylor Grant, news	The Robert Q. Lewis Show	Fulton Lewis Jr., news	The Chesterfield Supper Club
7:15	Elmer Davis, news		The Answer Man	Morgan Beatty, news
7:30	The Green Hornet	Club Fifteen	A. L. Alexander, poetry	The Hollywood Theater
7:45		Edward R. Murrow, news	Bill Brandt, sports	
8pm	Youth Asks the Government	Mystery Theater	The Mysterious Traveler	The Mel Torme Show
8:15	Edwin D. Canham, news			
8:30	America's Town Meeting of the Air	Mr. and Mrs. North	Official Detective	Carmen Cavallaro Orchestra
8:45				
9pm		We, the People	Gabriel Heatter, news	Pickens Party
9:15			The Mutual Newsreel	
9:30	The American String Quartet	Hit the Jackpot	The Lone Wolf	Call the Police
9:45				
10pm		Crusade for Children	Roger Kilgore, Public Defender	Meet Corliss Archer
10:15				
10:30	What Do People Think	Freddy Martin Orchestra	The Longines Symphonette	An Evening with Romberg
10:45	Summer Serenade			

EVENING — SUMMER, 1948

Wednesday

ABC	CBS	MBS	NBC	
Joe Hasel, sports	Eric Sevareid, news	Lyle Van, news	Kenneth Banghart, news	6pm
New York Tonight, Allen Prescott	Maynard C. Krueger, talk	Bob Elson Interviews	Bill Stern, sports	6:15
	Lum and Abner	Fred Vandeventer, news	Wayne Howell, news	6:30
	Lowell Thomas, news	Stan Lomax, sports	Three Star Extra	6:45
Taylor Grant, news	The Robert Q. Lewis Show	Fulton Lewis Jr., news	The Chesterfield Supper Club	7pm
Elmer Davis, news		The Answer Man	Morgan Beatty, news	7:15
The Lone Ranger	Club Fifteen	Robert S. Allen, news	World Over Playhouse	7:30
	Edward R. Murrow, news	Bill Brandt, sports	Richard Harkness, news	7:45
Xavier Cugat Orchestra	Mr. Chameleon	Can You Top This	Swing Time at the Savoy	8pm
				8:15
On Stage America	Dr. Christian	Boston Blackie	Jack and Cliff	8:30
				8:45
Abbott and Costello	County Fair	Gabriel Heatter, news	Hi Jinx	9pm
		The Mutual Newsreel		9:15
Go for the House	Harvest of Stars	High Adventure	Mr. District Attorney	9:30
				9:45
The Texaco Star Theater, Gordon MacRae	The Whistler	Bulldog Drummond	The Big Story	10pm
				10:15
On Trial	Capital Cloak Room	The Longines Symphonette	The New Adventures of the Thin Man	10:30
				10:45

EVENING — SUMMER, 1948

Thursday

	ABC	CBS	MBS	NBC
6pm	Joe Hasel, sports	Eric Severeid, news	Lyle Van, news	Kenneth Banghart, news
6:15	New York Tonight, Allen Prescott	An American Abroad	Bob Elson Interviews	Bill Stern, sports
6:30		Lum and Abner	Fred Vandeventer, news	Wayne Howell, news
6:45		Lowell Thomas, news	Stan Lomax, sports	Three Star Extra
7pm	Taylor Grant, news	The Robert Q. Lewis Show	Fulton Lewis Jr., news	The Chesterfield Supper Club
7:15	Elmer Davis, news		The Answer Man	Morgan Beatty, news
7:30	Rex Maupin Orchestra	Club Fifteen	A. L. Alexander, poetry	Serenade to America
7:45		Edward R. Murrow, news	Bill Brandt, sports	
8pm	The Front Page	Dr. Standish, Medical Examiner	Talent Jackpot	Roll Call
8:15				
8:30	Criminal Casebook	Mr. Keen, Tracer of Lost Persons	The Better Half	New Faces of 1948
8:45				
9pm	Child's World	Suspense	Gabriel Heatter, news	The Kraft Music Hall, Nelson Eddy
9:15			The Mutual Newsreel	
9:30	The Candid Microphone	Casey, Crime Photographer	The All-Star Revue	The Sealtest Village Store, Ilene Woods
9:45			Erskine Johnson, news	
10pm	Cavalcade of Sports	The Hallmark Playhouse	The Family Theater	The Bob Hawk Show
10:15				
10:30	Joe Hasel's Sports Page	Doorway to Life	The Longines Symphonette	Fred Waring Orchestra
10:45				

EVENTING — SUMMER, 1948

Friday

ABC	CBS	MBS	NBC	
Joe Hasel, sports	Eric Sevareid, news	Lyle Van, news	Kenneth Banghart, news	6pm
New York Tonight, Allen Prescott	Report from the UN	Bob Elson Interviews	Bill Stern, sports	6:15
	Lum and Abner	Fred Vandeventer, news	Wayne Howell, news	6:30
	Lowell Thomas, news	Stan Lomax, sports	Three Star Extra	6:45
Taylor Grant, news	The Robert Q. Lewis Show	Fulton Lewis Jr., news	The Chesterfield Supper Club	7pm
Elmer Davis, news		The Answer Man	Morgan Beatty, news	7:15
The Lone Ranger	Club Fifteen	Henry J. Taylor, news	The Melody Riders	7:30
	Edward R. Murrow, news	Bill Brandt, sports	Richard Harkness, news	7:45
The Fat Man	Mr. ace & JANE	The Smiths of Hollywood	The Cities Service Band of America	8pm
				8:15
This is Your FBI	Personal Appearance	Leave It to the Girls	Who Said That	8:30
				8:45
Break the Bank	My Favorite Husband	Gabriel Heatter, news	The NBC University Theater	9pm
		The Mutual Newsreel		9:15
The Sheriff	Musicomedy	Colonel Stoopnagle		9:30
				9:45
Dance Band Jamboree	Everybody Wins	Meet the Press	The Slapsy Maxie Rosenbloom Show	10pm
				10:15
	The Summer Spotlight Revue	The Longines Symphonette	The Colgate Sports Newsreel, Bill Stern	10:30
			Pro and Con	10:45

EVENING — SUMMER, 1948

Saturday

	ABC	CBS	MBS	NBC
6pm	Manhattan Close-Up	Bob Hite, news	Lyle Van, news	Kenneth Banghart, news
6:15	Bible Message	CBS Views the Press	Hy Gardner, news	The Art of Living
6:30	Harry Wismer, sports	Red Barber, sports	Fred Vandeventer, news	NBC Symphony Orchestra
6:45	Jack Beall, talk	Larry Lesueur, news	Stan Lomax, sports	
7pm	Treasury Bandstand	St. Louis Municipal Opera	Guess Who	
7:15				
7:30	Famous Jury Trials	Saturday Night Serenade	Grandstand Managers	Curtain Time
7:45			The Answer Man	
8pm	Red Dolan, Detective	Sing It Again	Twenty Questions	George Olsen Orchestra
8:15				
8:30	The Amazing Mr. Malone		Stop Me If You've Heard This One	Blue Barron Orchestra
8:45				
9pm	Gangbusters	The Morey Amsterdam Show	Three for the Money	Your Hit Parade
9:15				
9:30	What's My Name	It Pays to Be Ignorant		Can You Top This
9:45				
10pm	Musical Etchings	Let's Dance America	The Chicago Theater of the Air	Grand Ole Opry
10:15				
10:30	Hayloft Hoedown			The Radio City Playhouse
10:45				

DAYTIME — SUMMER, 1948

Sunday

	ABC	CBS	MBS	NBC
9am	Bert Bacharach, talk	News	Harry Hennessy, news	John McVane, news
9:15		From the Organ Loft	The Sermon of the Week	The Comic Weekly Man
9:30	Coast-to-Coast on a Bus		The Mutual Radio Chapel	
9:45		St. Paul's Trinity Choir		Music
10am	Message of Israel	The CBS Church of the Air	Henry Gladstone, news	Highlights of the Bible
10:15			Fix It Yourself	
10:30	The Southernaires Quarter		A. L. Alexander, poetry	The Horn and Hardart Children's Hour
10:45			Robin Morgan, songs	
11am	Brunch with the Fitzgeralds	Howard K. Smith, news	Lyle Van, news	
11:15		The Newsmakers	Brunch with Dorothy and Dick	
11:30	The Hour of Faith	The Salt Lake Tabernacle Choir		Charles F. McCarthy, news
11:45				Solitaire Time
12pm	George Putnam, news	Invitation to Learning	The Show Shop	Hi Jinx
12:15	Foreign Reporters			
12:30	The Piano Playhouse	The People's Platform	Melvin Elliott, news	The Eternal Light
12:45			Milton Rettenberg, piano	
1pm	Samuel Pettengell, news	Return Engagement	Michael O'Duffy, songs	America United
1:15	Edward Weeks, news		Your Hymnal	
1:30	National Vespers	Tell It Again	The Mutual Music Box	Stories By Olmsted
1:45				

DAYTIME — SUMMER, 1948

Monday-Friday

ABC	CBS	MBS	NBC	
The Breakfast Club	Bob Hite, news	Harry Hennessy, news	Peter Roberts, news	9am
	This is New York, Danny O'Neill	The Passing Parade	John McCaffrey, news	9:15
		Alfred W. McCann, food	The Norman Brokenshire Show	9:30
				9:45
My True Story	Missus Goes A Shopping	Henry Gladstone, news	Fred Waring Orchestra	10am
		Martha Deane, talk		10:15
Betty Crocker	Sing Along		The Road of Life	10:30
Music / Listening Post / Dorothy Kilgallen, gossip			Joyce Jordan, MD	10:45
Breakfast with Breneman	Arthur Godfrey Time	Prescott Robinson, news	This is Nora Drake	11am
		Tello-Test Quiz	We Love and Learn	11:15
Between the Bookends	Grand Slam	Heart's Desire	The Jack Berch Show	11:30
Walter Kiernan, news	Rosemary		Lora Lawton	11:45
Welcome, Travelers	Wendy Warren and the News	Kate Smith Speaks	Charles F. McCarthy, news	12pm
	Aunt Jenny's True Life Stories	Kate Smith Sings	Richard Harkness, news	12:15
Nancy Booth Craig, talk	The Romance of Helen Trent	Henry Gladstone, news	The Norman Brokenshire Show	12:30
	Our Gal Sunday	The Answer Man		12:45
H. R. Baukhage, news	Big Sister	Luncheon at Sardi's	Mary Margaret McBride, talk	1pm
Nancy Booth Craig, talk	Ma Perkins			1:15
Pat Barnes, talk	Young Dr. Malone	John Gambling Calling		1:30
	The Guiding Light	John B. Kennedy, news	Believe It or Not	1:45

DAYTIME — SUMMER, 1948

Sunday

	ABC	CBS	MBS	NBC
2pm	This Week Around the World	Public Affairs	The Five Mysteries	The First Piano Quartet
2:15				
2:30	Mr. President	Joseph C. Harsch, news	Lyle Van, news	The RCA Victor Show
2:45		Where the People Stand	The Periscope	
3pm	Harrison Wood, news	New York Philharmonic Orchestra	What's the Name of That Song	The Sheaffer Parade
3:15	American Almanac			
3:30	The Treasury Band Show		Life Begins at Eighty	One Man's Family
3:45				
4pm	Cal Tinney, news		The House of Mystery	The Quiz Kids
4:15	Johnny Thompson, songs			
4:30	Favorite Story	Make Mine Music	True Detective Mysteries	Living 1948
4:45				
5pm	Milton Cross Opera Album	Tommy Dorsey Orchestra	Under Arrest	Author Meets The Critics
5:15		Woody Herman Orchestra		
5:30	Counterspy	Sunday at the Chase	What Makes You Tick	Surprise Serenade
5:45				

DAYTIME — SUMMER, 1948

	Monday-Friday			
ABC	CBS	MBS	NBC	
Maggie McNellis, talk	The Second Mrs. Burton	Queen for a Day	Double or Nothing	*2pm*
	Perry Mason			*2:15*
Bride and Groom	This is Nora Drake	On Your Mark	Today's Children	*2:30*
	The Strange Romance of Evelyn Winters	On Your Mark (M, W, F) / Favorite Melodies (T, Th)	The Light of the World	*2:45*
Ladies Be Seated	David Harum	Movie Matinee	Life Can Be Beautiful	*3pm*
	Hilltop House		Ma Perkins	*3:15*
Second Honeymoon	House Party	Daily Dilemmas	Pepper Young's Family	*3:30*
			The Right to Happiness	*3:45*
Listen to This	Hint Hunt	Barbara Welles, talk	Mary Noble, Backstage Wife	*4pm*
			Stella Dallas	*4:15*
The Treasury Band Show	Galen Drake, talk	The Ladies Man	Lorenzo Jones	*4:30*
			Young Widder Brown	*4:45*
Challenge of the Yukon /	Music	Bill Harrington, songs	When a Girl Marries	*5pm*
Fun House		The Adventures of Superman	Portia Faces Life	*5:15*
Sky King /	Winner Take All	Adventure Parade	Just Plain Bill	*5:30*
The Sea Hound		The Tom Mix Ralston Straight Shooters	Front Page Farrell	*5:45*

DAYTIME — SUMMER, 1948

Saturday

	ABC	CBS	MBS	NBC
9am	Shoppers Special	Bob Hite, news	Harry Hennessey, news	The Triple B Ranch
9:15		This is New York, Danny O'Neill	Let's Go	
9:30			There's Always a Woman	The PAL Show
9:45		Galen Drake, talk		The NBC Stamp Club
10am	This is for You		Henry Gladstone, news	The Adventures of Frank Merriwell
10:15		The Garden Gate	The Charlotte Adams Show	
10:30	Johnny Thompson, songs	Mary Lee Taylor, cooking		Archie Andrews
10:45	Saturday Strings			
11am	The Abbott and Costello Children's Show	Let's Pretend	Prescott Robinson, news	Meet the Meeks
11:15			Tello-Test Quiz	
11:30	Don Gardiner, news	Junior Miss	Special Agent	Smilin' Ed's Buster Brown Gang
11:45	The Buddy Weed Trio			
12pm	The Freedom Gardener	The Armstrong Theater of Today	Keep Up with the Kids	Charles F. McCarthy, news
12:15				Irene and Rene Kuhn, talk
12:30	The American Farmer	Stars Over Hollywood	Henry Gladstone, news	Coffee with Congress
12:45			The Answer Man	
1pm	Maggie McNellis and Herb Sheldon, talk	Grand Central Station	Luncheon at Sardi's	The National Farm and Home Hour
1:15				
1:30	The Piano Playhouse	Give and Take	Public Affairs	Edward Tomlinson, news
1:45				Public Affairs

DAYTIME — SUMMER, 1948

Saturday

	ABC	CBS	MBS	NBC
2pm	Fascinating Rhythm	Bernie Cummins Orchestra	The US Air Force Band	Vincent Lopez Orchestra
2:15				
2:30	The Hitching Post	Columbia's Country Journal	On the Beam	The Veterans Advisor
2:45				
3pm	Speaking of Songs	Report from Overseas	Movie Matinee	Nature Sketches
3:15		Adventures in Science		Your Radio Reporter
3:30	ABC Symphony Orchestra	Cross-Section USA	Daily Dilemmas	McCritchie Orchestra
3:45				
4pm		Stan Dougherty Presents	Barbera Welles, talk	Horse Racing
4:15				
4:30	The Treasury Band Show	Treasury Bandstand	The Ladies Man	Mind Your Manners
4:45				
5pm	Horse Racing	Dave Stephens Orchestra	Take a Number	Dizzy Dean, sports
5:15				Lassie
5:30	Melodies to Remember	Make Way for Youth	True or False	Dr. I. Q. Jr.
5:45	Dorothy Fuldheim, news			

EVENING — FALL, 1948

Sunday

	ABC	CBS	MBS	NBC
6pm	Drew Pearson, news	The Prudential Family Hour of Stars	The Roy Rogers Show	The Catholic Hour
6:15	Don Gardiner, news			
6:30	The Greatest Story Ever Told	The Pause That Refreshes	Nick Carter, Master Detective	The Adventures of Ozzie and Harriet
6:45				
7pm	Go for the House	Gene Autry's Melody Ranch	Sherlock Holmes	The Lucky Strike Program, Jack Benny
7:15				
7:30	Carnegie Hall	Amos 'n' Andy	Behind the Front Page	The Phil Harris - Alice Faye Show
7:45				
8pm	Stop the Music	The Adventures of Sam Spade	A. L. Alexander's Mediation Board	The Charlie McCarthy Show
8:15				
8:30		Cabin B-13	It's a Living	The Fred Allen Show
8:45				
9pm	Walter Winchell's Jergens Journal	The Electric Theater	Secret Missions	The Manhattan Merry-Go-Round
9:15	Louella Parsons, gossip			
9:30	The Theater Guild on the Air	Our Miss Brooks	Jimmy Fidler, gossip	The American Album of Familiar Music
9:45			Twin Views of the News	
10pm		Lum and Abner	Hobby Lobby	Take It or Leave It
10:15				
10:30	Jimmy Fidler, gossip	Strike It Rich	Pat Hollis, songs	The Youth Opportunity Program
10:45	We CARE		Fix It Yourself	

EVENING — FALL, 1948

Monday

ABC	CBS	MBS	NBC	
Joe Hasel, news	Eric Severeid, news	Lyle Van, news	John McVane, news	6pm
Ethel and Albert	In My Opinion	Bob Elson Interviews	Bill Stern, sports	6:15
New York Tonight, Allen Prescott	Alka Seltzer Time, Bing Crosby Herb Shriner	Fred Vandeventer, news	Wayne Howell, news	6:30
	Lowell Thomas, news	Stan Lomax, sports	Three Star Extra	6:45
Taylor Grant, news	The Beulah Show	Fulton Lewis Jr., news	The Chesterfield Supper Club	7pm
Elmer Davis, news	The Jack Smith Show	The Answer Man	Morgan Beatty, news	7:15
The Lone Ranger	Club Fifteen	Henry J. Taylor, news	The Art Van Damme Quintet	7:30
	Edward R. Murrow, news	Bill Brandt, sports	H. V. Kaltenborn, news	7:45
The Railroad Hour	Inner Sanctum Mysteries	The Falcon	The Cavalcade of America	8pm
				8:15
	Arthur Godfrey's Talent Scouts	The Casebook of Gregory Hood	The Voice of Firestone	8:30
Henry J. Taylor, news		Hy Gardner, news (8:55pm)		8:45
Glen Osser Orchestra	The Lux Radio Theater	Gabriel Heatter, news	The Bell Telephone Hour	9pm
		The Mutual Newsreel		9:15
Stars in the Night		The Fishing and Hunting Club	Dr. I. Q., the Mental Banker	9:30
				9:45
Arthur Gaeth, news	My Friend Irma	Philo Vance	The Carnation Contented Hour	10pm
Earl Godwin, news				10:15
The Kay Starr Show	The Bob Hawk Show	The Longines Symphonette	The Radio City Playhouse	10:30
				10:45

EVENING — FALL, 1948

Tuesday

	ABC	CBS	MBS	NBC
6pm	Walter Kiernan, news	Eric Severeid, news	Lyle Van, news	John McVane, news
6:15	Ethel and Albert	Frontiers of Science	Bob Elson Interviews	Bill Stern, sports
6:30	New York Tonight, Allen Prescott	Alka Seltzer Time, Bing Crosby Herb Shriner	Fred Vandeventer, news	Wayne Howell, news
6:45		Lowell Thomas, news	Stan Lomax, sports	Three Star Extra
7pm	Taylor Grant, news	The Beulah Show	Fulton Lewis Jr., news	The Chesterfield Supper Club
7:15	Elmer Davis, news	The Jack Smith Show	The Answer Man	Morgan Beatty, news
7:30	Phillip Bovero Orchestra	Club Fifteen	A. L. Alexander, poetry	The Smoothies
7:45		Edward R. Murrow, news	Bill Brandt, sports	Richard Harkness, news
8pm	Youth Asks the Government	Mystery Theater	The Mysterious Traveler	The Mel Torme Show
8:15	Earl Godwin, news			
8:30	America's Town Meeting of the Air	Mr. and Mrs. North	Official Detective	A Date with Judy
8:45			Hy Gardner, news (8:55pm)	
9pm		We, the People	Gabriel Heatter, news	The Bob Hope Show
9:15			The Mutual Newsreel	
9:30	Detroit Symphony Orchestra	Life with Luigi	Under Arrest	Fibber Magee and Molly
9:45				
10pm		Hit the Jackpot	The American Forum of the Air	Big Town
10:15				
10:30	Let Freedom Ring	The Morey Amsterdam Show	The Longines Symphonette	People Are Funny
10:45	Serenade for Strings			

EVENING — FALL, 1948

Wednesday

ABC	CBS	MBS	NBC	
Walter Kiernan, news	Eric Severeid, news	Lyle Van, news	John McVane, news	6pm
Ethel and Albert	George C. McGhee, talk	Bob Elson Interviews	Bill Stern, sports	6:15
New York Tonight, Allen Prescott	Alka Seltzer Time, Bing Crosby Herb Shriner	Fred Vandeventer, news	Wayne Howell, news	6:30
	Lowell Thomas, news	Stan Lomax, sports	Three Star Extra	6:45
Taylor Grant, news	The Beulah Show	Fulton Lewis Jr., news	The Chesterfield Supper Club	7pm
Elmer Davis, news	The Jack Smith Show	The Answer Man	Morgan Beatty, news	7:15
The Lone Ranger	Club Fifteen	Henry J. Taylor, news	The Adrian Rollini Trio	7:30
	Edward R. Murrow, news	Bill Brandt, sports	H. V. Kaltenborn, news	7:45
Ted Mack's Original Amateur Hour	Mr. Chameleon	Stop Me If You've Heard This One	Blondie	8pm
				8:15
	Dr. Christian	High Adventure	The Great Gildersleeve	8:30
		Hy Gardner, news (8:55pm)		8:45
The Texaco Star Theater, Milton Berle	Your Song and Mine	Gabriel Heatter, news	Duffy's Tavern	9pm
		The Mutual Newsreel		9:15
You Bet Your Life	Harvest of Stars	Hollywood Story	Mr. District Attorney	9:30
				9:45
Philco Radio Time, Bing Crosby	Times A Wastin'	Bulldog Drummond	The Big Story	10pm
				10:15
Meredith Willson Orchestra	Capitol Cloak Room	The Longines Symphonette	Curtain Time	10:30
				10:45

EVENING — FALL, 1948

Thursday

	ABC	CBS	MBS	NBC
6pm	Walter Kiernan, news	Eric Severeid, news	Lyle Van, news	John McVane, news
6:15	Ethel and Albert	An American Abroad	Bob Elson Interviews	Bill Stern, sports
6:30	New York Tonight, Allen Prescott	Alka Seltzer Time, Bing Crosby Herb Shriner	Fred Vandeventer, news	Wayne Howell, news
6:45		Lowell Thomas, news	Stan Lomax, sports	Three Star Extra
7pm	Taylor Grant, news	The Beulah Show	Fulton Lewis Jr., news	The Chesterfield Supper Club
7:15	Elmer Davis, news	The Jack Smith Show	The Answer Man	Morgan Beatty, news
7:30	Final Edition	Club Fifteen	A. L. Alexander, poetry	The Art Van Damme Quintet
7:45		Edward R. Murrow, news	Bill Brandt, sports	Richard Harkness, news
8pm	Abbott and Costello	The FBI in Peace and War	Talent Jackpot	The Aldrich Family
8:15				
8:30	Personal Autograph	Mr. Keen, Tracer of Lost Persons	The Better Half	Maxwell House Coffee Time, Bing Crosby
8:45			Hy Gardner, news (8:55pm)	
9pm	Child's World	Suspense	Gabriel Heatter, news	The Kraft Music Hall, Al Jolson
9:15			The Mutual Newsreel	
9:30	The Candid Microphone	Casey, Crime Photographer	The All-Star Revue	The Sealtest Variety Theater, Dorothy Lamour
9:45				
10pm	Dance Band Jamboree	The Hallmark Playhouse	The Family Theater	The Camel Screen Guild Players
10:15				
10:30		The First Nighter Program	The Longines Symphonette	Fred Waring Orchestra
10:45	Harrison Wood, news			

EVENING — FALL, 1948

Friday

ABC	CBS	MBS	NBC	
Walter Kiernan, news	Eric Severeid, news	Lyle Van, news	John McVane, news	6pm
Ethel and Albert	Report from the UN	Bob Elson Interviews	Bill Stern, sports	6:15
New York Tonight, Allen Prescott	Alka Seltzer Time, Bing Crosby Herb Shriner	Fred Vandeventer, news	Wayne Howell, news	6:30
	Lowell Thomas, news	Stan Lomax, sports	Three Star Extra	6:45
Taylor Grant, news	The Beulah Show	Fulton Lewis Jr., news	The Chesterfield Supper Club	7pm
Elmer Davis, news	The Jack Smith Show	The Answer Man	Morgan Beatty, news	7:15
The Lone Ranger	Club Fifteen	Henry J. Taylor, news	Music for Tonight	7:30
	Edward R. Murrow, news	Bill Brandt, sports	H. V. Kaltenborn, news	7:45
The Fat Man	The Jack Carson Show	Great Scenes from Great Plays	The Cities Service Band of America	8pm
				8:15
This is Your FBI	Mr. ace & JANE	Leave It to the Girls	The Jimmy Durante Show	8:30
		Hy Gardner, news (8:55pm)		8:45
Break the Bank	The Ford Theater	Gabriel Heatter, news	Pabst Blue Ribbon Town, Eddie Cantor	9pm
		The Mutual Newsreel		9:15
The Sheriff		Lionel Hampton Orchestra	The Raleigh Cigarette Program, Red Skelton	9:30
				9:45
Madison Square Garden Boxing	The Phillip Morris Playhouse	Meet the Press	The Life of Riley	10pm
				10:15
Joe Hasel's Sports Page	Spotlight Revue	The Longines Symphonette	The Colgate Sports Newsreel, Bill Stern	10:30
			Pro and Con	10:45

EVENING — FALL, 1948

Saturday

	ABC	CBS	MBS	NBC
6pm	Manhattan Close-Up	Art Hannes, news	Lyle Van, news	Kenneth Banghart, news
6:15	The Brownee Sisters, songs	CBS Views the Press	John B. Kennedy, news	Sports Round-Up
6:30	Quizdom Class	Red Barber, sports	Fred Vandeventer, news	NBC Symphony Orchestra
6:45		Larry Lesueur, news	Stan Lomax, sports	
7pm	Joe Hasel, sports	My Favorite Husband	Guess Who	
7:15	George Putnam, news			
7:30	Famous Jury Trials	The Camel Caravan, Vaughn Monroe	The Answer Man	The Pet Milk Show, Vic Damone
7:45			Mel Allen, sports	
8pm	Johnny Fletcher	Sing It Again	Twenty Questions	The Hollywood Star Theater
8:15				
8:30	The Amazing Mr. Malone		Life Begins at Eighty	Truth or Consequences
8:45				
9pm	Gangbusters	Winner Take All	Gabriel Heatter, news	Your Hit Parade
9:15			The Lanny Ross Show	
9:30	What's My Name	It Pays to Be Ignorant	Lombardoland USA	The Judy Canova Show
9:45				
10pm	Whiz Quiz	Hometown Reunion	The Chicago Theater of the Air	A Day in the Life of Dennis Day
10:15				
10:30	Joe Beall, talk	The National Military Ball		Grand Ole Opry
10:45	Hayloft Hoedown			

DAYTIME — FALL, 1948

Sunday

	ABC	CBS	MBS	NBC
9am	Bert Bacharach, talk	News	News	W. W. Chaplin, news
9:15		From the Organ Loft	Robin Morgan, songs	The Comic Weekly Man
9:30	Coast-to-Coast on a Bus		The Mutual Radio Chapel	
9:45		St. Paul's Trinity Choir		Music
10am	Message of Israel	The CBS Church of the Air	Henry Gladstone, news	The National Radio Pulpit
10:15			The Handy Man	
10:30	The Southernaires Quartet		A. L. Alexander, poetry	The Horn and Hardart Children's Hour
10:45			Your Hymnal	
11am	Brunch with the Fitzgeralds	Howard K. Smith, news	Lyle Van, news	
11:15		The Newsmakers	Brunch with Dorothy and Dick	
11:30	The Hour of Faith	The Salt Lake Tabernacle Choir		Charles F. McCarthy, news
11:45				Solitaire Time
12pm	Texas Jim Robertson, songs	Invitation to Learning	The Show Shop	Hi Jinx
12:15	Robert Strudevant, news			
12:30	The Piano Playhouse	The People's Platform	Melvin Elliott, news	The Eternal Light
12:45			Milton Rettenberg, piano	
1pm	American Almanac	Joseph C. Harsch, news	William L. Shirer, news	America United
1:15	Edward Weeks, news	Where the People Stand	John B. Kennedy, news	
1:30	National Vespers	Tell It Again	The Canary Pet Shop	Author Meets the Critics
1:45			Your Hymnal	

DAYTIME — FALL, 1948

Monday-Friday

ABC	CBS	MBS	NBC	
The Breakfast Club	Bob Hite, news	Harry Hennessy, news	Clyde Kittell, news	9am
	Barnyard Follies	The Passing Parade	Ivan Sanderson, news	9:15
		Alfred W. McCann, food	The Norman Brokenshire Show	9:30
				9:45
My True Story	Missus Goes A Shopping	Henry Gladstone, news	Fred Waring Orchestra	10am
		Martha Deane, talk		10:15
Betty Crocker, cooking	Arthur Godfrey Time		The Road of Life	10:30
Music / Listening Post / Dorothy Kilgallen, gossip			The Brighter Day	10:45
Kay Kyser's College of Musical Knowledge		Prescott Robinson, news	This is Nora Drake	11am
		Victor Lindlahr, health	We Love and Learn	11:15
Between the Bookends	Grand Slam	Gabriel Heatter's Mailbag	The Jack Berch Show	11:30
What Makes You Tick	Rosemary	Tello-Test Quiz	Lora Lawton	11:45
Welcome, Travelers	Wendy Warren and the News	Kate Smith Speaks	Charles F. McCarthy, news	12pm
	Aunt Jenny's True Life Stories	Kate Smith Sings	Richard Harkness, news	12:15
Maggie McNellis and Herb Sheldon, talk	The Romance of Helen Trent	Henry Gladstone, news	The Norman Brokenshire Show	12:30
	Our Gal Sunday	The Answer Man		12:45
H. R. Baukhage, news	Big Sister	Luncheon at Sardi's	Mary Margaret McBride, talk	1pm
Nancy Booth Craig, talk	Ma Perkins			1:15
	Young Dr. Malone	The Hollywood Theater of Stars		1:30
	The Guiding Light			1:45

DAYTIME — FALL, 1948

Sunday

	ABC	CBS	MBS	NBC
2pm	This Week Around the World	Festival of Song	Deems Taylor Concert	Everyman's Story
2:15				
2:30	Mr. President	You Are There	Harry Hennessy, news	The NBC University Theater
2:45			Blackstone, the Magician	
3pm	Harrison Wood, news	New York Philharmonic Orchestra	Michael O'Duffy, songs	
3:15	The Future of America			
3:30	The Treasury Band Show		Juvenile Jury	One Man's Family
3:45				
4pm	Between the Bookends		The House of Mystery	The Quiz Kids
4:15	Johnny Thompson, songs			
4:30	Milton Cross Opera Album	Skyway to the Stars	True Detective Mysteries	Living 1948
4:45				
5pm	Quiet, Please	The Robert Q. Lewis Show	The Shadow	Pickens Party
5:15				
5:30	Counterspy	The Adventures of Phillip Marlowe	Quick as a Flash	The RCA Victor Show
5:45				

DAYTIME — FALL, 1948

Monday-Friday

ABC	CBS	MBS	NBC	
Breakfast in Hollywood	The Second Mrs. Burton	Queen for a Day	Double or Nothing	2pm
	Perry Mason			2:15
Bride and Groom	This is Nora Drake	On Your Mark	Today's Children	2:30
	The Strange Romance of Evelyn Winters		The Light of the World	2:45
Ladies Be Seated	David Harum	Movie Matinee	Life Can Be Beautiful	3pm
	Hilltop House		Ma Perkins	3:15
Galen Drake, talk	House Party	Daily Dilemmas	Pepper Young's Family	3:30
			The Right to Happiness	3:45
Second Honeymoon	Hint Hunt	Barbera Welles, talk	Mary Noble, Backstage Wife	4pm
			Stella Dallas	4:15
Pat Barnes, talk	Galen Drake, talk	The Ladies Man	Lorenzo Jones	4:30
Story for Today			Young Widder Brown	4:45
Challenge of the Yukon /	Treasury Bandstand	Adventure Parade	When a Girl Marries	5pm
The Green Hornet		The Adventures of Superman	Portia Faces Life	5:15
Sky King /	Winner Take All	Captain Midnight	Just Plain Bill	5:30
Jack Armstrong, the All-American Boy		The Tom Mix Ralston Straight Shooters	Front Page Farrell	5:45

DAYTIME — FALL, 1948

Saturday

	ABC	CBS	MBS	NBC
9am	Shoppers Special	Bob Hite, news	Harry Hennessy, news	The Triple B Ranch
9:15		This is New York, Danny O'Neill	Top Tunes of the Week	
9:30			The Lone Wolf	The PAL Show
9:45		Galen Drake, talk		The NBC Stamp Club
10am	This is for You		Henry Gladstone, news	Mary Lee Taylor, cooking
10:15		The Garden Gate	The Charlotte Adams Program	
10:30	Johnny Thompson, songs	Mary Lee Taylor, cooking		Archie Andrews
10:45	Saturday Strings			
11am	The Abbott and Costello Children's Show	Let's Pretend	Prescott Robinson, news	Meet the Meeks
11:15			John B. Kennedy, news	
11:30	Don Gardiner, news	Junior Miss	The Man on the Farm	Smilin' Ed's Buster Brown Gang
11:45	The Buddy Weed Trio			
12pm	Pat Barnes, talk	The Armstrong Theater of Today	Your Favorite Music	Charles F. McCarthy, news
12:15			Let's Go	Irene and Rene Kuhn, talk
12:30	The American Farmer	Grand Central Station	Henry Gladstone, news	Coffee with Congress
12:45			The Answer Man	
1pm	Maggie McNellis and Herb Sheldon, talk	County Fair	Luncheon at Sardi's	The National Farm and Home Hour
1:15				
1:30	The Bernie George Show	Give and Take	Sports	Edward Tomlinson, news
1:45				Public Affairs

DAYTIME — FALL, 1948

Saturday

	ABC	CBS	MBS	NBC
2pm	Harry Kogen Orchestra	Stars Over Hollywood		Vincent Lopez Orchestra
2:15				
2:30	Saturday Session	Columbia's Country Journal		Salute to Veterans
2:45	Sports			
3pm		Report from Overseas		Sports
3:15		Adventures in Science		
3:30		Sports		
3:45				
4pm				
4:15				
4:30				
4:45				
5pm		Tommy Ryan Orchestra	Take a Number	Dizzy Dean, sports
5:15				Lassie
5:30	Melodies to Remember	Red Barber's Club House	True or False	Dr. I. Q. Jr.
5:45	Dorothy Fuldheim, news			

LISTINGS FOR 1949

EVENING — WINTER, 1949

Sunday

	ABC	CBS	MBS	NBC
6pm	Drew Pearson, news	The Prudential Family Hour of Stars of Stars	The Roy Rogers Show	The Catholic Hour
6:15	Don Gardiner, news			
6:30	The Greatest Story Ever Told	Spotlight Revue	Nick Carter, Master Detective	The Adventures of Ozzie and Harriet
6:45				
7pm	Go for the House	The Lucky Strike Program, Jack Benny	The Falcon	The Youth Opportunity Program
7:15				
7:30	Carnegie Hall	Amos 'n' Andy	The Mayor of the Town	The Phil Harris - Alice Faye Show
7:45				
8pm	Stop the Music	The Adventures of Sam Spade	A. L. Alexander's Mediation Board	The Fred Allen Show
8:15				
8:30		Lum and Abner	Melvin Elliott, news	The NBC Theater
8:45			Robert S. Allen, news	
9pm	Walter Winchell, gossip	The Electric Theater	Under Arrest	The Manhattan Merry-Go-Round
9:15	Louella Parsons, gossip			
9:30	The Theater Guild on the Air	Our Miss Brooks	Jimmy Fidler, gossip	The American Album of Familiar Music
9:45			John B. Kennedy, news	
10pm		Life with Luigi	Secret Missions	Take It or Leave It
10:15				
10:30	Jimmy Fidler, gossip	It Pays to Be Ignorant	Box 13	Who Said That
10:45	George Sokolsky, news			

EVENING — WINTER, 1949

Monday

ABC	CBS	MBS	NBC	
Joe Hasel, sports	Eric Severeid, news	Lyle Van, news	Kenneth Banghart, news	6pm
Ethel and Albert	You and the World	Bob Elson Interviews	Bill Stern, sports	6:15
New York Tonight, Allen Prescott	Alka Seltzer Time, Herb Shriner	Fred Vandeventer, news	Rey Rodel, songs	6:30
	Lowell Thomas, news	Stan Lomax, sports	Three Star Extra	6:45
Taylor Grant, news	The Beulah Show	Fulton Lewis Jr., news	The Chesterfield Supper Club	7pm
Elmer Davis, news	The Jack Smith Show	The Answer Man	Morgan Beatty, news	7:15
The Lone Ranger	Club Fifteen	A. L. Alexander, poetry	The Smoothies	7:30
	Edward R. Murrow, news	Bill Brandt, sports	H. V. Kaltenborn, news	7:45
The Railroad Hour	Inner Sanctum Mysteries	The Casebook of Gregory Hood	The Cavalcade of America	8pm
				8:15
	Arthur Godfrey's Talent Scouts	Sherlock Holmes	The Voice of Firestone	8:30
Henry J. Taylor, news		Harry Herschfield, stories (8:55pm)		8:45
Let's Go to the Met	The Lux Radio Theater	Gabriel Heatter, news	The Bell Telephone Hour	9pm
		The Mutual Newsreel		9:15
Stars in the Night		The Fishing and Hunting Club	Dr. I. Q., The Mental Banker	9:30
				9:45
Arthur Gaeth, news	My Friend Irma	The American Forum of the Air	The Carnation Contented Hour	10pm
Earl Godwin, news				10:15
On Trial	The Bob Hawk Show	The Longines Symphonette	The Radio City Playhouse	10:30
				10:45

EVENING — WINTER, 1949

Tuesday

	ABC	CBS	MBS	NBC
6pm	Joe Hasel, sports	Eric Severeid, news	Lyle Van, news	Kenneth Banghart, news
6:15	Ethel and Albert	You and the World	Bob Elson Interviews	Bill Stern, sports
6:30	New York Tonight, Allen Prescott	Alka Seltzer Time, Herb Shriner	Fred Vandeventer, news	Rey Rodel, songs
6:45		Lowell Thomas, news	Stan Lomax, sports	Three Star Extra
7pm	Taylor Grant, news	The Beulah Show	Fulton Lewis Jr., news	The Chesterfield Supper Club
7:15	Elmer Davis, news	The Jack Smith Show	The Answer Man	Morgan Beatty, news
7:30	Counterspy	Club Fifteen	A. L. Alexander, poetry	The Hollywood Theater
7:45		Edward R. Murrow, news	Bill Brandt, sports	
8pm	Youth Asks the Government	Mystery Theater	The George O' Hanlon Show	This is Your Life
8:15	Earl Godwin, news			
8:30	America's Town Meeting of the Air	Mr. and Mrs. North	Share the Wealth	The Alan Young Show
8:45			Harry Herschfield, stories (8:55pm)	
9pm		We, the People	Gabriel Heatter, news	The Bob Hope Show
9:15			The Mutual Newsreel	
9:30	Edwin D. Canham, news	The Morey Amsterdam Show	The Bill Williams Show	Fibber Magee and Molly
9:45	Detroit Symphony Orchestra			
10pm		Hit the Jackpot	Let's Play Games	Big Town
10:15				
10:30	It's in the Family	Frankie Carle Orchestra	The Longines Symphonette	People Are Funny
10:45	It's Your Business			

EVENING — WINTER, 1949

Wednesday

ABC	CBS	MBS	NBC	
Joe Hasel, sports	Eric Severeid, news	Lyle Van, news	Kenneth Banghart, news	6pm
Ethel and Albert	You and the World	Bob Elson Interviews	Bill Stern, sports	6:15
New York Tonight, Allen Prescott	Alka Seltzer Time, Herb Shriner	Fred Vandeventer, news	Rey Rodel, songs	6:30
	Lowell Thomas, news	Stan Lomax, sports	Three Star Extra	6:45
Taylor Grant, news	The Beulah Show	Fulton Lewis Jr., news	The Chesterfield Supper Club	7pm
Elmer Davis, news	The Jack Smith Show	The Answer Man	Morgan Beatty, news	7:15
The Lone Ranger	Club Fifteen	A. L. Alexander, poetry	World Over Playhouse	7:30
	Edward R. Murrow, news	Bill Brandt, sports	H. V. Kaltenborn, news	7:45
Ted Mack's Original Amateur Hour	Mr. Chameleon	Can You Top This	Blondie	8pm
				8:15
	Dr. Christian	Boston Blackie	The Great Gildersleeve	8:30
		Harry Herschfield, stories (8:55pm)		8:45
The Texaco Star Theater, Milton Berle	County Fair	Gabriel Heatter, news	Duffy's Tavern	9pm
		The Mutual Newsreel		9:15
You Bet Your Life	Harvest of Stars	The Better Half	Mr. District Attorney	9:30
				9:45
Philco Radio Time, Bing Crosby	Beat the Clock	The Comedy Playhouse	The Big Story	10pm
				10:15
Meredith Willson Orchestra	Capitol Cloak Room	The Longines Symphonette	Curtain Time	10:30
				10:45

EVENING — WINTER, 1949

Thursday

	ABC	CBS	MBS	NBC
6pm	Joe Hasel, sports	Eric Severeid, news	Lyle Van, news	Kenneth Banghart, news
6:15	Ethel and Albert	You and the World	Bob Elson Interviews	Bill Stern, sports
6:30	New York Tonight, Allen Prescott	Alka Seltzer Time, Herb Shriner	Fred Vandeventer, news	Rey Rodel, songs
6:45		Lowell Thomas, news	Stan Lomax, sports	Three Star Extra
7pm	Taylor Grant, news	The Beulah Show	Fulton Lewis Jr., news	The Chesterfield Supper Club
7:15	Elmer Davis, news	The Jack Smith Show	The Answer Man	Morgan Beatty, news
7:30	Counterspy	Club Fifteen	A. L. Alexander, poetry	Serenade to America
7:45		Edward R. Murrow, news	Bill Brandt, sports	
8pm	Abbott and Costello	The FBI in Peace and War	Plantation Jubilee	The Aldrich Family
8:15				
8:30	Theater USA	Mr. Keen, Tracer of Lost Persons	The Western Hit Revue	Maxwell House Coffee Time, Burns and Allen
8:45			Harry Herschfield, stories (8:55pm)	
9pm	Our Job is Manhattan	Suspense	Gabriel Heatter, news	The Kraft Music Hall, Al Jolson
9:15			The Mutual Newsreel	
9:30	The Jo Stafford Show	Casey, Crime Photographer	The Mysterious Traveler	The Sealtest Variety Theater, Dorothy Lamour
9:45				
10pm	Child's World	The Hallmark Playhouse	Philo Vance	The Camel Screen Guild Players
10:15				
10:30	We CARE	The First Nighter Program	The Longines Symphonette	Fred Waring Orchestra
10:45	Harrison Wood, news			

EVENING — WINTER, 1949

Friday

ABC	CBS	MBS	NBC	
Joe Hasel, sports	Eric Severeid, news	Lyle Van, news	Kenneth Banghart, news	6pm
Ethel and Albert	You and the World	Bob Elson Interviews	Bill Stern, sports	6:15
New York Tonight, Allen Prescott	Alka Seltzer Time, Herb Shriner	Fred Vandeventer, news	Rey Rodel, songs	6:30
	Lowell Thomas, news	Stan Lomax, sports	Three Star Extra	6:45
Taylor Grant, news	The Beulah Show	Fulton Lewis Jr., news	The Chesterfield Supper Club	7pm
Elmer Davis, news	The Jack Smith Show	The Answer Man	Morgan Beatty, news	7:15
The Lone Ranger	Club Fifteen	A. L. Alexander, poetry	Bill Cochran, sports	7:30
	Edward R. Murrow, news	Bill Brandt, sports	H. V. Kaltenborn, news	7:45
The Fat Man	The Jack Carson Show	Great Scenes from Great Plays	The Cities Service Band of America	8pm
				8:15
This is Your FBI	My Favorite Husband	Yours for a Song	The Jimmy Durante Show	8:30
		Harry Herschfield, stories (8:55pm)		8:45
Break the Bank	The Ford Theater	Gabriel Heatter, news	Pabst Blue Ribbon Town, Eddie Cantor	9pm
		The Mutual Newsreel		9:15
The Sheriff		The Opera Concert	The Raleigh Cigarette Program, Red Skelton	9:30
				9:45
Madison Square Garden Boxing	The Phillip Morris Playhouse	Meet the Press	The Life of Riley	10pm
				10:15
Joe Hasel's Sports Page	The Pause That Refreshes	The Longines Symphonette	The Colgate Sports Newsreel, Bill Stern	10:30
			Pro and Con	10:45

EVENING — WINTER, 1949

Saturday

	ABC	CBS	MBS	NBC
6pm	Speaking of Songs	Griffin Bancroft, news	Lyle Van, news	Kenneth Banghart, news
6:15		CBS Views the Press	John B. Kennedy, news	Religion in the News
6:30	Quizdom Class	Red Barber, sports	Fred Vandeventer, news	NBC Symphony Orchestra
6:45		Larry Lesueur, news	Stan Lomax, sports	
7pm	The Treasury Band Show	Winner Take All	Guess Who	
7:15	Bert Andrews, news			
7:30	Hawthorne's Adventures	The Camel Caravan, Vaughn Monroe	H. R. Knickerbocker, news	The Pet Milk Show, Vic Damone
7:45			The Answer Man	
8pm	The Kay Starr Show	Gene Autry's Melody Ranch	Twenty Questions	The Hollywood Star Theater
8:15				
8:30	Famous Jury Trials	The Adventures of Phillip Marlowe	Take a Number	Truth or Consequences
8:45				
9pm	Little Herman	Gangbusters	Life Begins at Eighty	Your Hit Parade
9:15				
9:30	The Amazing Mr. Malone	Tales of Fatima	Lombardoland USA	The Judy Canova Show
9:45				
10pm	Phil Bovero Orchestra	Sing It Again	The Chicago Theater of the Air the Air	A Day In the Life of Dennis Day of Dennis Day
10:15				
10:30	Jack Beall, talk			Grand Ole Opry
10:45	Hayloft Hoedown			

DAYTIME — WINTER, 1949

Sunday

	ABC	CBS	MBS	NBC
9am	Bert Bacharach, talk	News	News	W. W. Chaplin, news
9:15		From the Organ Loft	Live a New Life	The Comic Weekly Man
9:30	Music Time		The Mutual Radio Chapel	
9:45		St. Paul's Trinity Choir		Music
10am	Message of Israel	The CBS Church of the Air	Henry Gladstone, news	The National Radio Pulpit
10:15			Fix It Yourself	
10:30	The Southernaires Quartet		Get More Out of Life	The Horn and Hardart Children's Hour
10:45			Your Hymnal	
11am	Brunch with the Fitzgeralds	Howard K. Smith, news	Lyle Van, news	
11:15		The Newsmakers	Brunch with Dorothy and Dick	
11:30	The Hour of Faith	The Salt Lake Tabernacle Choir		Charles F. McCarthy, news
11:45				Solitaire Time
12pm	George Putnam, news	Invitation to Learning	The Show Shop	Hi Jinx
12:15	Robert Strudevant, news			
12:30	The Piano Playhouse	The People's Platform	Melvin Elliott, news	The Eternal Light
12:45			Rendezvous with Ross	
1pm	American Almanac	Joseph C. Harsch, news	William L. Shirer, news	America United
1:15	Edward Weeks, news	Where the People Stand	The Canary Pet Shop	
1:30	National Vespers	Tell It Again	These Stories Are Yours	Author Meets The Critics
1:45			Songs By Great Singers	

DAYTIME — WINTER, 1949

Monday-Friday

ABC	CBS	MBS	NBC	
The Breakfast Club	Bob Hite, news	Harry Hennessy, news	Peter Roberts, news	9am
	This is New York, Danny O'Neill	Get More Out of Life	Ivan Sanderson, talk	9:15
		Alfred W. McCann, food	The Norman Brokenshire Show	9:30
	Missus Goes A Shopping			9:45
My True Story		Henry Gladstone, news	Fred Waring Orchestra	10am
	This is Bing Crosby	Martha Deane, talk		10:15
Betty Crocker, cooking	Arthur Godfrey Time		The Road of Life	10:30
Music / Eleanor and Anna Roosevelt, talk / Dorothy Kilgallen, gossip			The Brighter Day	10:45
Jane Jordan, home economics		Prescott Robinson, news	This is Nora Drake	11am
At Home with the Kirkwoods		Victor Lindlahr, health	We Love and Learn	11:15
Between the Bookends	Grand Slam	Gabriel Heatter's Mailbag	The Jack Berch Show	11:30
Galen Drake, talk	Rosemary	Tello-Test Quiz	Lora Lawton	11:45
Welcome, Travelers	Wendy Warren and the News	Kate Smith Speaks	Charles F. McCarthy, news	12pm
	Aunt Jenny's True Life Stories	Kate Smith Sings	Richard Harkness, news	12:15
Maggie McNellis and Herb Sheldon, talk	The Romance of Helen Trent	News	The Norman Brokenshire Show	12:30
	Our Gal Sunday	The Answer Man		12:45
Party Time	Big Sister	Luncheon at Sardi's	Mary Margaret McBride, talk	1pm
Nancy Booth Craig, talk	Ma Perkins			1:15
	Young Dr. Malone	The Hollywood Theater of Stars		1:30
Dorothy Dix at Home	The Guiding Light			1:45

DAYTIME — WINTER, 1949

Sunday

	ABC	CBS	MBS	NBC
2pm	This Week Around the World	The Longines Choraliers	Deems Taylor Concert	Here's to the Family
2:15				
2:30	Mr. President	You Are There	Harry Hennessy, news	The NBC University Theater
2:45			Blackstone, the Magician	
3pm	Harrison Wood, news	New York Philharmonic Orchestra	Michael O'Duffy, songs	
3:15	Betty Clark Sings			
3:30	Favorite Story		Juvenile Jury	One Man's Family
3:45				
4pm	The Future of America		The House of Mystery	The Quiz Kids
4:15	Johnny Thompson, songs			
4:30	The Metropolitan Opera Auditions	Skyway to the Stars	True Detective Mysteries	Living 1949
4:45				
5pm	Family Close-Up	The Longines Symphonette	The Shadow	Pickens Party
5:15				
5:30	Quiet, Please	Strike It Rich	Quick as a Flash	The RCA Victor Show
5:45				

DAYTIME — WINTER, 1949

Monday-Friday

ABC	CBS	MBS	NBC	
Breakfast in Hollywood	The Second Mrs. Burton	Queen for a Day	Double or Nothing	2pm
	Perry Mason		Hilltop House	2:15
Bride And Groom	This is Nora Drake	The Passing Parade	Today's Children	2:30
	What Makes You Tick	On Your Mark	The Light of the World	2:45
Ladies Be Seated	David Harum	Movie Matinee	Life Can Be Beautiful	3pm
	Hilltop House		Ma Perkins	3:15
House Party	Your Lucky Strike	Best Girl	Pepper Young's Family	3:30
			The Right to Happiness	3:45
Kay Kyser's College of Musical Knowledge	Hint Hunt	Barbera Welles, talk	Mary Noble, Backstage Wife	4pm
			Stella Dallas	4:15
Pat Barnes, talk	The Robert Q. Lewis Show	The Ladies Man	Lorenzo Jones	4:30
Story for Today			Young Widder Brown	4:45
Challenge of the Yukon /	Treasury Bandstand	Tele-Kid Test Quiz	When a Girl Marries	5pm
The Green Hornet		The Adventures of Superman	Portia Faces Life	5:15
Sky King /	Hits and Misses	Captain Midnight	Just Plain Bill	5:30
Jack Armstrong, the All-American Boy		The Tom Mix Ralston Straight Shooters	Front Page Farrell	5:45

DAYTIME — WINTER, 1949

Saturday

	ABC	CBS	MBS	NBC
9am	Shoppers Special	Bob Hite, news	Harry Hennessy, news	The Triple B Ranch
9:15		This is New York, Danny O'Neill	Get More Out of Life	
9:30			The Lanny Ross Show	The PAL Show
9:45		Galen Drake, talk	Let's Go	The NBC Stamp Club
10am	Concert of American Jazz		Henry Gladstone, news	Mary Lee Taylor, cooking
10:15		The Garden Gate	The Charlotte Adams Program	
10:30	The Big and Little Club	Theater of Romance		Archie Andrews
10:45	Saturday Strings		What Am I Offered	
11am	The Abbott and Costello Children's Show	Let's Pretend	Prescott Robinson, news	Meet the Meeks
11:15			Rendezvous with Ross	
11:30	Don Gardiner, news	Junior Miss	The Man on the Farm	Smilin' Ed's Buster Brown Gang
11:45	What's Right Today			
12pm	Pat Barnes, talk	The Armstrong Theater of Today	Your Favorite Music	Charles F. McCarthy, news
12:15			Dr. Kenrad's Unsolved Mysteries	Irene and Rene Kuhn, talk
12:30	The American Farmer	Grand Central Station	Henry Gladstone, news	Vincent Lopez Orchestra
12:45			The Answer Man	
1pm	Maggie McNellis and Herb Sheldon	Stars Over Hollywood	Luncheon at Sardi's	The National Farm and Home Hour
1:15				
1:30	The US Navy Band	Give and Take	Official Detective	RFD America
1:45				

DAYTIME — WINTER, 1949

Saturday

	ABC	CBS	MBS	NBC
2pm	The Metropolitan Opera	The Handy Man	John B. Kennedy, news	The Adventures of Frank Merriwell
2:15		Get More Out of Life	Lawrence Gould Orchestra	
2:30		Columbia's Country Journal	The Family Theater	Edward Tomlinson, news
2:45				Public Affairs
3pm		Report from Overseas	Proudly We Hail	Orchestras of the Nation
3:15		Adventures in Science		
3:30		Cross-Section USA	The Cisco Kid	
3:45				
4pm		Stan Dougherty Presents	Hobby Lobby	Art Mooney Orchestra
4:15				
4:30		Treasury Bandstand	Three's a Crowd	
4:45				Your Radio Reporter
5pm	Tea and Crumpets	Saturday at the Chase	Take a Number	Lassie
5:15				Wormwood Forest
5:30		Red Barber's Club House	True or False	Dr. I. Q. Jr.
5:45				

EVENING — SPRING, 1949

Sunday

	ABC	CBS	MBS	NBC
6pm	Drew Pearson, news	The Prudential Family Hour of Stars	The Roy Rogers Show	The Catholic Hour
6:15	Don Gardiner, news			
6:30	The Greatest Story Ever Told	The Adventures of Ozzie and Harriet	Nick Carter, Master Detective	The Martin and Lewis Show
6:45				
7pm	The Curt Massey Show	The Lucky Strike Program, Jack Benny	The Falcon	The Youth Opportunity Program
7:15				
7:30	Carnegie Hall	Amos 'n' Andy	The Mayor of the Town	The Phil Harris - Alice Faye Show
7:45				
8pm	Stop the Music	The Adventures of Sam Spade	A. L. Alexander's Mediation Board	The Fred Allen Show
8:15				
8:30		Lum and Abner	Melvin Elliott, news	The NBC Theater
8:45			Robert S. Allen, news	
9pm	Walter Winchell, gossip	The Electric Theater	Under Arrest	The Manhattan Merry-Go-Round
9:15	Louella Parsons, gossip			
9:30	The Theater Guild on the Air	Our Miss Brooks	Jimmy Fidler, gossip	The American Album of Familiar Music
9:45			John B. Kennedy, news	
10pm		Life with Luigi	Secret Missions	Take It or Leave It
10:15				
10:30	Jimmy Fidler, gossip	It Pays to Be Ignorant	My Name is Logan	Who Said That
10:45	George Sokolsky, news		Dr. Kenrad's Unsolved Mysteries	

EVENTING — SPRING, 1949

Monday

ABC	CBS	MBS	NBC	
Joe Hasel, sports	Eric Sevareid, news	Lyle Van, news	Kenneth Banghart, news	6pm
Ethel and Albert	You and the World	Bob Elson Interviews	Bill Stern, sports	6:15
New York Tonight, Allen Prescott	Alka Seltzer Time, Herb Shriner	Fred Vandeventer, news	Wayne Howell, news	6:30
	Lowell Thomas, news	Stan Lomax, sports	Three Star Extra	6:45
Taylor Grant, news	The Beulah Show	Fulton Lewis Jr., news	The Chesterfield Supper Club	7pm
Elmer Davis, news	The Jack Smith Show	The Answer Man	Morgan Beatty, news	7:15
The Lone Ranger	Club Fifteen	H. R. Knickerbocker, news	World Over Playhouse	7:30
	Edward R. Murrow, news	Bill Brandt, sports	H. V. Kaltenborn, news	7:45
The Railroad Hour	Inner Sanctum Mysteries	Straight Arrow	The Cavalcade of America	8pm
				8:15
	Arthur Godfrey's Talent Scouts	Sherlock Holmes	The Voice of Firestone	8:30
Henry J. Taylor, news		Bill Henry, news (8:55pm)		8:45
Let's Go to the Met	The Lux Radio Theater	Gabriel Heatter, news	The Bell Telephone Hour	9pm
		The Mutual Newsreel		9:15
Child's World		The Fishing and Hunting Club	Dr. I. Q., The Mental Banker	9:30
				9:45
Arthur Gaeth, news	My Friend Irma	The American Forum of the Air	The Carnation Contented Hour	10pm
Earl Godwin, news				10:15
On Trial	The Bob Hawk Show	The Longines Symphonette	The Radio City Playhouse	10:30
				10:45

EVENING — SPRING, 1949

Tuesday

	ABC	CBS	MBS	NBC
6pm	Joe Hasel, sports	Eric Severeid, news	Lyle Van, news	Kenneth Banghart, news
6:15	Ethel and Albert	You and the World	Bob Elson Interviews	Bill Stern, sports
6:30	New York Tonight, Allen Prescott	Alka Seltzer Time, Herb Shriner	Fred Vandeventer, news	Wayne Howell, news
6:45		Lowell Thomas, news	Stan Lomax, sports	Three Star Extra
7pm	Taylor Grant, news	The Beulah Show	Fulton Lewis Jr., news	The Chesterfield Supper Club
7:15	Elmer Davis, news	The Jack Smith Show	The Answer Man	Morgan Beatty, news
7:30	Counterspy	Club Fifteen	H. R. Knickerbocker, news	The Hollywood Theater
7:45		Edward R. Murrow, news	Bill Brandt, sports	
8pm	Art Mooney's Talent Tour	Mystery Theater	The Casebook of Gregory Hood	This is Your Life
8:15				
8:30	America's Town Meeting of the Air	Mr. and Mrs. North	Share the Wealth	The Alan Young Show
8:45			Bill Henry, news (8:55pm)	
9pm		We, the People	Gabriel Heatter, news	The Bob Hope Show
9:15			The Mutual Newsreel	
9:30	Edwin D. Canham, news	Strike It Rich	The Mysterious Traveler	Fibber Magee and Molly
9:45	Rex Maupin Entertains			
10pm		Hit the Jackpot	Philo Vance	Big Town
10:15				
10:30	It's in the Family	Mr. ace & JANE	The Longines Symphonette	People Are Funny
10:45	Let Freedom Ring			

EVENING — SPRING, 1949

Wednesday

ABC	CBS	MBS	NBC	
Joe Hasel, sports	Eric Sevareid, news	Lyle Van, news	Kenneth Banghart, news	6pm
Ethel and Albert	You and the World	Bob Elson Interviews	Bill Stern, sports	6:15
New York Tonight, Allen Prescott	Alka Seltzer Time, Herb Shriner	Fred Vandeventer, news	Wayne Howell, news	6:30
	Lowell Thomas, news	Stan Lomax, sports	Three Star Extra	6:45
Taylor Grant, news	The Beulah Show	Fulton Lewis Jr., news	The Chesterfield Supper Club	7pm
Elmer Davis, news	The Jack Smith Show	The Answer Man	Morgan Beatty, news	7:15
The Lone Ranger	Club Fifteen	H. R. Knickerbocker,	World Over Playhouse	7:30
	Edward R. Murrow, news	Bill Brandt, sports	H. V. Kaltenborn, news	7:45
Ted Mack's Original Amateur Hour	Mr. Chameleon	Can You Top This	Blondie	8pm
				8:15
	Dr. Christian	Boston Blackie	The Great Gildersleeve	8:30
		Bill Henry, news (8:55pm)		8:45
The Texaco Star Theater, Milton Berle	County Fair	Gabriel Heatter, news	Duffy's Tavern	9pm
		The Mutual Newsreel		9:15
You Bet Your Life	We CARE	The Family Theater	Mr. District Attorney	9:30
				9:45
Philco Radio Time, Bing Crosby	Beat the Clock	The Comedy Playhouse	The Big Story	10pm
				10:15
At Home with the Kirkwoods	Capitol Cloak Room	The Longines Symphonette	Curtain Time	10:30
				10:45

EVENING — SPRING, 1949

Thursday

	ABC	CBS	MBS	NBC
6pm	Joe Hasel, sports	Eric Severeid, news	Lyle Van, news	Kenneth Banghart, news
6:15	Ethel and Albert	You and the World	Bob Elson Interviews	Bill Stern, sports
6:30	New York Tonight, Allen Prescott	Alka Seltzer Time, Herb Shriner	Fred Vandeventer, news	Wayne Howell, news
6:45		Lowell Thomas, news	Stan Lomax, sports	Three Star Extra
7pm	Taylor Grant, news	The Beulah Show	Fulton Lewis Jr., news	The Chesterfield Supper Club
7:15	Elmer Davis, news	The Jack Smith Show	The Answer Man	Morgan Beatty, news
7:30	Counterspy	Club Fifteen	H. R. Knickerbocker, news	Serenade to America
7:45		Edward R. Murrow, news	Bill Brandt, sports	
8pm	Abbott and Costello	The FBI in Peace and War	The Five Mysteries	The Aldrich Family
8:15				
8:30	Theater USA	Mr. Keen, Tracer of Lost Persons	International Airport	Maxwell House Coffee Time, Burns and Allen
8:45			Bill Henry, news (8:55pm)	
9pm	Go for the House	Suspense	Gabriel Heatter, news	The Kraft Music Hall, Al Jolson
9:15			The Mutual Newsreel	
9:30	The Jo Stafford Show	Casey, Crime Photographer	The Better Half	The Sealtest Variety Theater, Dorothy Lamour
9:45				
10pm	Rex Maupin Entertains	The Hallmark Playhouse	This is Paris, Maurice Chevalier	The Camel Screen Guild Players
10:15				
10:30	We CARE	The First Nighter Program	The Longines Symphonette	Fred Waring Orchestra
10:45	Harrison Wood, news			

EVENING — SPRING, 1949

Friday

ABC	CBS	MBS	NBC	
Joe Hasel, sports	Eric Severeid, news	Lyle Van, news	Kenneth Banghart, news	6pm
Ethel and Albert	You and the World	Bob Elson Interviews	Bill Stern, sports	6:15
New York Tonight, Allen Prescott	Alka Seltzer Time, Herb Shriner	Fred Vandeventer, news	Wayne Howell, news	6:30
	Lowell Thomas, news	Stan Lomax, sports	Three Star Extra	6:45
Taylor Grant, news	The Beulah Show	Fulton Lewis Jr., news	The Chesterfield Supper Club	7pm
Elmer Davis, news	The Jack Smith Show	The Answer Man	Morgan Beatty, news	7:15
The Lone Ranger	Club Fifteen	H. R. Knickerbocker,	Bill Cochran, sports	7:30
	Edward R. Murrow, news	Bill Brandt, sports	H. V. Kaltenborn, news	7:45
The Fat Man	The Jack Carson Show	Experience Speaks	The Cities Service Band of America	8pm
				8:15
This is Your FBI	My Favorite Husband	Yours for a Song	The Jimmy Durante Show	8:30
		Bill Henry, news (8:55pm)		8:45
Break the Bank	The Ford Theater	Gabriel Heatter, news	Pabst Blue Ribbon Town, Eddie Cantor	9pm
		The Mutual Newsreel		9:15
The Sheriff		The Opera Concert	The Raleigh Cigarette Program, Red Skelton	9:30
				9:45
Madison Square Garden Boxing	The Phillip Morris Playhouse	Meet the Press	The Life of Riley	10pm
				10:15
Joe Hasel's Sports Page	Yours Truly, Johnny Dollar	The Longines Symphonette	The Colgate Sports Newsreel, Bill Stern	10:30
			Pro and Con	10:45

EVENING — SPRING, 1949

Saturday

	ABC	CBS	MBS	NBC
6pm	The Honeydreamers	Griffin Bancroft, news	Lyle Van, news	Kenneth Banghart, news
6:15	Bible Message	CBS Views the Press	John B. Kennedy, news	Religion in the News
6:30	Quizdom Class	Red Barber, sports	Fred Vandeventer, news	NBC Symphony Orchestra
6:45		Larry Lesueur, news	Stan Lomax, sports	
7pm	Harry Wismer, sports	Spotlight Revue	Guess Who	
7:15	Bert Andrews, news			
7:30	Phil Bovero Orchestra	The Camel Caravan, Vaughn Monroe	H. R. Knickerbocker, news	The Pet Milk Show, Vic Damone
7:45			The Answer Man	
8pm	Take a Chorus	Gene Autry's Melody Ranch	Twenty Questions	The Hollywood Star Theater
8:15				
8:30	Famous Jury Trials	The Adventures of Phillip Marlowe	Take a Number	Truth or Consequences
8:45				
9pm	Little Herman	Gangbusters	Life Begins at Eighty	Your Hit Parade
9:15				
9:30	Pat Novak for Hire	Tales of Fatima	Lombardoland USA	The Judy Canova Show
9:45				
10pm	Earl Godwin, news	Sing It Again	The Chicago Theater of the Air	A Day In the Life of Dennis Day
10:15	The Irving Fields Trio			
10:30	Jack Beall, talk			Grand Ole Opry
10:45	Hayloft Hoedown			

DAYTIME — SPRING, 1949

Sunday

	ABC	CBS	MBS	NBC
9am	Bert Bacharach, talk	News	News	W. W. Chaplin, news
9:15		From the Organ Loft	Live a New Life	The Comic Weekly Man
9:30	Music Time		The Mutual Radio Chapel	
9:45		St. Paul's Trinity Choir		Music
10am	Message of Israel	The CBS Church of the Air	Henry Gladstone, news	The National Radio Pulpit
10:15			Fix It Yourself	
10:30	The Southernaires Quartet		Get More Out of Life	The Horn and Hardart Children's Hour
10:45			Your Hymnal	
11am	Brunch with the Fitzgeralds	The Newsmakers	Henry Gladstone, news	
11:15		Howard K. Smith, news	Brunch with Dorothy and Dick	
11:30	The Hour of Faith	The Salt Lake Tabernacle Choir		Charles F. McCarthy, news
11:45				Solitaire Time
12pm	George Putnam, news	Invitation to Learning	The Show Shop	Hi Jinx
12:15	Robert Strudevant, news			
12:30	The Piano Playhouse	The People's Platform	Melvin Elliott, news	The Eternal Light
12:45			Rendezvous with Ross	
1pm	American Almanac	Charles Collingwood, news	William L. Shirer, news	America United
1:15	Edward Weeks, news	Where the People Stand	The Canary Pet Shop	
1:30	National Vespers	Tell It Again	Great Singers	Author Meets The Critics
1:45				

DAYTIME — SPRING, 1949

Monday-Friday

ABC	CBS	MBS	NBC	
The Breakfast Club	Bob Hite, news	Harry Hennessy, news	Peter Roberts, news	9am
	This is New York, Danny O'Neill	Meet the Menjous	Ivan Sanderson, talk	9:15
		Alfred W. McCann, food	The Norman Brokenshire Show	9:30
	Missus Goes A Shopping			9:45
My True Story		Henry Gladstone, news	Fred Waring Orchestra	10am
	This is Bing Crosby	Martha Deane, talk		10:15
Betty Crocker, cooking	Arthur Godfrey Time		The Road of Life	10:30
Music / Jane Jordan, economics / Dorothy Kilgallen, gossip / Modern Romances			The Brighter Day	10:45
		Prescott Robinson, news	Dr. Paul	11am
		Victor Lindlahr, health	We Love and Learn	11:15
Between the Bookends	Grand Slam	Against the Storm	The Jack Berch Show	11:30
Galen Drake, talk	Rosemary		Lora Lawton	11:45
Welcome, Travelers	Wendy Warren and the News	Kate Smith Speaks	Charles F. McCarthy, news	12pm
	Aunt Jenny's True Life Stories	Kate Smith Sings	Richard Harkness, news	12:15
Maggie McNellis and Herb Sheldon, talk	The Romance of Helen Trent	Henry Gladstone, news	The Norman Brokenshire Show	12:30
	Our Gal Sunday	The Answer Man		12:45
Party Time	Big Sister	Luncheon at Sardi's	Mary Margaret McBride, talk	1pm
Nancy Booth Craig, talk	Ma Perkins			1:15
	Young Dr. Malone	Get More Out of Life		1:30
Dorothy Dix at Home	The Guiding Light			1:45

DAYTIME — SPRING, 1949

Sunday

	ABC	CBS	MBS	NBC
2pm	This Week Around the World	The Longines Choraliers	Deems Taylor Concert	Homecoming
2:15				
2:30	Mr. President	You Are There	Harry Hennessy, news	The NBC University Theater
2:45			The Quiz Club	
3pm	Harrison Wood, news	New York Philharmonic Orchestra	Michael O'Duffy, songs	
3:15	Betty Clark Sings			
3:30	Phil Brestoff Orchestra		Juvenile Jury	One Man's Family
3:45				
4pm	Future of America		The House of Mystery	The Quiz Kids
4:15	Thinking Allowed			
4:30	Milton Cross Opera Album	Skyway to the Stars	True Detective Mysteries	Pickens Party
4:45				
5pm	Music of Today	The Longines Symphonette	The Shadow	The RCA Victor Show
5:15				
5:30	Quiet, Please	Broadway is My Beat	Quick as a Flash	Harvest of Stars
5:45				

DAYTIME — SPRING, 1949

Monday-Friday

ABC	CBS	MBS	NBC	
Breakfast in Hollywood	The Second Mrs. Burton	Queen for a Day	Double or Nothing	2pm
	Perry Mason			2:15
Bride And Groom	This is Nora Drake	The Passing Parade	Today's Children	2:30
	What Makes You Tick	Tello-Test Quiz	The Light of the World	2:45
Ladies Be Seated / Talk Your Way Out of It	David Harum	Movie Matinee	Life Can Be Beautiful	3pm
	Hilltop House		Ma Perkins	3:15
House Party	The Robert Q. Lewis Show	Best Girl	Pepper Young's Family	3:30
			The Right to Happiness	3:45
Kay Kyser's College of Musical Knowledge	Hint Hunt	Barbera Welles, talk	Mary Noble, Backstage Wife	4pm
			Stella Dallas	4:15
Pat Barnes, talk	Winner Take All	The Johnny Olsen Show	Lorenzo Jones	4:30
Eleanor and Anna Roosevelt, talk	Beat the Clock		Young Widder Brown	4:45
Challenge of the Yukon /	Galen Drake, talk	Straight Arrow /	When a Girl Marries	5pm
The Green Hornet		The Adventures of Superman	Portia Faces Life	5:15
Sky King /	Hits and Misses	Captain Midnight	Just Plain Bill	5:30
Jack Armstrong, the All-American Boy		The Tom Mix Ralston Straight Shooters	Front Page Farrell	5:45

DAYTIME — SPRING, 1949

Saturday

	ABC	CBS	MBS	NBC
9am	Shoppers Special	Bob Hite, news	Harry Hennessy, news	The Triple B Ranch
9:15		This is New York, Danny O'Neill	Get More Out of Life	
9:30			What Am I Offered	The PAL Show
9:45		Galen Drake, talk		The NBC Stamp Club
10am	Concert of American Jazz		Henry Gladstone, news	Archie Andrews
10:15		The Garden Gate	Gardening with Gambling	
10:30	This is for You	Tell It Again	Your Home Beautiful	Mary Lee Taylor, cooking
10:45			Let's Go	
11am	Junior Junction	Let's Pretend	Prescott Robinson, news	Meet the Meeks
11:15			Rendezvous with Ross	
11:30	What's My Name	Junior Miss	The Man on the Farm	Smilin' Ed's Buster Brown Gang
11:45				
12pm	The Girls Corp	The Armstrong Theater of Today	The Tremaynes, talk	Charles F. McCarthy, news
12:15				The Do It Yourself Club
12:30	The US Navy Band	Grand Central Station	Henry Gladstone, news	Vincent Lopez Orchestra
12:45			The Answer Man	
1pm	The Home Gardener	Stars Over Hollywood	Luncheon at Sardi's	The National Farm and Home Hour
1:15				
1:30	Pat Barnes, talk	Give and Take	Monica Lewin - Frank Farrell	RFD America
1:45				

DAYTIME — SPRING, 1949

Saturday

	ABC	CBS	MBS	NBC
2pm	Western Hits Revue	Get More Out of Life	Official Detective	Living 1949
2:15		The Handy Man		
2:30	Bruce Chase Orchestra	Columbia's Country Journal	The Affairs of Peter Salem	Edward Tomlinson, news
2:45				The UN is My Beat
3pm	The Treasury Band Show	Report from Overseas	The Cisco Kid	Orchestras of the Nation
3:15		Adventures in Science		
3:30		Cross-Section USA	Hopalong Cassidy	
3:45				
4pm	Tom Glazier's Ballad Box	Straight Facts for Veterans	Proudly We Hail	Your Health Today
4:15	Horse Racing	Horse Racing		Horse Racing
4:30	Two Billion Strong	Saturday at the Chase	Three's a Crowd	Public Affairs
4:45				Irene and Rene Kuhn, talk
5pm	Tea and Crumpets	Treasury Bandstand	Take a Number	Lassie
5:15				Wormwood Forest
5:30		Make Way for Youth	True or False	Bobby Byrnes Orchestra
5:45				

EVENING — SUMMER, 1949

Sunday

	ABC	CBS	MBS	NBC
6pm	Drew Pearson, news	The Prudential Family Hour of Stars	The Roy Rogers Show	The Catholic Hour
6:15	Don Gardiner, news			
6:30	Betty Clark Sings	Yours Truly, Johnny Dollar	Nick Carter, Master Detective	Hollywood Calling
6:45	Phil Bovero Orchestra			
7pm	Think Fast	Your Hit Parade on Parade	The Falcon	
7:15				
7:30	Carnegie Hall	Call the Police	The Saint	Guy Lombardo Orchestra
7:45				
8pm	Stop the Music	The Adventures of Sam Spade	A. L. Alexander's Mediation Board	The Four Star Playhouse
8:15				
8:30		Life with Luigi	Melvin Elliott, news	NBC Symphony Orchestra
8:45			Robert S. Allen, news	
9pm	The Burl Ives Show	Meet Corliss Archer	The Count of Monte Cristo	
9:15	Louella Parsons, gossip			
9:30	Chance of a Lifetime	Our Miss Brooks	Sheilah Graham, gossip	The Ethel Merman Show
9:45			Twin Views of the News	
10pm	Sheilah Graham and Erskine Johnson, gossip	Dress Parade	Murder By Experts	Who Said That
10:15	Between the Bookends			
10:30	George Henninger, organ	Dick Jurgens Orchestra	Smoke Rings	The Youth Opportunity Program
10:45	George Sokolsky, news			

EVENING — SUMMER, 1949

Monday

ABC	CBS	MBS	NBC	
Gene Kirby, sports	Richard Hotteltot, news	Lyle Van, news	Kenneth Banghart, news	6pm
New York Tonight, Allen Prescott	You and the World	Bob Elson Interviews	Bill Stern, sports	6:15
	Curt Massey, songs	Fred Vandeventer, news	Wayne Howell, news	6:30
Sammy Kaye's Showroom	Lowell Thomas, news	Stan Lomax, sports	Three Star Extra	6:45
Taylor Grant, news	The Beulah Show	Fulton Lewis Jr., news	The Chesterfield Supper Club	7pm
Albert Warner, news	The Jack Smith Show	The Answer Man	Morgan Beatty, news	7:15
The Lone Ranger	Spin to Win	Gabriel Heatter, news	Vincent Lopez Orchestra	7:30
	Larry Lesueur, news	Bill Brandt, sports	Richard Harkness, news	7:45
The Railroad Hour	Inner Sanctum Mysteries	Straight Arrow	One Man's Family	8pm
				8:15
Ella Mae Time	Young Love	The Affairs of Peter Salem	The Voice of Firestone	8:30
Henry J. Taylor, news		Charles Shaw, news (8:55pm)		8:45
Kate Smith Calls	Leave It to Joan	The Periscope	The Bell Telephone Hour	9pm
		A. L. Alexander, poetry		9:15
	Breakfast with Burrows	Secret Missions	Pickens Party	9:30
				9:45
Arthur Gaeth, news	The Straw Hat Concert	The American Forum of the Air	The Carnation Contented Hour	10pm
Kate Smith Calls				10:15
	The Nation's Defense	The Longines Symphonette	The Radio City Playhouse	10:30
				10:45

EVENING — SUMMER, 1949

Tuesday

	ABC	CBS	MBS	NBC
6pm	Gene Kirby, sports	Richard Hotteltot, news	Lyle Van, news	Kenneth Banghart, news
6:15	New York Tonight, Allen Prescott	You and the World	Bob Elson Interviews	Bill Stern, sports
6:30		Curt Massey, songs	Fred Vandeventer, news	Wayne Howell, news
6:45	Johnny Thompson, songs	Lowell Thomas, news	Stan Lomax, sports	Three Star Extra
7pm	Taylor Grant, news	The Beulah Show	Fulton Lewis Jr., news	The Chesterfield Supper Club
7:15	Albert Warner, news	The Jack Smith Show	The Answer Man	Morgan Beatty, news
7:30	Counterspy	Spin to Win	Gabriel Heatter, news	Vincent Lopez Orchestra
7:45		Larry Lesueur, news	Bill Brandt, sports	
8pm	Little Herman	Mystery Theater	The Casebook of Gregory Hood	Hogan's Daughter
8:15				
8:30	America's Town Meeting of the Air	Mr. and Mrs. North	Official Detective	Me and Janie
8:45			Charles Shaw, news (8:55pm)	
9pm		We, the People	John Steele, Adventurer	The Martin and Lewis Show
9:15				
9:30	Edwin D. Canham, news	It Pays to Be Ignorant	The Mysterious Traveler	The King's Men
9:45	Detroit Symphony Orchestra			
10pm		Hit the Jackpot	Philo Vance	Big Town
10:15				
10:30	As We See It	The Nation's Defense	The Longines Symphonette	A Life in Your Hands
10:45	It's Your Business			

EVENING — SUMMER, 1949

Wednesday

ABC	CBS	MBS	NBC	
Gene Kirby, sports	Richard Hotteltot, news	Lyle Van, news	Kenneth Banghart, news	6pm
New York Tonight, Allen Prescott	You and the World	Bob Elson Interviews	Bill Stern, sports	6:15
	Curt Massey, songs	Fred Vandeventer, news	Wayne Howell, news	6:30
Sammy Kaye's Showroom	Lowell Thomas, news	Stan Lomax, sports	Three Star Extra	6:45
Taylor Grant, news	The Beulah Show	Fulton Lewis Jr., news	The Chesterfield Supper Club	7pm
Albert Warner, news	The Jack Smith Show	The Answer Man	Morgan Beatty, news	7:15
The Lone Ranger	Spin to Win	Gabriel Heatter, news	Guy Lombardo Orchestra	7:30
	Larry Lesueur, news	Bill Brandt, sports	Richard Harkness, news	7:45
Ted Mack's Original Amateur Hour	Mr. Chameleon	Can You Top This	Chicken Every Sunday	8pm
				8:15
	Dr. Christian	Boston Blackie	Archie Andrews	8:30
		Charles Shaw, news (8:55pm)		8:45
Stars in the Night	The Lewisohn Stadium Concerts	The Hollywood Theater of Stars	The Henry Morgan Show	9pm
				9:15
Lawrence Welk High Life Revue		The Family Theater	Mr. District Attorney	9:30
				9:45
It's Time for Music		The Comedy Playhouse	The Big Story	10pm
				10:15
On Trial	Capitol Cloak Room	The Longines Symphonette	Curtain Time	10:30
				10:45

EVENING — SUMMER, 1949

Thursday

	ABC	CBS	MBS	NBC
6pm	Gene Kirby, sports	Richard Hotteltot, news	Lyle Van, news	Kenneth Banghart, news
6:15	New York Tonight, Allen Prescott	You and the World	Bob Elson Interviews	Bill Stern, sports
6:30		Curt Massey, songs	Fred Vandeventer, news	Wayne Howell, news
6:45	Johnny Thompson, songs	Lowell Thomas, news	Stan Lomax, sports	Three Star Extra
7pm	Taylor Grant, news	The Beulah Show	Fulton Lewis Jr., news	The Chesterfield Supper Club
7:15	Albert Warner, news	The Jack Smith Show	The Answer Man	Morgan Beatty, news
7:30	Counterspy	Spin to Win	Gabriel Heatter, news	Serenade to America
7:45		Larry Lesueur, news	Bill Brandt, sports	
8pm	Eye Sketch	Broadway is My Beat	The Five Mysteries	My Silent Partner
8:15				
8:30	The First Hundred Years	Mr. Keen, Tracer of Lost Persons	The Fishing and Hunting Club	Eight by Request
8:45			Charles Shaw, news (8:55pm)	
9pm	Play It Again	Escape	Meet Your Match	The Kraft Music Hall, Nelson Eddy
9:15				
9:30	Name the Movie	Casey, Crime Photographer	Sing for Your Supper	The James and Pamela Mason Show
9:45				
10pm	Rex Maupin Entertains	The First Nighter Program	This is Paris, Maurice Chevalier	Fred Waring Orchestra
10:15				
10:30	We CARE	The Nation's Defense	The Longines Symphonette	Dragnet
10:45	The Harmonaires			

EVENING — SUMMER, 1949

Friday

ABC	CBS	MBS	NBC	
Joe Hasel, sports	Richard Hotteltot, news	Lyle Van, news	Kenneth Banghart, news	6pm
New York Tonight, Allen Prescott	You and the World	Bob Elson Interviews	Bill Stern, sports	6:15
	Curt Massey, songs	Fred Vandeventer, news	Wayne Howell, news	6:30
Sammy Kaye's Showroom	Lowell Thomas, news	Stan Lomax, sports	Three Star Extra	6:45
Taylor Grant, news	The Beulah Show	Fulton Lewis Jr., news	The Chesterfield Supper Club	7pm
Albert Warner, news	The Jack Smith Show	The Answer Man	Morgan Beatty, news	7:15
The Lone Ranger	Spin to Win	Gabriel Heatter, news	Bill Cochran, sports	7:30
	Larry Lesueur, news	Bill Brandt, sports	Richard Harkness, news	7:45
The Fat Man	Summer in St. Louis	Plantation Jubilee	The Cities Service Band of America	8pm
				8:15
This is Your FBI		Xavier Cugat Orchestra	A Tree Grows in Brooklyn	8:30
		Charles Shaw, news (8:55pm)		8:45
Break the Bank	This is Broadway	The Opera Concert	The Screen Director's Playhouse	9pm
				9:15
The Sheriff		The Better Half	My Good Wife	9:30
				9:45
Heinie and His Band	Xavier Cugat Orchestra	Meet the Press	Dr. I. Q., the Mental Banker	10pm
				10:15
The Enchantment Hour	The Nation's Defense	The Longines Symphonette	The Colgate Sports Newsreel, Bill Stern	10:30
			Pro and Con	10:45

EVENING — SUMMER, 1949

Saturday

	ABC	CBS	MBS	NBC
6pm	Fantasy in Melody	Wayne Nelson, news	Lyle Van, news	Kenneth Banghart, news
6:15	Phil Bovero Orchestra	CBS Views the Press	The Spotlighters	The Art of Living
6:30	Harry Wismer, sports	Red Barber, sports	Fred Vandeventer, news	The NBC University Theater
6:45	Rendezvous with Music	Larry Lesueur, news	Stan Lomax, sports	
7pm	Here's Hollywood	The Green Lama	Frank Farrell, songs	
7:15	Bert Andrews, news		The Answer Man	
7:30	Bronislav Gimpel Orchestra	The Camel Caravan, Vaughn Monroe	True or False	Kay Armen Sings
7:45				
8pm	Buzz Adlam's Playroom	Gene Autry's Melody Ranch	Twenty Questions	Saturday Dance Date
8:15				
8:30	Two Billion Strong	The Adventures of Phillip Marlowe	Take a Number	Truth or Consequences
8:45				
9pm	Tommy Dorsey Orchestra	Gangbusters	Life Begins at Eighty	Your Hit Parade
9:15				
9:30	Phil Bovero Orchestra	Tales of Fatima	Lombardoland USA	Dangerous Assignment
9:45				
10pm	Musical Etchings	Sing It Again	The Chicago Theater of the Air	Richard Diamond, Private Detective
10:15	The Irving Fields Trio			
10:30	Richard Himber Orchestra			Grand Ole Opry
10:45				

DAYTIME — SUMMER, 1949

Sunday

	ABC	CBS	MBS	NBC
9am	Bert Bacharach, talk	News	News	W. W. Chaplin, news
9:15		From the Organ Loft	Live a New Life	The Comic Weekly Man
9:30	The Voice of Prophecy		The Mutual Radio Chapel	
9:45		St. Paul's Trinity Choir		Music
10am	Message of Israel	The CBS Church of the Air	Henry Gladstone, news	Highlights of the Bible
10:15			Jane Jordan, economics	
10:30	The Southernaires Quartet			The Horn and Hardart Children's Hour
10:45			Your Hymnal	
11am	Brunch with the Fitzgeralds	The Newsmakers	Henry Gladstone, news	
11:15		Howard K. Smith, news	The Longneckers	
11:30	The Hour of Faith	The Salt Lake Tabernacle Choir		Charles F. McCarthy, news
11:45				Solitaire Time
12pm	Fantasy in Melody	Invitation to Learning	The Show Shop	Hi Jinx
12:15	Robert Strudevant, news			
12:30	The Piano Playhouse	The People's Platform	Melvin Elliott, news	The Eternal Light
12:45			Rendezvous with Ross	
1pm	The Song Salesman	Charles Collingwood, news	The Enchanted Hour	America United
1:15	Hollywood Byline	Where the People Stand		
1:30	National Vespers	Treasury Bandstand	Michael O'Duffy, songs	Salute to the NBC Symphony
1:45				

DAYTIME — SUMMER, 1949

Monday-Friday

ABC	CBS	MBS	NBC	
The Breakfast Club	Bob Hite, news	Harry Hennessy, news	Peter Roberts, news	9am
	This is New York, Danny O'Neill	Meet the Menjous	The Norman Brokenshire Show	9:15
		Alfred W. McCann, food		9:30
	Missus Goes A Shopping		Inside the Doctor's Office	9:45
My True Story		Henry Gladstone, news	Welcome, Travelers	10am
	This is Bing Crosby	Martha Deane, talk		10:15
Betty Crocker, cooking	Arthur Godfrey Time		Marriage for Two	10:30
Music / Rosa Rio, organ			Thanks for Tomorrow	10:45
Modern Romances		Prescott Robinson, news	Dr. Paul	11am
		Tello-Test Quiz	We Love and Learn	11:15
Between the Bookends	Grand Slam	Against the Storm	The Jack Berch Show	11:30
Galen Drake, talk	Rosemary		Lora Lawton	11:45
Listen to This	Wendy Warren and the News	Kate Smith Speaks	Charles F. McCarthy, news	12pm
	Aunt Jenny's True Life Stories	Kate Smith Sings	Richard Harkness, news	12:15
	The Romance of Helen Trent	Henry Gladstone, news	The Hometowners	12:30
H. R. Baukhage, news	Our Gal Sunday	The Answer Man		12:45
Party Time	Big Sister	Luncheon at Sardi's	Mary Margaret McBride, talk	1pm
Nancy Booth Craig, talk	Ma Perkins			1:15
	Young Dr. Malone			1:30
Dorothy Dix at Home	The Guiding Light	Your Marriage		1:45

DAYTIME — SUMMER, 1949

Sunday

	ABC	CBS	MBS	NBC
2pm	This Week Around the World	The Longines Choraliers	Deems Taylor Concert	For Us, the Living
2:15				
2:30	Mr. President	Arms for Europe	Harry Hennessy, news	Design for Listening
2:45			David Snell, talk	
3pm	Harrison Wood, news	CBS Symphony Orchestra	Ernie Lee's Omega Show	
3:15	Chautauqua Symphony Orchestra			
3:30			True Detective Mysteries	The US Air Force Band
3:45				
4pm			The House of Mystery	Living 1949
4:15				
4:30	Milton Cross Opera Album	Art Mooney Orchestra	Martin Kane, Private Detective	The Silver Strings
4:45				
5pm	The US Navy Band	Music for You	Under Arrest	Surprise Serenade
5:15				
5:30	Buzz Adlam's Playroom	The Longines Symphonette	Mr. Fix-It	Voices and Events
5:45			Jimmy Powers, sports	

DAYTIME — SUMMER, 1949

Monday-Friday

ABC	CBS	MBS	NBC	
Breakfast in Hollywood	The Second Mrs. Burton	Queen for a Day	Double or Nothing	*2pm*
	Perry Mason			*2:15*
Bride and Groom	This is Nora Drake	Second Honeymoon	Today's Children	*2:30*
	The Brighter Day		The Light of the World	*2:45*
Ladies Be Seated	David Harum	The Tremaynes, talk	Life Can Be Beautiful	*3pm*
	Hilltop House		The Road of Life	*3:15*
Add a Line	Make-Believe Town, Hollywood	Best Girl	Pepper Young's Family	*3:30*
			The Right to Happiness	*3:45*
The Herb Sheldon Show	Beat the Clock	Barbera Welles, talk	Mary Noble, Backstage Wife	*4pm*
			Stella Dallas	*4:15*
Eleanor and Anna Roosevelt, talk	Winner Take All	The Johnny Olsen Show	Lorenzo Jones	*4:30*
Pat Barnes, talk			Young Widder Brown	*4:45*
Challenge of the Yukon /	Roger Bennett, talk	Bobby Benson /	When a Girl Marries	*5pm*
The Green Hornet		Ted Drake, Guardian of the Big Top	Portia Faces Life	*5:15*
Sky King /	Hits and Misses	Gabriel Heatter's Mailbag	Just Plain Bill	*5:30*
Johnny Lujack of Notre Dame		Top Tunes	Front Page Farrell	*5:45*

DAYTIME — SUMMER, 1949

Saturday

	ABC	CBS	MBS	NBC
9am	The Kelvin Keech Show	Bob Hite, news	Harry Hennessy, news	The Story Shop
9:15		This is New York, Danny O'Neill	Bing Crosby Records	
9:30	Shoppers Special		Tele-Kid Test Quiz	The PAL Show
9:45		Missus Goes A Shopping		The NBC Stamp Club
10am	Johnny Olsen's Get-Together	Roger Bennett, talk	Henry Gladstone, news	Fred Waring Orchestra
10:15			Frank Sinatra Records	
10:30		Music for You		Mary Lee Taylor, cooking
10:45			Let's Go	
11am	Modern Romances	Let's Pretend	Prescott Robinson, news	The Adventures of Frank Merriwell
11:15			Rendezvous with Ross	
11:30	Jay Stewart's Fun Fair	Junior Miss	Charmer and the Dell	Smilin' Ed's Buster Brown Gang
11:45				
12pm	The Girls Corp	The Armstrong Theater of Today	Man on the Farm	Charles F. McCarthy, news
12:15				Americans Abroad
12:30	What's My Name	Grand Central Station	Henry Gladstone, news	Vincent Lopez Orchestra
12:45			The Answer Man	
1pm	The Home Gardener	Stars Over Hollywood	Luncheon at Sardi's	The National Farm and Home Hour
1:15				
1:30	Pat Barnes, talk	Give and Take	The Tremaynes, talk	RFD America
1:45				

DAYTIME — SUMMER, 1949

Saturday

	ABC	CBS	MBS	NBC
2pm	The Western Hit Revue	County Fair	Julie and Red	Echoes from the Tropics
2:15				
2:30	Junior Junction	Farm News	The Damon Runyon Theater	Here's to Veterans
2:45		The Dell Trio		The UN is My Beat
3pm	The Treasury Band Show	Report from Overseas	International Airport	Ivan Sanderson, talk
3:15		Adventures in Science		
3:30	Fascinating Rhythm	Dave Stephens Orchestra	The Cisco Kid	Whitney Berquist Orchestra
3:45				
4pm	Chuck Foster Orchestra	George Towne Orchestra	Hopalong Cassidy	Your Health Today
4:15				Slim Bryant Orchestra
4:30	Horse Racing	Saturday at the Chase	Proudly We Hail	The University of Chicago Round Table
4:45				
5pm	Musical Contrasts	Henry Jerome Orchestra	The Summer Theater	Mind Your Manners
5:15		Horse Racing		
5:30		Make Way for Youth	Scattergood Baines	Guest Star
5:45				Horse Racing

EVENING — FALL, 1949

Sunday

	ABC	CBS	MBS	NBC
6pm	Drew Pearson, news	The Prudential Family Hour of Stars	The Roy Rogers Show	The Catholic Hour
6:15	Don Gardiner, news			
6:30	Author Meets the Critics	Our Miss Brooks	Nick Carter, Master Detective	Hollywood Calling
6:45				
7pm	Think Fast	The Lucky Strike Program, Jack Benny	The Falcon	
7:15				
7:30	Ralph Norman Orchestra	Amos 'n' Andy	The Saint	The Phil Harris - Alice Faye Show
7:45				
8pm	Stop the Music	The Charlie McCarthy Show	A. L. Alexander's Mediation Board	The Adventures of Sam Spade
8:15				
8:30		The Red Skelton Show	Melvin Elliott, news	The Theater Guild on the Air
8:45			Robert S. Allen, news	
9pm	Walter Winchell, gossip	Meet Corliss Archer	The Opera Concert	
9:15	Louella Parsons, gossip			
9:30	Chance of a Lifetime	The Youth Opportunity Program	Sheilah Graham, gossip	The American Album of Familiar Music
9:45			Twin Views of the News	
10pm	Jimmy Fidler, gossip	The Carnation Contented Hour	The Damon Runyon Theater	Take It or Leave It
10:15	Between the Bookends			
10:30	Cliff Cameron, organ	Johnny Long Orchestra		The Pet Milk Show
10:45	George Sokolsky, news		The Visiting Nurse Service Show	

EVENING — FALL, 1949

Monday

ABC	CBS	MBS	NBC	
Walter Kiernan, news	Eric Severeid, news	Lyle Van, news	Kenneth Banghart, news	6pm
New York Tonight, Allen Prescott	You and the World	Bob Elson Interviews	Bill Stern, sports	6:15
	Curt Massey, songs	Fred Vandeventer, news	Wayne Howell, news	6:30
Sammy Kaye's Showroom	Fulton Oursler, news	Stan Lomax, sports	Three Star Extra	6:45
Taylor Grant, news	The Beulah Show	Fulton Lewis Jr., news	Light Up Time, Frank Sinatra	7pm
Elmer Davis, news	The Jack Smith Show	The Answer Man	John W. Vandercook, news	7:15
The Lone Ranger	Club Fifteen	Gabriel Heatter, news	Echoes from the Tropics	7:30
	Edward R. Murrow, news	I Love a Mystery	H. V. Kaltenborn, news	7:45
Rex Maupin Orchestra	Inner Sanctum Mysteries	Straight Arrow	The Railroad Hour	8pm
				8:15
Ella Maetime, songs	Arthur Godfrey's Talent Scouts	The Affairs of Peter Salem	The Voice of Firestone	8:30
Henry J. Taylor, news		Bill Henry, news (8:55pm)		8:45
Kate Smith Calls	The Lux Radio Theater	Murder By Experts	The Bell Telephone Hour	9pm
				9:15
		Secret Missions	The Cities Service Band of America	9:30
				9:45
Arthur Gaeth, news	My Friend Irma	Public Affairs	The Screen Director's Playhouse	10pm
Kate Smith Calls				10:15
	The Bob Hawk Show	The Longines Symphonette	The Ethel Merman Show	10:30
				10:45

EVENING — FALL, 1949

Tuesday

	ABC	CBS	MBS	NBC
6pm	Walter Kiernan, news	Eric Severeid, news	Lyle Van, news	Kenneth Banghart, news
6:15	New York Tonight, Allen Prescott	You and the World	Bob Elson Interviews	Bill Stern, sports
6:30		Curt Massey, songs	Fred Vandeventer, news	Wayne Howell, news
6:45	Johnny Thompson, songs	Fulton Oursler, news	Stan Lomax, sports	Three Star Extra
7pm	Taylor Grant, news	The Beulah Show	Fulton Lewis Jr., news	Light Up Time, Frank Sinatra
7:15	Elmer Davis, news	The Jack Smith Show	The Answer Man	John W. Vandercook, news
7:30	Counterspy	Club Fifteen	Gabriel Heatter, news	Hotel Orchestra
7:45		Edward R. Murrow, news	I Love a Mystery	Richard Harkness, news
8pm	Carnegie Hall	Mystery Theater	The Count of Monte Cristo	The Cavalcade of America
8:15				
8:30	America's Town Meeting of the Air	Mr. and Mrs. North	Official Detective	Me and James
8:45			Bill Henry, news (8:55pm)	
9pm		We, the People	John Steele, Adventurer	The Bob Hope Show
9:15				
9:30	Christian Science News	Life with Luigi	The Mysterious Traveler	Fibber Magee and Molly
9:45	We CARE			
10pm	Time for Defense	Hit the Jackpot	Philo Vance	Big Town
10:15				
10:30	As We See It	Jimmy Dorsey Orchestra	The Longines Symphonette	People Are Funny
10:45	Let Freedom Ring			

EVENING — FALL, 1949

Wednesday

ABC	CBS	MBS	NBC	
Walter Kiernan, news	Eric Severeid, news	Lyle Van, news	Kenneth Banghart, news	6pm
New York Tonight, Allen Prescott	You and the World	Bob Elson Interviews	Bill Stern, sports	6:15
	Curt Massey, songs	Fred Vandeventer, news	Wayne Howell, news	6:30
Sammy Kaye's Showroom	Fulton Oursler, news	Stan Lomax, sports	Three Star Extra	6:45
Taylor Grant, news	The Beulah Show	Fulton Lewis Jr., news	Light Up Time, Frank Sinatra	7pm
Elmer Davis, news	The Jack Smith Show	The Answer Man	John W. Vandercook, news	7:15
The Lone Ranger	Club Fifteen	Gabriel Heatter, news	Guy Lombardo Orchestra	7:30
	Edward R. Murrow, news	I Love a Mystery	H. V. Kaltenborn, news	7:45
The Amazing Mr. Malone	Mr. Chameleon	Can You Top This	This is Your Life	8pm
				8:15
Sherlock Holmes	Dr. Christian	International Airport	The Great Gildersleeve	8:30
		Bill Henry, news (8:55pm)		8:45
Starring Boris Karloff	You Bet Your Life	The Hollywood Theater of Stars	Break the Bank	9pm
				9:15
The Croupier	The Bing Crosby Chesterfield Show	The Family Theater	Mr. District Attorney	9:30
				9:45
Lawrence Welk High Life Revue	Burns and Allen	Scattergood Baines	The Big Story	10pm
				10:15
On Trial	Capitol Cloak Room	The Longines Symphonette	Curtain Time	10:30
				10:45

EVENING — FALL, 1949

Thursday

	ABC	CBS	MBS	NBC
6pm	Walter Kiernan, news	Eric Severeid, news	Lyle Van, news	Kenneth Banghart, news
6:15	New York Tonight, Allen Prescott	You and the World	Bob Elson Interviews	Bill Stern, sports
6:30		Curt Massey, songs	Fred Vandeventer, news	Wayne Howell, news
6:45	Johnny Thompson, songs	Fulton Oursler, news	Stan Lomax, sports	Three Star Extra
7pm	Taylor Grant, news	The Beulah Show	Fulton Lewis Jr., news	Light Up Time, Frank Sinatra
7:15	Elmer Davis, news	The Jack Smith Show	The Answer Man	John W. Vandercook, news
7:30	Counterspy	Club Fifteen	Gabriel Heatter, news	Serenade to America
7:45		Edward R. Murrow, news	I Love a Mystery	Richard Harkness, news
8pm	Blondie	The FBI in Peace and War	California Caravan	The Aldrich Family
8:15				
8:30	A Date with Judy	Mr. Keen, Tracer of Lost Persons	The Fishing and Hunting Club	Father Knows Best
8:45			Bill Henry, news (8:55pm)	
9pm	Ted Mack's Original Amateur Hour	Suspense	The Comedy Playhouse	The Camel Screen Guild Players
9:15				
9:30		Casey, Crime Photographer		Duffy's Tavern
9:45				
10pm	Name the Movie	The Hallmark Playhouse	The Better Half	The Chesterfield Supper Club
10:15	Robert Montgomery Speaking			
10:30	Someone You Know	The First Nighter Program	The Longines Symphonette	Dragnet
10:45				

EVENING — FALL, 1949

Friday

ABC	CBS	MBS	NBC	
Walter Kiernan, news	Eric Severeid, news	Lyle Van, news	Kenneth Banghart, news	6pm
New York Tonight, Allen Prescott	You and the World	Bob Elson Interviews	Bill Stern, sports	6:15
	Curt Massey, songs	Fred Vandeventer, news	Wayne Howell, news	6:30
Sammy Kaye's Showroom	Fulton Oursler, news	Stan Lomax, sports	Three Star Extra	6:45
Taylor Grant, news	The Beulah Show	Fulton Lewis Jr., news	Light Up Time, Frank Sinatra	7pm
Elmer Davis, news	The Jack Smith Show	The Answer Man	John W. Vandercook, news	7:15
The Lone Ranger	Club Fifteen	Gabriel Heatter, news	Echoes from the Tropics	7:30
	Edward R. Murrow, news	I Love a Mystery	H. V. Kaltenborn, news	7:45
The Fat Man	The Goldbergs	Bandstand USA	The Henry Morgan Show	8pm
				8:15
This is Your FBI	My Favorite Husband	The Harry Gray Show	The Martin and Lewis Show	8:30
		Bill Henry, news (8:55pm)		8:45
The Adventures of Ozzie and Harriet	Leave It to Joan	Mystery is My Hobby	The Life of Riley	9pm
				9:15
The Sheriff	Crime Correspondent	Meet the Press	The Jimmy Durante Show	9:30
				9:45
Madison Square Garden Boxing	Young Love	Proudly We Hail	Dr. I. Q., the Mental Banker	10pm
				10:15
Joe Hasel's Sports Page	Capitol Cloak Room	The Longines Symphonette	The Colgate Sports Newsreel, Bill Stern	10:30
			Pro and Con	10:45

EVENING — FALL, 1949

Saturday

	ABC	CBS	MBS	NBC
6pm	Albert Warner, news	Bill Shaedel news	Lyle Van, news	Kenneth Banghart, news
6:15	The Church and the Nation	CBS Views the Press	Sidney Walton, news	Bill Cochran, sports
6:30	Harry Wismer, sports	Red Barber, sports	Fred Vandeventer, news	NBC Symphony Orchestra
6:45	The Harmonaires	Larry Lesueur, news	Stan Lomax, sports	
7pm	Rex Koury, organ	Lum and Abner	Frank Farrell, songs	
7:15	Bert Andrews, news		The Answer Man	
7:30	Russ Hodges, sports	The Camel Caravan, Vaughn Monroe	Quick as a Flash	Richard Diamond, Private Detective
7:45	Buzz Adlam's Playroom			
8pm	Chandu, the Magician	Gene Autry's Melody Ranch	Twenty Questions	The Hollywood Star Theater
8:15				
8:30	The Casebook of Gregory Hood	The Adventures of Phillip Marlowe	Take a Number	Truth or Consequences
8:45				
9pm	Dick Jurgens Orchestra	Gangbusters	Meet Your Match	Your Hit Parade
9:15				
9:30	Hollywood Byline	Escape	Lombardoland USA	A Day In the Life of Dennis Day
9:45				
10pm	Voices That Live	Sing It Again	The Chicago Theater of the Air	The Judy Canova Show
10:15				
10:30	Saturday at the Shamrock			Grand Ole Opry
10:45				

DAYTIME — FALL, 1949

Sunday

	ABC	CBS	MBS	NBC
9am	Bert Bacharach, talk	News	Harry Hennessy, news	News
9:15		From the Organ Loft	Live a New Life	The Comic Weekly Man
9:30	The Voice of Prophecy		The Mutual Radio Chapel	
9:45		St. Paul's Trinity Choir		Music
10am	Message of Israel	The CBS Church of the Air	Henry Gladstone, news	The National Radio Pulpit
10:15			Get More Out of Life	
10:30	The Southernaires Quartet			The Horn and Hardart Children's Hour
10:45			Your Hymnal	
11am	Victor Lindlahr, health	The Newsmakers	Henry Gladstone, news	
11:15	Frank and Ernest, religion	Howard K. Smith, news	Brunch with Dorothy and Dick	
11:30	The Hour of Faith	The Salt Lake Tabernacle Choir		Charles F. McCarthy, news
11:45				Solitaire Time
12pm	Brunch with the Fitzgeralds	Invitation to Learning	The Show Shop	Mr. Fix-It
12:15				On the Village Green
12:30	The Piano Playhouse	The People's Platform	Marvin Elliott, news	Tex and Jinx, talk
12:45			John M. Wyatt, news	
1pm	The Fine Arts Quartet	Charles Collingwood, news	Sidney Walton, news	Expedition's End
1:15	We CARE	Where the Public Stands	The Canary Pet Shop	
1:30	National Vespers	Treasury Bandstand	Michael O'Duffy, songs	The Quiz Kids
1:45				

DAYTIME — FALL, 1949

Monday-Friday

ABC	CBS	MBS	NBC	
The Breakfast Club	This is New York, Danny O'Neill	Harry Hennessy, news	Tex and Jinx, talk (8:30am)	9am
		Get More Out of Life	The Norman Brokenshire Show	9:15
		Alfred W. McCann, food		9:30
	Missus Goes A Shopping		Inside the Doctor's Office	9:45
My True Story	This is Bing Crosby	Henry Gladstone, news	Welcome, Travelers	10am
	Arthur Godfrey Time	Martha Deane, talk		10:15
Betty Crocker, cooking			Marriage for Two	10:30
Victor Lindlahr, health			Dorothy Dix at Home	10:45
Modern Romances		Precott Robinson, news	We Love and Learn	11am
		Tello-Test Quiz	Dr. Paul	11:15
Pick a Date	Grand Slam	Red Benson's Movie Matinee	The Jack Berch Show	11:30
	Rosemary	Kate Smith Sings	Lora Lawton	11:45
House Party	Wendy Warren and the News	Kate Smith Speaks	Charles F. McCarthy, news	12pm
	Aunt Jenny's True Life Stories	The Quiz Club	The Norman Brokenshire Show	12:15
The Herb Sheldon Show	The Romance of Helen Trent	Henry Gladstone, news		12:30
	Our Gal Sunday	Luncheon at Sardi's		12:45
H. R. Baukhage, news	Big Sister		Mary Margaret McBride, talk	1pm
Nancy Booth Craig, talk	Ma Perkins			1:15
	Young Dr. Malone	The Hollywood Theater of Stars		1:30
	The Guiding Light			1:45

DAYTIME — FALL, 1949

Sunday

	ABC	CBS	MBS	NBC
2pm	This Week Around the World	The Longines Choraliers	Deems Taylor Concert	The NBC Theater
2:15				
2:30	Mr. President	Syncopation Piece	Harry Hennessy, news	
2:45			David Snell, talk	
3pm	Harrison Wood, news	New York Philharmonic Orchestra	Treasury Varieties	One Man's Family
3:15	Betty Clark Sings			
3:30	The Lutheran Hour		Juvenile Jury	The Quiz Kids
3:45				
4pm	Voices That Live		The House of Mystery	Living 1949
4:15				
4:30	Milton Cross Opera Album	You Are There	Martin Kane, Private Detective	The American Forum of the Air
4:45				
5pm	Family Close-Up	Music for You	The Shadow	The Radio City Playhouse
5:15				
5:30	The Greatest Story Ever Told	The Longines Symphonette	True Detective Mysteries	Harvest of Stars
5:45				

DAYTIME — FALL, 1949

Monday-Friday

ABC	CBS	MBS	NBC	
Breakfast in Hollywood	The Second Mrs. Burton	Queen for a Day	Double or Nothing	2pm
	Perry Mason			2:15
Bride and Groom	This is Nora Drake	Second Honeymoon	Today's Children	2:30
	The Brighter Day		The Light of the World	2:45
At Home with the Kirkwoods / Talk Your Way Out of It	David Harum	The Answer Man	Life Can Be Beautiful	3pm
	Hilltop House	Joe's Happiness Exchange	The Road of Life	3:15
Ladies Be Seated	The Garry Moore Show		Pepper Young's Family	3:30
			The Right to Happiness	3:45
Galen Drake, talk		Barbera Welles, talk	Mary Noble, Backstage Wife	4pm
Tune Time			Stella Dallas	4:15
Melody Promenade	Treasury Bandstand	Prince Charming	Lorenzo Jones	4:30
Pat Barnes, talk			Young Widder Brown	4:45
Challenge of the Yukon /	Galen Drake, talk	Bobby Benson /	When a Girl Marries	5pm
The Green Hornet		Straight Arrow	Portia Faces Life	5:15
Sky King /	Hits and Misses	Captain Midnight /	Just Plain Bill	5:30
Jack Armstrong, the All-American Boy		The Tom Mix Ralston Straight Shooters	Front Page Farrell	5:45

DAYTIME — FALL, 1949

Saturday

	ABC	CBS	MBS	NBC
9am	The Kelvin Keech Show	This is New York, Danny O'Neill	Harry Hennessy, news	The PAL Show
9:15			Sidney Walton, news	The NBC Stamp Club
9:30	Shopper's Special		Tele-Kid Test Quiz	People Are Funny
9:45		The Garden Gate		
10am	Introduction to Music	The Joe DiMaggio Show	Henry Gladstone, news	Fred Waring Orchestra
10:15			Fix It Yourself	
10:30	The Big and Little Club	Galen Drake, talk	Lorraine Sherwood, talk	Mary Lee Taylor, cooking
10:45			Let's Go	
11am	The US Navy Band	Let's Pretend	Prescott Robinson, news	Lassie
11:15			Bing Crosby Records	Tom, Timmy and Mae, songs
11:30	The Roger Dann Show	Junior Miss	Parade Preview	Smilin' Ed's Buster Brown Gang
11:45			Here's Heidi	
12pm	The Girl Corps	The Armstrong Theater of Today	The Man on the Farm	Charles F. McCarthy, news
12:15				Americans Abroad
12:30	The American Farmer	Grand Central Station	Henry Gladstone, news	Archie Andrews
12:45			The Answer Man	
1pm	The Home Gardener	Stars Over Hollywood	Luncheon at Sardi's	The National Farm and Home Hour
1:15				
1:30	Old, New, Borrowed, Blue	Give and Take	Win, Lose or Draw	Report on America
1:45			Sports	Report on Europe

DAYTIME — FALL, 1949

Saturday

	ABC	CBS	MBS	NBC
2pm	Sports	County Fair		Sports
2:15				
2:30		Sports		
2:45				
3pm				
3:15				
3:30				
3:45				
4pm				
4:15				
4:30				
4:45				
5pm	Tea and Crumpets			
5:15				
5:30		Mother Knows Best	The Cisco Kid	Guest Star
5:45				Confidential Close-Ups

LISTINGS FOR 1950

EVENING — WINTER, 1950

Sunday

	ABC	CBS	MBS	NBC
6pm	Drew Pearson, news	The Prudential Family Hour of Stars	The Roy Rogers Show	The Catholic Hour
6:15	Don Gardiner, news			
6:30	Music with the Hormel Girls	Our Miss Brooks	Nick Carter, Master Detective	The Henry Morgan Show
6:45				
7pm	Phil Bovero Orchestra	The Lucky Strike Program, Jack Benny	The Falcon	The Adventures of Christopher London
7:15				
7:30	The Amazing Mr. Malone	Amos 'n' Andy	The Saint	The Phil Harris - Alice Faye Show
7:45				
8pm	Stop the Music	The Charlie McCarthy Show	A. L. Alexander's Mediation Board	The Adventures of Sam Spade
8:15				
8:30		The Red Skelton Show	The Opera Concert	The Theater Guild on the Air
8:45				
9pm	Walter Winchell, gossip	Meet Corliss Archer	Melvin Elliott, news	
9:15	Louella Parsons, gossip		Rebuttal	
9:30	Chance of a Lifetime	The Youth Opportunity Program	Sheilah Graham, gossip	The American Album of Familiar Music
9:45			Twin Views of the News	
10pm	Jimmy Fidler, gossip	The Carnation Contented Hour	The Damon Runyon Theater	Take It or Leave It
10:15	Between the Bookends			
10:30	Jackie Robinson, sports	Joe Reichman Orchestra	Arthur Van Horn, news	The Pet Milk Show
10:45	George Sokolsky, news		David Snell, talk	

EVENING — WINTER, 1950

Monday

ABC	CBS	MBS	NBC	
Joe Hasel, sports	Eric Severeid, news	Lyle Van, news	Kenneth Banghart, news	6pm
New York Tonight, Allen Prescott	You and the World	Bob Elson Interviews	Bill Stern, sports	6:15
	Curt Massey, songs	Fred Vandeventer, news	Wayne Howell, news	6:30
Sammy Kaye's Showroom	Lowell Thomas, news	Stan Lomax, sports	Three Star Extra	6:45
Taylor Grant, news	The Beulah Show	Fulton Lewis Jr., news	Light Up Time, Frank Sinatra	7pm
Elmer Davis, news	The Jack Smith Show	The Answer Man	Morgan Beatty, news	7:15
The Lone Ranger	Club Fifteen	Gabriel Heatter, news	The Storyteller's Playhouse	7:30
	Edward R. Murrow, news	Sidney Walton, news	H. V. Kaltenborn, news	7:45
Ethel and Albert	Inner Sanctum Mysteries	Bobby Benson	The Railroad Hour	8pm
				8:15
Henry J. Taylor, news	Arthur Godfrey's Talent Scouts	The Affairs of Peter Salem	The Voice of Firestone	8:30
The Buddy Weed Trio		Bill Henry, news (8:55pm)		8:45
Kate Smith Calls	The Lux Radio Theater	Murder By Experts	The Bell Telephone Hour	9pm
				9:15
		The Five Mysteries	The Cities Service Band of America	9:30
				9:45
Arthur Gaeth, news	My Friend Irma	Frank Edwards, news	The Martin and Lewis Show	10pm
Phil Brestoff Orchestra		The Mutual Newsreel		10:15
Music By Ralph Norman	The Bob Hawk Show	The Longines Symphonette	Dial Dave Garroway	10:30
				10:45

EVENING — WINTER, 1950

Tuesday

	ABC	CBS	MBS	NBC
6pm	Joe Hasel, sports	Eric Severeid, news	Lyle Van, news	Kenneth Banghart, news
6:15	New York Tonight, Allen Prescott	You and the World	Bob Elson Interviews	Bill Stern, sports
6:30		Curt Massey, songs	Fred Vandeventer, news	Wayne Howell, news
6:45	Johnny Thompson, songs	Lowell Thomas, news	Stan Lomax, sports	Three Star Extra
7pm	Taylor Grant, news	The Beulah Show	Fulton Lewis Jr., news	Light Up Time, Frank Sinatra
7:15	Elmer Davis, news	The Jack Smith Show	The Answer Man	Morgan Beatty, news
7:30	Counterspy	Club Fifteen	Gabriel Heatter, news	Everyman's Story
7:45		Edward R. Murrow, news	Galen Drake, news	Richard Harkness, news
8pm	Carnegie Hall	Mystery Theater	The New Adventures of Michael Shayne	The Cavalcade of America
8:15				
8:30	Gentlemen of the Press	Mr. and Mrs. North	Official Detective	The Baby Snooks Show
8:45			Bill Henry, news (8:55pm)	
9pm	America's Town Meeting of the Air	Life with Luigi	Mystery is My Hobby	The Bob Hope Show
9:15				
9:30	Edwin D. Canham, news	Escape	The Mysterious Traveler	Fibber Magee and Molly
9:45	We CARE			
10pm	Time for Defense	Pursuit	Frank Edwards, news	Big Town
10:15			The Mutual Newsreel	
10:30	It's Your Business	Frankie Carle Orchestra	The Longines Symphonette	People Are Funny
10:45	Robert R. Nathan, news			

EVENING — WINTER, 1950

Wednesday

ABC	CBS	MBS	NBC	
Joe Hasel, sports	Eric Sevareid, news	Lyle Van, news	Kenneth Banghart, news	6pm
New York Tonight, Allen Prescott	You and the World	Bob Elson Interviews	Bill Stern, sports	6:15
	Curt Massey, songs	Fred Vandeventer, news	Wayne Howell, news	6:30
Sammy Kaye's Showroom	Lowell Thomas, news	Stan Lomax, sports	Three Star Extra	6:45
Taylor Grant, news	The Beulah Show	Fulton Lewis Jr., news	Light Up Time, Frank Sinatra	7pm
Elmer Davis, news	The Jack Smith Show	The Answer Man	Morgan Beatty, news	7:15
The Lone Ranger	Club Fifteen	Gabriel Heatter, news	Guy Lombardo Orchestra	7:30
	Edward R. Murrow, news	Sidney Walton, news	H. V. Kaltenborn, news	7:45
Dr. I. Q., the Mental Banker	Mr. Chameleon	Can You Top This	This is Your Life	8pm
				8:15
The Casebook of Gregory Hood	Dr. Christian	Boston Blackie	The Great Gildersleeve	8:30
		Bill Henry, news (8:55pm)		8:45
Sherlock Holmes	You Bet Your Life	Mr. Feathers	Break the Bank	9pm
				9:15
Buzz Adlam's Playroom	The Bing Crosby Chesterfield Show	The Family Theater	Mr. District Attorney	9:30
				9:45
Lawrence Welk High Life Revue	Burns and Allen	Frank Edwards, news	The Big Story	10pm
		The Mutual Newsreel		10:15
On Trial	Lum and Abner	The Longines Symphonette	Curtain Time	10:30
				10:45

EVENING — WINTER, 1950

Thursday

	ABC	CBS	MBS	NBC
6pm	Joe Hasel, sports	Eric Sevareid, news	Lyle Van, news	Kenneth Banghart, news
6:15	New York Tonight, Allen Prescott	You and the World	Bob Elson Interviews	Bill Stern, sports
6:30		Curt Massey, songs	Fred Vandeventer, news	Wayne Howell, news
6:45	Johnny Thompson, songs	Lowell Thomas, news	Stan Lomax, sports	Three Star Extra
7pm	Taylor Grant, news	The Beulah Show	Fulton Lewis Jr., news	Light Up Time, Frank Sinatra
7:15	Elmer Davis, news	The Jack Smith Show	The Answer Man	Morgan Beatty, news
7:30	Counterspy	Club Fifteen	Gabriel Heatter, news	Great Moments in Opera
7:45		Edward R. Murrow, news	Galen Drake, news	
8pm	Blondie	The FBI in Peace and War	Philo Vance	The Aldrich Family
8:15				
8:30	A Date with Judy	Mr. Keen, Tracer of Lost Persons	Sports for All	Father Knows Best
8:45			Bill Henry, news (8:55pm)	
9pm	Ted Mack's Original Amateur Hour	Suspense	The Comedy Playhouse	The Camel Screen Guild Players
9:15				
9:30		Casey, Crime Photographer		Duffy's Tavern
9:45	Robert Montgomery Speaking			
10pm	Author Meets the Critics	The Hallmark Playhouse	Frank Edwards, news	The Chesterfield Supper Club
10:15			The Mutual Newsreel	
10:30	Let's Go to the Met	The Skippy Hollywood Theater	The Longines Symphonette	Dragnet
10:45				

EVENING — WINTER, 1950

Friday

ABC	CBS	MBS	NBC	
Joe Hasel, sports	Eric Severeid, news	Lyle Van, news	Kenneth Banghart, news	6pm
New York Tonight, Allen Prescott	You and the World	Bob Elson Interviews	Bill Stern, sports	6:15
	Curt Massey, songs	Fred Vandeventer, news	Wayne Howell, news	6:30
Sammy Kaye's Showroom	Lowell Thomas, news	Stan Lomax, sports	Three Star Extra	6:45
Taylor Grant, news	The Beulah Show	Fulton Lewis Jr., news	Light Up Time, Frank Sinatra	7pm
Elmer Davis, news	The Jack Smith Show	The Answer Man	Morgan Beatty, news	7:15
The Lone Ranger	Club Fifteen	Gabriel Heatter, news	Reading for Pleasure	7:30
	Edward R. Murrow, news	Sidney Walton, news	H. V. Kaltenborn, news	7:45
The Fat Man	The Goldbergs	The Kate Smith Show	The Halls of Ivy	8pm
				8:15
This is Your FBI	My Favorite Husband		We, the People	8:30
		Bill Henry, news (8:55pm)		8:45
The Adventures of Ozzie and Harriet	Leave It to Joan	Box 13	The Screen Director's Playhouse	9pm
				9:15
The Sheriff	The Show Goes On, Robert Q. Lewis	Meet the Press	The Jimmy Durante Show	9:30
				9:45
Madison Square Garden Boxing		Frank Edwards, news	The Life of Riley	10pm
		The Mutual Newsreel		10:15
Joe Hasel's Sports Page	Capital Cloak Room	The Longines Symphonette	The Colgate Sports Newsreel, Bill Stern	10:30
			Pro and Con	10:45

EVENING — WINTER, 1950

Saturday

	ABC	CBS	MBS	NBC
6pm	Albert Warner, news	Bill Schaedel, news	Lyle Van, news	Kenneth Banghart, news
6:15	The Church and the Nation	CBS Views the News	Bill Lang, news	Religion in the News
6:30	Harry Wismer, sports	Red Barber's Club House	Fred Vandeventer, news	NBC Symphony Orchestra
6:45	The Roger Renner Trio	Larry Lesueur, news	Stan Lomax, sports	
7pm	Rex Koury, organ	Young Love	Frank Farrell, talk	
7:15	Bert Andrews, news		The Answer Man	
7:30	Chandu, the Magician	The Camel Caravan, Vaughn Monroe	Comedy of Errors	Archie Andrews
7:45				
8pm	The Adventures of Superman	Gene Autry's Melody Ranch	Twenty Questions	The Hollywood Star Theater
8:15				
8:30	Hollywood Byline	The Adventures of Phillip Marlowe	Take a Number	Truth or Consequences
8:45				
9pm	The Rayburn and Finch Show	Gangbusters	Meet Your Match	Your Hit Parade
9:15				
9:30		Broadway is My Beat	Lombardoland USA	A Day in the Life of Dennis Day
9:45				
10pm	Voices That Live	Sing It Again	The Chicago Theater of the Air	The Judy Canova Show
10:15				
10:30	Saturday at the Shamrock			Grand Ole Opry
10:45				

DAYTIME — WINTER, 1950

Sunday

	ABC	CBS	MBS	NBC
9am	Bert Bacharach, talk	News	Harry Hennessy, news	News
9:15		From the Organ Loft	The Quiz Club	The Comic Weekly Man
9:30	The Voice of Prophecy		The Mutual Radio Chapel	
9:45		St. Paul's Trinity Choir		Music
10am	Message of Israel	The CBS Church of the Air	Henry Gladstone, news	The National Radio Pulpit
10:15			Perry Como Records	
10:30	The Southernaires Quartet			The Horn and Hardart Children's Hour
10:45			Your Hymnal	
11am	Foreign Reporter	The Newsmakers	Henry Gladstone, news	
11:15	Frank and Ernest, religion	Winston Burdett, news	Brunch with Dorothy and Dick	
11:30	The Hour of Faith	The Salt Lake Tabernacle Choir		Charles F. McCarthy, news
11:45				Solitaire Time
12pm	Fantasy in Melody	Get More Out of Life	The Cisco Kid	Melody Parade
12:15				
12:30	The Piano Playhouse	The People's Platform	Melvin Elliott, news	Tex and Jinx, talk
12:45			John M. Wyatt, news	
1pm	Dr. William Ward Ayer, talk	Charles Collingwood, news	Sidney Walton, news	The Eternal Light
1:15		Where the Public Stands	The Canary Pet Shop	
1:30	National Vespers	Invitation to Learning	The Show Shop	The Quiz Kids
1:45				

DAYTIME — WINTER, 1950

Monday-Friday

ABC	CBS	MBS	NBC	
The Breakfast Club	This is New York, Danny O'Neil	Harry Hennessy, news	Tex and Jinx, talk (8:30am)	*9am*
		Meet the Menjous	The Norman Brokenshire Show	*9:15*
		Alfred W. McCann, food		*9:30*
	Missus Goes A Shopping		Inside the Doctor's Office	*9:45*
My True Story	This is Bing Crosby	Henry Gladstone, news	Welcome, Travelers	*10am*
	Arthur Godfrey Time	Martha Deane, talk		*10:15*
Betty Crocker, cooking			Marriage for Two	*10:30*
Victor Lindlahr, health			Dorothy Dix at Home	*10:45*
Modern Romances		Precott Robinson, news	We Love and Learn	*11am*
		Tello-Test Quiz	Dial Dave Garroway	*11:15*
Quick as a Flash	Grand Slam	Sidney Walton, news	The Jack Berch Show	*11:30*
	Rosemary	Kate Smith Sings	David Harum	*11:45*
Ladies Be Seated	Wendy Warren and the News	Kate Smith Speaks	Charles F. McCarthy, news	*12pm*
	Aunt Jenny's True Life Stories	Rod Hedrickson, news	The Norman Brokenshire Show	*12:15*
The Herb Sheldon Show	The Romance of Helen Trent	Henry Gladstone, news		*12:30*
	Our Gal Sunday	Luncheon at Sardi's		*12:45*
H. R. Baukhage, news	Big Sister		Mary Margaret McBride, talk	*1pm*
Nancy Booth Craig, talk	Ma Perkins			*1:15*
	Young Dr. Malone	The Hollywood Theater of Stars		*1:30*
Art Baker's Notebook	The Guiding Light			*1:45*

DAYTIME — WINTER, 1950

Sunday

	ABC	CBS	MBS	NBC
2pm	This Week Around the World	Sammy Kaye's Sunday Serenade	Deems Taylor Concert	The NBC Theater
2:15				
2:30	Mr. President	Galen Drake, talk	John Steele, Adventurer	
2:45		Jack Sterling, talk		
3pm	Harrison Wood, news	New York Philharmonic Orchestra	Bill Lang, news	One Man's Family
3:15	Betty Clark, songs		The National Guard Show	
3:30	The Lutheran Hour		Juvenile Jury	The Quiz Kids
3:45				
4pm	Voices That Live		Hopalong Cassidy	Edwin C. Hill, news
4:15				Facts Unlimited
4:30	Milton Cross Opera Album	You Are There	Martin Kane, Private Detective	The American Forum of the Air
4:45				
5pm	Think Fast	Earn Your Vacation	The Shadow	Richard Diamond, Private Detective
5:15				
5:30	The Greatest Story Ever Told	Strike It Rich	True Detective Mysteries	Harvest of Stars
5:45				

DAYTIME — WINTER, 1950

Monday-Friday

ABC	CBS	MBS	NBC	
Welcome to Hollywood	The Second Mrs. Burton	Ladies Fair	Double or Nothing	*2pm*
	Perry Mason			*2:15*
Bride and Groom	This is Nora Drake	Queen for a Day	Today's Children	*2:30*
	The Brighter Day		The Light of the World	*2:45*
Pick a Date	Nona from Nowhere	Second Honeymoon	Life Can Be Beautiful	*3pm*
	Hilltop House		The Road of Life	*3:15*
Hannibal Cobb	House Party	The Answer Man	Pepper Young's Family	*3:30*
		Gabriel Heatter's Mailbag	The Right to Happiness	*3:45*
The Carter Family, songs	The Garry Moore Show	Barbera Welles, talk	Mary Noble, Backstage Wife	*4pm*
Tune Time			Stella Dallas	*4:15*
Melody Promenade		Dean Cameron, talk	Lorenzo Jones	*4:30*
Pat Barnes, talk			Young Widder Brown	*4:45*
Challenge of the Yukon /	Galen Drake, talk	Bobby Benson /	When a Girl Marries	*5pm*
The Green Hornet		Straight Arrow	Portia Faces Life	*5:15*
Sky King /	Hits and Misses	Bobby Benson /	Just Plain Bill	*5:30*
Jack Armstrong, the All-American Boy		The Tom Mix Ralston Straight Shooters	Front Page Farrell	*5:45*

DAYTIME — WINTER, 1950

Saturday

	ABC	CBS	MBS	NBC
9am	No School Today	This is New York, Danny O'Neil	Harry Hennessy, news	Tom, Timmy and Mae, songs
9:15			Bill Lang, news	The PAL Show
9:30	Conversation with Casey		Tele-Kid Test Quiz	People Are Funny
9:45		Missus Goes A Shopping		
10am	At Home with Music	Galen Drake, talk	Henry Gladstone, news	Fred Waring Orchestra
10:15			Get More Out of Life	
10:30	Junior Junction	The Joe DiMaggio Show		Mary Lee Taylor, cooking
10:45			Let's Go	
11am	Joe Franklin's Record Shop	Let's Pretend	Prescott Robinson, news	Lassie
11:15			Bing Crosby Records	The NBC Stamp Club
11:30	The Roger Dann Show	Junior Miss	The Quiz Club	Smilin' Ed's Buster Brown Gang
11:45			Lorraine Sherwood, talk	
12pm	The Ranch Boys Trio	The Armstrong Theater of Today	The Man on the Farm	The Mystery Chef
12:15				Public Affairs
12:30	The American Farmer	Grand Central Station	Henry Gladstone, news	Vincent Lopez Orchestra
12:45			The Answer Man	
1pm	Concert of American Jazz	Stars Over Hollywood	Luncheon at Sardi's	The National Farm and Home Hour
1:15				
1:30	Old, New, Borrowed, Blue	Give and Take	Symphonies for Youth	Here's to Veterans
1:45				Voices Down the Wind

DAYTIME — WINTER, 1950

Saturday

	ABC	CBS	MBS	NBC
2pm	The Metropolitan Opera	County Fair		Voices and Events
2:15				
2:30		Get More Out of Life	International Airport	Whitney Berquist Orchestra
2:45				
3pm		Report from Overseas	California Melodies	Orchestras of the Nation
3:15		Adventures in Science		
3:30		CBS Farm News	Proudly We Hail	
3:45		Cross-Section USA		
4pm		Treasury Bandstand	The Count of Monte Cristo	Living 1950
4:15				
4:30		Noro Morales Orchestra	Crime Fighters	The University of Chicago Round Table
4:45				
5pm	The Jacques Fray Show	George Towne Orchestra	True or False	Slim Bryant's Wildcats
5:15				
5:30	Tea and Crumpets	Musical Notebook	Incredible, But True	Guest Star
5:45			Hollywood Quiz	Confidential Close-Ups

EVENING — SPRING, 1950

Sunday

	ABC	CBS	MBS	NBC
6pm	Drew Pearson, news	My Favorite Husband	The Roy Rogers Show	The Catholic Hour
6:15	Don Gardiner, news			
6:30	Music with the Hormel Girls	Our Miss Brooks	Nick Carter, Master Detective	The Henry Morgan Show
6:45				
7pm	Voices That Live	The Lucky Strike Program, Jack Benny	The Falcon	The Adventures of Christopher London
7:15				
7:30	The Amazing Mr. Malone	Amos 'n' Andy	The Saint	The Phil Harris - Alice Faye Show
7:45				
8pm	Stop the Music	The Charlie McCarthy Show	A. L. Alexander's Mediation Board	The Adventures of Sam Spade
8:15				
8:30		The Red Skelton Show	Melvin Elliott, news	The Theater Guild on the Air
8:45			David Snell, talk	
9pm	Walter Winchell, gossip	Meet Corliss Archer	The Opera Concert	
9:15	Louella Parsons, gossip			
9:30	Chance of a Lifetime	The Youth Opportunity Program	Sheilah Graham, gossip	The American Album of Familiar Music
9:45			Twin Views of the News	
10pm	Jimmy Fidler, gossip	The Carnation Contented Hour	The Damon Runyon Theater	Take It or Leave It
10:15	Get More Out of Life			
10:30	Jackie Robinson, sports	We Take Your Word	Arthur Van Horn, news	The Pet Milk Show
10:45	George Sokolsky, news		Incredible, But True	

EVENING — SPRING, 1950

Monday

ABC	CBS	MBS	NBC	
Joe Hasel, sports	Allan Jackson, news	Lyle Van, news	Kenneth Banghart, news	6pm
Art Baker's Notebook	You and Your Health	Bob Elson Interviews	Bill Stern, sports	6:15
The Herb Sheldon Show	Curt Massey, songs	Fred Vandeventer, news	Here's Morgan	6:30
	Lowell Thomas, news	Stan Lomax, sports	Three Star Extra	6:45
Taylor Grant, news	The Beulah Show	Fulton Lewis Jr., news	Light Up Time, Frank Sinatra	7pm
Elmer Davis, news	The Jack Smith Show	The Answer Man	Morgan Beatty, news	7:15
The Lone Ranger	Club Fifteen	Gabriel Heatter, news	The Storyteller's Playhouse	7:30
	Edward R. Murrow, news	Tello-Test Quiz	H. V. Kaltenborn, news	7:45
Ethel and Albert	The Hollywood Star Theater	Bobby Benson	The Railroad Hour	8pm
				8:15
Henry J. Taylor, news	Arthur Godfrey's Talent Scouts	The Affairs of Peter Salem	The Voice of Firestone	8:30
Phil Bovero Orchestra		Bill Henry, news (8:55pm)		8:45
Melody Rendezvous	The Lux Radio Theater	Murder By Experts	The Bell Telephone Hour	9pm
				9:15
Earl Wilson's Broadway Column		The Five Mysteries	The Cities Service Band of America	9:30
				9:45
The Ted Malone Show	My Friend Irma	Frank Edwards, news	The Martin and Lewis Show	10pm
		Calling All Detectives		10:15
Strictly from Dixie	The Bob Hawk Show	The Longines Symphonette	Dangerous Assignment	10:30
				10:45

EVENING — SPRING, 1950

Tuesday

	ABC	CBS	MBS	NBC
6pm	Joe Hasel, sports	Allan Jackson, news	Lyle Van, news	Kenneth Banghart, news
6:15	Art Baker's Notebook	You and Your Health	Bob Elson Interviews	Bill Stern, sports
6:30	The Herb Sheldon Show	Curt Massey, songs	Fred Vandeventer, news	Here's Morgan
6:45		Lowell Thomas, news	Stan Lomax, sports	Three Star Extra
7pm	Taylor Grant, news	The Beulah Show	Fulton Lewis Jr., news	Light Up Time, Frank Sinatra
7:15	Elmer Davis, news	The Jack Smith Show	The Answer Man	Morgan Beatty, news
7:30	Counterspy	Club Fifteen	Gabriel Heatter, news	Everyman's Story
7:45		Edward R. Murrow, news	Tello-Test Quiz	
8pm	Carnegie Hall	Mystery Theater	Philo Vance	The Cavalcade of America
8:15				
8:30	Gentlemen of the Press	Mr. and Mrs. North	Official Detective	The Baby Snooks Show
8:45			Bill Henry, news (8:55pm)	
9pm	America's Town Meeting of the Air	Life with Luigi	Mystery is My Hobby	The Bob Hope Show
9:15				
9:30	Edwin D. Canham, news	Yours Truly, Johnny Dollar	The Mysterious Traveler	Fibber Magee and Molly
9:45	We CARE			
10pm	Time for Defense	The Adventures of Phillip Marlowe	Frank Edwards, news	Big Town
10:15			Calling All Detectives	
10:30	This is Our Town	Pursuit	The Longines Symphonette	People Are Funny
10:45	As We See It			

EVENING — SPRING, 1950

Wednesday

ABC	CBS	MBS	NBC	
Joe Hasel, sports	Allan Jackson, news	Lyle Van, news	Kenneth Banghart, news	6pm
Art Baker's Notebook	You and Your Health	Bob Elson Interviews	Bill Stern, sports	6:15
The Herb Sheldon Show	Curt Massey, songs	Fred Vandeventer, news	Here's Morgan	6:30
	Lowell Thomas, news	Stan Lomax, sports	Three Star Extra	6:45
Taylor Grant, news	The Beulah Show	Fulton Lewis Jr., news	Light Up Time, Frank Sinatra	7pm
Elmer Davis, news	The Jack Smith Show	The Answer Man	Morgan Beatty, news	7:15
The Lone Ranger	Club Fifteen	Gabriel Heatter, news	The Wayne Howell Show	7:30
	Edward R. Murrow, news	Tello-Test Quiz		7:45
Dr. I. Q., the Mental Banker	Mr. Chameleon	Can You Top This	This is Your Life	8pm
				8:15
The Casebook of Gregory Hood	Dr. Christian	Boston Blackie	The Great Gildersleeve	8:30
		Bill Henry, news (8:55pm)		8:45
Sherlock Holmes	You Bet Your Life	Two-Thousand Plus	Break the Bank	9pm
				9:15
Earl Wilson's Broadway Column	The Bing Crosby Chesterfield Show	The Family Theater	Mr. District Attorney	9:30
				9:45
Lawrence Welk High Life Revue	Burns and Allen	Frank Edwards, news	The Big Story	10pm
		Calling All Detectives		10:15
On Trial	Lum and Abner	The Longines Symphonette	Richard Diamond, Private Detective	10:30
				10:45

EVENING — SPRING, 1950

Thursday

	ABC	CBS	MBS	NBC
6pm	Joe Hasel, sports	Allan Jackson, news	Lyle Van, news	Kenneth Banghart, news
6:15	Art Baker's Notebook	You and Your Health	Bob Elson Interviews	Bill Stern, sports
6:30	The Herb Sheldon Show	Curt Massey, songs	Fred Vandeventer, news	Here's Morgan
6:45		Lowell Thomas, news	Stan Lomax, sports	Three Star Extra
7pm	Taylor Grant, news	The Beulah Show	Fulton Lewis, Jr., news	Light Up Time, Frank Sinatra
7:15	Elmer Davis, news	The Jack Smith Show	The Answer Man	Morgan Beatty, news
7:30	Counterspy	Club Fifteen	Gabriel Heatter, news	Serenade to America
7:45		Edward R. Murrow, news	Tello-Test Quiz	
8pm	Blondie	The FBI in Peace and War	The Cisco Kid	The Aldrich Family
8:15				
8:30	A Date with Judy	Mr. Keen, Tracer of Lost Persons	Sports for All	Father Knows Best
8:45			Bill Henry, news (8:55pm)	
9pm	Ted Mack's Original Amateur Hour	Suspense	The Limerick Show	The Camel Screen Guild Players
9:15				
9:30		Casey, Crime Photographer	The Kirkwood - Goodman Show	Duffy's Tavern
9:45	Robert Montgomery Speaking			
10pm	Author Meets the Critics	The Hallmark Playhouse	Frank Edwards, news	The Chesterfield Supper Club
10:15			Calling All Detectives	
10:30	Public Affairs	The Skippy Hollywood Theater	The Longines Symphonette	Dragnet
10:45				

EVENING — SPRING, 1950

Friday

	ABC	CBS	MBS	NBC	
	Joe Hasel, sports	Allan Jackson, news	Lyle Van, news	Kenneth Banghart, news	6pm
	Art Baker's Notebook	You and Your Health	Bob Elson Interviews	Bill Stern, sports	6:15
	The Herb Sheldon Show	Curt Massey, songs	Fred Vandeventer, news	Here's Morgan	6:30
		Lowell Thomas, news	Stan Lomax, sports	Three Star Extra	6:45
	Taylor Grant, news	The Beulah Show	Fulton Lewis Jr., news	Light Up Time, Frank Sinatra	7pm
	Elmer Davis, news	The Jack Smith Show	The Answer Man	Morgan Beatty, news	7:15
	The Lone Ranger	Club Fifteen	Gabriel Heatter, news	Reading for Pleasure	7:30
		Edward R. Murrow, news	Tello-Test Quiz	H. V. Kaltenborn, news	7:45
	The Fat Man	The Show Goes On, Robert Q. Lewis	The Kate Smith Show	The Halls of Ivy	8pm
					8:15
	This is Your FBI			We, the People	8:30
			Bill Henry, news (8:55pm)		8:45
	The Adventures of Ozzie and Harriet	Up for Parole	Box 13	The Screen Director's Playhouse	9pm
					9:15
	The Sheriff	Broadway is My Beat	Meet the Press	The Jimmy Durante Show	9:30
					9:45
	Madison Square Garden Boxing	Escape	Frank Edwards, news	The Life of Riley	10pm
			Calling All Detectives		10:15
	Joe Hasel's Sports Page	Capital Cloak Room	The Longines Symphonette	The Colgate Sports Newsreel, Bill Stern	10:30
				Pro and Con	10:45

EVENING — SPRING, 1950

Saturday

	ABC	CBS	MBS	NBC
6pm	Albert Warner, news	Bill Slater, news	Lyle Van, news	Kenneth Banghart, news
6:15	The Roger Renner Trio	CBS Views the News	Tello-Test Quiz	Religion in the News
6:30	Harry Wismer, sports	Red Barber's Club House	Fred Vandeventer, news	The NBC Spring Concert
6:45	Vera Massey, songs	Larry Lesueur, news	Stan Lomax, sports	
7pm	Rex Koury, organ	Young Love	History in the Making	
7:15	Bert Andrews, news		The Answer Man	
7:30	Chandu, the Magician	The Camel Caravan, Vaughn Monroe	Comedy of Errors	The Joe DiMaggio Show
7:45				
8pm	Dixieland Jambake	Gene Autry's Melody Ranch	Twenty Questions	Dimension X
8:15				
8:30	Hollywood Byline	The Goldbergs	Get More Out of Life	Truth or Consequences
8:45				
9pm	Playhouse of Favorites	Gangbusters	True or False	Your Hit Parade
9:15				
9:30	Earl Wilson's Broadway Column	Arthur Godfrey's Digest	Lombardoland USA	A Day in the Life of Dennis Day
9:45				
10pm	The Rayburn and Finch Show	Sing It Again	The Chicago Theater of the Air	The Judy Canova Show
10:15				
10:30				Grand Ole Opry
10:45				

DAYTIME — SPRING, 1950

Sunday

	ABC	CBS	MBS	NBC
9am	Music Time	News	Harry Hennessy, news	News
9:15		From the Organ Loft	A Faith to Live By	The Comic Weekly Man
9:30	The Voice of Prophecy		The Mutual Radio Chapel	
9:45		St. Paul's Trinity Choir		Music
10am	Message of Israel	The CBS Church of the Air	Henry Gladstone, news	The National Radio Pulpit
10:15			The Quiz Club	
10:30	Negro College Choirs		Arthur Van Horn, news	The Horn and Hardart Children's Hour
10:45			Your Hymnal	
11am	Foreign Reporter	The Newsmakers	Henry Gladstone, news	
11:15	Frank and Ernest, religion	Winston Burdett, news	Brunch with Dorothy and Dick	
11:30	The Hour of Faith	The Salt Lake Tabernacle Choir		Charles F. McCarthy, news
11:45				Solitaire Time
12pm	Next Week in New York, Bert Bacharach	Invitation to Learning	Junior Celebrities	Tex and Jinx, talk
12:15				
12:30	The Piano Playhouse	The People's Platform	Melvin Elliott, news	The Eternal Light
12:45			John M. Wyatt, news	
1pm	Dr. William Ward Ayer, talk	Charles Collingwood, news	Frank Farrell, news	The American Forum of the Air
1:15		Where the Public Stands	The Canary Pet Shop	
1:30	National Vespers	The Record Parade	Treasury Varieties	The Quiz Kids
1:45				

DAYTIME — SPRING, 1950

Monday-Friday

ABC	CBS	MBS	NBC	
The Breakfast Club	This is New York, Danny O'Neill	Harry Hennessy, news	Tex and Jinx, talk (8:30am)	9am
		The Answer Man	The Norman Brokenshire Show	9:15
		Alfred W. McCann, food		9:30
	Missus Goes A Shopping		Anne Haywood, talk / The Wayne Howell Show Welcome, Travelers	9:45
My True Story	This is Bing Crosby	Henry Gladstone, news		10am
	Arthur Godfrey Time	Martha Deane, talk		10:15
Betty Crocker, cooking			Double or Nothing	10:30
Victor Lindlahr, health				10:45
Modern Romances		Precott Robinson, news	We Love and Learn	11am
		The Rudy Vallee Show	Dial Dave Garroway	11:15
Quick as a Flash	Grand Slam		The Jack Berch Show	11:30
	Rosemary	Kate Smith Sings	David Harum	11:45
Ladies Be Seated	Wendy Warren and the News	Kate Smith Speaks	Charles F. McCarthy, news	12pm
	Aunt Jenny's True Life Stories	The Lanny Ross Show	The Norman Brokenshire Show	12:15
The Herb Sheldon Show	The Romance of Helen Trent	Henry Gladstone, news		12:30
	Our Gal Sunday	Luncheon at Sardi's		12:45
H. R. Baukhage, news	Big Sister		Mary Margaret McBride, talk	1pm
Nancy Booth Craig, talk	Ma Perkins			1:15
	Young Dr. Malone	Meet the Menjous		1:30
	The Guiding Light	Gabriel Heatter's Mailbag		1:45

DAYTIME — SPRING, 1950

Sunday

	ABC	CBS	MBS	NBC
2pm	This Week Around the World	The Longines Choraliers	Deems Taylor Concert	The NBC Theater
2:15				
2:30	Mr. President	You Are There	Bobby Benson	
2:45				
3pm	Vacation Time	New York Philharmonic Orchestra	The Show Shop	One Man's Family
3:15	Phil Brestoff Orchestra			
3:30	The Lutheran Hour		Juvenile Jury	The Quiz Kids
3:45				
4pm	Sammy Kaye's Sunday Serenade		Hopalong Cassidy	Nightbeat
4:15				
4:30	Milton Cross Opera Album	The Longines Symphonette	Martin Kane, Private Detective	High Adventure
4:45				
5pm	Juvenile Choir	Music for You	The Shadow	Voices and Events
5:15				
5:30	The Greatest Story Ever Told	Earn Your Vacation	True Detective Mysteries	Harvest of Stars
5:45				

DAYTIME — SPRING, 1950

Monday-Friday

ABC	CBS	MBS	NBC	
Welcome to Hollywood	The Second Mrs. Burton	Ladies Fair	Double or Nothing	2pm
	Perry Mason			2:15
Hannibal Cobb	This is Nora Drake	Queen for a Day	Today's Children	2:30
	The Brighter Day		The Light of the World	2:45
Bride and Groom	Nona from Nowhere	Second Honeymoon	Life Can Be Beautiful	3pm
	Hilltop House		The Road of Life	3:15
Pick a Date	House Party	Poole's Paradise	Pepper Young's Family	3:30
			The Right to Happiness	3:45
Surprise Package	Strike It Rich	Barbera Welles, talk	Mary Noble, Backstage Wife	4pm
			Stella Dallas	4:15
Happy Landing	Treasury Bandstand	Dean Cameron, talk	Lorenzo Jones	4:30
Pat Barnes, talk			Young Widder Brown	4:45
Challenge of the Yukon /	Galen Drake, talk	Mark Trail /	When a Girl Marries	5pm
The Green Hornet		Straight Arrow	Portia Faces Life	5:15
Sky King /	Hits and Misses	Tele-Kid Test Quiz /	Just Plain Bill	5:30
Jack Armstrong, the All-American Boy		The Tom Mix Ralston Straight Shooters	Front Page Farrell	5:45

DAYTIME — SPRING, 1950

Saturday

	ABC	CBS	MBS	NBC
9am	No School Today	This is New York, Danny O'Neill	Harry Hennessy, news	Tom, Timmy and Mae, songs
9:15			Behind the Story	The PAL Show
9:30			The McCanns at Home	People Are Funny
9:45		Missus Goes A Shopping		
10am		Galen Drake, talk	Henry Gladstone, news	Fred Waring Orchestra
10:15			Get More Out of Life	
10:30		The Garden Gate		Mary Lee Taylor, cooking
10:45			Let's Go	
11am	Joe Franklin's Record Shop	Let's Pretend	Your Home Beautiful	Lassie
11:15			Prescott Robinson, news	The NBC Stamp Club
11:30	At Home with Music	Junior Miss	Get More Out of Life	Smilin' Ed's Buster Brown Gang
11:45			Tele-Kid Test Quiz	
12pm	The Home Gardener	The Armstrong Theater of Today	The Man on the Farm	Critic's Corner
12:15				Public Affairs
12:30	The American Farmer	Grand Central Station	Henry Gladstone, news	Vincent Lopez Orchestra
12:45			The Answer Man	
1pm	The US Navy Band	Stars Over Hollywood	Luncheon at Sardi's	The National Farm and Home Hour
1:15				
1:30	The Roger Dann Show	Give and Take	The B and D Club	The University of Chicago Round Table
1:45				

DAYTIME — SPRING, 1950

Saturday

	ABC	CBS	MBS	NBC
2pm	Let's Go to the Opera	County Fair		Recovery Story
2:15				
2:30		Get More Out of Life		The University Glee Club
2:45				
3pm		Report from Overseas	Bobby Benson	Orchestras of the Nation
3:15		Adventures in Science		
3:30	Phil Bovero Orchestra	CBS Farm News	International Airport	
3:45		Cross-Section USA		
4pm	Horse Racing	Horse Racing	The Count of Monte Cristo	Living 1950
4:15	The Three Suns	Facts for Veterans		
4:30	The Treasury Band Show	Musical Notebook	Mr. Dynamic	Ralph Flannagan Orchestra
4:45				
5pm	Tea and Crumpets	Philadelphia Symphony Orchestra	John Steele, Adventurer	The Green Cross Song Festival
5:15				
5:30			Stars Over Broadway	The US Air Force Band
5:45			Get More Out of Life	Confidential Close-Ups

EVENING — SUMMER, 1950

Sunday

	ABC	CBS	MBS	NBC
6pm	Drew Pearson, news	My Favorite Husband	The Roy Rogers Show	The Catholic Hour
6:15	Don Gardiner, news			
6:30	Phil Brestoff Orchestra	The Steve Allen Show	Nick Carter, Master Detective	Western Caravan
6:45				
7pm	Voices That Live	Guy Lombardo Orchestra	The Affairs of Peter Salem	1000 Reward
7:15				
7:30	The Amazing Mr. Malone	Hit the Jackpot	Melvin Elliott, news	The Saint
7:45			David Snell, talk	
8pm	Stop the Music	The Pause That Refreshes	The Singing Marshall	The Adventures of Sam Spade
8:15				
8:30		Much Ado About Doolittle	Under Arrest	NBC Symphony Orchestra
8:45				
9pm	The Vic Damone Show	Rate Your Mate	The Opera Concert	
9:15	Louella Parsons, gossip			
9:30	Crossroads	The Youth Opportunity Program	Gabriel Heatter, news	Top Secret
9:45			George Fielding Eliot, comment	
10pm	Jimmy Blaine, songs	The Carnation Contented Hour	The Damon Runyon Theater	Take It or Leave It
10:15	Love Letters to Music			
10:30	Jackie Robinson, sports	Treasury Bandstand	Arthur Van Horn, news	The Pet Milk Show
10:45	George Sokolsky, news		Incredible, But True	

EVENING — SUMMER, 1950

Monday

ABC	CBS	MBS	NBC	
Joe Hasel, sports	Allan Jackson, news	Lyle Van, news	Kenneth Banghart, news	6pm
Dorian St. George, news	You and Your Health	Bob Elson Interviews	Bill Stern, sports	6:15
The Herb Sheldon Show	Curt Massey, songs	Fred Vandeventer, news	Tex and Jinx, talk	6:30
	Lowell Thomas, news	Stan Lomax, sports	Three Star Extra	6:45
Taylor Grant, news	The Garry Moore Show	Fulton Lewis Jr., news	One Man's Family	7pm
Elmer Davis, news		The Answer Man	Morgan Beatty, news	7:15
The Lone Ranger	Stepping Out	Gabriel Heatter, news	The Storyteller's Playhouse	7:30
	Larry Lesueur, news	A. L. Alexander, poetry	Mindy Carson, songs	7:45
Ethel and Albert	The Hollywood Star Theater	Bobby Benson	The Railroad Hour	8pm
				8:15
Henry J. Taylor, news	Broadway is My Beat	Crime Fighters	The Voice of Firestone	8:30
Joe Hasel, sports		Bill Henry, news (8:55pm)		8:45
Musical Rendezvous	Too Many Cooks	Murder By Experts	The Bell Telephone Hour	9pm
				9:15
Rex Maupin Orchestra	Granby's Green Acres	Korean War News Roundup	The Cities Service Band of America	9:30
				9:45
United or Not	Leave It to Joan	Frank Edwards, news	Nightbeat	10pm
		Raymond Gram Swing, news		10:15
John Hicks, news	Xavier Cugat Orchestra	The Longines Symphonette	The First Piano Quartet	10:30
Between the Bookends				10:45

EVENING — SUMMER, 1950

Tuesday

	ABC	CBS	MBS	NBC
6pm	Russ Hodges, sports	Allan Jackson, news	Lyle Van, news	Kenneth Banghart, news
6:15	Dorian St. George, news	You and Your Health	Bob Elson Interviews	Bill Stern, sports
6:30	The Herb Sheldon Show	Curt Massey, songs	Fred Vandeventer, news	Tex and Jinx, talk
6:45		Lowell Thomas, news	Stan Lomax, sports	Three Star Extra
7pm	Taylor Grant, news	The Garry Moore Show	Fulton Lewis Jr., news	One Man's Family
7:15	Elmer Davis, news		The Answer Man	Morgan Beatty, news
7:30	Counterspy	Stepping Out	Gabriel Heatter, news	Leopold Stokowski Orchestra
7:45		Larry Lesueur, news	A. L. Alexander, poetry	
8pm	Paul Whiteman Presents	Mystery Theater	The Count of Monte Cristo	Who Said That
8:15				
8:30	Gentlemen of the Press	Satan's Waiting	Official Detective	Starlight Concert
8:45			Bill Henry, news (8:55pm)	
9pm	America's Town Meeting of the Air	Life with Luigi	Mystery is My Hobby	The Penny Singleton Show
9:15				
9:30	Edwin D. Canham, news	The Candid Microphone	The Mysterious Traveler	Presenting Charles Boyer
9:45	We CARE			
10pm	Time for Defense	America's Position	Frank Edwards, news	Big Town
10:15			The Mutual Newsreel	
10:30	John Hicks, news	Xavier Cugat Orchestra	The Longines Symphonette	A Life in Your Hands
10:45	Between the Bookends			

EVENING — SUMMER, 1950

Wednesday

ABC	CBS	MBS	NBC	
Russ Hodges, sports	Allan Jackson, news	Lyle Van, news	Kenneth Banghart, news	6pm
Dorian St. George, news	You and Your Health	Bob Elson Interviews	Bill Stern, sports	6:15
The Herb Sheldon Show	Curt Massey, songs	Fred Vandeventer, news	Tex and Jinx, talk	6:30
	Lowell Thomas, news	Stan Lomax, sports	Three Star Extra	6:45
Taylor Grant, news	The Garry Moore Show	Fulton Lewis Jr., news	One Man's Family	7pm
Elmer Davis, news		The Answer Man	Morgan Beatty, news	7:15
The Lone Ranger	Stepping Out	Gabriel Heatter, news	Don Cherry, songs	7:30
	Larry Lesueur, news	A. L. Alexander, poetry	Mindy Carson, songs	7:45
Dr. I. Q., the Mental Banker	Mr. Chameleon	The Hidden Truth	Dangerous Assignment	8pm
				8:15
The Cliché Club	Dr. Christian	Boston Blackie	The Falcon	8:30
		Bill Henry, news (8:55pm)		8:45
Detour	It Pays to Be Ignorant	Information, Please	Break the Bank	9pm
				9:15
Chandu, the Magician	The ABC's of Music, Robert Q. Lewis	The Family Theater	Mr. District Attorney	9:30
				9:45
Lawrence Welk High Life Revue	Jan Garber Orchestra	Frank Edwards, news	The Big Story	10pm
		Raymond Gram Swing, news		10:15
John Hicks, news	The Dixieland Jazz Concert	The Longines Symphonette	Richard Diamond, Private Detective	10:30
Between the Bookends				10:45

EVENING — SUMMER, 1950

Thursday

	ABC	CBS	MBS	NBC
6pm	Russ Hodges, sports	Allan Jackson, news	Lyle Van, news	Kenneth Banghart, news
6:15	Dorian St. George, talk	You and Your Health	Bing Crosby Records	Bill Stern, sports
6:30	The Herb Sheldon Show	Curt Massey, songs	Fred Vandeventer, news	Tex and Jinx, talk
6:45		Lowell Thomas, news	Stan Lomax, sports	Three Star Extra
7pm	Taylor Grant, news	The Garry Moore Show	Fulton Lewis Jr., news	One Man's Family
7:15	Elmer Davis, news		The Answer Man	Morgan Beatty, news
7:30	Counterspy	Stepping Out	Gabriel Heatter, news	The Gai Paris Music Hall
7:45		Larry Lesueur, news	A. L. Alexander, poetry	
8pm	The Casebook of Gregory Hood	The Lineup	The Cisco Kid	The Quick and the Dead
8:15				
8:30	Inner Sanctum Mysteries	Mr. Keen, Tracer of Lost Persons	Mr. Feathers	Father Knows Best
8:45			Bill Henry, news (8:55pm)	
9pm	Ted Mack's Original Amateur Hour	Somebody Knows	The Limerick Show	The Cass Daley Show
9:15				
9:30		Casey, Crime Photographer	The Reporters Round Up	Duffy's Tavern
9:45	Paul Harvey, news			
10pm	Author Meets the Critics	Yours Truly, Johnny Dollar	Frank Edwards, news	Dragnet
10:15			The Mutual Newsreel	
10:30	John Hicks, news	The Skippy Hollywood Theater	The Longines Symphonette	Sara's Private Caper
10:45	Between the Bookends			

EVENING — SUMMER, 1950

Friday

ABC	CBS	MBS	NBC	
Russ Hodges, sports	Allan Jackson, news	Lyle Van, news	Kenneth Banghart, news	6pm
Dorian St. George, talk	You and Your Health	Bob Elson Interviews	Bill Stern, sports	6:15
The Herb Sheldon Show	Curt Massey, songs	Fred Vandeventer, news	Tex and Jinx, talk	6:30
	Lowell Thomas, news	Stan Lomax, sports	Three Star Extra	6:45
Taylor Grant, news	The Garry Moore Show	Fulton Lewis Jr., news	One Man's Family	7pm
Elmer Davis, news		The Answer Man	Morgan Beatty, news	7:15
The Lone Ranger	Stepping Out	Gabriel Heatter, news	Alvy West Orchestra	7:30
	Larry Lesueur, news	A. L. Alexander, poetry		7:45
The Fat Man	The Adventures of Phillip Marlowe	The Kate Smith Show	Stars and Starters	8pm
				8:15
This is Your FBI	Up for Parole		We, the People	8:30
		Bill Henry, news (8:55pm)		8:45
The Adventures of the Thin Man	Songs for Sale	Box 13	Dimension X	9pm
				9:15
The Sheriff		The Kirkwood - Goodman Show	Confidentially Yours	9:30
				9:45
The Treasury Band Show	Escape	Frank Edwards, news	Wanted	10pm
		Raymond Gram Swing, news		10:15
John Hicks, news	Capital Cloak Room	The Longines Symphonette	The Colgate Sports Newsreel, Bill Stern	10:30
Between the Bookends			Pro and Con	10:45

EVENING — SUMMER, 1950

Saturday

	ABC	CBS	MBS	NBC
6pm	Jack Beall, news	Joe Wershba, news	Lyle Van, news	Kenneth Banghart, news
6:15	Cliff Cameron, organ	CBS Views the News	Marvin Miller, stories	Bob Considine, talk
6:30	Harry Wismer, sports	The Saturday Sports Review	Fred Vandeventer, news	NBC Symphony Orchestra
6:45	Rex Koury, organ	Larry Lesueur, news	Stan Lomax, sports	
7pm	The Dell Trio	Winner Take All	History in the Making	Voices and Events
7:15	Bert Andrews, news		The Answer Man	
7:30	Buzz Adlam's Playroom	The Camel Caravan, Vaughn Monroe	Comedy of Errors	The Joe DiMaggio Show
7:45				
8pm	Dixieland Jambake	Gene Autry's Melody Ranch	Twenty Questions	Saturday Dance Date
8:15				
8:30	Hollywood Byline	T-Man	Take a Number	Truth or Consequences
8:45				
9pm	The Norman Brokenshire Show	Gangbusters	True or False	Your Hit Parade
9:15				
9:30	Phil Bovero Orchestra	Tommy Dorsey Orchestra	Lombardoland USA	Tales of the Texas Rangers
9:45				
10pm	Al Trace Orchestra	Sing It Again	The Chicago Theater of The Air	The Chamber Music Society of Lower Basin Street
10:15				
10:30	Dance Band Jamboree			Grand Ole Opry
10:45				

DAYTIME — SUMMER, 1950

Sunday

	ABC	CBS	MBS	NBC
9am	Music Time	News	Harry Hennessy, news	News
9:15		From the Organ Loft	A Faith to Live By	The Comic Weekly Man
9:30	The Voice of Prophecy		The Mutual Radio Chapel	
9:45		St. Paul's Trinity Choir		Music
10am	Message of Israel	The CBS Church of the Air	Henry Gladstone, news	The National Radio Pulpit
10:15			The Stars of Song	
10:30	Negro College Choirs			The Horn and Hardart Children's Hour
10:45			Your Hymnal	
11am	Foreign Reporter	The Newsmakers	Henry Gladstone, news	
11:15	Frank and Ernest, religion	Winston Burdett, news	Brunch with Dorothy and Dick	
11:30	The Hour of Faith	The Salt Lake Tabernacle Choir		Charles F. McCarthy, news
11:45				Solitaire Time
12pm	Next Week in New York, Bert Bacharach	Invitation to Learning	John Steele, Adventurer	Tex and Jinx, talk
12:15				
12:30	The Piano Playhouse	The People's Platform	Melvin Elliott, news	The Arthur Treacher Show
12:45			John M. Wyatt, news	
1pm	Dr. William Ward Ayer, talk	Charles Collingwood, news	William Hillman, news	The American Forum of the Air
1:15		Where the Public Stands	The Show Shop	
1:30	National Vespers	Starlight Operetta		The Eternal Light
1:45				

DAYTIME — SUMMER, 1950

Monday-Friday

ABC	CBS	MBS	NBC	
The Breakfast Club	This is New York, Danny O'Neill	Harry Hennessy, news	Tex and Jinx, talk (8:30am)	*9am*
		Tello-Test Quiz	Bing Crosby Records	*9:15*
		Alfred W. McCann, food		*9:30*
	Missus Goes A Shopping			*9:45*
My True Story	This is Bing Crosby	Henry Gladstone, news	Welcome, Travelers	*10am*
	Arthur Godfrey Time	Martha Deane, talk		*10:15*
Betty Crocker, cooking			Double or Nothing	*10:30*
John B. Kennedy, news				*10:45*
Modern Romances		Precott Robinson, news	We Love and Learn	*11am*
		The Rudy Vallee Show	Report from the Pentagon	*11:15*
Quick as a Flash	Grand Slam		The Jack Berch Show	*11:30*
	Rosemary	Kate Smith Sings	David Harum	*11:45*
Johnny Olsen's Luncheon Club	Wendy Warren and the News	Kate Smith Speaks	Charles F. McCarthy, news	*12pm*
	Aunt Jenny's True Life Stories	The Lanny Ross Show	The Skitch Henderson Show	*12:15*
The Herb Sheldon Show	The Romance of Helen Trent	Henry Gladstone, news		*12:30*
	Our Gal Sunday	Luncheon at Sardi's		*12:45*
H. R. Baukhage, news	Big Sister		Mary Margaret McBride, talk	*1pm*
Nancy Booth Craig, talk	Ma Perkins			*1:15*
	Young Dr. Malone	The Answer Man		*1:30*
	The Guiding Light	Gabriel Heatter's Mailbag		*1:45*

DAYTIME — SUMMER, 1950

Sunday

	ABC	CBS	MBS	NBC
2pm	This Week Around the World	Syncopation Piece	Deems Taylor Concert	The NBC Theater
2:15				
2:30	Mr. President	Teddy Powell Orchestra	Challenge of the Yukon	
2:45				
3pm	Music with the Hormel Girls	Invitation to Music	Bobby Benson	The Truitts
3:15				
3:30	The Lutheran Hour		Hashknife Hartley and Sleepy Stevens	The Quiz Kids
3:45				
4pm	The Old Fashioned Revival Hour		Hopalong Cassidy	Cloak and Dagger
4:15				
4:30		The Longines Symphonette	Martin Kane, Private Detective	High Adventure
4:45				
5pm	Sammy Kaye's Sunday Serenade	Tex Beneke Orchestra	The Shadow	The Big Guy
5:15				
5:30	Think Fast	The Main Street Music Hall	True Detective Mysteries	Harvest of Stars
5:45				

DAYTIME — SUMMER, 1950

Monday-Friday

ABC	CBS	MBS	NBC	
Welcome to Hollywood	The Second Mrs. Burton	Ladies Fair	Double or Nothing	2pm
	Perry Mason			2:15
Chance of a Lifetime	This is Nora Drake	Queen for a Day	Live Like a Millionaire	2:30
	The Brighter Day			2:45
Bride and Groom	Nona from Nowhere	Second Honeymoon	Life Can Be Beautiful	3pm
	Hilltop House		The Road of Life	3:15
Hannibal Cobb	Winner Take All	Tello-Test Quiz	Pepper Young's Family	3:30
			The Right to Happiness	3:45
The Norman Brokenshire Show	Strike It Rich	Barbera Welles, talk	Mary Noble, Backstage Wife	4pm
			Stella Dallas	4:15
Conversation with Casey	Treasury Bandstand	Dean Cameron, talk	Lorenzo Jones	4:30
Pat Barnes, talk			Young Widder Brown	4:45
Fun House	Galen Drake, talk	Buddy Rogers Orchestra	When a Girl Marries	5pm
			Portia Faces Life	5:15
The Adventures of Superman /	Hits and Misses	Vincent Lopez Orchestra	Just Plain Bill	5:30
Space Patrol / The Green Hornet			Front Page Farrell	5:45

DAYTIME — SUMMER, 1950

Saturday

	ABC	CBS	MBS	NBC
9am	No School Today	This is New York, Danny O'Neill	Harry Hennessy, news	Platter Playground
9:15			Frank Sinatra Records	
9:30		Galen Drake, talk	The McCanns at Home	Coffee in Washington
9:45				
10am		The Carnation Family Party	Henry Gladstone, news	Mind Your Manners
10:15			Tele-Kid Test Quiz	
10:30		Look Your Best		Mary Lee Taylor, cooking
10:45			Let's Go	
11am	Joe Franklin's Record Shop	Let's Pretend	Prescott Robinson, news	Archie Andrews
11:15			The Rudy Vallee Show	
11:30	At Home with Music	Junior Miss		Smilin' Ed's Buster Brown Gang
11:45			Bing Crosby Records	
12pm	The Home Gardener	The Armstrong Theater of Today	Lorraine Sherwood, talk	Charles F. McCarthy, news
12:15				Perry Como Records
12:30	The American Farmer	Grand Central Station	Henry Gladstone, news	Vincent Lopez Orchestra
12:45			The Answer Man	
1pm	The US Navy Band	Stars Over Hollywood	California Caravan	The National Farm and Home Hour
1:15				
1:30	The Roger Dann Show	Give and Take	The B and D Club	The University of Chicago Round Table
1:45				

DAYTIME — SUMMER, 1950

Saturday

	ABC	CBS	MBS	NBC
2pm	Let's Go to the Opera	Music with the Hormel Girls		Voices Down the Wind
2:15				
2:30		Dave Stephens Orchestra		The US Army Band
2:45				
3pm	Concert of American Jazz	Report from Overseas	The Alan Kent Show	Pioneers of Music
3:15		Music You Know		
3:30	The Music of Today	Lennie Herman Orchestra		
3:45				
4pm	Horse Racing	South American Way		The Wayne Howell Show
4:15		Facts for Veterans		
4:30	The Treasury Band Show	George Olsen Orchestra	Vincent Lopez Orchestra	Slim Bryant Orchestra
4:45				
5pm	Tea and Crumpets	Stan Dougherty Orchestra	Bobby Benson	Al Goodman Orchestra
5:15				
5:30		Roy Stevens Orchestra	Stars Over Broadway	The Sport of Kings
5:45	The Club Choral Singers		Twin Views of the News	Confidential Close-Ups

EVENING — FALL, 1950

Sunday

	ABC	CBS	MBS	NBC
6pm	Drew Pearson, news	Rate Your Mate	The Roy Rogers Show	From the Files of the UN
6:15	Don Gardiner, news			
6:30	The Norman Brokenshire Show	Our Miss Brooks	Nick Carter, Master Detective	
6:45				
7pm	Sammy Kaye's Sunday Serenade	The Lucky Strike Program, Jack Benny	The Affairs of Peter Salem	1000 Reward
7:15				
7:30	The Cliché Club	Amos 'n' Andy	Juvenile Jury	The Phil Harris - Alice Faye Show
7:45				
8pm	Stop the Music	The Charlie McCarthy Show	The Singing Marshall	Tales of the Texas Rangers
8:15				
8:30		The Red Skelton Show	Melvin Elliott, news	The Theater Guild on the Air
8:45			David Snell, news	
9pm	Walter Winchell, gossip	Meet Corliss Archer	The Opera Concert	
9:15	Louella Parsons, gossip			
9:30	Crossroads	The Youth Opportunity Program	Gabriel Heatter, news	The American Album of Familiar Music
9:45			War Review	
10pm	The Botany Song Shop, Ginny Simms	The Carnation Contented Hour	Information, Please	The $64 Question
10:15	Jimmy Blaine, songs			
10:30	Jackie Robinson, sports	The Longines Choraliers	Arthur Van Noon, news	Meet Me in St. Louis
10:45	George Sokolsky, news		The Forty Plus Forum	

EVENING — FALL, 1950

Monday

ABC	CBS	MBS	NBC	
Joe Hasel, sports	Allan Jackson, news	Lyle Van, news	Kenneth Banghart, news	6pm
Dorian St. George, news	You and the World	Bob Elson Interviews	Bill Stern, sports	6:15
The Norman Brokenshire Show	Curt Massey, songs	Fred Vandeventer, news	Here's Morgan	6:30
	Lowell Thomas, news	Stan Lomax, sports	Three Star Extra	6:45
Taylor Grant, news	The Beulah Show	Fulton Lewis Jr., news	The Longines Symphonette	7pm
Elmer Davis, news	The Jack Smith Show	The Answer Man		7:15
The Lone Ranger	Club Fifteen	Gabriel Heatter, news	Morgan Beatty, news	7:30
	Edward R. Murrow, news	The Kirkwood - Goodman Show	One Man's Family	7:45
Inner Sanctum Mysteries	The Hollywood Star Playhouse	Bobby Benson	The Railroad Hour	8pm
				8:15
Henry J. Taylor, news	Arthur Godfrey's Talent Scouts	Crime Fighters	The Voice of Firestone	8:30
The Dell Trio		Bill Henry, news (8:55pm)		8:45
Martha Lou Harp, songs	The Lux Radio Theater	Murder By Experts	The Bell Telephone Hour	9pm
Paul Harvey, news				9:15
Johnny Desmond Goes to College		War Front, Home Front	The Cities Service Band of America	9:30
				9:45
United or Not	My Friend Irma	Frank Edwards, news	NBC Symphony Orchestra	10pm
		A. L. Alexander, poetry		10:15
The Longines Symphonette	The Bob Hawk Show	The Opera Concert		10:30
				10:45

EVENING — FALL, 1950

Tuesday

	ABC	CBS	MBS	NBC
6pm	Joe Hasel, sports	Allan Jackson, news	Lyle Van, news	Kenneth Banghart, news
6:15	Dorian St. George, news	You and the World	Bob Elson Interviews	Bill Stern, sports
6:30	The Norman Brokenshire Show	Curt Massey, songs	Fred Vandeventer, news	Here's Morgan
6:45		Lowell Thomas, news	Stan Lomax, sports	Three Star Extra
7pm	Taylor Grant, news	The Beulah Show	Fulton Lewis Jr., news	The Longines Symphonette
7:15	Elmer Davis, news	The Jack Smith Show	The Answer Man	
7:30	Armstrong of the SBI	Club Fifteen	Gabriel Heatter, news	Morgan Beatty, news
7:45		Edward R. Murrow, news	The Kirkwood - Goodman Show	One Man's Family
8pm	The Metropolitan Opera Auditions	Mystery Theater	The Count of Monte Cristo	The Cavalcade of America
8:15				
8:30	Time for Defense	Mr. and Mrs. North	Official Detective	The Baby Snooks Show
8:45			Bill Henry, news (8:55pm)	
9pm	America's Town Meeting of the Air	Life with Luigi	John Steele, Adventurer	The Bob Hope Show
9:15				
9:30	Edwin D. Canham, news	Truth or Consequences	The Mysterious Traveler	Fibber Magee and Molly
9:45	The Fine Arts Quartet			
10pm	On Trial	Dollar A Minute	Frank Edwards, news	Big Town
10:15			A. L. Alexander, poetry	
10:30	The Longines Symphonette	Capitol Cloak Room	The Show Shop	People Are Funny
10:45				

EVENING — FALL, 1950

Wednesday

ABC	CBS	MBS	NBC	
Joe Hasel, sports	Allan Jackson, news	Lyle Van, news	Kenneth Banghart, news	6pm
Dorian St. George, news	You and the World	Bob Elson Interviews	Bill Stern, sports	6:15
The Norman Brokenshire Show	Curt Massey, songs	Fred Vandeventer, news	Here's Morgan	6:30
	Lowell Thomas, news	Stan Lomax, sports	Three Star Extra	6:45
Taylor Grant, news	The Beulah Show	Fulton Lewis Jr., news	The Longines Symphonette	7pm
Elmer Davis, news	The Jack Smith Show	The Answer Man		7:15
The Lone Ranger	Club Fifteen	Gabriel Heatter, news	Morgan Beatty, news	7:30
	Edward R. Murrow, news	The Kirkwood - Goodman Show	One Man's Family	7:45
Dr. I. Q., the Mental Banker	Mr. Chameleon	The Hidden Truth	The Halls of Ivy	8pm
				8:15
Bob Barcley, American Agent	Dr. Christian	Boston Blackie	The Great Gildersleeve	8:30
		Bill Henry, news (8:55pm)		8:45
Detour	Honest Harold	Two-Thousand Plus	You Bet Your Life	9pm
				9:15
Manhattan Maharajah	The Bing Crosby Chesterfield Show	The Family Theater	Mr. District Attorney	9:30
				9:45
Lawrence Welk High Life Revue	The Wednesday Night Fights	Frank Edwards, news	The Big Story	10pm
		A. L. Alexander, poetry		10:15
The Longines Symphonette		The Show Shop	Richard Diamond, Private Detective	10:30
				10:45

EVENING — FALL, 1950

Thursday

	ABC	CBS	MBS	NBC
6pm	Joe Hasel, sports	Allan Jackson, news	Lyle Van, news	Kenneth Banghart, news
6:15	Dorian St. George, news	You and the World	Bob Elson Interviews	Bill Stern, sports
6:30	The Norman Brokenshire Show	Curt Massey, songs	Fred Vandeventer, news	Here's Morgan
6:45		Lowell Thomas, news	Stan Lomax, sports	Three Star Extra
7pm	Taylor Grant, news	The Beulah Show	Fulton Lewis Jr., news	The Longines Symphonette
7:15	Elmer Davis, news	The Jack Smith Show	The Answer Man	
7:30	Armstrong of the SBI	Club Fifteen	Gabriel Heatter, news	Morgan Beatty, news
7:45		Edward R. Murrow, news	The Kirkwood - Goodman Show	One Man's Family
8pm	The Screen Guild Theater	The FBI in Peace and War	The Cisco Kid	The Aldrich Family
8:15				
8:30		Mr. Keen, Tracer of Lost Persons	The Rod and Gun Club	Father Knows Best
8:45			Bill Henry, news (8:55pm)	
9pm	Ted Mack's Original Amateur Hour	Suspense	The Damon Runyon Theater	Dragnet
9:15				
9:30		Casey, Crime Photographer	Mutual Reporter's Round-Up	We, the People
9:45	Robert Montgomery Speaking			
10pm	Hollywood Byline	The Hallmark Playhouse	Frank Edwards, news	Top Secret
10:15			A. L. Alexander, poetry	
10:30	The Longines Symphonette	Jimmy Dorsey Orchestra	The Show Shop	Presenting Charles Boyer
10:45				

EVENING — FALL, 1950

Friday

ABC	CBS	MBS	NBC	
Joe Hasel, sports	Allan Jackson, news	Lyle Van, news	Kenneth Banghart, news	6pm
Dorian St. George, news	You and the World	Bob Elson Interviews	Bill Stern, sports	6:15
The Norman Brokenshire Show	Curt Massey, songs	Fred Vandeventer, news	Here's Morgan	6:30
	Lowell Thomas, news	Stan Lomax, sports	Three Star Extra	6:45
Taylor Grant, news	The Beulah Show	Fulton Lewis Jr., news	The Longines Symphonette	7pm
Elmer Davis, news	The Jack Smith Show	The Answer Man		7:15
The Lone Ranger	Club Fifteen	Gabriel Heatter, news	Morgan Beatty, news	7:30
	Edward R. Murrow, news	The Kirkwood - Goodman Show	One Man's Family	7:45
The Fat Man	Songs for Sale	Bandstand USA	The New Adventures of Nero Wolfe	8pm
				8:15
This is Your FBI		Guy Lombardo Orchestra	The Man Called X	8:30
		Bill Henry, news (8:55pm)		8:45
The Adventures of Ozzie and Harriet	Up for Parole	True or False	Nightbeat	9pm
				9:15
The Sheriff	Broadway is My Beat	The Kirkwood - Goodman Show	Duffy's Tavern	9:30
				9:45
Madison Square Garden Boxing	We Take Your Word	Frank Edwards, news	The Life of Riley	10pm
		A. L. Alexander, poetry		10:15
Joe Hasel's Sports Page	New York Story	The Show Shop	Colgate Sports Newsreel, Bill Stern	10:30
			Pro and Con	10:45

EVENING — FALL, 1950

Saturday

	ABC	CBS	MBS	NBC
6pm	Albert Warner, news	Joe Wershba, news	Lyle Van, news	Kenneth Banghart, news
6:15	Faith for the Future	CBS Views the Press	The Forty Plus Forum	Herman Herkman, sports
6:30	Harry Wismer, sports	Red Barber, sports	Fred Vandeventer, news	NBC Symphony Orchestra
6:45	It's Your Business	Larry Lesueur, news	Stan Lomax, sports	
7pm	The AFL-CIO Program	Yours Truly, Johnny Dollar	History in the Making	
7:15	Bert Andrews, news		The Answer Man	
7:30	Buzz Adlam's Playroom	The Camel Caravan, Vaughn Monroe	Comedy of Errors	
7:45				
8pm	Shoot the Moon	Gene Autry's Melody Ranch	Twenty Questions	The Cass Daley Show
8:15				
8:30	Merry-Go-Round, Jimmy Blaine	Hopalong Cassidy	Take a Number	Hedda Hopper's Hollywood
8:45				
9pm	What Makes You Tick	Gangbusters	Hawaii Calls	Your Hit Parade
9:15				
9:30	Can You Top This	My Favorite Husband	Lombardoland USA	A Day in the Life of Dennis Day
9:45				
10pm	Saturday at the Shamrock	Sing It Again	The Chicago Theater of the Air	The Judy Canova Show
10:15				
10:30	Dixieland Jambake			Grand Ole Opry
10:45				

DAYTIME — FALL, 1950

Sunday

	ABC	CBS	MBS	NBC
9am	Milton Cross Opera Album	News	Harry Hennessy, news	News
9:15		From the Organ Loft	Heartbeat in the News	The Comic Weekly Man
9:30	The Voice of Prophecy		The Mutual Radio Chapel	
9:45		St. Paul's Trinity Choir		Music
10am	Message of Israel	The CBS Church of the Air	Henry Gladstone, news	The National Radio Pulpit
10:15			Get More Out of Life	
10:30	Negro College Choirs		The Stars of Song	The Horn and Hardart Children's Hour
10:45			Your Hymnal	
11am	Next Week in New York, Bert Bacharach	The Salt Lake Tabernacle Choir	Henry Gladstone, news	
11:15			Brunch with Dorothy and Dick	
11:30	Christian in Action	Invitation to Learning		Charles F. McCarthy, news
11:45				Solitaire Time
12pm	The Treasury Band Show	The People's Platform	Junior Celebrities	Tex and Jinx, talk
12:15				
12:30	The Piano Playhouse	Howard K. Smith, news	Melvin Elliott, news	The Eternal Light
12:45		Charles Collingwood, news	Roy King, news	
1pm	Dr. William Ward Ayer, talk	Invitation to Music	The Canary Pet Shop	The American Forum of the Air
1:15			The Show Shop	
1:30	National Vespers			The Quiz Kids
1:45			Stan Lomax, sports	

DAYTIME — FALL, 1950

Monday-Friday

ABC	CBS	MBS	NBC	
The Breakfast Club	This is New York, Danny O'Neill	Harry Hennessy, news	Tex and Jinx, talk (8:30am)	*9am*
		Tello-Test Quiz		*9:15*
		Alfred W. McCann, food	Bing Crosby Records	*9:30*
	Tommy Riggs and Betty Lou			*9:45*
My True Story	Arthur Godfrey Time	Henry Gladstone, news	Welcome, Travelers	*10am*
		Martha Deane, talk		*10:15*
Betty Crocker, cooking			Double or Nothing	*10:30*
Victor Lindlahr, health				*10:45*
Modern Romances		Precott Robinson, news	Break the Bank	*11am*
		The Rudy Vallee Show		*11:15*
Quick as a Flash	Grand Slam		The Jack Berch Show	*11:30*
	Rosemary	Kate Smith Sings	David Harum	*11:45*
Johnny Olsen's Luncheon Club	Wendy Warren and the News	Kate Smith Speaks	Charles F. McCarthy, news	*12pm*
	Aunt Jenny's True Life Stories	Music / Get More Out of Life	Skitch's Scrapbook	*12:15*
The Herb Sheldon Show	The Romance of Helen Trent	Henry Gladstone, news	Eleanor Roosevelt, talk	*12:30*
	Our Gal Sunday	Luncheon at Sardi's		*12:45*
Mary Margaret McBride, talk	Big Sister			*1pm*
	Ma Perkins		Dial Dave Garroway	*1:15*
	Young Dr. Malone	The Hollywood Theater of Stars	George Hicks, news	*1:30*
	The Guiding Light		We Love and Learn	*1:45*

DAYTIME — FALL, 1950

Sunday

	ABC	CBS	MBS	NBC
2pm	This Week Around the World		Ben Pollack Orchestra	The Catholic Hour
2:15				
2:30	Mr. President	The Longines Symphonette	Proudly We Hail	Voices and Events
2:45				
3pm	Music with the Hormel Girls	Escape	Bobby Benson	The NBC University Theater
3:15				
3:30	The Lutheran Hour	Make-Believe Town, Hollywood	Hashknife Hartley and Sleepy Stevens	The Quiz Kids
3:45				
4pm	The Old Fashioned Revival Hour	Earn Your Vacation	Under Arrest	The Falcon
4:15				
4:30		Arthur Godfrey's Digest	Martin Kane, Private Detective	Cloak and Dagger
4:45				
5pm	Author Meets the Critics	Syncopated Piece	The Shadow	The Big Guy
5:15				
5:30	The Greatest Story Ever Told	Music for You	True Detective Mysteries	Charlie Wild, Private Detective
5:45				

DAYTIME — FALL, 1950

Monday-Friday

ABC	CBS	MBS	NBC	
Welcome to Hollywood	The Second Mrs. Burton	Buddy Rogers Orchestra	Double or Nothing	*2pm*
	Perry Mason			*2:15*
John B. Kennedy, news	This is Nora Drake	Queen for a Day	Live Like a Millionaire	*2:30*
Peace of Mind	The Brighter Day			*2:45*
Chance of a Lifetime	Nona from Nowhere	Second Honeymoon	Life Can Be Beautiful	*3pm*
	Hilltop House		The Road of Life	*3:15*
Hannibal Cobb	House Party	Tello-Test Quiz	Pepper Young's Family	*3:30*
Talk Back with Happy Felton			The Right to Happiness	*3:45*
Nancy Booth Craig, talk	Strike It Rich	Barbera Welles, talk	Mary Noble, Backstage Wife	*4pm*
			Stella Dallas	*4:15*
Music	Missus Goes A Shopping	Dean Cameron, talk	Lorenzo Jones	*4:30*
Pat Barnes, talk			Young Widder Brown	*4:45*
The Jimmy Wakely Show	Galen Drake, talk	Mark Trail /	When a Girl Marries	*5pm*
		Straight Arrow	Portia Faces Life	*5:15*
Blackhawk / Space Patrol /	Hits and Misses	Challenge of The Yukon /	Just Plain Bill	*5:30*
The Adventures of Superman		Sky King	Front Page Farrell	*5:45*

DAYTIME — FALL, 1950

Saturday

	ABC	CBS	MBS	NBC
9am	No School Today	This is New York, Danny O'Neill	Harry Hennessy, news	Platter Playground
9:15			Get More Out of Life	
9:30		Galen Drake, talk	The McCanns at Home	Boston Symphony Dress Rehearsal
9:45				
10am		The Carnation Family Party	Henry Gladstone, news	Mind Your Manners
10:15			Bill Lang, news	
10:30		The Coke Club, Morton Downey	Tele-Kid Test Quiz	Mary Lee Taylor, cooking
10:45			Let's Go	
11am	Junior Junction	Let's Pretend	Prescott Robinson, news	Archie Andrews
11:15			The Rudy Vallee Show	
11:30	Joe Franklin's Record Shop	Junior Miss		Prom Date
11:45			Bing Crosby Records	
12pm	The Ranch Boys Trio	The Armstrong Theater of Today	The Man on the Farm	Perry Como Records
12:15				
12:30	The American Farmer	Grand Central Station	Henry Gladstone, news	Vincent Lopez Orchestra
12:45			The Answer Man	
1pm	The US Navy Band	Stars Over Hollywood	Lorraine Sherwood, talk	The National Farm and Home Hour
1:15				
1:30	Concert of American Jazz	Give and Take	Tune Time	Sports
1:45			Sports	

DAYTIME — FALL, 1950

Saturday

	ABC	CBS	MBS	NBC
2pm		Music with the Hormel Girls		
2:15	Sports			
2:30		Sports		
2:45				
3pm				
3:15				
3:30				
3:45				
4pm				
4:15				
4:30				
4:45				
5pm	Tea and Crumpets			
5:15				
5:30		Saturday at the Chase	The Alan Kent Show	The Wayne Howell Show
5:45	The Club Choral Singers		Twin Views of the News	

LISTINGS FOR 1951

EVENING — WINTER, 1951

Sunday

	ABC	CBS	MBS	NBC
6pm	Drew Pearson, news	Charlie Wild, Private Detective	The Roy Rogers Show	The Big Show
6:15	Don Gardiner, news			
6:30	The Ted Mack Family Hour	Our Miss Brooks	Nick Carter, Master Detective	
6:45				
7pm	Sammy Kaye's Sunday Serenade	The Lucky Strike Program, Jack Benny	The Affairs of Peter Salem	
7:15				
7:30	Mystery File	Amos 'n' Andy	Juvenile Jury	The Phil Harris - Alice Faye Show
7:45				
8pm	Stop the Music	The Charlie McCarthy Show	A. L. Alexander's Mediation Board	Hedda Hopper's Hollywood
8:15				
8:30		The Red Skelton Show	Melvin Elliott, news	The Theater Guild on the Air
8:45			Sidney Walton, news	
9pm	Walter Winchell, gossip	Meet Corliss Archer	The Opera Concert	
9:15	Louella Parsons, gossip			
9:30	The American Album of Familiar Music	The Youth Opportunity Program	Gabriel Heatter, news	Tales of the Texas Rangers
9:45			The Forty Plus Forum	
10pm	The Botany Song Shop, Ginny Simms	The Carnation Contented Hour	Information, Please	The $64 Question
10:15	Jimmy Blaine, songs			
10:30	George Sokolsky, news	The Longines Choraliers	Arthur Van Horn, news	The American Forum of the Air
10:45	Get More Out of Life		Outwitting Your Years	

EVENING — WINTER, 1951

Monday

ABC	CBS	MBS	NBC	
Joe Hasel, sports	Allan Jackson, news	Lyle Van, news	Bob Edwards, news	*6pm*
Dorian St. George, talk	You and the World	Bob Elson Interviews	The Answer Man	*6:15*
The Norman Brokenshire Show	Curt Massey, songs	Fred Vandeventer, news	Wayne Howell, news	*6:30*
	Lowell Thomas, news	Stan Lomax, sports	Three Star Extra	*6:45*
Taylor Grant, news	The Beulah Show	Fulton Lewis Jr., news	The Longines Symphonette	*7pm*
Elmer Davis, news	The Jack Smith Show	The Mutual Newsreel		*7:15*
The Lone Ranger	Club Fifteen	Gabriel Heatter, news	Morgan Beatty, news	*7:30*
	Edward R. Murrow, news	The Kirkwood - Goodman Show	One Man's Family	*7:45*
Inner Sanctum Mysteries	The Hollywood Star Playhouse	The Cisco Kid	The Railroad Hour	*8pm*
				8:15
Henry J. Taylor, news	Arthur Godfrey's Talent Scouts	Crime Fighters	The Voice of Firestone	*8:30*
World News		Bill Henry, news (8:55pm)		*8:45*
Martha Lou Harp, songs	The Lux Radio Theater	Murder By Experts	The Bell Telephone Hour	*9pm*
Manhattan Maharajah				*9:15*
Johnny Desmond Goes to College		War Front, Home Front	The Cities Service Band of America	*9:30*
				9:45
Ralph Flanagan Orchestra	My Friend Irma	Frank Edwards, news	NBC Symphony Orchestra	*10pm*
		A. L. Alexander, poetry		*10:15*
United or Not	The Bob Hawk Show	The Show Shop		*10:30*
				10:45

EVENING — WINTER, 1951

Tuesday

	ABC	CBS	MBS	NBC
6pm	Joe Hasel, sports	Allan Jackson, news	Lyle Van, news	Bob Edwards, news
6:15	Dorian St. George, talk	You and the World	Bob Elson Interviews	The Answer Man
6:30	The Norman Brokenshire Show	Curt Massey, songs	Fred Vandeventer, news	Wayne Howell, news
6:45		Lowell Thomas, news	Stan Lomax, sports	Three Star Extra
7pm	Taylor Grant, news	The Beulah Show	Fulton Lewis Jr., news	The Longines Symphonette
7:15	Elmer Davis, news	The Jack Smith Show	The Mutual Newsreel	
7:30	Armstrong of the SBI	Club Fifteen	Gabriel Heatter, news	Morgan Beatty, news
7:45		Edward R. Murrow, news	The Kirkwood - Goodman Show	One Man's Family
8pm	Can You Top This	Mystery Theater	Mystery House	The Cavalcade of America
8:15				
8:30	I Fly Anything	Mr. and Mrs. North	Official Detective	The Baby Snooks Show
8:45			Bill Henry, news (8:55pm)	
9pm	America's Town Meeting of the Air	Life with Luigi	Arthur Van Horn, news	The Bob Hope Show
9:15			Bill Lang, news	
9:30		Truth or Consequences	The Mysterious Traveler	Fibber Magee and Molly
9:45	Edwin D. Canham, news			
10pm	The Metropolitan Opera Auditions	Rate Your Mate	Frank Edwards, news	Big Town
10:15			Get More Out of Life	
10:30	On Trial	Capitol Cloak Room	The Show Shop	People Are Funny
10:45				

EVENING — WINTER, 1951

Wednesday

ABC	CBS	MBS	NBC	
Joe Hasel, sports	Allan Jackson, news	Lyle Van, news	Bob Edwards, news	6pm
Dorian St. George, talk	You and the World	Bob Elson Interviews	The Answer Man	6:15
The Norman Brokenshire Show	Curt Massey, songs	Fred Vandeventer, news	Wayne Howell, news	6:30
	Lowell Thomas, news	Stan Lomax, sports	Three Star Extra	6:45
Taylor Grant, news	The Beulah Show	Fulton Lewis Jr., news	The Longines Symphonette	7pm
Elmer Davis, news	The Jack Smith Show	The Mutual Newsreel		7:15
The Lone Ranger	Club Fifteen	Gabriel Heatter, news	Morgan Beatty, news	7:30
	Edward R. Murrow, news	The Kirkwood - Goodman Show	One Man's Family	7:45
Bob Barcley, American Agent	Mr. Chameleon	The Hidden Truth	The Halls of Ivy	8pm
				8:15
The Fat Man	Dr. Christian	International Airport	The Great Gildersleeve	8:30
		Bill Henry, news (8:55pm)		8:45
Rogue's Gallery	Honest Harold	Two-Thousand Plus	You Bet Your Life	9pm
				9:15
Mr. President	The Bing Crosby Chesterfield Show	The Family Theater	Mr. District Attorney	9:30
				9:45
Lawrence Welk High Life Revue	The Wednesday Night Fights	Frank Edwards, news	The Big Story	10pm
		A. L. Alexander, poetry		10:15
Dance Orchestra		The Show Shop	The NBC University Theater	10:30
	Henry Jerome Orchestra			10:45

EVENING — WINTER, 1951

Thursday

	ABC	CBS	MBS	NBC
6pm	Joe Hasel, sports	Allan Jackson, news	Lyle Van, news	Bob Edwards, news
6:15	Dorian St. George, talk	You and the World	Bob Elson Interviews	The Answer Man
6:30	The Norman Brokenshire Show	Curt Massey, songs	Fred Vandeventer, news	Wayne Howell, news
6:45		Lowell Thomas, news	Stan Lomax, sports	Three Star Extra
7pm	Taylor Grant, news	The Beulah Show	Fulton Lewis Jr., news	The Longines Symphonette
7:15	Elmer Davis, news	The Jack Smith Show	The Mutual Newsreel	
7:30	Armstrong of the SBI	Club Fifteen	Gabriel Heatter, news	Morgan Beatty, news
7:45		Edward R. Murrow, news	The Kirkwood - Goodman Show	One Man's Family
8pm	The Screen Guild Theater	The FBI in Peace and War	The Damon Runyon Theater	The Aldrich Family
8:15				
8:30		Mr. Keen, Tracer of Lost Persons	The Rod and Gun Club	Father Knows Best
8:45			Bill Henry, news (8:55pm)	
9pm	Ted Mack's Original Amateur Hour	Suspense	The Count of Monte Cristo	Dragnet
9:15				
9:30		The Hallmark Playhouse	Mutual Reporter's Round-Up	We, the People
9:45	Robert Montgomery Speaking			
10pm	Time for Defense	The Lineup	Frank Edwards, news	The Screen Director's Playhouse
10:15			Get More Out of Life	
10:30	Rex Maupin Orchestra	Frankie Carle Orchestra	The Show Shop	
10:45				

EVENING — WINTER, 1951

Friday

ABC	CBS	MBS	NBC	
Joe Hasel, sports	Allan Jackson, news	Lyle Van, news	Bob Edwards, news	6pm
Dorian St. George, talk	You and the World	Bob Elson Interviews	The Answer Man	6:15
The Norman Brokenshire Show	Curt Massey, songs	Fred Vandeventer, news	Wayne Howell, news	6:30
	Lowell Thomas, news	Stan Lomax, sports	Three Star Extra	6:45
Taylor Grant, news	The Beulah Show	Fulton Lewis Jr., news	The Longines Symphonette	7pm
Elmer Davis, news	The Jack Smith Show	The Mutual Newsreel		7:15
The Lone Ranger	Club Fifteen	Gabriel Heatter, news	Morgan Beatty, news	7:30
	Edward R. Murrow, news	The Kirkwood - Goodman Show	One Man's Family	7:45
Richard Diamond, Private Detective	Songs for Sale	The Cisco Kid	The New Adventures of Nero Wolfe	8pm
				8:15
This is Your FBI		Guy Lombardo Orchestra	The Adventures of Sam Spade	8:30
		Bill Henry, news (8:55pm)		8:45
The Adventures of Ozzie and Harriet	Hear It Now	The Opera Concert	The Magnificent Montague	9pm
				9:15
The Sheriff		Elliot Lawrence Orchestra	Duffy's Tavern	9:30
				9:45
Madison Square Garden Boxing	We Take Your Word	Frank Edwards, news	The Life of Riley	10pm
		A. L. Alexander, poetry		10:15
Joe Hasel's Sports Page	New York Story	The Show Shop	The Colgate Sports Newsreel, Bill Stern	10:30
			Pro and Con	10:45

EVENING — WINTER, 1951

Saturday

	ABC	CBS	MBS	NBC
6pm	Saturday Strings	Joe Wershba, news	Lyle Van, news	NBC Symphony Orchestra
6:15	Una Mae Carlisle, songs	CBS Views the Press	Inside News	
6:30	Harry Wismer, sports	The Saturday Sports Review	Fred Vandeventer, news	
6:45	The AFL-CIO Program	Larry Lesueur, news	Stan Lomax, sports	
7pm	It's Your Business	Yours Truly, Johnny Dollar	History in the Making	
7:15	Bert Andrews, news		Twin Views of the News	
7:30	Buzz Adlam's Playroom	The Camel Caravan, Vaughn Monroe	Comedy of Errors	
7:45				
8pm	Shoot the Moon	Gene Autry's Melody Ranch	Twenty Questions	Dangerous Assignment
8:15				
8:30	Merry-Go-Round, Jimmy Blaine	Hopalong Cassidy	Take a Number	The Man Called X
8:45				
9pm	What Makes You Tick	Gangbusters	Hawaii Calls	Your Hit Parade
9:15				
9:30	Jay Stewart's Fun Fair	My Favorite Husband	Lombardoland USA	A Day in the Life of Dennis Day
9:45				
10pm	Saturday at the Shamrock	Sing It Again	The Chicago Theater of the Air	The Judy Canova Show
10:15				
10:30	Dixieland Jambake			Grand Ole Opry
10:45				

DAYTIME — WINTER, 1951

Sunday

	ABC	CBS	MBS	NBC
9am	Rev. Barnhouse, religion	News	News	News
9:15		From the Organ Loft	The Magic of Believing	The Comic Weekly Man
9:30	The Voice of Prophecy		The Mutual Radio Chapel	
9:45		St. Paul's Trinity Choir		Music
10am	Message of Israel	The CBS Church of the Air	Henry Gladstone, news	The National Radio Pulpit
10:15			Sidney Walton, news	
10:30	Negro College Choirs		The Stars of Song	The Horn and Hardart Children's Hour
10:45			Bill Lang, news	
11am	Brunch with Kelvin Keech	The Salt Lake Tabernacle Choir	Henry Gladstone, news	
11:15	Frank and Ernest, religion		Brunch with Dorothy and Dick	
11:30	Christian in Action	Invitation to Learning		Edwin C. Hill, news
11:45				Solitaire Time
12pm	This Week in New York, Bert Bacharach	The People's Platform	Junior Celebrities	Tex and Jinx, talk
12:15				
12:30	The Piano Playhouse	Howard K. Smith, news	Bill Hillman, news	The Eternal Light
12:45		Charles Collingwood, news	Top Tunes with Trendler	
1pm	Dr. William Ward Ayer, talk	New York Philharmonic Orchestra	The Canary Pet Shop	The American Forum of the Air
1:15			The Show Shop	
1:30	National Vespers			The Quiz Kids
1:45				

DAYTIME — WINTER, 1951

Monday-Friday

ABC	CBS	MBS	NBC	
The Breakfast Club	This is New York, Danny O'Neill	Harry Hennessy, news	Tex and Jinx, talk (8:30am)	9am
		This is Allyn Edwards		9:15
		Alfred W. McCann, food	Andre Baruch, talk	9:30
	Tommy Riggs and Betty Lou			9:45
My True Story	The Robert Q. Lewis Show	Cecil Brown, news	Welcome, Travelers	10am
		Martha Deane, talk		10:15
Betty Crocker, cooking			Double or Nothing	10:30
Victor Lindlahr, health				10:45
Modern Romances		Prescott Robinson, news	Break the Bank	11am
		Tello-Test Quiz		11:15
Quick as a Flash	Grand Slam	Queen for a Day	The Jack Berch Show	11:30
	Rosemary		Dial Dave Garroway	11:45
Johnny Olsen's Luncheon Club	Wendy Warren and the News	Kate Smith Speaks	Charles F. McCarthy, news	12pm
	Aunt Jenny's True Life Stories	Kate Smith Sings	Skitch's Scrapbook	12:15
The Herb Sheldon Show	The Romance of Helen Trent	Henry Gladstone, news	Eleanor Roosevelt, talk	12:30
	Our Gal Sunday	Luncheon at Sardi's		12:45
Mary Margaret McBride, talk	Big Sister			1pm
	Ma Perkins		Penthouse Matinee	1:15
	Young Dr. Malone	The Hollywood Theater of Stars	The Answer Man	1:30
	The Guiding Light		We Love and Learn	1:45

DAYTIME — WINTER, 1951

Sunday

	ABC	CBS	MBS	NBC
2pm	The Hour of Decision		Only Human	The Catholic Hour
2:15				
2:30	The Southernaires Quartet	The Longines Symphonette	David Snell, talk	Bob Considine, sports
2:45			George Fielding Elliot, comment	The First Piano Quartet
3pm	This Week Around the World	News from Washington	Bobby Benson	Music with the Hormel Girls
3:15		Larry Lesueur, news		
3:30	The Lutheran Hour	Your Tropical Trip	John Steele, Adventurer	The Quiz Kids
3:45				
4pm	The Old Fashioned Revival Hour	Dollar a Minute	Under Arrest	The Falcon
4:15				
4:30		Arthur Godfrey's Digest	Martin Kane, Private Detective	The Saint
4:45				
5pm	Author Meets the Critics	Meet Frank Sinatra	The Shadow	Counterspy
5:15				
5:30	The Greatest Story Ever Told		True Detective Mysteries	Mr. and Mrs. Blandings
5:45		Eric Severeid, news		

DAYTIME — WINTER, 1951

Monday-Friday

ABC	CBS	MBS	NBC	
Ilka Chase, talk	The Second Mrs. Burton	The Gloria Swanson Show	Double or Nothing	2pm
	Perry Mason			2:15
John B. Kennedy, news	This is Nora Drake	The Rudy Vallee Show	Live Like a Millionaire	2:30
David Amity	The Brighter Day			2:45
Welcome to Hollywood	Nora from Nowhere	Buddy Rogers Orchestra	Life Can Be Beautiful	3pm
	Winner Take All		The Road of Life	3:15
Hannibal Cobb	House Party	Tello-Test Quiz	Pepper Young's Family	3:30
Talk Back with Happy Felton			The Right to Happiness	3:45
Nancy Booth Craig, talk	Strike It Rich	Barbera Welles, talk	Mary Noble, Backstage Wife	4pm
			Stella Dallas	4:15
Pat Barnes, talk	Missus Goes A Shopping	Dean Cameron, talk	Lorenzo Jones	4:30
			Young Widder Brown	4:45
Chance of a Lifetime	Galen Drake, talk	Mark Trail /	When a Girl Marries	5pm
		Straight Arrow	Portia Faces Life	5:15
Big Jon and Sparkie	Hits and Misses	Clyde Beatty Adventures /	Just Plain Bill	5:30
		Sky King	Front Page Farrell	5:45

DAYTIME — WINTER, 1951

Saturday

	ABC	CBS	MBS	NBC
9am	No School Today	This is New York, Danny O'Neill	Bing Crosby Records	Platter Playground
9:15			The Quiz Club	
9:30		Galen Drake, talk	The McCanns at Home	Boston Symphony Dress Rehearsal
9:45		The Garden Gate		
10am		The Carnation Family Party	Henry Gladstone, news	Mind Your Manners
10:15			Bill Lang, news	
10:30		The Coke Club, Morton Downey	Tele-Kid Test Quiz	Mary Lee Taylor, cooking
10:45			Let's Go	
11am	Junior Junction	Let's Pretend	Prescott Robinson, news	Archie Andrews
11:15			Inside News	
11:30	The Bill Watson Show	The Somerset Maugham Theater	Proudly We Hail	Prom Date
11:45				
12pm	The Ranch Boys Trio	The Armstrong Theater of Today	The Man on the Farm	Perry Como Records
12:15				
12:30	The American Farmer	Grand Central Station	Henry Gladstone, news	Clem McCarthy's Record Derby
12:45			Get More Out of Life	
1pm	The US Navy Band	Stars Over Hollywood	Lorraine Sherwood, talk	The National Farm and Home Hour
1:15				
1:30	Concert of American Jazz	Give and Take	The Alan Kent Show	The University of Chicago Round Table
1:45	The Baron Elliott Octet			

DAYTIME — WINTER, 1951

Saturday

	ABC	CBS	MBS	NBC
2pm	The Metropolitan Opera	Music with the Hormel Girls		Battleground for Peace
2:15				
2:30		Galen Drake, talk		The Slim Byrant Show
2:45		Dave Stephens Orchestra		
3pm			The Leonard Feather Show	Radio City, USA
3:15		Adventures in Science		
3:30		Report from Overseas		The US Army Band
3:45		CBS Farm News		
4pm		Make Way for Youth		Musiciana
4:15				
4:30		Cross-Section USA	Horse Racing	
4:45			Music	
5pm		Radio Reporter's Scratchpad	Hashknife Hartley and Sleepy Stevens Stevens	The First Piano Quartet
5:15		Songs By Symington		
5:30	Tea and Crumpets	Saturday at the Chase	Challenge of the Yukon	The Wayne Howell Show
5:45	Club Time			

EVENTING — SPRING, 1951

Sunday

	ABC	CBS	MBS	NBC
6pm	Drew Pearson, news	Charlie Wild, Private Detective	The Roy Rogers Show	The Big Show
6:15	Don Gardiner, news			
6:30	QED Quiz	Our Miss Brooks	Nick Carter, Master Detective	
6:45				
7pm	Sammy Kaye's Sunday Serenade	The Lucky Strike Program, Jack Benny	The Hidden Truth	
7:15				
7:30	The Ted Mack Family Hour	Amos 'n' Andy	Melvin Elliott, news	The Phil Harris - Alice Faye Show
7:45			Incredible, But True	
8pm	Stop the Music	The Charlie McCarthy Show	A. L. Alexander's Mediation Board	Hedda Hopper's Hollywood
8:15				
8:30		The Red Skelton Show	The Affairs of Peter Salem	The Theater Guild on the Air
8:45				
9pm	Walter Winchell, gossip	Meet Corliss Archer	The Opera Concert	
9:15	Louella Parsons, gossip			
9:30	The American Album of Familiar Music	The Youth Opportunity Program	Gabriel Heatter, news	Tales of the Texas Rangers
9:45			David Snell, talk	
10pm	News	The Carnation Contented Hour	Information, Please	The $64 Question
10:15	Latin American Music			
10:30	George Sokolsky, news	The Longines Choraliers	Heartbeat in the News	Voices and Events
10:45	The Sunday Sports Review		Your Legal Advisor	

EVENING — SPRING, 1951

Monday

ABC	CBS	MBS	NBC	
The Allen Stuart Show	Allan Jackson, news	Lyle Van, news	Bob Edwards, news	6pm
	You and the World	Bob Elson Interviews	The Answer Man	6:15
	Curt Massey, songs	Fred Vandeventer, news	Bill Stern, sports	6:30
	Lowell Thomas, news	Stan Lomax, sports	Three Star Extra	6:45
Taylor Grant, news	The Beulah Show	Fulton Lewis Jr., news	The Longines Symphonette	7pm
Elmer Davis, news	The Jack Smith Show	Tello-Test Quiz		7:15
The Lone Ranger	Club Fifteen	Gabriel Heatter, news	Morgan Beatty, news	7:30
	Edward R. Murrow, news	Friendly Bandstand	One Man's Family	7:45
Inner Sanctum Mysteries	The Hollywood Star Playhouse		The Railroad Hour	8pm
				8:15
Henry J. Taylor, news	Arthur Godfrey's Talent Scouts		The Voice of Firestone	8:30
World News		Bill Henry, news (8:55pm)		8:45
United or Not	The Lux Radio Theater	Murder By Experts	The Bell Telephone Hour	9pm
				9:15
Dreamboat, Doris Drew		A. L. Alexander, poetry	The Cities Service Band of America	9:30
		The Mutual Newsreel		9:45
Ralph Flanagan Orchestra	My Friend Irma	Frank Edwards, news	NBC Symphony Orchestra	10pm
		The Show Shop		10:15
News of Tomorrow	The Bob Hawk Show			10:30
The Three Suns				10:45

EVENING — SPRING, 1951

Sunday

	ABC	CBS	MBS	NBC
6pm	Around the Clock	Allan Jackson, news	Lyle Van, news	Bob Edwards, news
6:15		You and the World	Bob Elson Interviews	The Answer Man
6:30		Curt Massey, songs	Fred Vandeventer, news	Bill Stern, sports
6:45		Lowell Thomas, news	Stan Lomax, sports	Three Star Extra
7pm	Taylor Grant, news	The Beulah Show	Fulton Lewis Jr., news	The Longines Symphonette
7:15	Elmer Davis, news	The Jack Smith Show	Tello-Test Quiz	
7:30	Armstrong of the SBI	Club Fifteen	Gabriel Heatter, news	Morgan Beatty, news
7:45		Edward R. Murrow, news	Bing Crosby Records	One Man's Family
8pm	Can You Top This	Mystery Theater	The Damon Runyon Theater	The Cavalcade of America
8:15				
8:30	I Fly Anything	Mr. and Mrs. North	Official Detective	The Baby Snooks Show
8:45			Bill Henry, news (8:55pm)	
9pm	America's Town Meeting of the Air	Life with Luigi	John Steele, Adventurer	The Bob Hope Show
9:15				
9:30		Truth or Consequences	Incredible, But True	Fibber Magee and Molly
9:45	Edwin D. Canham, news		The Mutual Newsreel	
10pm	Time for Defense	The Lineup	Frank Edwards, news	Big Town
10:15			The Show Shop	
10:30	News of Tomorrow	Capitol Cloak Room		People Are Funny
10:45	The Three Suns			

EVENING — SPRING, 1951

Monday

ABC	CBS	MBS	NBC	
The Allen Stuart Show	Allan Jackson, news	Lyle Van, news	Bob Edwards, news	*6pm*
	You and the World	Bob Elson Interviews	The Answer Man	*6:15*
	Curt Massey, songs	Fred Vandeventer, news	Bill Stern, sports	*6:30*
	Lowell Thomas, news	Stan Lomax, sports	Three Star Extra	*6:45*
Taylor Grant, news	The Beulah Show	Fulton Lewis Jr., news	The Longines Symphonette	*7pm*
Elmer Davis, news	The Jack Smith Show	Tello-Test Quiz		*7:15*
The Lone Ranger	Club Fifteen	Gabriel Heatter, news	Morgan Beatty, news	*7:30*
	Edward R. Murrow, news	Friendly Bandstand	One Man's Family	*7:45*
Bob Barcley, American Agent	Mr. Chameleon		The Halls of Ivy	*8pm*
				8:15
The Fat Man	Dr. Christian		The Great Gildersleeve	*8:30*
		Bill Henry, news (8:55pm)		*8:45*
Rogue's Gallery	Honest Harold	The Mysterious Traveler	You Bet Your Life	*9pm*
				9:15
Mr. President	The Bing Crosby Chesterfield Show	A. L. Alexander, poetry	Mr. District Attorney	*9:30*
		The Mutual Newsreel		*9:45*
Shoot the Moon	The Wednesday Night Fights	Frank Edwards, news	The Big Story	*10pm*
		The Show Shop		*10:15*
News of Tomorrow			NBC Presents: Short Story	*10:30*
The Three Suns	Henry Jerome Orchestra			*10:45*

EVENING — SPRING, 1951

Thursday

	ABC	CBS	MBS	NBC
6pm	Around the Clock	Allan Jackson, news	Lyle Van, news	Bob Edwards, news
6:15		You and the World	Bob Elson Interviews	The Answer Man
6:30		Curt Massey, songs	Fred Vandeventer, news	Bill Stern, sports
6:45		Lowell Thomas, news	Stan Lomax, sports	Three Star Extra
7pm	Taylor Grant, news	The Beulah Show	Fulton Lewis Jr., news	The Longines Symphonette
7:15	Elmer Davis, news	The Jack Smith Show	Tello-Test Quiz	
7:30	Armstrong of the SBI	Club Fifteen	Gabriel Heatter, news	Morgan Beatty, news
7:45		Edward R. Murrow, news	Bing Crosby Records	One Man's Family
8pm	The Screen Guild Theater	The FBI in Peace and War	Let's Do It Now	The Aldrich Family
8:15				
8:30		Mr. Keen, Tracer of Lost Persons	The Rod and Gun Club	Father Knows Best
8:45			Bill Henry, news (8:55pm)	
9pm	Ted Mack's Original Amateur Hour	Suspense	The Family Theater	Dragnet
9:15				
9:30		The Hallmark Playhouse	Incredible, But True	Counterspy
9:45	Robert Montgomery Speaking		The Mutual Newsreel	
10pm	Newstand Theater	The Phillip Morris Playhouse	Frank Edwards, news	The Screen Director's Playhouse
10:15			The Show Shop	
10:30	News of Tomorrow	Freddie Martin Orchestra		
10:45	The Three Suns			

EVENING — SPRING, 1951

Friday

ABC	CBS	MBS	NBC	
The Allen Stuart Show	Allan Jackson, news	Lyle Van, news	Bob Edwards, news	6pm
	You and the World	Bob Elson Interviews	The Answer Man	6:15
	Curt Massey, songs	Fred Vandeventer, news	Bill Stern, sports	6:30
	Lowell Thomas, news	Stan Lomax, sports	Three Star Extra	6:45
Taylor Grant, news	The Beulah Show	Fulton Lewis Jr., news	The Longines Symphonette	7pm
Elmer Davis, news	The Jack Smith Show	Tello-Test Quiz		7:15
The Lone Ranger	Club Fifteen	Gabriel Heatter, news	Morgan Beatty, news	7:30
	Edward R. Murrow, news	Friendly Bandstand	One Man's Family	7:45
Richard Diamond, Private Detective	Songs for Sale		The New Adventures of Nero Wolfe	8pm
				8:15
This is Your FBI			The Adventures of Sam Spade	8:30
		Bill Henry, news (8:55pm)		8:45
The Adventures of Ozzie and Harriet	Hear It Now	Two Thousand Plus	The Magnificent Montague	9pm
				9:15
The Sheriff		A. L. Alexander, poetry	Duffy's Tavern	9:30
		The Mutual Newsreel		9:45
Madison Square Garden Boxing	We Take Your Word	Frank Edwards, news	The Life of Riley	10pm
		The Show Shop		10:15
Joe Hasel's Sports Page	New York Story		The Colgate Sports Newsreel, Bill Stern	10:30
			Pro and Con	10:45

EVENING — SPRING, 1951

Saturday

	ABC	CBS	MBS	NBC
6pm	The Roger Renner Trio	Bob Hite, news	Lyle Van, news	Bob Edwards, news
6:15	Una Mae Carlisle, songs	CBS Views the Press	Inside News	The Answer Man
6:30	Harry Wismer, sports	The Saturday Sports Review	Fred Vandeventer, news	The NBC Spring Concert
6:45	The AFL-CIO Program	Larry Lesueur, news	Stan Lomax, sports	
7pm	Talking It Over	Yours Truly, Johnny Dollar	History in the Making	
7:15	Bert Andrews, news		Twin Views of the News	
7:30	The Cavalcade of Music	The Camel Caravan, Vaughn Monroe	Comedy of Errors	People Are Funny
7:45				
8pm		Gene Autry's Melody Ranch	Twenty Questions	Dangerous Assignment
8:15				
8:30		Hopalong Cassidy	Where to Retire	The Man Called X
8:45			Incredible, But True	
9pm		Gangbusters	Mutual Reporter's Round-Up	Your Hit Parade
9:15				
9:30		Broadway is My Beat	Magazine Theater	A Day in the Life of Dennis Day
9:45				
10pm		Sing It Again	The Chicago Theater of the Air	The Judy Canova Show
10:15				
10:30	Dixieland Jambake			Grand Ole Opry
10:45	The Three Suns			

DAYTIME — SPRING, 1951

Sunday

	ABC	CBS	MBS	NBC
9am	Rev. Barnhouse, religion	News	News	News
9:15		From the Organ Loft	Outwitting Your Years	The Comic Weekly Man
9:30	The Voice of Prophecy		The Mutual Radio Chapel	
9:45		St. Paul's Trinity Choir		Music
10am	Message of Israel	The CBS Church of the Air	Henry Gladstone, news	The National Radio Pulpit
10:15			The Stars of Song	
10:30	Negro College Choirs			The Horn and Hardart Children's Hour
10:45			Your Hymnal	
11am	Brunch with Kelvin Keech	The Salt Lake Tabernacle Choir	Henry Gladstone, news	
11:15	Frank and Ernest, religion		Brunch with Dorothy and Dick	
11:30	Christian in Action	Invitation to Learning		Edwin C. Hill, news
11:45				Citizens of the World
12pm	This Week in New York, Bert Bacharach	The People's Platform	Heatherton House	Tex and Jinx, talk
12:15				
12:30	The Piano Playhouse	Howard K. Smith, news	Bill Hillman, news	Great Shakespearean Moments
12:45		Charles Collingwood, news	Gabriel Heatter's Mailbag	
1pm	Dr. William Ward Ayer, talk	New York Philharmonic Orchestra	The Canary Pet Shop	The Quiz Kids
1:15			The Show Shop	
1:30	National Vespers			The American Forum of the Air
1:45				

DAYTIME — SPRING, 1951

Monday-Friday

ABC	CBS	MBS	NBC	
The Breakfast Club	This is New York, Danny O'Neill	Harry Hennessy, news	Tex and Jinx, talk (8:30am)	*9am*
		This is Allyn Edwards		*9:15*
		Alfred W. McCann, food	Andre Baruch, talk	*9:30*
	Tommy Riggs and Betty Lou			*9:45*
My True Story	Arthur Godfrey Time	Cecil Brown, news	Welcome, Travelers	*10am*
		Martha Deane, talk		*10:15*
Betty Crocker, cooking			Double or Nothing	*10:30*
Modern Romances				*10:45*
Victor Lindlahr, health		Prescott Robinson, news	Break the Bank	*11am*
David Amity		Tello-Test Quiz		*11:15*
Quick as a Flash	Grand Slam	Queen for a Day	The Jack Berch Show	*11:30*
	Rosemary		Dial Dave Garroway	*11:45*
Johnny Olsen's Luncheon Club	Wendy Warren and the News	Kate Smith Speaks	Charles F. McCarthy, news	*12pm*
	Aunt Jenny's True Life Stories	Kate Smith Sings	Skitch's Scrapbook	*12:15*
The Herb Sheldon Show	The Romance of Helen Trent	Henry Gladstone, news	Eleanor Roosevelt, talk	*12:30*
	Our Gal Sunday	Luncheon at Sardi's		*12:45*
Mary Margaret McBride, talk	Big Sister			*1pm*
	Ma Perkins		Pickens Party	*1:15*
	Young Dr. Malone	The Gloria Swanson Show	The Answer Man	*1:30*
	The Guiding Light		The Woman in My House	*1:45*

DAYTIME — SPRING, 1951

Sunday

	ABC	CBS	MBS	NBC
2pm	Sunday Notebook		Only Human	The Catholic Hour
2:15				
2:30	Christian Science Monitor	The Longines Symphonette	Top Tunes with Trendler	Bob Considine, sports
2:45	Between the Bookends			The Girl from Paris
3pm	This Week Around the World	News from Washington		Music with the Hormel Girls
3:15		Larry Lesueur, news		
3:30	The Hour of Decision	Your Tropical Trip		David Lawrence, news
3:45				John Cameron, Swayze, news
4pm	The Old Fashioned Revival Hour	Dollar a Minute		The Falcon
4:15				
4:30		Rate Your Mate	Martin Kane, Private Detective	The Saint
4:45				
5pm	Author Meets the Critics	Meet Frank Sinatra	The Shadow	The Phil Regan Show
5:15				
5:30	The Greatest Story Ever Told		True Detective Mysteries	Mr. and Mrs. Blandings
5:45		Ed Morgan, news		

DAYTIME — SPRING, 1951

Monday-Friday

ABC	CBS	MBS	NBC	
Ilka Chase, talk	The Second Mrs. Burton	Prescott Robinson, news	Double or Nothing	*2pm*
	Perry Mason	Cedric Foster, news		*2:15*
Sweeney and March	This is Nora Drake	Heatherton House	Live Like a Millionaire	*2:30*
Frances Scully, gossip	The Brighter Day			*2:45*
Welcome to Hollywood	Hilltop House	Buddy Rogers Orchestra	Life Can Be Beautiful	*3pm*
	King's Row		The Road of Life	*3:15*
Hannibal Cobb	House Party	The Jean Sablon Show	Pepper Young's Family	*3:30*
Talk Back with Happy Felton			The Right to Happiness	*3:45*
Dean Cameron, talk	Strike It Rich	Barbera Welles, talk	Mary Noble, Backstage Wife	*4pm*
			Stella Dallas	*4:15*
Nancy Booth Craig, talk	Missus Goes A Shopping	The Frank Bishop Show	Lorenzo Jones	*4:30*
			Young Widder Brown	*4:45*
Big Jon and Sparkie	Galen Drake, talk	Mark Trail /	When a Girl Marries	*5pm*
		Straight Arrow	Portia Faces Life	*5:15*
	Hits and Misses	Clyde Beatty Adventures /	Just Plain Bill	*5:30*
		Sky King	Front Page Farrell	*5:45*

DAYTIME — SPRING, 1951

Saturday

	ABC	CBS	MBS	NBC
9am	No School Today	This is New York, Danny O'Neill	Harry Hennesey, news	Platter Playground
9:15			Where to Retire	
9:30		Galen Drake, talk	The McCanns at Home	Boston Symphony Dress Rehearsal
9:45		The Garden Gate		
10am		Make Way for Youth	Henry Gladstone, news	Mind Your Manners
10:15			Bill Lang, news	
10:30		The Coke Club, Morton Downey	Let's Go	Mary Lee Taylor, cooking
10:45			Cecil Brown, news	
11am	Junior Junction	Let's Pretend	Your Home Beautiful	Archie Andrews
11:15			Inside News	
11:30	Bible Messages	The Somerset Maugham Theater	The Singing Marshall	Star's Review of the Hits
11:45	The Bill Watson Show			
12pm	The Home Gardener	The Armstrong Theater of Today	The Man on the Farm	Perry Como Records
12:15				
12:30	The American Farmer	Grand Central Station	Henry Gladstone, news	The US Marine Band
12:45			Lorraine Sherwood, talk	
1pm	The US Navy Band	Stars Over Hollywood	Festival of Opera	The National Farm and Home Hour
1:15				
1:30	The Baron Elliott Octet	Alias Jane Doe		The University of Chicago Round Table
1:45				

DAYTIME — SPRING, 1951

Saturday

	ABC	CBS	MBS	NBC
2pm	The Metropolitan Opera	Music with the Hormel Girls		Musiciana
2:15				
2:30		Galen Drake, talk		The House of Music
2:45		Plan for Survival		
3pm		Operation Ex-GI		
3:15		Adventures in Science		
3:30		Report from Overseas		
3:45		CBS Farm News	Country Capers	
4pm		Horse Racing		
4:15		Lee Castle Orchestra		
4:30		Cross-Section USA		
4:45			The Stars of Song	
5pm	Tea and Crumpets	Radio Reporter's Scratchpad	Friendly Bandstand	
5:15		Price of Peace		
5:30	Vacationland, USA	Saturday at the Chase		Living 1951
5:45	Club Time			

EVENING — SUMMER, 1951

Sunday

	ABC	CBS	MBS	NBC
6pm	Drew Pearson, news	The Atlantic City String Band	Challenge of the Yukon	You Can't Take It With You
6:15	Don Gardiner, news			
6:30	QED Quiz	St. Louis Municipal Opera	Nick Carter, Master Detective	Archie Andrews
6:45				
7pm	Buzz Adlam's Playroom	Guy Lombardo Orchestra	Wild Bill Hickok	The Quiz Kids
7:15				
7:30	The Ted Mack Family Hour	Fiesta	Melvin Elliott, news	The New Theater
7:45			Bill Lang, news	
8pm	Stop the Music	The Mario Lanza Show	This is Europe	
8:15				
8:30		The Youth Opportunity Program	The Sunday Concert	The Theater Guild on the Air
8:45				
9pm	Patti Page, songs	Broadway is My Beat	The Opera Concert	
9:15	Jane Wyman, gossip			
9:30	The Law and You	Melody Ballroom, Jo Stafford	Gabriel Heatter, news	Mr. I. A. Moto
9:45	Dr. Gino's Musicale		George Fielding Eliot, comment	
10pm	Paul Harvey, news	Music for You	Magazine Theater	The $64 Question
10:15	Gloria Parker, news			
10:30	George Sokolsky, news	The Longines Choraliers	The Health Clinic	The American Forum of the Air
10:45	My Lucky Stars		These Stories Are Yours	

EVENING — SUMMER, 1951

Monday

ABC	CBS	MBS	NBC	
The Allen Stuart Show	Allan Jackson, news	News on the Human Side	Bob Edwards, news	6pm
	You and the World	Tello-Test Quiz	The Answer Man	6:15
	Curt Massey, songs	Fred Vandeventer, news	Bill Stern, sports	6:30
	Ron Cochran, news	Stan Lomax, sports	Three Star Extra	6:45
Taylor Grant, news	Robert Q. Lewis's Waxworks	Fulton Lewis Jr., news	The Longines Symphonette	7pm
Quincy Howe, news		Behind the Story		7:15
The Lone Ranger		Gabriel Heatter, news	Morgan Beatty, news	7:30
	Don Hollenbeck, news	Bing Crosby Records	One Man's Family	7:45
The Man from Homicide	How To	War Front, Home Front	The Railroad Hour	8pm
				8:15
Henry J. Taylor, news	Arthur Godfrey's Talent Scouts	Crime Fighters	The Voice of Firestone	8:30
The Lonesome Road		Bill Henry, news (8:55pm)		8:45
United or Not	Theater of Romance	Murder By Experts	The Bell Telephone Hour	9pm
				9:15
Ghost Stories	Meet Millie	A. L. Alexander, poetry	The Cities Service Band of America	9:30
		The Mutual Newsreel		9:45
Art Waner Orchestra	The Straw Hat Concerts	Frank Edwards, news	Boston Pops Orchestra	10pm
		The Show Shop		10:15
News of Tomorrow	Dance Orchestra			10:30
Martha Lou Harp, songs	Galen Drake, talk			10:45

EVENING — SUMMER, 1951

Tuesday

	ABC	CBS	MBS	NBC
6pm	The Allen Stuart Show	Allan Jackson, news	News on the Human Side	Bob Edwards, news
6:15		You and the World	Tello-Test Quiz	The Answer Man
6:30		Curt Massey, songs	Fred Vandeventer, news	Bill Stern, sports
6:45		Ron Cochran, news	Stan Lomax, sports	Three Star Extra
7pm	Taylor Grant, news	Robert Q. Lewis's Waxworks	Fulton Lewis Jr., news	The Longines Symphonette
7:15	Quincy Howe, news		Behind the Story	
7:30	Mr. Mercury		Gabriel Heatter, news	Morgan Beatty, news
7:45		Don Hollenbeck, news	Bing Crosby Records	One Man's Family
8pm	Chance of a Lifetime	Operation Underground	The Count of Monte Cristo	American Portraits
8:15				
8:30	The Sea Hound	Mr. and Mrs. North	Official Detective	Carmen Dragon
8:45			Bill Henry, news (8:55pm)	
9pm	America's Town Meeting of the Air	Pursuit	John Steele, Adventurer	It's Higgins, Sir
9:15				
9:30		The Bickersons	The Health Clinic	The Jack Pearl Show
9:45	Edwin D. Canham, news		The Mutual Newsreel	
10pm	Time for Defense	Capital Cloak Room	Frank Edwards, news	Big Town
10:15			The Show Shop	
10:30	News of Tomorrow	Dance Orchestra		Summer Time Serenade
10:45	Martha Lou Harp, songs	Galen Drake, talk		

EVENING — SUMMER, 1951

Wednesday

ABC	CBS	MBS	NBC	
The Allen Stuart Show	Allan Jackson, news	News on the Human Side	Bob Edwards, news	*6pm*
	You and the World	Tello-Test Quiz	The Answer Man	*6:15*
	Curt Massey, songs	Fred Vandeventer, news	Bill Stern, sports	*6:30*
	Ron Cochran, news	Stan Lomax, sports	Three Star Extra	*6:45*
Taylor Grant, news	Robert Q. Lewis's Waxworks	Fulton Lewis Jr., news	The Longines Symphonette	*7pm*
Quincy Howe, news		Behind the Story		*7:15*
The Lone Ranger		Gabriel Heatter, news	Morgan Beatty, news	*7:30*
	Don Hollenbeck, news	Bing Crosby Records	One Man's Family	*7:45*
Bob Barcley, American Agent	Rocky Jordan	The Hidden Truth	Pete Kelly's Blues	*8pm*
				8:15
The Fat Man	Dr. Christian	International Airport	The Private Files of Rex Saunders	*8:30*
		Bill Henry, news (8:55pm)		*8:45*
Rogue's Gallery	Escape	The Mysterious Traveler	It Pays to Be Ignorant	*9pm*
				9:15
Mr. President	Yours Truly, Johnny Dollar	A. L. Alexander, poetry	Mr. District Attorney	*9:30*
		The Mutual Newsreel		*9:45*
The Treasury Band Show	The Wednesday Night Fights	Frank Edwards, news	The Big Story	*10pm*
		The Show Shop		*10:15*
News of Tomorrow	Dance Orchestra		Meredith Willson's Music Room	*10:30*
Martha Lou Harp, songs	Galen Drake, talk			*10:45*

EVENING — SUMMER, 1951

Thursday

	ABC	CBS	MBS	NBC
6pm	The Allen Stuart Show	Allan Jackson, news	News on the Human Side	Bob Edwards, news
6:15		You and the World	Tello-Test Quiz	The Answer Man
6:30		Curt Massey, songs	Fred Vandeventer, news	Bill Stern, sports
6:45		Ron Cochran, news	Stan Lomax, sports	Three Star Extra
7pm	Taylor Grant, news	Robert Q. Lewis's Waxworks	Fulton Lewis Jr., news	The Longines Symphonette
7:15	Quincy Howe, news		Behind the Story	
7:30	The Silver Eagle		Gabriel Heatter, news	Morgan Beatty, news
7:45		Don Hollenbeck, news	Bing Crosby Records	One Man's Family
8pm	Newstand Theater	The FBI in Peace and War	The Damon Runyon Theater	The Truitts
8:15				
8:30	The Hollywood Star Playhouse	The Nation's Nightmare		Dimension X
8:45			Bill Henry, news (8:55pm)	
9pm	Ted Mack's Original Amateur Hour	The Lineup	The Family Theater	Dragnet
9:15				
9:30		The Phillip Morris Playhouse	Incredible, But True	Counterspy
9:45	Foreign Reporter		The Mutual Newsreel	
10pm	The All-Sergeant Jazz Band	Dance Orchestra	Frank Edwards, news	The Screen Director's Playhouse
10:15			The Show Shop	
10:30	News of Tomorrow			
10:45	Martha Lou Harp, songs	Galen Drake, talk		

EVENING — SUMMER, 1951

Friday

ABC	CBS	MBS	NBC	
The Allen Stuart Show	Allan Jackson, news	News on the Human Side	Bob Edwards, news	6pm
	You and the World	Tello-Test Quiz	The Answer Man	6:15
	Curt Massey, songs	Fred Vandeventer, news	Bill Stern, sports	6:30
	Ron Cochran, news	Stan Lomax, sports	Three Star Extra	6:45
Taylor Grant, news	Robert Q. Lewis's Waxworks	Fulton Lewis Jr., news	The Longines Symphonette	7pm
Quincy Howe, news		Behind the Story		7:15
The Lone Ranger		Gabriel Heatter, news	Morgan Beatty, news	7:30
	Don Hollenbeck, news	Bing Crosby Records	One Man's Family	7:45
Defense Attorney	The Spade Cooley Show	Mystery is My Hobby	The Man Called X	8pm
				8:15
This is Your FBI		Miguelito Valdez Orchestra	Nightbeat	8:30
		Bill Henry, news (8:55pm)		8:45
A Life in Your Hands	The Rayburn and Finch Show	Mutual Reporter's Round Up	Inspector Thorne	9pm
				9:15
The Sheriff		A. L. Alexander, poetry	Mr. Keen, Tracer of Lost Persons	9:30
		The Mutual Newsreel		9:45
Dance Orchestra	New York Story	Frank Edwards, news	Roy Shield and Company	10pm
		The Show Shop		10:15
Orrin Tucker Orchestra	Dance Orchestra		The Colgate Sports Newsreel, Bill Stern	10:30
	Galen Drake, talk		Pro and Con	10:45

EVENTING — SUMMER, 1951

Saturday

	ABC	CBS	MBS	NBC
6pm	The Roger Renner Trio	Bob Hite, news	Lyle Van, news	Bob Edwards, news
6:15	Una Mae Carlisle, songs	The Atlantic City String Band	Incredible, But True	The Answer Man
6:30	Harry Wismer, sports	The Saturday Sports Review	Fred Vandeventer, news	The NBC Summer Concert
6:45	The AFL-CIO Program	Larry Lesueur, news	Stan Lomax, sports	
7pm	It's Your Business	Your Tropical Trip	History in the Making	
7:15	Bert Andrews, news		Twin Views of the News	
7:30	The Cavalcade of Music	The Camel Caravan, Vaughn Monroe	Comedy of Errors	Living 1951
7:45				
8pm		Gene Autry's Melody Ranch	Twenty Questions	The Musical Merry-Go-Round
8:15				
8:30		The Adventures of Philip Marlowe	Take a Number	The Magnificent Montague
8:45				
9pm		Gangbusters	Hawaii Calls	Al Goodman Musical Album
9:15				
9:30		Mr. Aladdin	Lombardoland USA	Bob and Ray
9:45				
10pm		Songs for Sale	The Chicago Theater of the Air	
10:15				
10:30	Dixieland Jambake			Grand Ole Opry
10:45	The Can-Do Club			

DAYTIME — SUMMER, 1951

Sunday

	ABC	CBS	MBS	NBC
9am	Rev. Barnhouse, religion	Keyboard Concerts	News	News
9:15		News	Where to Retire	The Comic Weekly Man
9:30	The Voice of Prophecy	From the Organ Loft	The Mutual Radio Chapel	
9:45				Music
10am	Message of Israel	The CBS Church of the Air	Henry Gladstone, news	The National Radio Pulpit
10:15			The Health Clinic	
10:30	Negro College Choirs		The Stars of Song	The Horn and Hardart Children's Hour
10:45			Your Hymnal	
11am	Brunch with Kelvin Keech	The Salt Lake Tabernacle Choir	Henry Gladstone, news	
11:15	Frank and Ernest, religion		Brunch with Dorothy and Dick	
11:30	Christian in Action	Invitation to Learning		Edwin C. Hill, news
11:45				This is My Favorite
12pm	Next Week in New York	The People's Platform	Heatherton House	Tex and Jinx, talk
12:15				
12:30	The Piano Playhouse	Howard K. Smith, news	Bill Hillman, news	The Eternal Light
12:45		Larry Lesueur, news	In the Neighborhood	
1pm	Dr. William Ward Ayer, talk	Your Invitation to Music	Fred Vandeventer, news	Yesterday, Today and Tomorrow
1:15			In the Doctor's Office	
1:30	National Vespers		The Show Shop	Salute to the NBC Symphony
1:45				

DAYTIME — SUMMER, 1951

Monday-Friday

ABC	CBS	MBS	NBC	
The Breakfast Club	This is New York, Danny O'Neill	Harry Hennessy, news	Tex and Jinx, talk (8:30am)	*9am*
		This is Allyn Edwards		*9:15*
		Alfred W. McCann, food	Andre Baruch, talk	*9:30*
	Tommy Riggs and Betty Lou			*9:45*
My True Story	Arthur Godfrey Time	Cecil Brown, news	Welcome, Travelers	*10am*
		Martha Deane, talk		*10:15*
Betty Crocker, cooking			Double or Nothing	*10:30*
Modern Romances				*10:45*
The Strange Romance of Evelyn Winters		Prescott Robinson, news	Break the Bank	*11am*
David Amity		Tello-Test Quiz		*11:15*
When a Girl Marries	Grand Slam	Queen for a Day	The Jack Berch Show	*11:30*
Lone Journey	Rosemary		Dial Dave Garroway	*11:45*
Thy Neighbor's Voice	Wendy Warren and the News	Curt Massey, songs	Charles F. McCarthy, news	*12pm*
Headlines in the News	Aunt Jenny's True Life Stories	Kate Smith Sings	Skitch's Scrapbook	*12:15*
The Herb Sheldon Show	The Romance of Helen Trent	Henry Gladstone, news	Eleanor Roosevelt, talk	*12:30*
	Our Gal Sunday	Luncheon at Sardi's		*12:45*
Mary Margaret McBride, talk	Big Sister			*1pm*
	Ma Perkins		Pickens Party	*1:15*
	Young Dr. Malone	The Gloria Swanson Show	The Answer Man	*1:30*
	The Guiding Light		Eve Young, songs	*1:45*

DAYTIME — SUMMER, 1951

Sunday

	ABC	CBS	MBS	NBC
2pm	Sunday Notebook		The Jean Sablon Show	The Catholic Hour
2:15				
2:30	Christian Science Monitor	The Longines Symphonette	Two-Thousand Plus	Bob Considine, sports
2:45	Altar Bound			The Girl from Paris
3pm	Sammy Kaye's Sunday Serenade	News from Washington	Hashknife Hartley and Sleepy Stevens	Music with the Hormel Girls
3:15		Larry Lesueur, news		
3:30	The Hour of Decision	Music from Pittsburgh	The Singing Marshall	David Lawrence, news
3:45				John Cameron Swayze, news
4pm	The Old Fashioned Revival Hour	Music from Hollywood	Bobby Benson	The Saint
4:15				
4:30		Music from St. Louis	Under Arrest	Martin Kane, Private Detective
4:45				
5pm	Country Style	The Main Street Music Hall	The Shadow	The Whisperer
5:15				
5:30	This Week Around the World	The Phil Regan Show	True Detective Mysteries	Now Hear This
5:45				

DAYTIME — SUMMER, 1951

Monday-Friday

ABC	CBS	MBS	NBC	
Ilka Chase, talk	The Second Mrs. Burton	Prescott Robinson, news	Double or Nothing	2pm
	Perry Mason	Pat Barnes and Barbera, talk		2:15
The Perfect Husband	This is Nora Drake	Heatherton House	Live Like a Millionaire	2:30
	The Brighter Day			2:45
Family Circle	Hilltop House	Buddy Rogers Orchestra	Life Can Be Beautiful	3pm
	King's Row		The Road of Life	3:15
	House Party	Ladies Fair	Pepper Young's Family	3:30
			The Right to Happiness	3:45
Dean Cameron, talk	Strike It Rich	Barbera Welles, talk	Mary Noble, Backstage Wife	4pm
			Stella Dallas	4:15
Manhattan Maharajah	Missus Goes A Shopping	Talk Back with Happy Felton	Young Widder Brown	4:30
			The Woman in My House	4:45
Big Jon and Sparkie	Galen Drake, talk	Bobby Sherwood Orchestra /	Just Plain Bill	5pm
		Challenge of the Yukon	Front Page Farrell	5:15
Between the Bookends	Hits and Misses	The Singing Marshall /	Lorenzo Jones	5:30
Paul Harvey, news		Bobby Benson	Bob and Ray	5:45

DAYTIME — SUMMER, 1951

Saturday

	ABC	CBS	MBS	NBC
9am	No School Today	This is New York, Danny O'Neill	Harry Hennesey, news	The Walt Disney Program
9:15			The Health Clinic	
9:30		Galen Drake, talk	The McCanns at Home	Jackie Robinson, sports
9:45		The Garden Gate		
10am		Lee Kelton Orchestra	Henry Gladstone, news	Mind Your Manners
10:15			Martha Deane, talk	
10:30		Dave Stephens Orchestra		Mary Lee Taylor, cooking
10:45				
11am	Junior Junction	Let's Pretend	Prescott Robinson, news	Hollywood Love Story
11:15			The Health Clinic	
11:30	Bible Messages	Make Believe Town	Lorraine Sherwood, talk	My Secret Story
11:45	The Bill Watson Show			
12pm	The Home Gardener	The Armstrong Theater of Today	The Man on the Farm	The Windshield Wiper
12:15				Perry Como Records
12:30	The American Farmer	Grand Central Station	Henry Gladstone, news	Star's Reviews of the Hits
12:45			Let's Go	
1pm	The US Navy Band	Stars Over Hollywood	The Festival of Opera	The National Farm and Home Hour
1:15				
1:30	Vincent Lopez Orchestra	Alias Jane Doe		Rio Rhythms
1:45				

DAYTIME — SUMMER, 1951

Saturday

	ABC	CBS	MBS	NBC
2pm	Music of Today	Music with the Hormel Girls		Musiciana
2:15				
2:30	Happy Hayloft	Salute to the Navy		The House of Music
2:45		Plan for Survival		
3pm	Pan-American Union Concert	CBS Farm News		
3:15		Adventures in Science		
3:30	Concert of American Jazz	Report from Overseas		
3:45		Chuck Foster Orchestra		
4pm	Marines in Review	Joe Richman Orchestra	The Frank Bishop Show	
4:15			The Gus Lesnevich Show	
4:30	Roseland Ballroom Orchestra	Cross-Section USA		
4:45				
5pm	Tea and Crumpets	Radio Reporter's Scratchpad	Bobby Sherwood Orchestra	
5:15		The Price of Peace		
5:30	Altar Bound	Lee Castle Orchestra	Challenge of the Yukon	Big City Serenade
5:45	Club Time			

EVENING — FALL, 1951

Sunday

	ABC	CBS	MBS	NBC
6pm	Drew Pearson, news	My Friend Irma	Challenge of the Yukon	Tales of the Texas Rangers
6:15	Don Gardiner, news			
6:30	Stage 52	Our Miss Brooks	Nick Carter, Master Detective	The Big Show
6:45				
7pm		The Lucky Strike Program, Jack Benny	Under Arrest	
7:15				
7:30	The Ted Mack Family Hour	Amos 'n' Andy	Melvin Elliott, news	
7:45			Bill Lang, news	
8pm	Stop the Music	The Charlie McCarthy Show	The Singing Marshall	The Phil Harris - Alice Faye Show
8:15				
8:30		The Youth Opportunity Program	The Enchanted Hour	The Theater Guild on the Air
8:45				
9pm	Walter Winchell, gossip	Meet Corliss Archer	The Opera Concert	
9:15	Louella Parsons, gossip			
9:30	Hollywood Stars on Stage	The Carnation Contented Hour	Report from the Pentagon	The Eddie Cantor Show
9:45			George Fielding Elliot, comment	
10pm	Paul Harvey, news	Music for You	The Hidden Truth	The Silent Men
10:15	Gloria Parker, news			
10:30	George Sokolsky, news	The Longines Choraliers	The Health Clinic	The Jubilee Show
10:45	Dr. Gino's Musicale		These Stories Are Yours	

EVENING — FALL, 1951

Monday

ABC	CBS	MBS	NBC	
Walter Kiernan, news	Allan Jackson, news	News on the Human Side	Kenneth Banghart, news	6pm
The Allen Stuart Show	You and the World	Tello-Test Quiz	The Answer Man	6:15
	Curt Massey, songs	Fred Vandeventer, news	Bill Stern, sports	6:30
	Lowell Thomas, news	Stan Lomax, sports	Three Star Extra	6:45
Taylor Grant, news	The Beulah Show	Fulton Lewis Jr., news	The Longines Symphonette	7pm
Elmer Davis, news	The Jack Smith Show	Behind the Story		7:15
The Lone Ranger	Club Fifteen	Gabriel Heatter, news	Morgan Beatty, news	7:30
	Edward R. Murrow, news	The Mark Rogers Show	One Man's Family	7:45
The Big Hand	Suspense		The Railroad Hour	8pm
				8:15
Henry J. Taylor, news	Arthur Godfrey's Talent Scouts		The Voice of Firestone	8:30
Lonesome Road		Bill Henry, news (8:55pm)		8:45
Paul Whiteman's Teen Club	The Lux Radio Theater	Murder By Experts	The Bell Telephone Hour	9pm
				9:15
		Mystery House	The Cities Service Band of America	9:30
				9:45
News of Tomorrow	The Bob Hawk Show	Frank Edwards, news	The Mario Lanza Show	10pm
Martha Lou Harp, songs		The Show Shop		10:15
Art Waner Orchestra	Robert Q. Lewis's Waxworks		The Man Called X	10:30
				10:45

EVENING — FALL, 1951

Tuesday

	ABC	CBS	MBS	NBC
6pm	Walter Kiernan, news	Allan Jackson, news	News on the Human Side	Kenneth Banghart, news
6:15	The Allen Stuart Show	You and the World	Tello-Test Quiz	The Answer Man
6:30		Curt Massey, songs	Fred Vandeventer, news	Bill Stern, sports
6:45		Lowell Thomas, news	Stan Lomax, sports	Three Star Extra
7pm	Taylor Grant, news	The Beulah Show	Fulton Lewis Jr., news	The Longines Symphonette
7:15	Elmer Davis, news	The Jack Smith Show	Behind the Story	
7:30	Mr. Mercury	Club Fifteen	Gabriel Heatter, news	Morgan Beatty, news
7:45		Edward R. Murrow, news	The Mark Rogers Show	One Man's Family
8pm	Newstand Theater	People Are Funny		The Cavalcade of America
8:15				
8:30	Chance of a Lifetime	Mr. And Mrs. North		The Tums Hollywood Theater
8:45			Bill Henry, news (8:55pm)	
9pm	America's Town Meeting of the Air	Life with Luigi	John Steele, Adventurer	The Bob Hope Show
9:15				
9:30		Pursuit	The Health Clinic	Fibber Magee and Molly
9:45	Edwin D. Canham, news		Incredible, But True	
10pm	News of Tomorrow	Meet Millie	Frank Edwards, news	Big Town
10:15	Martha Lou Harp, songs		The Show Shop	
10:30	United or Not	Robert Q. Lewis's Waxworks		The Phillip Morris Playhouse on Broadway
10:45				

EVENING — FALL, 1951

Wednesday

ABC	CBS	MBS	NBC	
Walter Kiernan, news	Allan Jackson, news	News on the Human Side	Kenneth Banghart, news	6pm
The Allen Stuart Show	You and the World	Tello-Test Quiz	The Answer Man	6:15
	Curt Massey, songs	Fred Vandeventer, news	Bill Stern, sports	6:30
	Lowell Thomas, news	Stan Lomax, sports	Three Star Extra	6:45
Taylor Grant, news	The Beulah Show	Fulton Lewis Jr., news	The Longines Symphonette	7pm
Elmer Davis, news	The Jack Smith Show	Behind the Story		7:15
The Lone Ranger	Club Fifteen	Gabriel Heatter, news	Morgan Beatty, news	7:30
	Edward R. Murrow, news	The Mark Rogers Show	One Man's Family	7:45
Mystery Theater	Mr. Chameleon		The Halls of Ivy	8pm
				8:15
The Top Guy	Dr. Christian		The Great Gildersleeve	8:30
		Bill Henry, news (8:55pm)		8:45
Rogue's Gallery	The Red Skelton Show	Two-Thousand Plus	You Bet Your Life	9pm
				9:15
Mr. President	The Bing Crosby Chesterfield Show	The Family Theater	The Big Story	9:30
				9:45
News of Tomorrow	The Wednesday Night Fights	Frank Edwards, news	Barrie Craig, Confidential Investigator	10pm
Martha Lou Harp, songs		The Show Shop		10:15
The Can-Do Club	Henry Jerome Orchestra		Meredith Willson's Music Room	10:30
Art Waner Orchestra				10:45

EVENING — FALL, 1951

Thursday

	ABC	CBS	MBS	NBC
6pm	Walter Kiernan, news	Allan Jackson, news	News on the Human Side	Kenneth Banghart, news
6:15	The Allen Stuart Show	You and the World	Tello-Test Quiz	The Answer Man
6:30		Curt Massey, songs	Fred Vandeventer, news	Bill Stern, sports
6:45		Lowell Thomas, news	Stan Lomax, sports	Three Star Extra
7pm	Taylor Grant, news	The Beulah Show	Fulton Lewis Jr., news	The Longines Symphonette
7:15	Elmer Davis, news	The Jack Smith Show	Behind the Story	
7:30	The Silver Eagle	Club Fifteen	Gabriel Heatter, news	Morgan Beatty, news
7:45		Edward R. Murrow, news	The Mark Rogers Show	One Man's Family
8pm	Defense Attorney	The FBI in Peace and War		Father Knows Best
8:15				
8:30	The Hollywood Star Playhouse	The Hallmark Playhouse		Mr. Keen, Tracer of Lost Persons
8:45			Bill Henry, news (8:55pm)	
9pm	Ted Mack's Original Amateur Hour	Hearthstone of the Death Squad	The Rod and Gun Club	Dragnet
9:15				
9:30		Operation Underground	Mutual Reporter's Round-Up	Counterspy
9:45	Foreign Reporter			
10pm	News of Tomorrow	The Lineup	Frank Edwards, news	Your Hit Parade
10:15	Martha Lou Harp, songs		The Show Shop	
10:30	The All-Sergeant Jazz Band	Robert Q. Lewis's Waxworks		Al Goodman Musical Album
10:45				

EVENING — FALL, 1951

Friday

ABC	CBS	MBS	NBC	
Walter Kiernan, news	Allan Jackson, news	News on the Human Side	Kenneth Banghart, news	6pm
The Allen Stuart Show	You and the World	Tello-Test Quiz	The Answer Man	6:15
	Curt Massey, songs	Fred Vandeventer, news	Bill Stern, sports	6:30
	Lowell Thomas, news	Stan Lomax, sports	Three Star Extra	6:45
Taylor Grant, news	The Beulah Show	Fulton Lewis Jr., news	The Longines Symphonette	7pm
Elmer Davis, news	The Jack Smith Show	Behind the Story		7:15
The Lone Ranger	Club Fifteen	Gabriel Heatter, news	Morgan Beatty, news	7:30
	Edward R. Murrow, news	The Mark Rogers Show	One Man's Family	7:45
Richard Diamond, Private Detective	The Grantland Rice Story		The Roy Rogers Show	8pm
	Musicland USA			8:15
This is Your FBI			The Martin and Lewis Show	8:30
		Bill Henry, news (8:55pm)		8:45
The Adventures of Ozzie and Harriet	The Big Time, Georgie Price	The Mysterious Traveler	Duffy's Tavern	9pm
				9:15
Mr. District Attorney	Paul Weston Orchestra	Magazine Theater	You Can't Take It With You	9:30
				9:45
Madison Square Garden Boxing	Capitol Cloakroom	Frank Edwards, news	Missions of the World	10pm
		The Show Shop	News	10:15
Joe Hasel's Sports Page	Dance Orchestra		Bill Stern Sports	10:30
			Pro and Con	10:45

EVENING — FALL, 1951

Saturday

	ABC	CBS	MBS	NBC
6pm	Una Mae Carlisle, songs	Joe Wershba, news	News on the Human Side	Kenneth Banghart, news
6:15	Faith for the Future	Treasury Bandstand	Incredible, But True	H. V. Kaltenborn, news
6:30	Harry Wismer, sports	The Saturday Sports Review	Fred Vandeventer, news	NBC Symphony Orchestra
6:45	As We See It	Larry Lesueur, news	Stan Lomax, sports	
7pm	The Chamber of Commerce	Yours Truly, Johnny Dollar	History in the Making	
7:15	Bert Andrews, news		Twin Views of the News	
7:30	The Great Adventure	The Camel Caravan, Vaughn Monroe	Comedy of Errors	Archie Andrews
7:45				
8pm	ABC Dancing Party	Gene Autry's Melody Ranch	Twenty Questions	The Magnificent Montague
8:15				
8:30		Hopalong Cassidy	Take a Number	Bob and Ray
8:45				
9pm		Gangbusters	Hawaii Calls	The Judy Canova Show
9:15				
9:30		Broadway is My Beat	Lombardoland USA	Grand Ole Opry
9:45				
10pm	Saturday at the Shamrock	Robert Q. Lewis's Waxworks	The Chicago Theater of the Air	Dangerous Assignment
10:15				
10:30	The Treasury Band Show			Jane Ace, Disc Jockey
10:45				

DAYTIME — FALL, 1951

Sunday

	ABC	CBS	MBS	NBC
9am	Rev. Barnhouse, religion	St. Paul's Trinity Choir	News	News
9:15		News	Where to Retire	The Comic Weekly Man
9:30	The Voice of Prophecy	From the Organ Loft	The Mutual Radio Chapel	
9:45				Music
10am	Message of Israel	The CBS Church of the Air	Henry Gladstone, news	The National Radio Pulpit
10:15			The Health Clinic	
10:30	Negro College Choirs		In the Neighborhood	The Horn and Hardart Children's Hour
10:45			Your Hymnal	
11am	Charles Antell, talk	The Salt Lake Tabernacle Choir	Henry Gladstone, news	
11:15	Frank and Ernest, religion		Brunch with Dorothy and Dick	
11:30	Christian in Action	Invitation to Learning		Charles F. McCarthy, news
11:45				This is My Favorite Music
12pm	Concert of Europe	The People's Platform	Heatherton House	
12:15				
12:30	The Piano Playhouse	Howard K. Smith, news	Melvin Elliott, news	The Eternal Light
12:45		Charles Collingwood, news	The Canary Pet Shop	
1pm	Dr. William Ward Ayer, talk	String Serenade	Fred Vandeventer, news	Yesterday, Today and Tomorrow
1:15			In the Doctor's Office	
1:30	National Vespers	Starlight Melodies	The Show Shop	What's the Score
1:45				

DAYTIME — FALL, 1951

Monday-Friday

ABC	CBS	MBS	NBC	
The Breakfast Club	This is New York, Danny O'Neil	Harry Hennessy, news	Tex and Jinx, talk (8:30am)	9am
		John Gambling's Second Breakfast		9:15
		Alfred W. McCann, food	Andre Baruch, talk	9:30
	Tommy Riggs and Betty Lou			9:45
My True Story	Arthur Godfrey Time	Henry Gladstone, news	Welcome, Travelers	10am
		Martha Deane, talk		10:15
Betty Crocker, cooking			Double or Nothing	10:30
Against the Storm				10:45
Lone Journey		Ladies Fair	Strike It Rich	11am
When a Girl Marries				11:15
Break the Bank	Grand Slam	Queen for a Day	King's Row	11:30
	Rosemary		Dial Dave Garroway	11:45
The Jack Berch Show	Wendy Warren and the News	Curt Massey, songs	The Kate Smith Program	12pm
Victor Lindlahr, health	Aunt Jenny's True Life Stories	Guest Time / Jimmy Carroll, songs		12:15
The Herb Sheldon Show	The Romance of Helen Trent	Henry Gladstone, news		12:30
	Our Gal Sunday	Luncheon at Sardi's	Skitch's Scrapbook	12:45
Mary Margaret McBride, talk	Big Sister			1pm
	Ma Perkins			1:15
	Young Dr. Malone	The Gloria Swanson Show	The Answer Man	1:30
	The Guiding Light		Pickens Party	1:45

DAYTIME — FALL, 1951

Sunday

	ABC	CBS	MBS	NBC
2pm	Marines in Review	The Longines Symphonette		The Catholic Hour
2:15				
2:30	Christian Science Monitor	New York Philharmonic Orchestra	The Jean Sablon Show	The American Forum of the Air
2:45	Between the Bookends			
3pm	This Week Around the World		The Count of Monte Crisco	Music with the Hormel Girls
3:15				
3:30	The Hour of Decision		Official Detective	David Lawrence, news
3:45				John Cameron Swayze, news
4pm	The Old Fashioned Revival Hour	Saved by the Mail	The Affairs of Peter Salem	The Saint
4:15		Edwin C. Hill, news		
4:30		The Frankie Laine Show	Wild Bill Hickok	Martin Kane, Private Detective
4:45				
5pm	Sammy Kaye's Sylvania Serenade	Arthur Godfrey's Digest	The Shadow	The Whisperer
5:15		Treasury Bandstand		
5:30	The Greatest Story Ever Told	How To	True Detective Mysteries	Now Hear This
5:45				

DAYTIME — FALL, 1951

Monday-Friday

ABC	CBS	MBS	NBC	
Manhattan Maharajah	Second Mrs. Burton	Prescott Robinson, news	Double or Nothing	2pm
Late News	Perry Mason	Pat Barnes and Barbera, talk		2:15
Family Circle	This is Nora Drake	A. L. Alexander's Mediation Board	Live Like a Millionaire	2:30
	The Brighter Day			2:45
	Hilltop House	Rambling with Gambling	Life Can Be Beautiful	3pm
	House Party		The Road of Life	3:15
The Story of Mary Marlin		Heatherton House	Pepper Young's Family	3:30
The Strange Romance of Evelyn Winters			The Right to Happiness	3:45
Valiant Lady	Strike It Rich	Barbera Welles, talk	Mary Noble, Backstage Wife	4pm
Marriage for Two			Stella Dallas	4:15
Dean Cameron, talk	Missus Goes A Shopping	Talk Back with Happy Felton	Young Widder Brown	4:30
			The Woman in My House	4:45
Big Jon and Sparkie	Galen Drake, talk	Bobby Sherwood Orchestra / Challenge of the Yukon	Just Plain Bill	5pm
			Front Page Farrell	5:15
Mark Trail /	Hits and Misses	Sky King /	Lorenzo Jones	5:30
Fun Factory		Clyde Beatty's Adventures	Bob and Ray	5:45

DAYTIME — FALL, 1951

Saturday

	ABC	CBS	MBS	NBC
9am	No School Today	This is New York, Danny O'Neill	Harry Hennessy, news	The Frank Luther Show
9:15			The Health Clinic	
9:30		Galen Drake, talk	The McCanns at Home	Jackie Robinson, sports
9:45				
10am		Lee Kelton Orchestra	Henry Gladstone, news	Mind Your Manners
10:15			Martha Deane, talk	
10:30	Space Patrol	Make Way for Youth		Mary Lee Taylor, cooking
10:45				
11am	Junior Junction	Let's Pretend	Prescott Robinson, news	Hollywood Love Story
11:15			Here's to Vets	
11:30	The Eddie Fisher Show	Give and Take	Lorraine Sherwood, talk	My Secret Story
11:45				
12pm	The Home Gardener	The Armstrong Theater of Today	The Man on the Farm	The Windshield Wiper
12:15				Perry Como Records
12:30	The American Farmer	Stars Over Hollywood	Henry Gladstone, news	Star's Reviews of the Hits
12:45			Let's Go	
1pm	The US Navy Band	Grand Central Station	The Armed Forces Review	The National Farm and Home Hour
1:15			The Mystery Singer	
1:30	Vincent Lopez Orchestra	City Hospital	Win, Lose or Draw	Uncle Sam's Playhouse
1:45			Sports	

DAYTIME — FALL, 1951

Saturday

	ABC	CBS	MBS	NBC
2pm	Sports	Music with the Hormel Girls		
2:15				
2:30		Sports Round-Up		The House of Music
2:45				
3pm		CBS Farm News		
3:15		Adventures in Science		
3:30		Report from Overseas		
3:45		Griff Williams Orchestra		
4pm		Stan Dougherty Orchestra		
4:15		Horse Racing		
4:30		Cross-Section USA		
4:45			Between the Games	
5pm	Roseland Ballroom Orchestra		Bobby Sherwood Orchestra	
5:15		Don Grimes Orchestra		The Music Hall of Fame
5:30		Sports Scores	The Gus Lesnevich Show	Sports Round-Up
5:45	Club Time	Operation Ex-GI		Bob Considine, sports

LISTINGS FOR 1952

EVENING — WINTER, 1952

Sunday

	ABC	CBS	MBS	NBC
6pm	Drew Pearson, news	My Friend Irma	The Gabby Hayes Show	Tales of the Texas Rangers
6:15	Don Gardiner, news			
6:30	Vancouver Symphony Orchestra	Our Miss Brooks	Nick Carter, Master Detective	The Big Show
6:45				
7pm		The Lucky Strike Program, Jack Benny	The Affairs of Peter Salem	
7:15				
7:30	The Great Adventure	Amos 'n' Andy	Melvin Elliott, news	
7:45			The Magic of Believing	
8pm	Stop the Music	The Charlie McCarthy Show	Official Detective	The Phil Harris - Alice Faye Show
8:15				
8:30		The Phillip Morris Playhouse on Broadway	Magazine Theater	The Theater Guild on the Air
8:45				
9pm	Walter Winchell, gossip	Meet Corliss Archer	The Opera Concert	
9:15	Café Istanbul			
9:30		Meet Millie	The John J. Anthony Program	The $64 Question
9:45	The Three Suns			
10pm	Paul Harvey, news	The People Act	Out of the Thunder	Tin Pan Valley
10:15	Gloria Parker, news			
10:30	George Sokolsky, news	The Longines Choraliers		The Eileen Christie Show
10:45	Dr. Gino's Musicale		The Health Clinic	

EVENING — WINTER, 1952

Monday

ABC	CBS	MBS	NBC	
Walter Kiernan, news	Allan Jackson, news	News on the Human Side	Richard Harkness, news	6pm
The Allen Stuart Show	You and the World	Kyle MacDonell, songs	The Answer Man	6:15
	Curt Massey, songs	Fred Vandeventer, news	Bill Stern, sports	6:30
	Lowell Thomas, news	Stan Lomax, sports	Three Star Extra	6:45
Taylor Grant, news	The Beulah Show	Fulton Lewis Jr., news	The Longines Symphonette	7pm
Elmer Davis, news	The Jack Smith Show	Behind the Story		7:15
The Lone Ranger	Club Fifteen	Gabriel Heatter, news	Morgan Beatty, news	7:30
	Edward R. Murrow, news	The Health Clinic	One Man's Family	7:45
Henry J. Taylor, news	Suspense	Woman of the Year	The Railroad Hour	8pm
John Daly, news				8:15
The Big Hand	Arthur Godfrey's Talent Scouts	Crime Does Not Pay	The Voice of Firestone	8:30
		Bill Henry, news (8:55pm)		8:45
Paul Whiteman's Teen Club	The Lux Radio Theater	The Mutual Newsreel	The Bell Telephone Hour	9pm
		I Love a Mystery		9:15
		War Front, Home Front	The Cities Service Band of America	9:30
				9:45
News of Tomorrow	The Bob Hawk Show	Frank Edwards, news	Musical Album	10pm
Martha Lou Harp, songs		The Health Clinic		10:15
Time for Defense	Robert Q. Lewis's Waxworks	The Show Shop	Dangerous Assignment	10:30
				10:45

EVENING — WINTER, 1952

Tuesday

	ABC	CBS	MBS	NBC
6pm	Walter Kiernan, news	Allan Jackson, news	News on the Human Side	Richard Harkness, news
6:15	The Allen Stuart Show	You and the World	Jimmy Carroll, songs	The Answer Man
6:30		Curt Massey, songs	Fred Vandeventer, news	Bill Stern, sports
6:45		Lowell Thomas, news	Stan Lomax, sports	Three Star Extra
7pm	Taylor Grant, news	The Beulah Show	Fulton Lewis Jr., news	The Longines Symphonette
7:15	Elmer Davis, news	The Jack Smith Show	Behind the Story	
7:30	The Silver Eagle	Peggy Lee, songs	Gabriel Heatter, news	Morgan Beatty, news
7:45		Edward R. Murrow, news	The Health Clinic	One Man's Family
8pm	Newstand Theater	People Are Funny	The Black Museum	The Cavalcade of America
8:15				
8:30	The Metropolitan Opera Auditions	Mr. and Mrs. North	The Story of Dr. Kildare	The Tums Hollywood Theater
8:45			Bill Henry, news (8:55pm)	
9pm	America's Town Meeting of the Air	Life with Luigi	The Mutual Newsreel	The Bob Hope Show
9:15			I Love a Mystery	
9:30		Pursuit	The Mysterious Traveler	Fibber Magee and Molly
9:45	Edwin D. Canham, news			
10pm	News of Tomorrow	The Lineup	Frank Edwards, news	The Eddie Cantor Show
10:15	Martha Lou Harp, songs		The Health Clinic	
10:30	United or Not	Robert Q. Lewis's Waxworks	The Show Shop	The Man Called X
10:45				

EVENING — WINDER, 1952

Wednesday

ABC	CBS	MBS	NBC	
Walter Kiernan, news	Allan Jackson, news	News on the Human Side	Richard Harkness, news	6pm
The Allen Stuart Show	You and the World	Kyle MacDonell, songs	The Answer Man	6:15
	Curt Massey, songs	Fred Vandeventer, news	Bill Stern, sports	6:30
	Lowell Thomas, news	Stan Lomax, sports	Three Star Extra	6:45
Taylor Grant, news	The Beulah Show	Fulton Lewis Jr., news	The Longines Symphonette	7pm
Elmer Davis, news	The Jack Smith Show	Behind the Story		7:15
The Lone Ranger	Club Fifteen	Gabriel Heatter, news	Morgan Beatty, news	7:30
	Edward R. Murrow, news	The Health Clinic	One Man's Family	7:45
Mystery Theater	Big Town	The MGM Musical Comedy Theater of the Air	The Halls of Ivy	8pm
				8:15
The Top Guy	Dr. Christian		The Great Gildersleeve	8:30
		Bill Henry, news (8:55pm)		8:45
The Third Man	The Red Skelton Show	The Mutual Newsreel	You Bet Your Life	9pm
		I Love a Mystery		9:15
Mr. President	The Bing Crosby Chesterfield Show	The Family Theater	The Big Story	9:30
				9:45
Rogue's Gallery	The Wednesday Night Fights	Frank Edwards, news	Barrie Craig, Confidential Investigator	10pm
		The Health Clinic		10:15
Art Waner Orchestra	Henry Jerome Orchestra	The Show Shop	Meredith Willson's Music Room	10:30
				10:45

EVENING — WINTER, 1952

Thursday

	ABC	CBS	MBS	NBC
6pm	Walter Kiernan, news	Allan Jackson, news	News on the Human Side	Richard Harkness, news
6:15	The Allen Stuart Show	You and the World	Jimmy Carroll, songs	The Answer Man
6:30		Curt Massey, songs	Fred Vandeventer, news	Bill Stern, sports
6:45		Lowell Thomas, news	Stan Lomax, sports	Three Star Extra
7pm	Taylor Grant, news	The Beulah Show	Fulton Lewis Jr., news	The Longines Symphonette
7:15	Elmer Davis, news	The Jack Smith Show	Behind the Story	
7:30	The Silver Eagle	Peggy Lee, songs	Gabriel Heatter, news	Morgan Beatty, news
7:45		Edward R. Murrow, news	The Health Clinic	One Man's Family
8pm	The Redhead	The FBI in Peace and War	The Modern Adventures of Casanova	Father Knows Best
8:15				
8:30	Defense Attorney	The Hallmark Playhouse	The Hardy Family	Mr. Keen, Tracer of Lost Persons
8:45			Bill Henry, news (8:55pm)	
9pm	Ted Mack's Original Amateur Hour	Mr. Chameleon	The Rod and Gun Club	Dragnet
9:15				
9:30		Stars in the Air	Mutual Reporter's Round-Up	Counterspy
9:45	Foreign Reporter			
10pm	News of Tomorrow	Hollywood Sound Stage	Frank Edwards, news	Your Hit Parade
10:15	The Can-Do Club		The Health Clinic	
10:30	Henry Jerome Orchestra	Robert Q. Lewis's Waxworks	The Show Shop	The Hollywood Music Box
10:45				

EVENING — WINTER, 1952

Friday

ABC	CBS	MBS	NBC	
Walter Kiernan, news	Allan Jackson, news	News on the Human Side	Richard Harkness, news	6pm
The Allen Stuart Show	You and the World	Kyle MacDonell, songs	The Answer Man	6:15
	Curt Massey, songs	Fred Vandeventer, news	Bill Stern, sports	6:30
	Lowell Thomas, news	Stan Lomax, sports	Three Star Extra	6:45
Taylor Grant, news	The Beulah Show	Fulton Lewis Jr., news	The Longines Symphonette	7pm
Elmer Davis, news	The Jack Smith Show	Behind the Story		7:15
The Lone Ranger	Club Fifteen	Gabriel Heatter, news	Morgan Beatty, news	7:30
	Edward R. Murrow, news	The Health Clinic	One Man's Family	7:45
Richard Diamond, Private Detective	Musicland USA	Maisie	The Roy Rogers Show	8pm
				8:15
This is Your FBI	The Big Time, Georgie Price	The Gracie Fields Show	The Martin and Lewis Show	8:30
		Bill Henry, news (8:55pm)		8:45
The Adventures of Ozzie and Harriet	Paul Weston Orchestra	The Mutual Newsreel	The Mario Lanza Show	9pm
		I Love a Mystery		9:15
Mr. District Attorney	Robert Q. Lewis's Waxworks	The Armed Forces Review	NBC Presents: Short Story	9:30
				9:45
Madison Square Garden Boxing	Capitol Cloak Room	Frank Edwards, news	Nightbeat	10pm
		The Health Clinic		10:15
Joe Hasel's Sports Page	Dance Orchestra	The Show Shop	Bill Stern Sports	10:30
			Pro and Con	10:45

EVENING — WINTER, 1952

Saturday

	ABC	CBS	MBS	NBC
6pm	Una Mae Carlisle, songs	Joe Wershba, news	News on the Human Side	Kenneth Banghart, news
6:15	Alert America	UN on the Record	The Health Clinic	H. V. Kaltenborn, news
6:30	Harry Wismer, sports	The Saturday Sports Review	Fred Vandeventer, news	NBC Symphony Orchestra
6:45	Allen Stuart, talk	Larry Lesueur, news	Stan Lomax, sports	
7pm	Cavalcade of Music	Saturday at the Chase	History in the Making	
7:15			Twin Views of the News	
7:30	Henry Jerome Orchestra	Operation Underground	Comedy of Errors	Archie Andrews
7:45				
8pm	It's Your Business	Gene Autry's Melody Ranch	Twenty Questions	Jane Ace, Disc Jockey
8:15	The CIO and You			
8:30	ABC Dancing Party	Hopalong Cassidy	The MGM Theater of the Air	Bob and Ray
8:45				
9pm		Gangbusters		The Judy Canova Show
9:15				
9:30		Broadway is My Beat	Lombardoland USA	Grand Ole Opry
9:45				
10pm	The International Jazz Club	Robert Q. Lewis's Waxworks	The Chicago Theater of the Air	The Camel Caravan, Vaughn Monroe
10:15				
10:30	Bert Andrews, news			Al Goodman Musical Album
10:45	The Three Suns			

DAYTIME — WINTER, 1952

Sunday

	ABC	CBS	MBS	NBC
9am	Rev. Barnhouse, religion	St. Paul's Trinity Choir	News	News
9:15		News	The Magic of Believing	The Comic Weekly Man
9:30	The Voice of Prophecy	From the Organ Loft	The Mutual Radio Chapel	
9:45				Music
10am	Message of Israel	The CBS Church of the Air	Henry Gladstone, news	The National Radio Pulpit
10:15			The Health Clinic	
10:30	Negro College Choirs		Lorraine Sherwood, talk	The Horn and Hardart Children's Hour
10:45			Your Hymnal	
11am	The Fine Arts Quartet	The Salt Lake Tabernacle Choir	Henry Gladstone, news	
11:15	Frank and Ernest, religion		Brunch with Dorothy and Dick	
11:30	Christian in Action	Invitation to Learning		Charles F. McCarthy, news
11:45				Pickens Party
12pm	Concert of Europe	The People's Platform	Your Investment Dollar	This is My Favorite Music
12:15			The Stars of Song	
12:30	The Piano Playhouse	Howard K. Smith, news	Melvin Elliott, news	The Eternal Light
12:45		Bill Costello, news	The Canary Pet Shop	
1pm	Dr. William Ward Ayer, talk	String Serenade	Festival of Opera	Leon Parson, news
1:15				Mike 95
1:30	National Vespers	Herbert Hoover, talk		The Endless Frontier
1:45				

DAYTIME — WINTER, 1952

Monday-Friday

ABC	CBS	MBS	NBC	
The Breakfast Club	This is New York, Danny O'Neill	Robert Hurleigh, news	Tex and Jinx, talk (8:30am)	9am
		John Gambling's Second Breakfast		9:15
		Alfred W. McCann, food	Andre Baruch, talk	9:30
	Tommy Riggs and Betty Lou			9:45
My True Story	Arthur Godfrey Time	Henry Gladstone, news	Welcome, Travelers	10am
		Martha Deane, talk		10:15
Betty Crocker, cooking			Double or Nothing	10:30
Against the Storm				10:45
Lone Journey		Ladies Fair	Strike It Rich	11am
When a Girl Marries				11:15
Break the Bank	Grand Slam	Queen for a Day	King's Row	11:30
	Rosemary		Dial Dave Garroway	11:45
The Jack Berch Show	Wendy Warren and the News	Curt Massey, songs	The Kate Smith Program	12pm
Victor Lindlahr, health	Aunt Jenny's True Life Stories	Heatherton House		12:15
The Herb Sheldon Show	The Romance of Helen Trent	Henry Gladstone, news		12:30
	Our Gal Sunday	Luncheon at Sardi's	Skitch's Scrapbook	12:45
Mary Margaret McBride, talk	Big Sister			1pm
	Ma Perkins			1:15
	Young Dr. Malone	Barbara Welles, talk	The Answer Man	1:30
	The Guiding Light		Pickens Party	1:45

DAYTIME — WINTER, 1952

Sunday

	ABC	CBS	MBS	NBC
2pm	Marines in Review	The Longines Symphonette		The Catholic Hour
2:15				
2:30	Christian Science Monitor	New York Philharmonic Orchestra		The American Forum of the Air
2:45				
3pm	The Baptist Hour			Music with the Hormel Girls
3:15				
3:30	The Hour of Decision			Earl Godwin, news
3:45				John Cameron Swayze, news
4pm	The Old Fashioned Revival Hour	Saved by the Mail	Bobby Benson	The Falcon
4:15		Edwin C. Hill, news		
4:30		It's Always Sunday	Under Arrest	Martin Kane, Private Detective
4:45				
5pm	Sammy Kaye's Sylvania Serenade	Arthur Godfrey's Digest	The Shadow	Whitehall 1212
5:15		Treasury Bandstand		
5:30	The Greatest Story Ever Told	Hearthstone of the Death Squad	True Detective Mysteries	The Silent Men
5:45				

DAYTIME — WINTER, 1952

Monday-Friday

ABC	CBS	MBS	NBC	
News	The Second Mrs. Burton	Prescott Robinson, news	Double or Nothing	2pm
Manhattan Maharajah	Perry Mason	Carl Warren, talk		2:15
Family Circle	This is Nora Drake	A. L. Alexander's Mediation Board	Live Like a Millionaire	2:30
	The Brighter Day			2:45
Marriage for Two	Hilltop House	Rambling with Gambling	Life Can Be Beautiful	3pm
The Story of Mary Marlin	House Party		The Road of Life	3:15
Joyce Jordan, MD		Pat Barnes and Barbara, talk	Pepper Young's Family	3:30
The Strange Romance of Evelyn Winters	Radie Harris, gossip		The Right to Happiness	3:45
Valiant Lady	Chicagoans Orchestra	Dick Willard, talk	Mary Noble, Backstage Wife	4pm
Thy Neighbor's Voice		Tello-Test Quiz	Stella Dallas	4:15
Dean Cameron, talk	Galen Drake, talk	The Merry Mailman	Young Widder Brown	4:30
			The Woman in My House	4:45
Big Jon and Sparkie	John Henry Faulk, talk	The Green Hornet / Sergeant Preston of the Yukon	Just Plain Bill	5pm
Mark Trail			Front Page Farrell	5:15
Fun Factory /		Sky King /	Lorenzo Jones	5:30
Tom Corbett, Space Cadet		Wild Bill Elliott	Bob and Ray	5:45

DAYTIME — WINTER, 1952

Saturday

	ABC	CBS	MBS	NBC
9am	No School Today	This is New York, Danny O'Neill	Harry Hennessy, news	Howdy Doody (8:30am)
9:15			The Health Clinic	
9:30		Galen Drake, talk	The McCanns at Home	Jackie Robinson, sports
9:45				
10am			Henry Gladstone, news	The Top Ten
10:15			Martha Deane, talk	
10:30	Space Patrol	Make Way for Youth		Mary Lee Taylor, cooking
10:45				
11am	Junior Junction	Let's Pretend	Prescott Robinson, news	The Somerset Maugham Theater
11:15			Bing Crosby Records	
11:30	The Eddie Fisher Show	Give and Take	Lorraine Sherwood, talk	Hollywood Love Story
11:45				
12pm	The Home Gardener	The Armstrong Theater of Today	The Man on the Farm	The Windshield Wiper
12:15				Perry Como Records
12:30	The American Farmer	Stars Over Hollywood	Henry Gladstone, news	Star's Reviews of the Hits
12:45			Let's Go	
1pm	The US Navy Band	Grand Central Station	Buster Crabbe's Western Jamboree	The National Farm and Home Hour
1:15				
1:30	Vincent Lopez Orchestra	City Hospital	The Show Shop	Uncle Sam's Playhouse
1:45		Bill Lang, news		

DAYTIME — WINTER, 1952

Saturday

	ABC	CBS	MBS	NBC
2pm	The Metropolitan Opera	Music with the Hormel Girls	Bobby Sherwood Orchestra	
2:15				
2:30		Chicagoans Orchestra		The House of Music
2:45		Operation Ex-GI		
3pm		Report from Overseas		
3:15		Adventures in Science		
3:30		CBS Farm News		
3:45		Griff Williams Orchestra		
4pm		Stan Dougherty Orchestra	Rambling with Gambling	
4:15				
4:30		Cross-Section USA	Rudy Mercer and Ted Haig	
4:45				
5pm	Great Moments in Opera	Dave Stephens Orchestra		
5:15				
5:30	At Home with Music	Treasury Bandstand	The Gus Lesnevich Show	
5:45	Club Time			Bob Considine, sports

EVENING — SPRING, 1952

Sunday

	ABC	CBS	MBS	NBC
6pm	George Sokolsky, news	My Friend Irma	The Gabby Hayes Show	Tales of the Texas Rangers
6:15	Don Gardiner, news			
6:30	Vancouver Symphony Orchestra	Our Miss Brooks	Nick Carter, Master Detective	The Chase
6:45				
7pm		The Lucky Strike Program, Jack Benny	The Affairs of Peter Salem	The First Nighter Program
7:15				
7:30	The Great Adventure	Amos 'n' Andy	Melvin Elliott, news	Stars in Khaki 'n' Blue
7:45			The Magic of Believing	
8pm	Stop the Music	The Charlie McCarthy Show	Official Detective	The Phil Harris - Alice Faye Show
8:15				
8:30		The Phillip Morris Playhouse on Broadway	Magazine Theater	The Theater Guild on the Air
8:45				
9pm	Drew Pearson, news	The Screen Guild Theater	The Opera Concert	
9:15	Meet Corliss Archer			
9:30		Meet Millie	The John J. Anthony Program	The $64 Question
9:45	The Three Suns			
10pm	Paul Harvey, news	The People Act	Out of the Thunder	The American Forum of the Air
10:15	Gloria Parker, news			
10:30	William Tusher, news	The Longines Choraliers		Welcome, Travelers
10:45	Dr. Gino's Musicale		Your Voice of America	

EVENING — SPRING, 1952

Monday

ABC	CBS	MBS	NBC	
Walter Kiernan, news	Allan Jackson, news	News on the Human Side	Richard Harkness, news	6pm
The Allen Stuart Show	You and the World	Kyle MacDonell, songs	Bill Stern, sports	6:15
	Curt Massey, songs	Fred Vandeventer, news	Lockwood Doty, sports	6:30
	Lowell Thomas, news	Stan Lomax, sports	Three Star Extra	6:45
Taylor Grant, news	The Beulah Show	Fulton Lewis Jr., news	The Longines Symphonette	7pm
Elmer Davis, news	The Jack Smith Show	Dorothy and Dick, talk		7:15
The Lone Ranger	Club Fifteen	Gabriel Heatter, news	Morgan Beatty, news	7:30
	Edward R. Murrow, news	Bing Crosby Records	One Man's Family	7:45
Henry J. Taylor, news	Suspense	Woman of the Year	The Railroad Hour	8pm
John Daly, news				8:15
The Big Hand	Arthur Godfrey's Talent Scouts	Crime Does Not Pay	The Voice of Firestone	8:30
		Bill Henry, news (8:55pm)		8:45
Paul Whiteman's Teen Club	The Lux Radio Theater	The Mutual Newsreel	The Bell Telephone Hour	9pm
		Bing Crosby Records		9:15
		War Front, Home Front	The Cities Service Band of America	9:30
				9:45
News of Tomorrow	The Bob Hawk Show	Frank Edwards, news	Bold Venture	10pm
Martha Lou Harp, songs		I Love a Mystery		10:15
Time for Defense	Robert Q. Lewis's Waxworks	The Show Shop	Dangerous Assignment	10:30
				10:45

EVENING — SPRING, 1952

Tuesday

	ABC	CBS	MBS	NBC
6pm	Walter Kiernan, news	Allan Jackson, news	News on the Human Side	Richard Harkness, news
6:15	The Allen Stuart Show	You and the World	Jimmy Carroll, songs	Bill Stern, sports
6:30		Curt Massey, songs	Fred Vandeventer, news	Phil Rizzuto, sports
6:45		Lowell Thomas, news	Stan Lomax, sports	Three Star Extra
7pm	Taylor Grant, news	The Beulah Show	Fulton Lewis Jr., news	The Longines Symphonette
7:15	Elmer Davis, news	The Jack Smith Show	Dorothy and Dick, talk	
7:30	The Silver Eagle	Peggy Lee, songs	Gabriel Heatter, news	Morgan Beatty, news
7:45		Edward R. Murrow, news	Bing Crosby Records	One Man's Family
8pm	Newstand Theater	People Are Funny	The Black Museum	The Cavalcade of America
8:15				
8:30	Escape with Me	Mr. and Mrs. North	The Story of Dr. Kildare	Barrie Craig, Confidential Investigator
8:45			Bill Henry, news (8:55pm)	
9pm	America's Town Meeting of the Air	Life with Luigi	The Mutual Newsreel	The Bob Hope Show
9:15			Bing Crosby Records	
9:30		The Lineup	The Mysterious Traveler	Fibber Magee and Molly
9:45	Edwin D. Canham, news			
10pm	News of Tomorrow	Candidates and Issues	Frank Edwards, news	The Eddie Cantor Show
10:15	Martha Lou Harp, songs		I Love a Mystery	
10:30	United or Not	Robert Q. Lewis's Waxworks	The Show Shop	The Man Called X
10:45				

EVENING — SPRING, 1952

Wednesday

ABC	CBS	MBS	NBC	
Walter Kiernan, news	Allan Jackson, news	News on the Human Side	Richard Harkness, news	6pm
The Allen Stuart Show	You and the World	Kyle MacDonell, songs	Bill Stern, sports	6:15
	Curt Massey, songs	Fred Vandeventer, news	Lockwood Doty, sports	6:30
	Lowell Thomas, news	Stan Lomax, sports	Three Star Extra	6:45
Taylor Grant, news	The Beulah Show	Fulton Lewis Jr., news	The Longines Symphonette	7pm
Elmer Davis, news	The Jack Smith Show	Dorothy and Dick, talk		7:15
The Lone Ranger	Club Fifteen	Gabriel Heatter, news	Morgan Beatty, news	7:30
	Edward R. Murrow, news	Bing Crosby Records	One Man's Family	7:45
Mystery Theater	Big Town	The MGM Musical Comedy Theater of the Air	The Halls of Ivy	8pm
				8:15
The Top Guy	Dr. Christian		The Great Gildersleeve	8:30
		Bill Henry, news (8:55pm)		8:45
The Third Man	The Red Skelton Show	The Mutual Newsreel	You Bet Your Life	9pm
		Bing Crosby Records		9:15
Crossfire	The Bing Crosby Chesterfield Show	The Family Theater	The Big Story	9:30
				9:45
Mr. President	The Wednesday Night Fights	Frank Edwards, news	The Silent Men	10pm
		I Love a Mystery		10:15
Art Waner Orchestra	Henry Jerome Orchestra	The Show Shop	Meredith Willson Music Room	10:30
				10:45

EVENING — SPRING, 1952

Thursday

	ABC	CBS	MBS	NBC
6pm	Walter Kiernan, news	Allan Jackson, news	News on the Human Side	Richard Harkness, news
6:15	The Allen Stuart Show	You and the World	Jimmy Carroll, songs	Bill Stern, sports
6:30		Curt Massey, songs	Fred Vandeventer, news	Phil Rizzuto, sports
6:45		Lowell Thomas, news	Stan Lomax, sports	Three Star Extra
7pm	Taylor Grant, news	The Beulah Show	Fulton Lewis Jr., news	The Longines Symphonette
7:15	Elmer Davis, news	The Jack Smith Show	Dorothy and Dick, talk	
7:30	The Silver Eagle	Peggy Lee, songs	Gabriel Heatter, news	Morgan Beatty, news
7:45		Edward R. Murrow, news	Bing Crosby Records	One Man's Family
8pm	Café Istanbul	The FBI in Peace and War	The Modern Adventures of Casanova	Father Knows Best
8:15				
8:30	Defense Attorney	The Hallmark Playhouse	The Hardy Family	Nightbeat
8:45			Bill Henry, news (8:55pm)	
9pm	Ted Mack's Original Amateur Hour	Mr. Chameleon	The Rod and Gun Club	Dragnet
9:15				
9:30		Stars in the Air	Mutual Reporter's Round-Up	Counterspy
9:45	I Covered the Story			
10pm	News of Tomorrow	Hollywood Sound Stage	Frank Edwards, news	Your Hit Parade
10:15	The Can-Do Club		I Love a Mystery	
10:30	Henry Jerome Orchestra	Presidential Profiles	The Show Shop	Welcome, Travelers
10:45				

EVENING — SPRING, 1952

Friday

ABC	CBS	MBS	NBC	
Walter Kiernan, news	Allan Jackson, news	News on the Human Side	Richard Harkness, news	6pm
The Allen Stuart Show	You and the World	Kyle MacDonell, songs	Bill Stern, sports	6:15
	Curt Massey, songs	Fred Vandeventer, news	Lockwood Doty, sports	6:30
	Lowell Thomas, news	Stan Lomax, sports	Three Star Extra	6:45
Taylor Grant, news	The Beulah Show	Fulton Lewis Jr., news	The Longines Symphonette	7pm
Elmer Davis, news	The Jack Smith Show	Dorothy and Dick, talk		7:15
The Lone Ranger	Club Fifteen	Gabriel Heatter, news	Morgan Beatty, news	7:30
	Edward R. Murrow, news	Bing Crosby Records	One Man's Family	7:45
Richard Diamond, Private Detective	Musicland USA	Maisie	The Roy Rogers Show	8pm
				8:15
This is Your FBI	The Big Time, Georgie Price	The Gracie Fields Show	Bob and Ray	8:30
		Bill Henry, news (8:55pm)		8:45
The Adventures of Ozzie and Harriet	The Doris Day Show	The Mutual Newsreel	The Mario Lanza Show	9pm
		Rukyeser Reports		9:15
Mr. District Attorney	Robert Q. Lewis's Waxworks	Great Day	NBC Presents: Short Story	9:30
				9:45
Madison Square Garden Boxing	Capitol Cloak Room	Frank Edwards, news	Tin Pan Valley	10pm
		I Love a Mystery		10:15
Joe Hasel's Sports Page	Dance Orchestra	The Show Shop	Bill Stern Sports	10:30
			Pro and Con	10:45

EVENING — SPRING, 1952

Saturday

	ABC	CBS	MBS	NBC
6pm	Una Mae Carlisle, songs	Joe Wershba, news	News on the Human Side	Kenneth Banghart, news
6:15	Dr. David Otis Fuller, health	UN on the Record	The Health Clinic	H. V. Kaltenborn, news
6:30	Harry Wismer, sports	The Saturday Sports Review	Fred Vandeventer, news	NBC Symphony Orchestra
6:45	The Allan Stuart Show	Larry Lesueur, news	Stan Lomax, sports	
7pm	Cavalcade of Music	Saturday at the Chase	History in the Making	
7:15			Twin Views of the News	
7:30	Henry Jerome Orchestra	Gunsmoke	Cavalcade of Music	Mind Your Manner
7:45				
8pm	Talking It Over	Gene Autry's Melody Ranch	Twenty Questions	Jane Ace, Disc Jockey
8:15	As We See It			
8:30	ABC Dancing Party	Tarzan	The MGM Theater of the Air	Truth or Consequences
8:45				
9pm		Gangbusters		The Judy Canova Show
9:15				
9:30		Broadway is My Beat	Lombardoland USA	Grand Ole Opry
9:45				
10pm	The International Jazz Club	Robert Q. Lewis's Waxworks	The Chicago Theater of the Air	The Camel Caravan, Vaughn Monroe
10:15				
10:30	Bert Andrews, news			The Chamber Music Society of Lower Basin Street
10:45	Dance Orchestra			

DAYTIME — SPRING, 1952

Sunday

	ABC	CBS	MBS	NBC
9am	Rev. Barnhouse, religion	St. Paul's Trinity Choir	News	News
9:15		News	The Magic of Believing	The Comic Weekly Man
9:30	The Voice of Prophecy	From the Organ Loft	The Mutual Radio Chapel	
9:45				Music
10am	Message of Israel	The CBS Church of the Air	Henry Gladstone, news	The National Radio Pulpit
10:15			Your Money at Work	
10:30	Negro College Choirs		Lorraine Sherwood, talk	The Horn and Hardart Children's Hour
10:45			Your Hymnal	
11am	The Fine Arts Quartet	The Salt Lake Tabernacle Choir	Henry Gladstone, news	
11:15	Frank and Ernest, religion		Brunch with Dorothy and Dick	
11:30	Christian in Action	Invitation to Learning		Charles F. McCarthy, news
11:45				Stars for Defense
12pm	Here Comes the Band	The People's Platform	Your Investment Dollar	This is My Favorite Music
12:15			The Stars of Song	
12:30	The Herald of Truth	Howard K. Smith, news	Melvin Elliott, news	The Eternal Light
12:45		Bill Costello, news	The Canary Pet Shop	
1pm	Dr. William Ward Ayer, talk	String Serenade	Festival of Opera	Leon Parson, news
1:15				Mike 95
1:30	National Vespers	Syncopation Piece		Medicine, USA
1:45				

DAYTIME — SPRING, 1952

Monday-Friday

ABC	CBS	MBS	NBC	
The Breakfast Club	This is New York, Danny O'Neill	Robert Hurleigh, news	Tex and Jinx, talk (8:30am)	9am
		John Gambling's Second Breakfast		9:15
	The Joan Edwards Show	Alfred W. McCann, food	The Herb Sheldon Show	9:30
				9:45
My True Story	Arthur Godfrey Time	Henry Gladstone, news	Welcome, Travelers	10am
		Martha Deane, talk		10:15
Whispering Streets			Double or Nothing	10:30
Against the Storm				10:45
Lone Journey		Ladies Fair	Strike It Rich	11am
When a Girl Marries				11:15
Break the Bank	Grand Slam	Queen for a Day	Bob and Ray	11:30
	Rosemary		Dial Dave Garroway	11:45
The Jack Berch Show	Wendy Warren and the News	Curt Massey, songs	The Kate Smith Program	12pm
Victor Lindlahr, health	Aunt Jenny's True Life Stories	Dick Willard, songs		12:15
Caravan	The Romance of Helen Trent	Henry Gladstone, news		12:30
	Our Gal Sunday	Luncheon at Sardi's	Skitch's Scrapbook	12:45
Mary Margaret McBride, talk	Big Sister			1pm
	Ma Perkins			1:15
	Young Dr. Malone	Barbara Welles, talk	The Answer Man	1:30
	The Guiding Light		The Herb Sheldon Show	1:45

DAYTIME — SPRING, 1952

Sunday

	ABC	CBS	MBS	NBC
2pm	Music	The Longines Symphonette		The Catholic Hour
2:15				
2:30	Christian Science Monitor	New York Philharmonic Orchestra		America's Music
2:45	Between the Bookends			
3pm	The Baptist Hour			Where the Public Stands
3:15				Four Story Theater
3:30	The Hour of Decision		Top Tunes with Tendler	Bob Considine, sports
3:45				John Cameron Swayze, news
4pm	The Old Fashioned Revival Hour	Music for You	Under Arrest	The Falcon
4:15				
4:30		Hearthstone of the Death Squad	The Private Files of Matthew Bell	Martin Kane, Private Detective
4:45				
5pm	Sammy Kaye's Sylvania Serenade	Arthur Godfrey's Digest	The Shadow	The Hollywood Star Playhouse
5:15		Treasury Bandstand		
5:30	The Greatest Story Ever Told	Robert Trout, news	True Detective Mysteries	Whitehall 1212
5:45		Larry Lesueur, news		

DAYTIME — SPRING, 1952

Monday-Friday

ABC	CBS	MBS	NBC	
The Tom Reddy Show	The Second Mrs. Burton	Prescott Robinson, news	Pickens Party	*2pm*
	Perry Mason	Carl Warren, talk	Meredith Willson's Music Room	*2:15*
Family Circle	This is Nora Drake	The Answer Man	Live Like a Millionaire	*2:30*
	The Brighter Day			*2:45*
Ladies Be Seated	Hilltop House	Rambling with Gambling	Life Can Be Beautiful	*3pm*
	House Party		The Road of Life	*3:15*
The Story of Mary Marlin		Pat Barnes and Barbara, talk	Pepper Young's Family	*3:30*
The Strange Romance of Evelyn Winters	Radie Harris, gossip		The Right to Happiness	*3:45*
Betty Crocker, cooking	The Johnson Family	Dick Willard, talk	Mary Noble, Backstage Wife	*4pm*
Dean Cameron, talk	Tommy Riggs and Betty Lou	Tello-Test Quiz	Stella Dallas	*4:15*
	Galen Drake, talk	Heatherton House	Young Widder Brown	*4:30*
Music			The Woman in My House	*4:45*
Big Jon and Sparkie	John Henry Faulk, talk	Bobby Benson / The Green Hornet /	Just Plain Bill	*5pm*
Mark Trail		Sergeant Preston of the Yukon	Front Page Farrell	*5:15*
Fun Factory		Sky King	Lorenzo Jones	*5:30*
Tom Corbett, Space Cadet		Wild Bill Elliott	The Doctor's Wife	*5:45*

DAYTIME — SPRING, 1952

Saturday

	ABC	CBS	MBS	NBC
9am	No School Today	This is New York, Danny O'Neill	Harry Hennessy, news	Howdy Doody (8:30am)
9:15				
9:30		Galen Drake, talk	The McCanns at Home	Jackie Robinson, sports
9:45				
10am			Henry Gladstone, news	Archie Andrews
10:15			Martha Deane, talk	
10:30	Space Patrol	The Quiz Kids		Mary Lee Taylor, cooking
10:45				
11am	Junior Junction	Let's Pretend	Your Home Beautiful	My Secret Story
11:15			Prescott Robinson, news	
11:30	The Eddie Fisher Show	Give and Take	Lorraine Sherwood, talk	Hollywood Love Story
11:45				
12pm	The Home Gardener	The Armstrong Theater of Today	The Man on the Farm	Perry Como Records
12:15				
12:30	Music	Stars Over Hollywood	Henry Gladstone, news	Star's Reviews of the Hits
12:45			Ruth and Phillip Hunter, talk	
1pm		Grand Central Station	Informal Sonatas	The National Farm and Home Hour
1:15				
1:30	Vincent Lopez Orchestra	City Hospital	The Show Shop	Uncle Sam's Playhouse
1:45				

DAYTIME — SPRING, 1952

Saturday

	ABC	CBS	MBS	NBC
2pm	The Metropolitan Opera	Music with the Hormel Girls		
2:15				
2:30		Peggy Lee, songs	Bobby Sherwood Orchestra	The House of Music
2:45		Operation Ex-GI		
3pm		Report from Overseas		
3:15		Adventures in Science		
3:30		CBS Farm News		
3:45		Griff Williams Orchestra		
4pm		The US Air Force Band	Rambling with Gambling	
4:15				Horse Racing
4:30		Cross-Section USA	Music We Like	The House of Music
4:45				
5pm	Roseland Ballroom Orchestra	Dave Stephens Orchestra		
5:15				
5:30		Treasury Bandstand	Down You Go	A Helping Hand
5:45	Club Time			The Terrea Lea Show

EVENING — SUMMER, 1952

Sunday

	ABC	CBS	MBS	NBC
6pm	George Sokolsky, news	Music for You	Sergeant Preston of the Yukon	Tales of the Texas Rangers
6:15	Don Gardiner, news			
6:30	The Piano Playhouse	Syncopation Piece	Nick Carter, Master Detective	The First Nighter Program
6:45				
7pm	Phil Bovero Orchestra	December Bride	The Affairs of Peter Salem	The Hollywood Bowl
7:15				
7:30	Time Capsule	The Doris Day Show	Melvin Elliott, news	
7:45			Blackstone, the Magician	
8pm	The American Music Hall	The Frank Fontaine Show	The Lutheran Hour	Meredith Willson's Music Room
8:15				
8:30		The Phillip Morris Playhouse on Broadway	The Enchanted Hour	Best Plays
8:45				
9pm	Drew Pearson, news	Meet Millie	The Opera Concert	
9:15	Melody Highway			
9:30		Inner Sanctum Mysteries		NBC String Symphony
9:45	Alistair Cooke, comment			
10pm	Paul Harvey, news	Dance Orchestra	The Radio Bible Class	Meet the Press
10:15	Gloria Parker, news			
10:30	William Tusher, news		The Back to God Hour	The American Forum of the Air
10:45	Bob Edge, sports			

EVENING — SUMMER, 1952

Monday

ABC	CBS	MBS	NBC	
Walter Kiernan, news	Allan Jackson, news	News on the Human Side	Richard Harkness, news	6pm
The Allen Stuart Show	You and the World	Dorothy and Dick, talk	Bill Stern, sports	6:15
	Curt Massey, songs	Fred Vandeventer, news	Lockwood Doty, sports	6:30
	Edward P. Morgan, news	Stan Lomax, sports	Three Star Extra	6:45
Taylor Grant, news	Robert Q. Lewis's Waxworks	Fulton Lewis Jr., news	Guy Lombardo Orchestra	7pm
Quincy Howe, news		Bing Crosby Records		7:15
The Lone Ranger		Gabriel Heatter, news	Morgan Beatty, news	7:30
	Larry Lesueur, news	The Mutual Newsreel	One Man's Family	7:45
Henry J. Taylor, news	Horatio Hornblower	Stars in the Night	The Railroad Hour	8pm
John Daly, news				8:15
The Big Hand	Arthur Godfrey's Talent Scouts	Crime Does Not Pay	The Voice of Firestone	8:30
		Bill Henry, news (8:55pm)		8:45
Paul Whiteman's Teen Club	Theater of Romance	Crime Fighters	The Bell Telephone Hour	9pm
				9:15
	The Steve Allen Show	War Front, Home Front	The Cities Service Band of America	9:30
				9:45
John Daly, news	Walk a Mile	Frank Edwards, news	Bold Venture	10pm
Spotlight, New York		I Love a Mystery		10:15
	Dance Orchestra	The Show Shop	Dangerous Assignment	10:30
				10:45

EVENING — SUMMER, 1952

Tuesday

	ABC	CBS	MBS	NBC
6pm	Walter Kiernan, news	Allan Jackson, news	News on the Human Side	Richard Harkness, news
6:15	The Allen Stuart Show	You and the World	Dorothy and Dick, talk	Bill Stern, sports
6:30		Curt Massey, songs	Fred Vandeventer, news	Phil Rizzuto, sports
6:45		Edward P. Morgan, news	Stan Lomax, sports	Three Star Extra
7pm	Taylor Grant, news	Robert Q. Lewis's Waxworks	Fulton Lewis Jr., news	Guy Lombardo Orchestra
7:15	Quincy Howe, news		Bing Crosby Records	
7:30	The Silver Eagle	Peggy Lee, songs	Gabriel Heatter, news	Morgan Beatty, news
7:45		Larry Lesueur, news	The Mutual Newsreel	One Man's Family
8pm	The Mayor of Times Square	People Are Funny	The Jimmie Carroll Show	The Scarlet Pimpernel
8:15				
8:30	Escape with Me	Mr. and Mrs. North	The Story of Dr. Kildare	Barrie Craig, Confidential Investigator
8:45			Bill Henry, news (8:55pm)	
9pm	America's Town Meeting of the Air	Life with Luigi	Official Detective	Meet Your Match
9:15				
9:30		The Steve Allen Show	The Mysterious Traveler	Truth or Consequences
9:45	Edwin D. Canham, news			
10pm	John Daly, news	The Straw Hat Concert	Frank Edwards, news	The Capital Concert
10:15	Spotlight, New York		I Love a Mystery	
10:30		Dance Orchestra	The Show Shop	Stan Kenton Orchestra
10:45				

EVENING — SUMMER, 1952

Wednesday

ABC	CBS	MBS	NBC	
Walter Kiernan, news	Allan Jackson, news	News on the Human Side	Richard Harkness, news	6pm
The Allen Stuart Show	You and the World	Dorothy and Dick, talk	Bill Stern, sports	6:15
	Curt Massey, songs	Fred Vandeventer, news	Lockwood Doty, sports	6:30
	Edward P. Morgan, news	Stan Lomax, sports	Three Star Extra	6:45
Taylor Grant, news	Robert Q. Lewis's Waxworks	Fulton Lewis Jr., news	Guy Lombardo Orchestra	7pm
Quincy Howe, news		Bing Crosby Records		7:15
The Lone Ranger		Gabriel Heatter, news	Morgan Beatty, news	7:30
	Larry Lesueur, news	The Mutual Newsreel	One Man's Family	7:45
Postmark USA	Hearthstone of the Death Squad	Music for a Half Hour	What's My Line	8pm
				8:15
Barry Valentino Orchestra	Dr. Christian	Great Day	The Great Gildersleeve	8:30
		Bill Henry, news (8:55pm)		8:45
Mr. President	Yours Truly, Johnny Dollar	The Hidden Truth	You Bet Your Life	9pm
				9:15
Crossfire	The Steve Allen Show	The Family Theater	The Hollywood Music Box	9:30
				9:45
John Daly, news	The Wednesday Night Fights	Frank Edwards, news	Promenade Concert	10pm
Spotlight, New York		I Love a Mystery		10:15
	Henry Jerome Orchestra	The Show Shop	Portrait of a City	10:30
				10:45

EVENING — SUMMER, 1952

Thursday

	ABC	CBS	MBS	NBC
6pm	Walter Kiernan, news	Allan Jackson, news	News on the Human Side	Richard Harkness, news
6:15	The Allen Stuart Show	You and the World	Dorothy and Dick, talk	Bill Stern, sports
6:30		Curt Massey, songs	Fred Vandeventer, news	Phil Rizzuto, sports
6:45		Richard P. Morgan, news	Stan Lomax, sports	Three Star Extra
7pm	Taylor Grant, news	Robert Q. Lewis's Waxworks	Fulton Lewis Jr., news	Guy Lombardo Orchestra
7:15	Quincy Howe, news		Bing Crosby Records	
7:30	The Silver Eagle	Peggy Lee, songs	Gabriel Heatter, news	Morgan Beatty, news
7:45		Larry Lesueur, news	The Mutual Newsreel	One Man's Family
8pm	Mr. Broadway	Mr. Keen, Tracer of Lost Persons	Jazz Nocturne	A Life in Your Hands
8:15				
8:30	Defense Attorney	The FBI in Peace and War	The Hardy Family	The Chase
8:45			Bill Henry, news (8:55pm)	
9pm	Ted Mack's Original Amateur Hour	Mr. Chameleon	The Rod and Gun Club	Dragnet
9:15				
9:30		The Steve Allen Show	Mutual Reporter's Round-Up	Counterspy
9:45	I Covered the Story			
10pm	John Daly, news	Dance Orchestra	Frank Edwards, news	Nightbeat
10:15	Spotlight, New York		I Love a Mystery	
10:30			The Show Shop	Welcome, Travelers
10:45				

EVENING — SUMMER, 1952

Friday

ABC	CBS	MBS	NBC	
Walter Kiernan, news	Allan Jackson, news	News on the Human Side	Richard Harkness, news	6pm
The Allen Stuart Show	You and the World	Dorothy and Dick, talk	Bill Stern, sports	6:15
	Curt Massey, songs	Fred Vandeventer, news	Lockwood Doty, sports	6:30
	Richard P. Morgan, news	Stan Lomax, sports	Three Star Extra	6:45
Taylor Grant, news	Robert Q. Lewis's Waxworks	Fulton Lewis Jr., news	Guy Lombardo Orchestra	7pm
Quincy Howe, news		Bing Crosby Records		7:15
The Lone Ranger		Gabriel Heatter, news	Morgan Beatty, news	7:30
	Larry Lesueur, news	The Mutual Newsreel	One Man's Family	7:45
The Top Guy	Musicland USA	Symphonic Strings	The Roy Shield Revue	8pm
				8:15
This is Your FBI		The Gracie Fields Show	Bob and Ray	8:30
		Bill Henry, news (8:55pm)		8:45
Newstand Theater	The Doris Day Show	Magazine Theater	The Mario Lanza Show	9pm
				9:15
Ralph Norman Orchestra	The Steve Allen Show	The Hall of Fantasy	Music By Mantovani	9:30
				9:45
John Daly, news	Capitol Cloak Room	Frank Edwards, news	Hy Gardner Calling	10pm
Spotlight, New York		I Love a Mystery	Words in the Night	10:15
	The US Air Force Band	The Show Shop	Bill Stern Sports	10:30
			Pro and Con	10:45

EVENING — SUMMER, 1952

Saturday

	ABC	CBS	MBS	NBC
6pm	Una Mae Carlisle, songs	Joe Wershba, news	News on the Human Side	Kenneth Banghart, news
6:15		Alfredo Antonini Orchestra	Rukeyser Reports	Earl Godwin, news
6:30	Bob Finnigan, sports	The Saturday Sports Review	Fred Vandeventer, news	NBC Summer Symphony
6:45	The Allan Stuart Show	Larry Lesueur, news	Stan Lomax, sports	
7pm	Cavalcade of Music	Saturday at the Chase	History in the Making	
7:15			From the Pentagon	
7:30	Henry Jerome Orchestra	Gunsmoke	Down You Go	Vladimir Horowitz Classical Music
7:45				
8pm	It's Your Business	Gene Autry's Melody Ranch	Twenty Questions	Jane Ace, Disc Jockey
8:15	The CIO and You			
8:30	ABC Dancing Party	Tarzan	The MGM Theater of the Air	Stars in Khaki 'n' Blue
8:45				
9pm		Gangbusters		Ohio River Jamboree
9:15				
9:30	The International Jazz Club	Broadway is My Beat	Lombardoland USA	Grand Ole Opry
9:45				
10pm	John Daly, news	Robert Q. Lewis's Waxworks	The Chicago Theater of the Air	Reuben, Reuben
10:15	Spotlight, New York			
10:30				The Chamber Music Society of Lower Basin Street
10:45				

DAYTIME — SUMMER, 1952

Sunday

	ABC	CBS	MBS	NBC
9am	Rev. Barnhouse, religion	Keyboard Concert	News	News
9:15		News	The Magic of Believing	The Comic Weekly Man
9:30	The Voice of Prophecy	From the Organ Loft	The Mutual Radio Chapel	
9:45				Music
10am	Message of Israel	The CBS Church of the Air	Henry Gladstone, news	The National Radio Pulpit
10:15			Faith in Our Time	
10:30	Negro College Choirs		Lorraine Sherwood, talk	The Horn and Hardart Children's Hour
10:45			Your Hymnal	
11am	Brunch Time	The Salt Lake Tabernacle Choir	Henry Gladstone, news	
11:15	Frank and Ernest, religion		Brunch with Dorothy and Dick	
11:30	Christian in Action	Invitation to Learning		Charles F. McCarthy, news
11:45				Songs of the Wild
12pm	Sunday News Special	The People's Platform	The US Military Academy Band	This is My Favorite Music
12:15	Words of Power			
12:30	The Herald of Truth	Howard K. Smith, news	Melvin Elliott, news	The Eternal Light
12:45		Bill Costello, news	The Men's Corner	
1pm	Dr. William Ward Ayer, talk	Your Invitation to Music	Festival of Opera	Sunday News Desk
1:15				
1:30	National Vespers			Medicine, USA
1:45				

DAYTIME — SUMMER, 1952

Monday-Friday

ABC	CBS	MBS	NBC	
The Breakfast Club	This is New York, Danny O'Neill	Robert Hurleigh, news	Tex and Jinx, talk (8:30am)	9am
		John Gambling's Second Breakfast		9:15
	The Joan Edwards Show	Alfred W. McCann, food	Young Dr. Malone	9:30
			The Brighter Day	9:45
My True Story	Arthur Godfrey Time	Henry Gladstone, news	Welcome, Travelers	10am
		Martha Deane, talk		10:15
Whispering Streets			The Herb Sheldon Show	10:30
When a Girl Marries				10:45
The Tom Reddy Show		Prescott Robinson, news	Strike It Rich	11am
		Tello-Test Quiz		11:15
Break the Bank	Grand Slam	Queen for a Day	Bob and Ray	11:30
	Rosemary		Dial Dave Garroway	11:45
The Jack Berch Show	Wendy Warren and the News	Curt Massey, songs	The Kate Smith Program	12pm
Gordon Fraser, news	Aunt Jenny's True Life Stories	Bruce and Dan, songs		12:15
Kitchen Kapers	The Romance of Helen Trent	Henry Gladstone, news		12:30
	Our Gal Sunday	Luncheon at Sardi's	Skitch's Scrapbook	12:45
Mary Margaret McBride, talk	Big Sister			1pm
	Ma Perkins			1:15
	Young Dr. Malone	Barbara Welles, talk	Merrill Mueller, news	1:30
	The Guiding Light		The Herb Sheldon Show	1:45

DAYTIME — SUMMER, 1952

Sunday

	ABC	CBS	MBS	NBC
2pm	Music			The Catholic Hour
2:15				
2:30	Christian Science Monitor	On a Sunday Afternoon		Sammy Kaye's Sylvania Serenade
2:45	Women in Uniform			
3pm	The Baptist Hour	Music		Where the Public Stands
3:15				Intermezzo
3:30	The Hour of Decision	The Main Street Music Hall		Bob Considine, sports
3:45				Critic at Large
4pm	The Old Fashioned Revival Hour	Charlie Spivak Orchestra	The Green Hornet	The Falcon
4:15				
4:30		Pick the Winner	Under Arrest	Martin Kane, Private Detective
4:45				
5pm	Chautauqua Symphony Orchestra	Arthur Godfrey's Digest	The Shadow	The Hollywood Star Playhouse
5:15				
5:30	This Week Around the World	Robert Trout, news	True Detective Mysteries	Whitehall 1212
5:45		Larry Lesueur, news		

DAYTIME — SUMMER, 1952

Monday-Friday

ABC	CBS	MBS	NBC	
The Eddie Dunn Show	The Second Mrs. Burton	Prescott Robinson, news	Pickens Party	*2pm*
	Perry Mason	Carl Warren, talk	Meredith Willson's Music Room	*2:15*
	This is Nora Drake	Paula Stone, talk	Live Like a Millionaire	*2:30*
	The Brighter Day	Pat Barnes and Barbera, talk		*2:45*
	Hilltop House	Rambling with Gambling	Life Can Be Beautiful	*3pm*
	House Party		The Road of Life	*3:15*
The Tennessee Ernie Ford Show			Pepper Young's Family	*3:30*
	Cedric Adams, news		The Right to Happiness	*3:45*
Cal Tinney, talk	The Johnson Family	Ladies Fair	Mary Noble, Backstage Wife	*4pm*
	Tommy Riggs and Betty Lou		Stella Dallas	*4:15*
Dean Cameron, talk	The Housewives' League	Take a Number	Young Widder Brown	*4:30*
			The Woman in My House	*4:45*
Us Browns	John Henry Faulk, talk	Heatherton House	Just Plain Bill	*5pm*
			Front Page Farrell	*5:15*
Big Jon and Sparkie		Bobby Benson	Lorenzo Jones	*5:30*
Dan Peterson, talk			The Doctor's Wife	*5:45*

DAYTIME — SUMMER, 1952

Saturday

	ABC	CBS	MBS	NBC
9am	No School Today	This is New York, Danny O'Neill	Harry Hennessy, news	Howdy Doody (8:30am)
9:15			Bing Crosby Records	
9:30		The Housewives' League	The McCanns at Home	Jackie Robinson, sports
9:45				
10am		Galen Drake, talk	Henry Gladstone, news	Archie Andrews
10:15			Martha Deane, talk	
10:30	Space Patrol	Smilin Ed's Buster Brown Gang		Mary Lee Taylor, cooking
10:45				
11am	Junior Junction	Let's Pretend	Your Home Beautiful	My Secret Story
11:15			Lorraine Sherwood, talk	
11:30	The Eddie Fisher Show	Give and Take	Farm Quiz	Hollywood Love Story
11:45				
12pm	The Home Gardener	The Armstrong Theater of Today	The Man on the Farm	Perry Como Records
12:15				
12:30	Beauty Hints	Stars Over Hollywood	Henry Gladstone, news	Star's Reviews of the Hits
12:45	News		Ruth and Phillip Hunter, talk	
1pm	The US Navy Band	Grand Central Station	Festival of Opera	The National Farm and Home Hour
1:15				
1:30	Vincent Lopez Orchestra	City Hospital		Uncle Sam's Playhouse
1:45				

DAYTIME — SUMMER, 1952

Saturday

	ABC	CBS	MBS	NBC
2pm	Front and Center	Music with the Hormel Girls		
2:15				
2:30	Time for Defense	Chicagoans Orchestra		Afternoon of a Composer
2:45				
3pm	The US Air Force Band	Report from Overseas		
3:15		Adventures in Science		
3:30		CBS Farm News		
3:45		Radio Reporter's Scratchpad		
4pm	Looking Into Space	Stan Dougherty Orchestra		
4:15				
4:30	Recorded Music	The US Air Force Band	Music We Like	
4:45				
5pm	Roseland Ballroom Orchestra	Dave Stephens Orchestra		
5:15				
5:30		Treasury Bandstand	Pee Wee Reese Orchestra	The Author Speaks
5:45	Club Time			Terrea Lee, songs

EVENING — FALL, 1952

Sunday

	ABC	CBS	MBS	NBC
6pm	Drew Pearson, news	December Bride	Nick Carter, Master Detective	The Scarlet Pimpernel
6:15	Don Gardiner, news			
6:30	Music	Our Miss Brooks	Official Detective	Juvenile Jury
6:45				
7pm		The Lucky Strike Program, Jack Benny	Lights On, Votes Out	Meet Your Match
7:15	The Three Suns			
7:30	George Sokolsky, news	Amos 'n' Andy	Melvin Elliott, news	The Aldrich Family
7:45	Looking into Space		The US Air Force Band	
8pm	The American Music Hall	The Charlie McCarthy Show	Hawaii Calls	The Phil Harris - Alice Faye Show
8:15				
8:30	Café Istanbul	The Phillip Morris Playhouse on Broadway	The Voice of Prophecy	The Theater Guild on the Air
8:45				
9pm	Walter Winchell, gossip	The Hallmark Playhouse	The Opera Concert	
9:15	Taylor Grant, news			
9:30	Melody Highway	Escape	The John J. Anthony Program	Dragnet
9:45	Alistair Cooke, comment			
10pm	Paul Harvey, news	The Longines Choraliers	The Radio Bible Class	Barrie Craig: Confidential Investigator
10:15	Gloria Parker, news			
10:30	Time Capsule	The Eddie Fisher Show	The Back to God Hour	Meet the Press
10:45				

EVENING — FALL, 1952

Monday

ABC	CBS	MBS	NBC	
Walter Kiernan, news	Allan Jackson, news	News on the Human Side	Kenneth Banghart, news	6pm
The Allen Stuart Show	You and the World	Dorothy and Dick, talk	Bill Stern, sports	6:15
	Curt Massey, songs	Fred Vandeventer, news	Bob and Ray	6:30
	Lowell Thomas, news	Stan Lomax, sports	Three Star Extra	6:45
Taylor Grant, news	The Beulah Show	Fulton Lewis Jr., news	The Longines Symphonette	7pm
Elmer Davis, news	The Jack Smith Show	Bing Crosby Records		7:15
The Lone Ranger	Club Fifteen	Gabriel Heatter, news	Morgan Beatty, news	7:30
	Edward R. Murrow, news	The Mutual Newsreel	One Man's Family	7:45
Henry J. Taylor, news	Suspense	Woman of the Year	The Railroad Hour	8pm
Bob Edge's Outdoor Talks				8:15
Dinner with the Fitzgeralds	Arthur Godfrey's Talent Scouts	Crime Does Not Pay	The Voice of Firestone	8:30
		Bill Henry, news (8:55pm)		8:45
Tommy Henrich's All-Star Show	The Lux Radio Theater	Mutual Reporter's Round-Up	The Bell Telephone Hour	9pm
				9:15
		On and Off the Record	The Cities Service Band of America	9:30
				9:45
John Daly, news	The Bob Hawk Show	Frank Edwards, news	Bold Venture	10pm
Spotlight, New York		I Love a Mystery		10:15
	Dance Orchestra	The Show Shop	Dangerous Assignment	10:30
				10:45

EVENING — FALL, 1952

Tuesday

	ABC	CBS	MBS	NBC
6pm	Walter Kiernan, news	Allan Jackson, news	News on the Human Side	Kenneth Banghart, news
6:15	The Allen Stuart Show	You and the World	Dorothy and Dick, talk	Bill Stern, sports
6:30		Curt Massey, songs	Fred Vandeventer, news	Bob and Ray
6:45		Lowell Thomas, news	Stan Lomax, sports	Three Star Extra
7pm	Taylor Grant, news	The Beulah Show	Fulton Lewis Jr., news	The Longines Symphonette
7:15	Elmer Davis, news	The Jack Smith Show	Bing Crosby Records	
7:30	The Silver Eagle	Club Fifteen	Gabriel Heatter, news	Morgan Beatty, news
7:45		Edward R. Murrow, news	The Mutual Newsreel	One Man's Family
8pm	Michael Shayne, Private Detective	People Are Funny	The Black Museum	The Cavalcade of America
8:15				
8:30	Paul Whiteman's Teen Club	Mr. and Mrs. North	The Story of Dr. Kildare	The Red Skelton Show
8:45				
9pm	America's Town Meeting of the Air	Life with Luigi	The Search That Never Ends	The Martin and Lewis Show
9:15				
9:30		My Friend Irma	On and Off the Record	Fibber Magee and Molly
9:45	Edwin D. Canham, news			
10pm	John Daly, news	The Doris Day Show	Frank Edwards, news	Two for the Money
10:15	Spotlight, New York		I Love a Mystery	
10:30		Dance Orchestra	The Show Shop	The First Nighter Program
10:45				

EVENING — FALL, 1952

Wednesday

ABC	CBS	MBS	NBC	
Walter Kiernan, news	Allan Jackson, news	News on the Human Side	Kenneth Banghart, news	6pm
The Allen Stuart Show	You and the World	Dorothy and Dick, talk	Bill Stern, sports	6:15
	Curt Massey, songs	Fred Vandeventer, news	Bob and Ray	6:30
	Lowell Thomas, news	Stan Lomax, sports	Three Star Extra	6:45
Taylor Grant, news	The Beulah Show	Fulton Lewis Jr., news	The Longines Symphonette	7pm
Elmer Davis, news	The Jack Smith Show	Bing Crosby Records		7:15
The Lone Ranger	Club Fifteen	Gabriel Heatter, news	Morgan Beatty, news	7:30
	Edward R. Murrow, news	The Mutual Newsreel	One Man's Family	7:45
Mystery Theater	The FBI in Peace and War	The MGM Musical Comedy Theater of the Air	Walk a Mile	8pm
				8:15
Life Begins at Eighty	Dr. Christian		The Great Gildersleeve	8:30
				8:45
Mr. President	The Lineup	The Family Theater	You Bet Your Life	9pm
				9:15
Crossfire	What's My Line	On and Off the Record	The Big Story	9:30
				9:45
John Daly, news	The Wednesday Night Fights	Frank Edwards, news	Jason and the Golden Fleece	10pm
Spotlight, New York		I Love a Mystery		10:15
		The Show Shop	Al Goodman Musical Album	10:30
	Henry Jerome Orchestra			10:45

EVENING — FALL, 1952

Thursday

	ABC	CBS	MBS	NBC
6pm	Walter Kiernan, news	Allan Jackson, news	News on the Human Side	Kenneth Banghart, news
6:15	The Allen Stuart Show	You and the World	Dorothy and Dick, talk	Bill Stern, sports
6:30		Curt Massey, songs	Fred Vandeventer, news	Bob and Ray
6:45		Lowell Thomas, news	Stan Lomax, sports	Three Star Extra
7pm	Taylor Grant, news	The Beulah Show	Fulton Lewis Jr., news	The Longines Symphonette
7:15	Elmer Davis, news	The Jack Smith Show	Bing Crosby Records	
7:30	The Silver Eagle	Club Fifteen	Gabriel Heatter, news	Morgan Beatty, news
7:45		Edward R. Murrow, news	The Mutual Newsreel	One Man's Family
8pm	Defense Attorney	Meet Millie	The Modern Adventures of Casanova	The Roy Rogers Show
8:15				
8:30	The Top Guy	Junior Miss	The Hardy Family	Father Knows Best
8:45				
9pm	Escape with Me	Theater of Romance	The Rod and Gun Club	Truth or Consequences
9:15				
9:30	News As It Happened	The General Electric Show, Bing Crosby	On and Off the Record	The Eddie Cantor Show
9:45				
10pm	John Daly, news	Autumn in New York, Jimmy Carroll	Frank Edwards, news	Guy Lombardo Orchestra
10:15	Spotlight, New York		I Love a Mystery	
10:30		Dance Orchestra	The Show Shop	Pickens Party
10:45				

EVENING — FALL, 1952

Friday

ABC	CBS	MBS	NBC	
Walter Kiernan, news	Allan Jackson, news	News on the Human Side	Kenneth Banghart, news	6pm
The Allen Stuart Show	You and the World	Dorothy and Dick, talk	Bill Stern, sports	6:15
	Curt Massey, songs	Fred Vandeventer, news	Bob and Ray	6:30
	Lowell Thomas, news	Stan Lomax, sports	Three Star Extra	6:45
Taylor Grant, news	The Beulah Show	Fulton Lewis Jr., news	The Longines Symphonette	7pm
Elmer Davis, news	The Jack Smith Show	Bing Crosby Records		7:15
The Lone Ranger	Club Fifteen	Gabriel Heatter, news	Morgan Beatty, news	7:30
	Edward R. Murrow, news	The Mutual Newsreel	One Man's Family	7:45
Crime Letter from Dan Dodge	Mr. Keen, Tracer of Lost Persons	Maisie	Your Hit Parade	8pm
				8:15
This is Your FBI	Gunsmoke	The Gracie Fields Show	Music By Mantovani	8:30
				8:45
The Adventures of Ozzie and Harriet	Mr. Chameleon	The Great Day	Best Plays	9pm
				9:15
Meet Corliss Archer	Horatio Hornblower	On and Off the Record		9:30
				9:45
Madison Square Garden Boxing	Capitol Cloak Room	Frank Edwards, news	Hy Gardner Calling	10pm
		I Love a Mystery	Words in the Night	10:15
	Dance Orchestra	The Show Shop	Radio City Preview	10:30
			Sam Haye's Tips	10:45

EVENING — FALL, 1952

Saturday

	ABC	CBS	MBS	NBC
6pm	Una Mae Carlisle, songs	Joe Wershba, news	News on the Human Side	Kenneth Banghart, news
6:15	Faith for the Future	UN on the Record	Rukeyser Reports	Earl Godwin, news
6:30	Bob Finnigan, sports	The Saturday Sports Review	Fred Vandeventer, news	NBC Symphony Orchestra
6:45	The Allen Stuart Show	Larry Lesueur, news	Stan Lomax, sports	
7pm	Cavalcade of Music	Broadway is My Beat	History in the Making	
7:15			Report from the Pentagon	
7:30	Henry Jerome Orchestra	The Camel Caravan, Vaughn Monroe	Down You Go	Vladimir Horowitz Classical Music
7:45				
8pm	It's Your Business	Gene Autry's Melody Ranch	Twenty Questions	Inside Bob and Ray
8:15	As We See It			
8:30	Spotlight, New York	Tarzan	The MGM Theater of the Air	Dude Ranch Jamboree
8:45				
9pm		Gangbusters		Pee Wee King Orchestra
9:15				
9:30		The Steve Allen Show	Lombardoland USA	Grand Ole Opry
9:45				
10pm			The Chicago Theater of the Air	Reuben, Reuben
10:15				
10:30		Ray Sinatra Orchestra		The Duke of Paducah and Opry Songs
10:45				

DAYTIME — FALL, 1952

Sunday

	ABC	CBS	MBS	NBC
9am	Bible Study	St. Paul's Trinity Choir	News	News
9:15		News	The Magic of Believing	The Comic Weekly Man
9:30	The Voice of Prophecy	From the Organ Loft	The Mutual Radio Chapel	
9:45				Faith in Action
10am	Message of Israel	The CBS Church of the Air	Henry Gladstone, news	The National Radio Pulpit
10:15			Your Money at Work	
10:30	Negro College Choirs		Lorraine Sherwood, talk	The Horn and Hardart Children's Hour
10:45			Your Hymnal	
11am	Brunch Time	The Salt Lake Tabernacle Choir	Henry Gladstone, news	
11:15	Beauty Talk		Brunch with Dorothy and Dick	
11:30	Christian in Action	Invitation to Learning		Peter Roberts, news
11:45				Pickens Party
12pm	Sunday News Special	Bill Costello's News Story	The Men's Corner	Hollywood, USA
12:15	Bob Edge's Outdoor Talks		The Family Rosary Crusade	
12:30	The Herald of Truth	Howard K. Smith, news	Bill Cunningham, news	The Eternal Light
12:45		Bill Costello, news	The Canary Pet Shop	
1pm	Dr. William Ward Ayer, talk	String Serenade	Festival of Opera	Youth Wants to Know
1:15				
1:30	National Vespers	Galen Drake, talk		Pro and Con
1:45		Syncopation Piece		Your Voice of Freedom

DAYTIME — FALL, 1952

Monday-Friday

ABC	CBS	MBS	NBC	
The Breakfast Club	This is New York, Danny O'Neil	Harry Hennessy, news	Tex and Jinx, talk (8:30am)	9am
		John Gambling's Second Breakfast		9:15
	The Joan Edwards Show	The McCanns at Home	The Herb Sheldon Show	9:30
			The Brighter Day	9:45
My True Story	Arthur Godfrey Time	Henry Gladstone, news	Welcome, Travelers	10am
		Martha Deane, talk		10:15
Whispering Streets			The Herb Sheldon Show	10:30
When a Girl Marries			Victor Lindlahr, health	10:45
The Tom Reddy Show		Ladies Fair	Strike It Rich	11am
				11:15
Break the Bank	Grand Slam	Queen for a Day	Bob and Ray	11:30
	Rosemary		Dial Dave Garroway	11:45
The Jack Berch Show	Wendy Warren and the News	Curt Massey, songs	Faye Emerson, talk	12pm
Maggie McNellis, talk	Aunt Jenny's True Life Stories	Bruce and Dan, songs		12:15
Kitchen Kapers	The Romance of Helen Trent	Henry Gladstone, news		12:30
	Our Gal Sunday	Luncheon at Sardi's	Skitch's Scrapbook	12:45
Mary Margaret McBride, talk	Big Sister			1pm
	Ma Perkins			1:15
	Young Dr. Malone	Barbara Welles, talk	The Conrad Nagel Show	1:30
	The Guiding Light			1:45

DAYTIME — FALL, 1952

Sunday

	ABC	CBS	MBS	NBC
2pm	The Piano Playhouse	The Longines Symphonette		The Catholic Hour
2:15				
2:30	Christian Science Monitor	Your Invitation to Music		Sammy Kaye's Sylvania Serenade
2:45	Women in Uniform			
3pm	Marines in Review			Music with the Hormel Girls
3:15				
3:30	The Hour of Decision		Your Money at Work	Bob Considine, news
3:45			News	Critic at Large
4pm	The Old Fashioned Revival Hour	America Calling	Under Arrest	The Chase
4:15				
4:30		The Quiz Kids	The Private Files of Matthew Bell	Martin Kane, Private Detective
4:45				
5pm	This Week Around the World	Arthur Godfrey's Digest	The Shadow	The Hollywood Star Playhouse
5:15				
5:30	The Greatest Story Ever Told	Robert Trout, news	True Detective Mysteries	Counterspy
5:45		Larry Lesueur, news		

DAYTIME — FALL, 1952

Monday-Friday

ABC	CBS	MBS	NBC	
The Eddie Dunn Show	The Second Mrs. Burton	A. L. Alexander's Mediation Board	The Herb Sheldon Show	2pm
	Perry Mason			2:15
Betty Crocker, cooking	This is Nora Drake	Paula Stone, talk	Every Day	2:30
It's Up to You	The Brighter Day	The Answer Man	Kukla, Fran and Ollie	2:45
The Eddie Dunn Show	Hilltop House	Rambling with Gambling	Life Can Be Beautiful	3pm
	House Party		The Road of Life	3:15
The Tennessee Ernie Ford Show		Pat Barnes and Barbara, talk	Pepper Young's Family	3:30
	Aunt Jemima Home Folks	Tello-Test Quiz	The Right to Happiness	3:45
Cal Tinney, talk	The Emily Kimbrough Show	The Jack Kirkwood Show	Mary Noble, Backstage Wife	4pm
			Stella Dallas	4:15
Dean Cameron, talk	The Housewives' League	The Merry Mailman	Young Widder Brown	4:30
			The Woman in My House	4:45
Bobby Sherwood Orchestra	John Henry Faulk, talk	Bobby Benson / The Green Hornet	Just Plain Bill	5pm
		Sergeant Preston of the Yukon	Front Page Farrell	5:15
Big Jon and Sparkie		Wild Bill Hickok	Lorenzo Jones	5:30
Dan Peterson, talk		Sky King	The Doctor's Wife	5:45

DAYTIME — FALL, 1952

Saturday

	ABC	CBS	MBS	NBC
9am	No School Today	This is New York, Danny O'Neill	Harry Hennessy, news	Howdy Doody (8:30am)
9:15			Bing Crosby Records	
9:30		The Housewives' League	The McCanns at Home	Jackie Robinson, sports
9:45				
10am		Galen Drake, talk	Henry Gladstone, news	Archie Andrews
10:15		The Space Adventures of Super Noodle	Martha Deane, talk	
10:30	Space Patrol	The Stamp Club		Mary Lee Taylor, cooking
10:45		The Children's Hour		
11am	Junior Junction	Let's Pretend	Prescott Robinson, news	My Secret Story
11:15			Lorraine Sherwood, talk	
11:30	The Eddie Fisher Show	Give and Take	Farm Quiz	Hollywood Love Story
11:45				
12pm	The Home Gardener	The Armstrong Theater of Today	The Man on the Farm	Perry Como Records
12:15				
12:30	Beauty Hints	Stars Over Hollywood	Henry Gladstone, news	Star's Reviews of the Hits
12:45	News		Let's Go	
1pm	The US Navy Band	Fun For All, Arlene Francis	The Show Shop	The National Farm and Home Hour
1:15				
1:30	Vincent Lopez Orchestra	City Hospital		Uncle Sam's Playhouse
1:45				

DAYTIME — FALL, 1952

Saturday

	ABC	CBS	MBS	NBC
2pm	Sports	Music with the Hormel Girls	Sports	Sports
2:15				
2:30		Sports Round-Up		
2:45				
3pm		Sports		
3:15				
3:30				
3:45				
4pm				
4:15				
4:30				
4:45				
5pm			Rambling with Gambling	
5:15				
5:30	At Home with Music	Saturday at the Chase	Music We Like	Sports Round-Up
5:45	Club Time			Pickens Party

LISTINGS FOR 1953

EVENING — WINTER, 1953

Sunday

	ABC	CBS	MBS	NBC
6pm	Drew Pearson, news	December Bride	Nick Carter, Master Detective	The Scarlet Pimpernel
6:15	Don Gardiner, news			
6:30	Music	Our Miss Brooks	The Squad Room	Juvenile Jury
6:45				
7pm		The Lucky Strike Program, Jack Benny	The US Marine Band	My Son Jeep
7:15				
7:30	George Sokolsky, news	Amos 'n' Andy	Serenade in Blue	The Aldrich Family
7:45	Alistair Cooke, comment			
8pm	The American Music Hall	The Charlie McCarthy Show	The Lutheran Hour	The Phil Harris - Alice Faye Show
8:15				
8:30		My Little Margie	The Voice of Prophecy	The Theater Guild on the Air
8:45				
9pm	Walter Winchell, gossip	The Hallmark Hall of Fame	Jazz Nocturne	
9:15	Taylor Grant, news			
9:30	The Adventurer	Escape	America in the Year Ahead	Dragnet
9:45				
10pm	Paul Harvey, news	Music for You	The Radio Bible Class	Barrie Craig, Confidential Investigator
10:15	Gloria Parker, songs			
10:30	Time Capsule	Thinking Out Loud	The Back to God Hour	Meet the Press
10:45		UN Report		

EVENING — WINTER, 1953

Monday

ABC	CBS	MBS	NBC	
Walter Kiernan, news	Allan Jackson, news	News on the Human Side	Kenneth Banghart, news	6pm
The Allen Stuart Show	You and the World	Dorothy and Dick, talk	Bill Stern, sports	6:15
	Curt Massey, songs	Fred Vandeventer, news	Bob and Ray	6:30
	Lowell Thomas, news	Stan Lomax, sports	Three Star Extra	6:45
Taylor Grant, news	The Beulah Show	Fulton Lewis Jr., news	The Longines Symphonette	7pm
Elmer Davis, news	Junior Miss	The Answer Man		7:15
The Lone Ranger	Club Fifteen	Gabriel Heatter, news	Morgan Beatty, news	7:30
	Edward R. Murrow, news	The Mutual Newsreel	One Man's Family	7:45
Henry J. Taylor, news	Suspense	The Falcon	The Railroad Hour	8pm
Bob Edge's Outdoor Talks				8:15
Dinner with the Fitzgeralds	Arthur Godfrey's Talent Scouts	The Hall of Fantasy	The Voice of Firestone	8:30
		Bill Henry, news (8:55pm)		8:45
The Metropolitan Opera Auditions	The Lux Radio Theater	Mutual Reporter's Round-Up	The Bell Telephone Hour	9pm
				9:15
The ABC Radio Workshop		On and Off the Record	The Cities Service Band of America	9:30
				9:45
News of Tomorrow	The Bob Hawk Show	Frank Edwards, news	Encore, Robert Merrill	10pm
Spotlight, New York		Once in Every Family		10:15
	Cedric Adams, news	The Show Shop	Dangerous Assignment	10:30
	The Three Suns			10:45

EVENING — WINTER, 1953

Tuesday

	ABC	CBS	MBS	NBC
6pm	Walter Kiernan, news	Allan Jackson, news	News on the Human Side	Kenneth Banghart, news
6:15	The Allen Stuart Show	You and the World	Dorothy and Dick, talk	Bill Stern, sports
6:30		Curt Massey, songs	Fred Vandeventer, news	Bob and Ray
6:45		Lowell Thomas, news	Stan Lomax, sports	Three Star Extra
7pm	Taylor Grant, news	The Beulah Show	Fulton Lewis Jr., news	The Longines Symphonette
7:15	Elmer Davis, news	Junior Miss	The Answer Man	
7:30	The Silver Eagle	Club Fifteen	Gabriel Heatter, news	Morgan Beatty, news
7:45		Edward R. Murrow, news	The Mutual Newsreel	One Man's Family
8pm	Sparring Partners	People Are Funny	That Hammer Guy	The Cavalcade of America
8:15				
8:30	Paul Whiteman's Teen Club	Mr. and Mrs. North	High Adventure	The Red Skelton Show
8:45				
9pm	America's Town Meeting of the Air	Life with Luigi	The Search That Never Ends	The Martin and Lewis Show
9:15				
9:30		My Friend Irma	On and Off the Record	Fibber Magee and Molly
9:45	Edwin D. Canham, news			
10pm	News of Tomorrow	The Doris Day Show	Frank Edwards, news	Two for the Money
10:15	Spotlight, New York		Mr. Mystery	
10:30		Cedric Adams, news	The Show Shop	The First Nighter Program
10:45		The Three Suns		

EVENING — WINTER, 1953

Wednesday

ABC	CBS	MBS	NBC	
Walter Kiernan, news	Allan Jackson, news	News on the Human Side	Kenneth Banghart, news	6pm
The Allen Stuart Show	You and the World	Dorothy and Dick, talk	Bill Stern, sports	6:15
	Curt Massey, songs	Fred Vandeventer, news	Bob and Ray	6:30
	Lowell Thomas, news	Stan Lomax, sports	Three Star Extra	6:45
Taylor Grant, news	The Beulah Show	Fulton Lewis Jr., news	The Longines Symphonette	7pm
Elmer Davis, news	Junior Miss	The Answer Man		7:15
The Lone Ranger	Club Fifteen	Gabriel Heatter, news	Morgan Beatty, news	7:30
	Edward R. Murrow, news	The Mutual Newsreel	One Man's Family	7:45
Mystery Theater	The FBI in Peace and War	The Crime Files of Flamond	Walk a Mile	8pm
				8:15
Life Begins at Eighty	Dr. Christian	Crime Fighters	The Great Gildersleeve	8:30
				8:45
Mr. President	The Philip Morris Playhouse on Broadway	The Family Theater	You Bet Your Life	9pm
				9:15
Crossfire	What's My Line	On and Off the Record	The Big Story	9:30
				9:45
News of Tomorrow	The Lineup	Frank Edwards, news	The Bob Hope Show	10pm
Spotlight, New York		Ruby Mercer Orchestra		10:15
	Cedric Adams, news	The Show Shop	Al Goodman Musical Album	10:30
	Henry Jerome Orchestra			10:45

EVENING — WINTER, 1953

Thursday

	ABC	CBS	MBS	NBC
6pm	Walter Kiernan, news	Allan Jackson, news	News on the Human Side	Kenneth Banghart, news
6:15	The Allan Stuart Show	You and the World	Dorothy and Dick, talk	Bill Stern, sports
6:30		Curt Massey, songs	Fred Vandeventer, news	Bob and Ray
6:45		Lowell Thomas, news	Stan Lomax, sports	Three Star Extra
7pm	Taylor Grant, news	The Beulah Show	Fulton Lewis Jr., news	The Longines Symphonette
7:15	Elmer Davis, news	Junior Miss	The Answer Man	
7:30	The Silver Eagle	Club Fifteen	Gabriel Heatter, news	Morgan Beatty, news
7:45		Edward R. Murrow, news	The Mutual Newsreel	One Man's Family
8pm	The Top Guy	Meet Millie	Official Detective	The Roy Rogers Show
8:15				
8:30	Heritage	On Stage	John Steele, Adventurer	Father Knows Best
8:45				
9pm	Tales of Tomorrow	Time for Love	The Rod and Gun Club	Truth or Consequences
9:15				
9:30	Michael Shayne, Private Detective	The General Electric Show, Bing Crosby	On and Off the Record	The Eddie Cantor Show
9:45				
10pm	News of Tomorrow	The Youth Opportunity Program	Frank Edwards, news	The Judy Canova Show
10:15	Spotlight, New York		Mr. Mystery	
10:30		Cedric Adams, news	The Show Shop	Pickens Party
10:45		Dance Orchestra		

EVENING — WINTER, 1953

Friday

ABC	CBS	MBS	NBC	
Walter Kiernan, news	Allan Jackson, news	News on the Human Side	Kenneth Banghart, news	6pm
The Allan Stuart Show	You and the World	Dorothy and Dick, talk	Bill Stern, sports	6:15
	Curt Massey, songs	Fred Vandeventer, news	Bob and Ray	6:30
	Lowell Thomas, news	Stan Lomax, sports	Three Star Extra	6:45
Taylor Grant, news	The Beulah Show	Fulton Lewis Jr., news	The Longines Symphonette	7pm
Elmer Davis, news	Junior Miss	The Answer Man		7:15
The Lone Ranger	Club Fifteen	Gabriel Heatter, news	Morgan Beatty, news	7:30
	Edward R. Murrow, news	The Mutual Newsreel	One Man's Family	7:45
Crime Letter from Dan Dodge	Mr. Keen, Tracer of Lost Persons	The Movie Jackpot	Your Hit Parade	8pm
				8:15
This is Your FBI	Yours Truly, Johnny Dollar	True or False	Name That Tune	8:30
				8:45
The Adventures of Ozzie and Harriet	There's Music in the Air	The Great Day	Best Plays	9pm
				9:15
Meet Corliss Archer		On and Off the Record		9:30
				9:45
Madison Square Garden Boxing	Capitol Cloak Room	Frank Edwards, news	Hy Gardner Calling	10pm
		Ruby Mercer Orchestra	Words in the Night	10:15
	Cedric Adams, news	The Show Shop	Radio City Preview	10:30
	Dance Orchestra		Pro and Con	10:45

EVENING — WINTER, 1953

Saturday

	ABC	CBS	MBS	NBC
6pm	Una Mae Carlisle, songs	Joe Wershba, news	News on the Human Side	Kenneth Banghart, news
6:15	The Buddy Weed Trio	UN on the Record	Rukeyser Reports	H. V. Kaltenborn, news
6:30	Bob Finnigan, sports	The Saturday Sports Review	Fred Vandeventer, news	NBC Symphony Orchestra
6:45	The Allan Stuart Show	Larry Lesueur, news	Stan Lomax, sports	
7pm	Cavalcade of Music	Broadway is My Beat	Al Helfer, sports	
7:15			Report from the Pentagon	
7:30	Dinner at the Green Room	The Camel Caravan, Vaughn Monroe	Down You Go	Vladimir Horowitz Classical Music
7:45				
8pm	The CIO and You	Gene Autry's Melody Ranch	Twenty Questions	Inside Bob and Ray
8:15	Industry Reports			
8:30	ABC Dancing Party	Tarzan	Take a Number	Reuben, Reuben
8:45				
9pm		Gangbusters	The New England Barn Dance	Pee Wee King Orchestra
9:15				
9:30		Gunsmoke	Lombardoland USA	Grand Ole Opry
9:45				
10pm	Spotlight, New York	Saturday Night, Country Style	The Chicago Theater of the Air	Checkerboard Fun Festival
10:15				
10:30		Ray Sinatra Orchestra		Meredith Willson's Music Room
10:45				

DAYTIME — WINTER, 1953

Sunday

	ABC	CBS	MBS	NBC
9am	Bible Study	St. Paul's Trinity Choir	News	News
9:15		News	The Magic of Believing	The Comic Weekly Man
9:30	The Voice of Prophecy	From the Organ Loft	The Mutual Radio Chapel	
9:45				Faith in Action
10am	Message of Israel	The CBS Church of the Air	Henry Gladstone, news	The National Radio Pulpit
10:15			Bing Crosby Records	
10:30	Negro College Choirs		Faith in Our Time	The Horn and Hardart Children's Hour
10:45			Your Hymnal	
11am	Brunch Time	The Salt Lake Tabernacle Choir	Henry Gladstone, news	
11:15	Beauty Talk		The Bromfield Farm Report	
11:30	Christian in Action	Invitation to Learning	Mr. and Mrs. Dick Gordon, talk	Peter Roberts, news
11:45				Pickens Party
12pm	Sunday News Special	Bill Costello's News Story	Your Investment Dollar	Hollywood, USA
12:15	Looking into Space		The Men's Corner	
12:30	The Herald of Truth	Howard K. Smith, news	Bill Cunningham, news	The Eternal Light
12:45		Bill Costello, news	The Canary Pet Shop	
1pm	Dr. William Ward Ayer, talk	String Serenade	Festival of Opera	Youth Wants to Know
1:15				
1:30	National Vespers	Syncopation Piece		Proudly We Hail
1:45				

DAYTIME — WINTER, 1953

Monday-Friday

ABC	CBS	MBS	NBC	
The Breakfast Club	This is New York, Danny O'Neill	Robert Hurleigh, news	Tex and Jinx, talk (8:30am)	9am
		John Gambling's Second Breakfast		9:15
	Bea Wain and Andre Baruch, talk	The McCanns at Home	The Jim Coy Show	9:30
				9:45
My True Story	Arthur Godfrey Time	Cecil Brown, news	Welcome, Travelers	10am
		Martha Deane, talk		10:15
Whispering Streets			The Herb Sheldon Show	10:30
When a Girl Marries			Victor Lindlahr, health	10:45
Live Like a Millionaire		Ladies Fair	Strike It Rich	11am
				11:15
Break the Bank	Grand Slam	Queen for a Day	Bob and Ray	11:30
	Rosemary		The Bob Hope Show	11:45
The Jack Berch Show	Wendy Warren and the News	Curt Massey, songs	Faye Emerson, talk	12pm
Maggie McNellis, talk	Aunt Jenny's True Life Stories	Bruce and Dan, songs		12:15
	The Romance of Helen Trent	Henry Gladstone, news		12:30
Charles F. McCarthy, news	Our Gal Sunday	Luncheon at Sardi's	Skitch's Scrapbook	12:45
Mary Margaret McBride, talk	The Road of Life			1pm
	Ma Perkins			1:15
	Young Dr. Malone	Barbara Welles, talk	The Conrad Nagel Show	1:30
	The Guiding Light			1:45

DAYTIME — WINTER, 1953

Sunday

	ABC	CBS	MBS	NBC
2pm	The Church in the Home	The Longines Symphonette		The Catholic Hour
2:15				
2:30	Christian Science Monitor	New York Philharmonic Orchestra		The American Forum of the Air
2:45				
3pm	Dr. James McGinley, health			Where the Public Stands
3:15				Youth Brings You Music
3:30	The Hour of Decision		Your Money at Work	Bob Considine, news
3:45			News	Critic at Large
4pm	The Old Fashioned Revival Hour	America Calling	Under Arrest	The Chase
4:15				
4:30		The Quiz Kids	Dear Margie, It's Murder	Jason and the Golden Fleece
4:45				
5pm	This Week Around the World	Arthur Godfrey's Digest	The Shadow	The Hollywood Star Playhouse
5:15				
5:30	The Greatest Story Ever Told	Robert Trout, news	True Detective Mysteries	Counterspy
5:45		Larry Lesueur, news		

DAYTIME — WINTER, 1953

Monday-Friday

ABC	CBS	MBS	NBC	
The Eddie Dunn Show	The Second Mrs. Burton	A. L. Alexander's Mediation Board	News	*2pm*
	Perry Mason		The Herb Sheldon Show	*2:15*
	This is Nora Drake	The Mae McGuire Show / Paula Stone, talk	Dial Dave Garroway	*2:30*
	The Brighter Day	The Answer Man	Kukla, Fran and Ollie	*2:45*
	Hilltop House	Rambling with Gambling	Life Can Be Beautiful	*3pm*
National Health Aids	House Party		The Road of Life	*3:15*
The Tennessee Ernie Ford Show		Pat Barnes and Barbara, talk	Pepper Young's Family	*3:30*
	Aunt Jemima Home Folks	Tello-Test Quiz	The Right to Happiness	*3:45*
Cal Tinney, talk	The Emily Kimbrough Show	The Jack Kirkwood Show	Mary Noble, Backstage Wife	*4pm*
			Stella Dallas	*4:15*
Dean Cameron, talk	The Housewives' League	The Merry Mailman	Young Widder Brown	*4:30*
			The Woman in My House	*4:45*
Big Jon and Sparkie	John Henry Faulk, talk	Bobby Benson	Just Plain Bill	*5pm*
Bobby Sherwood Orchestra		Sergeant Preston of the Yukon	Front Page Farrell	*5:15*
		Wild Bill Hickok	Lorenzo Jones	*5:30*
		Sky King	The Doctor's Wife	*5:45*

DAYTIME — WINTER, 1953

Saturday

	ABC	CBS	MBS	NBC
9am	No School Today	This is New York, Danny O'Neill	Harry Hennessy, news	Howdy Doody (8:30am)
9:15			Bing Crosby Records	
9:30		The Housewives' League	The McCanns at Home	Mind Your Manners
9:45				
10am		Galen Drake, talk	Henry Gladstone, news	Archie Andrews
10:15		The Space Adventures of Super Noodle	Martha Deane, talk	
10:30	Space Patrol	The Stamp Club		Mary Lee Taylor, cooking
10:45		Robert Q. Lewis's Waxworks		
11am	The Jack Owens Show	Grand Central Station	Prescott Robinson, news	My Secret Story
11:15			Lorraine Sherwood, talk	
11:30	The Eddie Fisher Show	Give and Take	Farm Quiz	Hollywood Love Story
11:45				
12pm	The Home Gardener	The Armstrong Theater of Today	The Man on the Farm	Arthur Barriault, news
12:15				Buster Crabbe, talk
12:30	Beauty Hints	Stars Over Hollywood	Henry Gladstone, news	Perry Como Records
12:45	News		Country Editor	
1pm	Mary Margaret McBride, talk	Fun For All, Arlene Francis	The Affairs of Peter Salem	The National Farm and Home Hour
1:15				
1:30	Vincent Lopez Orchestra	City Hospital	Symphonies for Youth	Public Affairs
1:45				

DAYTIME — WINTER, 1953

Saturday

	ABC	CBS	MBS	NBC
2pm	The Metropolitan Opera	Music with the Hormel Girls		Kaleidoscope
2:15				
2:30		Let's Pretend	The US Marine Band	
2:45				
3pm		Report from Overseas	Bandstand USA	
3:15		Adventures in Science		
3:30		CBS Farm News	The Sports Parade	
3:45		Radio Reporter's Scratchpad		
4pm		Woody Herman Orchestra	Salute to the Nation	
4:15				
4:30		Washington, USA	The Mae McGuire Show	
4:45				
5pm	Roseland Ballroom Orchestra	The Eddie Fisher Show	The Show Shop	Treasury of Music
5:15				
5:30		Saturday at the Chase		Musical Barometer
5:45	Club Time			Pickens Party

EVENING — SPRING, 1953

Sunday

	ABC	CBS	MBS	NBC
6pm	Drew Pearson, news	Baker's Theater of Stars	Nick Carter, Master Detective	Bob Considine, sports
6:15	Norman Brokenshire, news			Meet the Veep
6:30	George Sokolsky, news	Our Miss Brooks	The Squad Room	My Favorite Story
6:45	Alistair Cooke, comment			
7pm	Don Cornell, songs	The Lucky Strike Program, Jack Benny	Treasury Varieties	My Son Jeep
7:15	The American Music Hall			
7:30		Amos 'n' Andy	Melvin Elliott, news	The Aldrich Family
7:45			Norman Brokenshire, news	
8pm		The Charlie McCarthy Show	The Lutheran Hour	The Phil Harris - Alice Faye Show
8:15				
8:30		My Little Margie	The Voice of Prophecy	The Theater Guild on the Air
8:45				
9pm	Walter Winchell, gossip	The Hallmark Hall of Fame	The US Marine Band	
9:15	Taylor Grant, news			
9:30	Freedom, USA	Escape	Answers for Americans	Dragnet
9:45				
10pm	The Adventurer	The Quiz Kids	The Radio Bible Class	Barrie Craig, Confidential Investigator
10:15				
10:30	Discovery	Thinking Out Loud	The Back to God Hour	Meet the Press
10:45	Paul Harvey, news	The UN Report		

EVENTS — SPRING, 1953

Monday

ABC	CBS	MBS	NBC	
Walter Kiernan, news	Allan Jackson, news	News on the Human Side	Kenneth Banghart, news	*6pm*
Bobby Sherwood Orchestra	Dwight Cooke, talk	Dorothy and Dick, talk	Bill Stern, sports	*6:15*
	Curt Massey, songs	Fred Vandeventer, news	Bob and Ray	*6:30*
	Lowell Thomas, news	Stan Lomax, sports	Three Star Extra	*6:45*
Taylor Grant, news	The Beulah Show	Fulton Lewis Jr., news	The Longines Symphonette	*7pm*
Elmer Davis, news	Junior Miss	The Answer Man		*7:15*
The Lone Ranger	Club Fifteen	Gabriel Heatter, news	Morgan Beatty, news	*7:30*
	Edward R. Murrow, news	Norman Brokenshire, news	One Man's Family	*7:45*
Henry J. Taylor, news	Suspense	The Falcon	The Railroad Hour	*8pm*
Bob Edge's Outdoor Talks				*8:15*
The American Concert Stage	Arthur Godfrey's Talent Scouts	The Hall of Fantasy	The Voice of Firestone	*8:30*
		Bill Henry, news (8:55pm)		*8:45*
	The Lux Radio Theater	Mutual Reporter's Round-Up	The Bell Telephone Hour	*9pm*
				9:15
		The Eugenia Baird Show	The Cities Service Band of America	*9:30*
The Jan Peerce Show				*9:45*
Gordon Fraser, news	The Bob Hawk Show	Frank Edwards, news	The Dinah Shore Show	*10pm*
Spotlight, New York		The Elton Britt Show	Words in the Night	*10:15*
	Cedric Adams, news	The Show Shop	Al Goodman Music Album	*10:30*
	The Three Suns			*10:45*

EVENING — SPRING, 1953

Tuesday

	ABC	CBS	MBS	NBC
6pm	Walter Kiernan, news	Allan Jackson, news	News on the Human Side	Kenneth Banghart, news
6:15	Bobby Sherwood Orchestra	Dwight Cooke, talk	Dorothy and Dick, talk	Bill Stern, sports
6:30		Curt Massey, songs	Fred Vandeventer, news	Bob and Ray
6:45		Lowell Thomas, news	Stan Lomax, sports	Three Star Extra
7pm	Taylor Grant, news	The Beulah Show	Fulton Lewis Jr., news	The Longines Symphonette
7:15	Elmer Davis, news	Junior Miss	The Answer Man	
7:30	The Silver Eagle	Club Fifteen	Gabriel Heatter, news	Morgan Beatty, news
7:45		Edward R. Murrow, news	The Mutual Newsreel	One Man's Family
8pm	SRO	People Are Funny	That Hammer Guy	Stars from Paris
8:15				
8:30	Paul Whiteman's Teen Club	Mr. and Mrs. North	High Adventure	The Red Skelton Show
8:45				
9pm	America's Town Meeting of the Air	Yours Truly, Johnny Dollar	The Search That Never Ends	The Martin and Lewis Show
9:15				
9:30		My Friend Irma	The Eugenia Baird Show	Fibber Magee and Molly
9:45	Edwin D. Canham, news			
10pm	Gordon Fraser, news	Louella Parsons, gossip	Frank Edwards, news	Two for the Money
10:15	Spotlight, New York	The Doris Day Show	The Elton Britt Show	
10:30		Cedric Adams, news	The Show Shop	The First Nighter Program
10:45		The Three Suns		

EVENING — SPRING, 1953

Wednesday

ABC	CBS	MBS	NBC	
Walter Kiernan, news	Allan Jackson, news	News on the Human Side	Kenneth Banghart, news	6pm
Bobby Sherwood Orchestra	Dwight Cooke, talk	Dorothy and Dick, talk	Bill Stern, sports	6:15
	Curt Massey, songs	Fred Vandeventer, news	Bob and Ray	6:30
	Lowell Thomas, news	Stan Lomax, sports	Three Star Extra	6:45
Taylor Grant, news	The Beulah Show	Fulton Lewis Jr., news	The Longines Symphonette	7pm
Elmer Davis, news	Junior Miss	The Answer Man		7:15
The Lone Ranger	Club Fifteen	Gabriel Heatter, news	Morgan Beatty, news	7:30
	Edward R. Murrow, news	Norman Brokenshire, news	One Man's Family	7:45
Mystery Theater	The FBI in Peace and War	The Crime Files of Flamond	Walk a Mile	8pm
				8:15
Life Begins at Eighty	Dr. Christian	Crime Fighters	The Great Gildersleeve	8:30
				8:45
Mr. President	The Philip Morris Playhouse on Broadway	The Family Theater	You Bet Your Life	9pm
				9:15
Crossfire	What's My Line	The Eugenia Baird Show	The Big Story	9:30
				9:45
Gordon Fraser, news	December Bride	Frank Edwards, news	The Bob Hope Show	10pm
Spotlight, New York		The Elton Britt Show		10:15
	Cedric Adams, news	The Show Shop	Dangerous Assignment	10:30
	Henry Jerome Orchestra			10:45

EVENTING — SPRING, 1953

Thursday

	ABC	CBS	MBS	NBC
6pm	Walter Kiernan, news	Allan Jackson, news	News on the Human Side	Kenneth Banghart, news
6:15	Bobby Sherwood Orchestra	Dwight Cooke, talk	Dorothy and Dick, talk	Bill Stern, sports
6:30		Curt Massey, songs	Fred Vandeventer, news	Bob and Ray
6:45		Lowell Thomas, news	Stan Lomax, sports	Three Star Extra
7pm	Taylor Grant, news	The Beulah Show	Fulton Lewis Jr., news	The Longines Symphonette
7:15	Elmer Davis, news	Junior Miss	The Answer Man	
7:30	The Silver Eagle	Club Fifteen	Gabriel Heatter, news	Morgan Beatty, news
7:45		Edward R. Murrow, news	The Mutual Newsreel	One Man's Family
8pm	The Top Guy	Meet Millie	Official Detective	The Roy Rogers Show
8:15				
8:30	Heritage	On Stage	John Steele, Adventurer	Father Knows Best
8:45				
9pm	The ABC Radio Workshop	Time for Love	Life is Worth Living	Truth or Consequences
9:15				
9:30	Time Capsule	The General Electric Theater, Bing Crosby	The Eugenia Baird Show	The Eddie Cantor Show
9:45				
10pm	Gordon Fraser, news	The Youth Opportunity Program	Frank Edwards, news	The Judy Canova Show
10:15	Spotlight, New York		The Elton Britt Show	
10:30		Cedric Adams, news	The Show Shop	Pickens Party
10:45		Dance Orchestra		

EVENING — SPRING, 1953

Friday

ABC	CBS	MBS	NBC	
Walter Kiernan, news	Allan Jackson, news	News on the Human Side	Kenneth Banghart, news	6pm
Bobby Sherwood Orchestra	Dwight Cooke, talk	Dorothy and Dick, talk	Bill Stern, sports	6:15
	Curt Massey, songs	Fred Vandeventer, news	Bob and Ray	6:30
	Lowell Thomas, news	Stan Lomax, sports	Three Star Extra	6:45
Taylor Grant, news	The Beulah Show	Fulton Lewis Jr., news	The Longines Symphonette	7pm
Elmer Davis, news	Junior Miss	The Answer Man		7:15
The Lone Ranger	Club Fifteen	Gabriel Heatter, news	Morgan Beatty, news	7:30
	Edward R. Murrow, news	Norman Brokenshire, news	One Man's Family	7:45
Michael Shayne, Private Detective	Mr. Keen, Tracer of Lost Persons	Take a Number	Your Hit Parade	8pm
				8:15
Fun For All, Arlene Francis	Mr. Chameleon	True or False	Best Plays	8:30
				8:45
The Adventures of Ozzie and Harriet	There's Music in the Air	The Rod and Gun Club		9pm
				9:15
Meet Corliss Archer		The Eugenia Baird Show	Name That Tune	9:30
				9:45
Madison Square Garden Boxing	Capitol Cloak Room	Frank Edwards, news	The Dinah Shore Show	10pm
		The Elton Britt Show	Words in the Night	10:15
	Cedric Adams, news	The Show Shop	Radio City Preview	10:30
	Dance Orchestra		Pro and Con	10:45

EVENING — SPRING, 1953

Saturday

	ABC	CBS	MBS	NBC
6pm	Horse Racing	Joe Wershba, news	News on the Human Side	Kenneth Banghart, news
6:15	The International Jazz Club	UN on the Record	Facts Forum	H. V. Kaltenborn, news
6:30		The Saturday Sports Review	Fred Vandeventer, news	The NBC Spring Concert
6:45	As We See It	Larry Lesueur, news	Stan Lomax, sports	
7pm	It's Your Business	Broadway is My Beat	Rukeyser Reports	
7:15	The Three Suns		Report from the Pentagon	
7:30	Dinner at the Green Room	The Camel Caravan, Vaughn Monroe	Down You Go	Vladimir Horowitz Classical Music
7:45				
8pm	ABC Dancing Party	Gene Autry's Melody Ranch	Twenty Questions	Inside Bob and Ray
8:15				
8:30		Tarzan	The Virginia Barn Dance	Medicine, USA
8:45				
9pm		Gangbusters	The New England Barn Dance	Pee Wee King Orchestra
9:15				
9:30		Gunsmoke	Lombardoland USA	Grand Ole Opry
9:45				
10pm	Spotlight, New York	Saturday Night, Country Style	The Chicago Theater of the Air	Treasury of Music
10:15				
10:30		Ray Sinatra Orchestra		Meredith Willson's Music Room
10:45				

DAYTIME — SPRING, 1953

Sunday

	ABC	CBS	MBS	NBC
9am	Bible Study	St. Paul's Trinity Choir	News	News
9:15		News	Where to Retire	The Comic Weekly Man
9:30	The Voice of Prophecy	From the Organ Loft	The Mutual Radio Chapel	
9:45				Faith in Action
10am	Message of Israel	The CBS Church of the Air	Henry Gladstone, news	The National Radio Pulpit
10:15			Norman Brokenshire, news	
10:30	Negro College Choirs		Faith in Our Time	The Horn and Hardart Children's Hour
10:45			Your Hymnal	
11am	Brunch Time	The Salt Lake Tabernacle Choir	Henry Gladstone, news	
11:15	Beauty Talk		Norman Brokenshire, news	
11:30	Christian in Action	Invitation to Learning	Mr. and Mrs. Dick Gordon, talk	Peter Roberts, news
11:45				Pickens Party
12pm	Sunday News Special	Bill Costello's News Story	Your Investment Dollar	Sammy Kaye's Sunday Serenade
12:15	Mrs. Ada Siegel, talk		The Men's Corner	
12:30	The Herald of Truth	Howard K. Smith, news	Bill Cunningham, news	The Eternal Light
12:45		Bill Costello, news	The Canary Pet Shop	
1pm	Dr. William Ward Ayer, talk	Anthony Antonini Orchestra	Fred Vandeventer, news	Youth Wants to Know
1:15		String Symphony	The Lanny Ross Show	
1:30	National Vespers	Let's Find Out	Festival of Opera	Citizens Union Searchlight
1:45				

DAYTIME — SPRING, 1953

Monday-Friday

ABC	CBS	MBS	NBC	
The Breakfast Club	This is New York, Danny O'Neill	Robert Hurleigh, news	Tex and Jinx, talk (8:30am)	9am
		John Gambling's Second Breakfast		9:15
	The Joan Edwards Show	The McCanns at Home	The Jim Coy Show	9:30
				9:45
My True Story	Arthur Godfrey Time	Cecil Brown, news	Welcome, Travelers	10am
		Martha Deane, talk		10:15
Whispering Streets			Stan Freeman, piano	10:30
When a Girl Marries			Victor Lindlahr, health	10:45
Live Like a Millionaire		Ladies Fair	Strike It Rich	11am
				11:15
Turn to a Friend	Grand Slam	Queen for a Day	The Phrase That Pays	11:30
	Rosemary		The Bob Hope Show	11:45
The Jack Berch Show	Wendy Warren and the News	Curt Massey, songs	Faye Emerson, talk	12pm
Maggie McNellis, talk	Aunt Jenny's True Life Stories	The Music Box		12:15
	The Romance of Helen Trent	Henry Gladstone, news		12:30
Charles F. McCarthy, news	Our Gal Sunday	Luncheon at Sardi's	Skitch's Scrapbook	12:45
Mary Margaret McBride, talk	The Road of Life			1pm
	Ma Perkins			1:15
	Young Dr. Malone	Barbara Welles, talk	The Herb Sheldon Show	1:30
	The Guiding Light			1:45

DAYTIME — SPRING, 1953

Sunday

	ABC	CBS	MBS	NBC
2pm	The Church in the Home	The Longines Symphonette		The Catholic Hour
2:15				
2:30	Christian Science Monitor	New York Philharmonic Orchestra		The American Forum of the Air
2:45				
3pm	Dr. James McGinley, health			Critic at Large
3:15				Carnival of Books
3:30	The Hour of Decision		Your Money at Work	Bob Considine, news
3:45			News	Where the Public Stands
4pm	The Old Fashioned Revival Hour	Music for You	Under Arrest	GI Joe
4:15				
4:30		Arthur Godfrey's Digest	Dear Margie, It's Murder	Jason and the Golden Fleece
4:45				
5pm	This Week Around the World		The Shadow	The Chase
5:15				
5:30	The Greatest Story Ever Told	Frank Black Orchestra	True Detective Mysteries	Counterspy
5:45		Bill Downs, news		

DAYTIME — SPRING, 1953

Monday-Friday

ABC	CBS	MBS	NBC	
The Eddie Dunn Show	The Second Mrs. Burton	A. L. Alexander's Mediation Board		*2pm*
	Perry Mason			*2:15*
	This is Nora Drake	Cedric Foster, news / Paula Stone, talk	Dial Dave Garroway	*2:30*
	The Brighter Day	The Answer Man	Kukla, Fran and Ollie	*2:45*
	Hilltop House	Rambling with Gambling	Life Can Be Beautiful	*3pm*
	House Party		The Road of Life	*3:15*
Lum and Abner		Pat Barnes and Barbara, talk	Pepper Young's Family	*3:30*
The Tennessee Ernie Ford Show	Aunt Jemima Home Folks	Tello-Test Quiz	The Right to Happiness	*3:45*
Cal Tinney, talk	The Emily Kimbrough Show	Bruce and Dan, songs	Mary Noble, Backstage Wife	*4pm*
			Stella Dallas	*4:15*
Dean Cameron, talk	Galen Drake, talk	The Merry Mailman	Young Widder Brown	*4:30*
			The Woman in My House	*4:45*
Big Jon and Sparkie	John Henry Faulk, talk	Bobby Benson	Just Plain Bill	*5pm*
John Conte, talk		Sergeant Preston of the Yukon	Front Page Farrell	*5:15*
		Wild Bill Hickok	Lorenzo Jones	*5:30*
		Sky King	The Doctor's Wife	*5:45*

DAYTIME — SPRING, 1953

Saturday

	ABC	CBS	MBS	NBC
9am	No School Today	This is New York, Danny O'Neill	Harry Hennessy, news	Howdy Doody (8:30am)
9:15			Norman Brokenshire, news	
9:30			The McCanns at Home	The Ezio Pinza Show
9:45				
10am		Galen Drake, talk	Henry Gladstone, news	Archie Andrews
10:15			Martha Deane, talk	
10:30	Space Patrol	The Stamp Club		Mary Lee Taylor, cooking
10:45		Robert Q. Lewis's Waxworks		
11am	Platterbrains	Grand Central Station	Prescott Robinson, news	My Secret Story
11:15			Lorraine Sherwood, talk	
11:30	The Eddie Fisher Show	Give and Take	Farm Quiz	Modern Romances
11:45				
12pm	The Home Gardener	The Armstrong Theater of Today	The Man on the Farm	Perry Como Records
12:15				
12:30	Beauty Hints	Stars Over Hollywood	Henry Gladstone, news	The Jim Coy Show
12:45	The US Air Force Band		Norman Brokenshire, news	
1pm	Mary Margaret McBride, talk	Fun For All, Arlene Francis	Home and Garden	The National Farm and Home Hour
1:15				
1:30		City Hospital	Symphonies for Youth	Dr. Gino's Musicale
1:45				

DAYTIME — SPRING, 1953

Saturday

	ABC	CBS	MBS	NBC
2pm	The Metropolitan Opera	Music with the Hormel Girls		Kaleidoscope
2:15				
2:30		Let's Pretend	Country Editor	
2:45				
3pm		Report from Overseas	Bandstand USA	
3:15		Adventures in Science		
3:30		CBS Farm News	Great Day	
3:45		Radio Reporter's Scratchpad		
4pm		The Eddie Fisher Show	The Affairs of Peter Salem	
4:15				
4:30		Washington, USA	College Choirs	
4:45				
5pm		Treasury Bandstand	The Show Shop	It's a Problem
5:15				
5:30		Saturday at the Chase		The UN Story
5:45				Pickens Party

EVENING — SUMMER, 1953

Sunday

	ABC	CBS	MBS	NBC
6pm	Drew Pearson, news	Gene Autry's Melody Ranch	Nick Carter, Master Detective	Bob Considine, sports
6:15	Don Cornell, songs			Meet the Veep
6:30	George Sokolsky, news	Summer in St. Louis	The Squad Room	Wayne King Orchestra
6:45	Vacationland, USA			
7pm	The American Music Hall	Guy Lombardo Orchestra	Treasury Varieties	Music By Mantovani
7:15				
7:30		Richard Diamond, Private Detective	The US Air Force Band	The American Forum of the Air
7:45				
8pm		Junior Miss	The Lutheran Hour	The Tony Martin Show
8:15				
8:30		My Little Margie	The Voice of Prophecy	Best Plays
8:45				
9pm	Taylor Grant, news	December Bride	The US Marine Band	
9:15	Austin Kiplinger, economics			
9:30	Call Me Freedom	Escape	How's the Family	Confession
9:45				
10pm	Clarence Manton, talk	The Robert Q. Lewis Show	The Radio Bible Class	Barrie Craig, Confidential Investigator
10:15	Alistair Cooke, comment			
10:30	Chatauqua Symphony Orchestra	Listen to Korea	The Back to God Hour	Meet the Press
10:45		John Derr, sports		

EVENING — SUMMER, 1951

Monday

ABC	CBS	MBS	NBC	
Walter Kiernan, news	Allan Jackson, news	News on the Human Side	Kenneth Banghart, news	6pm
Bobby Sherwood Orchestra	Curt Massey, songs	Dorothy and Dick, talk	Bill Stern, sports	6:15
	Dwight Cooke, talk	Fred Vandeventer, news	Tex and Jinx, talk	6:30
	Lowell Thomas, news	Stan Lomax, sports	Three Star Extra	6:45
Charles Woods, news	Family Skeleton	Fulton Lewis Jr., news	Guy Lombardo Orchestra	7pm
Quincy Howe, news	The Johnny Mercer Show	The Answer Man		7:15
The Lone Ranger		Gabriel Heatter, news	Morgan Beatty, news	7:30
	Edward R. Murrow, news	The Elton Britt Show	One Man's Family	7:45
Henry J. Taylor, news	Crime Classics	The Falcon	The Railroad Hour	8pm
Bob Edge's Outdoor Talks				8:15
The American Concert Stage	Arthur Godfrey's Talent Scouts	The Hall of Fantasy	The Voice of Firestone	8:30
		Bill Henry, news (8:55pm)		8:45
	The Lux Summer Theater	Mutual Reporter's Round-Up	The Bell Telephone Hour	9pm
				9:15
		The Eugenia Baird Show	The Cities Service Band of America	9:30
The Jan Peerce Show				9:45
Gordon Fraser, news	Walk a Mile	Frank Edwards, news	Hollywood Searchlight	10pm
Spotlight, New York		The Mutual Newsreel		10:15
	The Bill Cullen Show	The Show Shop	Stars from Paris	10:30
				10:45

EVENING — SUMMER, 1953

Tuesday

	ABC	CBS	MBS	NBC
6pm	Walter Kiernan, news	Allan Jackson, news	News on the Human Side	Kenneth Banghart, news
6:15	Bobby Sherwood Orchestra	Curt Massey, songs	Dorothy and Dick, talk	Bill Stern, sports
6:30		Dwight Cooke, talk	Fred Vandeventer, news	Tex and Jinx, talk
6:45		Lowell Thomas, news	Stan Lomax, sports	Three Star Extra
7pm	Charles Woods, news	Family Skeleton	Fulton Lewis Jr., news	Guy Lombardo Orchestra
7:15	Quincy Howe, news	The Johnny Mercer Show	The Answer Man	
7:30	Captain Starr of Space		Gabriel Heatter, news	Morgan Beatty, news
7:45		Edward R. Murrow, news	The Elton Britt Show	One Man's Family
8pm	Three City By-Line	People Are Funny	That Hammer Guy	The Eddie Fisher Show
8:15	Sammy Kaye's Cameo Room			The Rosemary Clooney Show
8:30	Discovery	Mr. and Mrs. North	High Adventure	The First Nighter Program
8:45	Literary Greats			
9pm	America's Town Meeting of the Air	Yours Truly, Johnny Dollar	The Search That Never Ends	The Baron and the Bee
9:15				
9:30		The Twenty-First Precinct	The Eugenia Baird Show	Cousin Willie
9:45	Edwin D. Canham, news			
10pm	Gordon Fraser, news	Louella Parsons, gossip	Frank Edwards, news	Two for the Money
10:15	Spotlight, New York	Sammy Kaye Orchestra	The Mutual Newsreel	
10:30		Cedric Adams, news	The Show Shop	Stan Kenton Orchestra
10:45		The Milt Herth Trio		

EVENING — SUMMER, 1951

Wednesday

ABC	CBS	MBS	NBC	
Walter Kiernan, news	Allan Jackson, news	News on the Human Side	Kenneth Banghart, news	6pm
Bobby Sherwood Orchestra	Curt Massey, songs	Dorothy and Dick, talk	Bill Stern, sports	6:15
	Dwight Cooke, talk	Fred Vandeventer, news	Tex and Jinx, talk	6:30
	Lowell Thomas, news	Stan Lomax, sports	Three Star Extra	6:45
Charles Woods, news	Family Skeleton	Fulton Lewis Jr., news	Guy Lombardo Orchestra	7pm
Quincy Howe, news	The Johnny Mercer Show	The Answer Man		7:15
The Lone Ranger		Gabriel Heatter, news	Morgan Beatty, news	7:30
	Edward R. Murrow, news	The Elton Britt Show	One Man's Family	7:45
Three City Byline	The FBI in Peace and War	Deadline	My Son Jeep	8pm
Sammy Kaye's Cameo Room				8:15
The City of Times Square	Dr. Christian	Crime Fighters	The Great Gildersleeve	8:30
				8:45
Mr. President	The Philip Morris Playhouse on Broadway	The Family Theater	You Bet Your Life	9pm
				9:15
Crossfire	Rogers of the Gazette	The Eugenia Baird Show	Truth or Consequences	9:30
				9:45
Gordon Fraser, news	The Straw Hat Concerts	Frank Edwards, news	The Scarlet Pimpernel	10pm
Spotlight, New York		The Mutual Newsreel		10:15
	Cedric Adams, news	The Show Shop	Report from Washington	10:30
	Henry Jerome Orchestra			10:45

EVENING — SUMMER, 1953

Thursday

	ABC	CBS	MBS	NBC
6pm	Walter Kiernan, news	Allan Jackson, news	News on the Human Side	Kenneth Banghart, news
6:15	Bobby Sherwood Orchestra	Curt Massey, songs	Dorothy and Dick, talk	Bill Stern, sports
6:30		Dwight Cooke, talk	Fred Vandeventer, news	Tex and Jinx, talk
6:45		Lowell Thomas, news	Stan Lomax, sports	Three Star Extra
7pm	Charles Woods, news	Family Skeleton	Fulton Lewis Jr., news	Guy Lombardo Orchestra
7:15	Quincy Howe, news	The Johnny Mercer Show	The Answer Man	
7:30	Captain Starr of Space		Gabriel Heatter, news	Morgan Beatty, news
7:45		Edward R. Murrow, news	The Elton Britt Show	One Man's Family
8pm	Three City By-Line	Meet Millie	Official Detective	The Roy Rogers Show
8:15	Sammy Kaye's Cameo Room			
8:30	Heritage	The General Electric Theater	John Steele, Adventurer	Father Knows Best
8:45				
9pm	Mike Malloy, Private Eye	Theater of Romance	The Rod and Gun Club	Counterspy
9:15				
9:30	Time Capsule	On Stage	The Eugenia Baird Show	The Eddie Cantor Show
9:45				
10pm	Gordon Fraser, news	The Youth Opportunity Program	Frank Edwards, news	The Judy Canova Show
10:15	Spotlight, New York		The Mutual Newsreel	
10:30		Cedric Adams, news	The Show Shop	Pickens Party
10:45		Dance Orchestra		

EVENING — SUMMER, 1951

Friday

ABC	CBS	MBS	NBC	
Walter Kiernan, news	Allan Jackson, news	News on the Human Side	Kenneth Banghart, news	*6pm*
Bobby Sherwood Orchestra	Curt Massey, songs	Dorothy and Dick, talk	Bill Stern, sports	*6:15*
	Dwight Cooke, talk	Fred Vandeventer, news	Tex and Jinx, talk	*6:30*
	Lowell Thomas, news	Stan Lomax, sports	Three Star Extra	*6:45*
Charles Woods, news	Family Skeleton	Fulton Lewis Jr., news	Guy Lombardo Orchestra	*7pm*
Quincy Howe, news	The Johnny Mercer Show	The Answer Man		*7:15*
The Lone Ranger		Gabriel Heatter, news	Morgan Beatty, news	*7:30*
	Edward R. Murrow, news	The Elton Britt Show	One Man's Family	*7:45*
Three City By-Line	Mr. Keen, Tracer of Lost Persons	Take a Number	The Eddie Fisher Show	*8pm*
Sammy Kaye's Cameo Room			The Rosemary Clooney Show	*8:15*
Platterbrains	There's Music in the Air	True or False	Name That Tune	*8:30*
				8:45
What's the Name of That Song		Great Day	The Parade of Bands	*9pm*
				9:15
Bob Edge's Outdoor Talks	The Duke of Paducah and Opry Songs	The Eugenia Baird Show	Bob and Ray	*9:30*
Public Affairs				*9:45*
Gordon Fraser, news	Capitol Cloak Room	Frank Edwards, news	The All-American Sports Show	*10pm*
Spotlight, New York		The Mutual Newsreel		*10:15*
	Cedric Adams, news	The Show Shop	Radio City Preview	*10:30*
	The Milt Herth Trio		Pro and Con	*10:45*

EVENING — SUMMER, 1953

Saturday

	ABC	CBS	MBS	NBC
6pm	The AFL-CIO Program	Joe Wershba, news	News on the Human Side	Kenneth Banghart, news
6:15	It's Your Business	UN on the Record	Facts Forum	Henry Cassidy, news
6:30	Bob Finnegan, sports	The Saturday Sports Review	Fred Vandeventer, news	NBC Summer Symphony
6:45	Una Mae Carlisle, songs	Larry Lesueur, news	Stan Lomax, sports	
7pm	Disaster Strikes	Saturday at the Chase	Rukeyser Reports	
7:15	John McVane, news		Report from the Pentagon	
7:30	Dinner at the Green Room	The Camel Caravan, Vaughn Monroe	Where in the World	New Talent, USA
7:45				
8pm	ABC Dancing Party	Broadway is My Beat	Twenty Questions	
8:15				
8:30		Gangbusters	The Virginia Barn Dance	
8:45				
9pm		Gunsmoke	The New England Barn Dance	
9:15				
9:30		Saturday Night, Country Style	Lombardoland USA	Let's Go Dancing
9:45				
10pm	Spotlight, New York		The Chicago Theater of the Air	
10:15				
10:30		Dance Orchestra		
10:45				

DAYTIME — SUMMER, 1953

Sunday

	ABC	CBS	MBS	NBC
9am	Bible Study	The Music Room	News	News
9:15		News	Music	The Comic Weekly Man
9:30	The Voice of Prophecy	From the Organ Loft	The Mutual Radio Chapel	
9:45				Faith in Action
10am	Message of Israel	The CBS Church of the Air	Henry Gladstone, news	The National Radio Pulpit
10:15			Your Hymnal	
10:30	Negro College Choirs		Faith in Our Time	The Horn and Hardart Children's Hour
10:45			Bing Crosby Records	
11am	Brunch Time	The Salt Lake Tabernacle Choir	Henry Gladstone, news	
11:15	Beauty Talk		The Bromfield Report	
11:30	Christian in Action	Invitation to Learning	Mr. and Mrs. Dick Gordon, talk	Peter Roberts, news
11:45				The UN Story
12pm	The Gloria Parker Show	Bill Costello's News Story	Here's to Vets	Sammy Kaye's Sunday Serenade
12:15			The Men's Corner	
12:30		Howard K. Smith, news	Bill Cunningham, news	The Eternal Light
12:45		Bill Costello, news	Christian Science Monitor	
1pm	Dr. William Ward Ayer, talk	Let's Find Out	Music of Worship	Mind Your Manners
1:15				
1:30	Sunday Melodies	On a Sunday Afternoon	Festival of Opera	Citizens Union Searchlight
1:45				

DAYTIME — SUMMER, 1953

Monday-Friday

ABC	CBS	MBS	NBC	
The Breakfast Club	This is New York, Danny O'Neill	Robert Hurleigh, news	Tex and Jinx, talk (8:30am)	*9am*
		John Gambling's Second Breakfast		*9:15*
	The Joan Edwards Show	The McCanns at Home	The Jim Coy Show	*9:30*
				9:45
My True Story	Arthur Godfrey Time	Cecil Brown, news	Welcome, Travelers	*10am*
		Martha Deane, talk		*10:15*
Whispering Streets			The Bob Hope Show	*10:30*
When a Girl Marries			The Barrys	*10:45*
Live Like a Millionaire		Prescott Robinson, news	Strike It Rich	*11am*
		Your Musical Vote		*11:15*
Double or Nothing	Make Up Your Mind	Queen for a Day	The Phrase That Pays	*11:30*
	Rosemary		The Bob Hope Show	*11:45*
Turn to a Friend	Wendy Warren and the News	Curt Massey, songs	Faye Emerson, talk	*12pm*
	Aunt Jenny's True Life Stories	Guest Time		*12:15*
Martin Agronsky, news	The Romance of Helen Trent	Henry Gladstone, news		*12:30*
Charles F. McCarthy, news	Our Gal Sunday	The McCanns at Home	Skitch's Scrapbook	*12:45*
Mary Margaret McBride, talk	The Road of Life	Wonderful City		*1pm*
	Ma Perkins			*1:15*
	Young Dr. Malone	Barbara Welles, talk	The Herb Sheldon Show	*1:30*
	The Guiding Light			*1:45*

DAYTIME — SUMMER, 1953

Sunday

	ABC	CBS	MBS	NBC
2pm	The Church in the Home	The Longines Symphonette		The Catholic Hour
2:15				
2:30	Wings of Healing	World Music Festivals		Music for Relaxation
2:45				
3pm	Dr. James McGinley, health			Critic at Large
3:15				Carnival of Books
3:30	The Hour of Decision			Transatlantic Briefing
3:45				Where the Public Stands
4pm	The Old Fashioned Revival Hour	The World Today	Under Arrest	The Hollywood Bowl
4:15				
4:30		Arthur Godfrey's Digest	Dear Margie, It's Murder	
4:45				
5pm	This Week Around the World		The Shadow	NBC Summer Symphony
5:15				
5:30	This Week in Music	Johnny Long Orchestra	True Detective Mysteries	
5:45				

DAYTIME — SUMMER, 1953

Monday-Friday

ABC	CBS	MBS	NBC	
Maggie McNellis, talk	The Second Mrs. Burton	Ladies Fair		2pm
	Perry Mason			2:15
Betty Crocker, cooking / The Toni Gilbert Show	This is Nora Drake	Cedric Foster, news / Paula Stone, talk	Dial Dave Garroway	2:30
Between the Bookends	The Brighter Day	The Fred Robbins Show	Pickens Party	2:45
	Hilltop House	Rambling with Gambling	Life Can Be Beautiful	3pm
	House Party		The Road of Life	3:15
The Beth Hollond Show		Pat Barnes and Barbara, talk	Pepper Young's Family	3:30
	The Walter O'Keefe Show	Tello-Test Quiz	The Right to Happiness	3:45
The Jack Owens Show	The Emily Kimbrough Show	Bruce and Dan, songs	Mary Noble, Backstage Wife	4pm
			Stella Dallas	4:15
Dean Cameron, talk	Galen Drake, talk	The Merry Mailman	Young Widder Brown	4:30
			The Woman in My House	4:45
Big Jon and Sparkie	John Henry Faulk, talk	Bobby Benson	Just Plain Bill	5pm
John Conte, talk			Front Page Farrell	5:15
		Keynote Ranch	Lorenzo Jones	5:30
			The Doctor's Wife	5:45

DAYTIME — SUMMER, 1953

Saturday

	ABC	CBS	MBS	NBC
9am	No School Today	This is New York, Danny O'Neill	Harry Hennessy, news	Howdy Doody (8:30am)
9:15			The Key	
9:30		Galen Drake, talk	The McCanns at Home	The Ezio Pinza Show
9:45				
10am			Henry Gladstone, news	Archie Andrews
10:15		The Port of New York	Martha Deane, talk	
10:30	Space Patrol	Let's Pretend		Mary Lee Taylor, cooking
10:45				
11am	Chatauqua Symphony Orchestra	Grand Central Station	Prescott Robinson, news	My Secret Story
11:15			Lorraine Sherwood, talk	
11:30	The All-League Clubhouse	Give and Take	Home and Garden	Modern Romances
11:45				
12pm	The Home Gardener	The Armstrong Theater of Today	The Man on the Farm	The Jim Coy Show
12:15				
12:30	Beauty Hints	Stars Over Hollywood	Henry Gladstone, news	
12:45	The US Air Force Band		Norman Brokenshire, news	Your Navy Show
1pm	Mary Margaret McBride, talk	Fun For All, Arlene Francis	Farm Quiz	The National Farm and Home Hour
1:15				
1:30		City Hospital	The Ruby Mercer Show	Dr. Gino's Musicale
1:45				

DAYTIME — SUMMER, 1953

Saturday

	ABC	CBS	MBS	NBC
2pm	Playland USA	Music with the Hormel Girls		Kaleidoscope
2:15				
2:30		Chicagoans Orchestra	The Military Academy Band	
2:45				
3pm	The US Air Force Band	Report from Overseas	Bandstand USA	
3:15		Adventures in Science		
3:30		CBS Farm News	The Sports Parade	
3:45		Radio Reporter's Scratchpad		
4pm	Martha Lou Harp, songs	The US Army Band	Salute to the Nation	
4:15				
4:30	Marines in Review	The Brevard Music Festival	The Sounding Board	
4:45				
5pm	The Music Box	Washington, USA	The Show Shop	The Treasury of Immortal Performances
5:15				
5:30	Pauline Carter, piano	Saturday at the Chase		Stars in Action
5:45	Club Time			

EVENING — FALL, 1953

Sunday

	ABC	CBS	MBS	NBC
6pm	Don Gardiner, news	Gene Autry's Melody Ranch	Nick Carter, Master Detective	Bob Considine, sports
6:15	Paul Harvey, news			Let's Ask Hollywood
6:30	George Sokolsky, news	Our Miss Brooks	The Squad Room	The NBC Star Playhouse
6:45	Don Cornell, songs			
7pm	This Week Around the World	The Lucky Strike Program, Jack Benny	The Rod and Gun Club	
7:15				
7:30	What's the Name of That Song	Amos 'n' Andy	The US Air Force Band	The Marriage
7:45				
8pm	The American Music Hall	The General Electric Show, Bing Crosby	Hawaii Calls	Hollywood Story
8:15				
8:30		My Little Margie	The Voice of Prophecy	Theater Royal
8:45				
9pm	Walter Winchell, gossip	The Hallmark Hall of Fame	The Great Day	Stroke of Fate
9:15	Taylor Grant, news			
9:30	Call Me Freedom	The Charlie McCarthy Show	London Studio Melodies	The Six Shooter
9:45				
10pm	Paul Harvey, news	The Man of the Week	The Radio Bible Class	Last Man Out
10:15	The People Speak			
10:30	Bob Dini, songs	The UN Report	The Back to God Hour	Golden Treasury
10:45	Bob Edge's Outdoor Talks	John Derr, sports		

EVENING — FALL, 1953

Monday

ABC	CBS	MBS	NBC	
Walter Kiernan, news	Allan Jackson, news	News on the Human Side	Kenneth Banghart, news	6pm
Bobby Sherwood Orchestra	Curt Massey, songs	Dorothy and Dick, talk	Mel Allen, sports	6:15
The Nation's Business	Guest Book	Fred Vandeventer, news	Light Up Time, Jim Coy (6:25pm)	6:30
Bill Stern, sports	Lowell Thomas, news	Stan Lomax, sports	Three Star Extra	6:45
Taylor Grant, news	Family Skelton	Fulton Lewis Jr., news	The Longines Symphonette	7pm
Elmer Davis, news	The Beulah Show	Today's Business		7:15
The Lone Ranger	Junior Miss	Gabriel Heatter, news	Morgan Beatty, news	7:30
	Edward R. Murrow, news	Perry Como, songs	One Man's Family	7:45
Henry J. Taylor, news	Suspense	The Falcon	The Railroad Hour	8pm
Sammy Kaye's Cameo Room				8:15
Hollywood Stairway	Arthur Godfrey's Talent Scouts	Counterspy	The Voice of Firestone	8:30
Mike Malloy, Detective				8:45
Celebrity Table	The Lux Radio Theater	The Man from Time Square	The Bell Telephone Hour	9pm
				9:15
		I Was a Communist for the FBI	The Cities Service Band of America	9:30
				9:45
John W. Vandercook, news	The Camel Caravan, Vaughn Monroe	Frank Edwards, news	Fibber Magee and Molly	10pm
Rudolph Halley, news		The Mutual Newsreel	Can You Top This	10:15
Spotlight, New York	Cedric Adams, news	The Cisco Kid	The Stan Freeman Little Revue	10:30
	The Three Suns			10:45

EVENING — FALL, 1953

Tuesday

	ABC	CBS	MBS	NBC
6pm	Walter Kiernan, news	Allan Jackson, news	News on the Human Side	Kenneth Banghart, news
6:15	Bobby Sherwood Orchestra	Curt Massey, songs	Dorothy and Dick, talk	Mel Allen, sports
6:30	The Nation's Business	Guest Book	Fred Vandeventer, news	Light Up Time, Jim Coy (6:25pm)
6:45	Bill Stern, sports	Lowell Thomas, news	Stan Lomax, sports	Three Star Extra
7pm	Taylor Grant, news	Family Skelton	Fulton Lewis Jr., news	The Longines Symphonette
7:15	Elmer Davis, news	The Beulah Show	Today's Business	
7:30	Captain Starr of Space	The Longines Choraliers	Gabriel Heatter, news	Taylor Grant, news
7:45		Edward R. Murrow, news	Bonnie Lou, songs	One Man's Family
8pm	Three City By-Line	People Are Funny	Mickey Spillane Mystery	Coke Time, Eddie Fisher
8:15	Sammy Kaye's Cameo Room			The Dinah Shore Show
8:30	Hollywood Stairway	Mr. and Mrs. North	High Adventure	Barrie Craig: Confidential Investigator
8:45	Mike Malloy, Detective			
9pm	America's Town Meeting of the Air	Yours Truly, Johnny Dollar	The Man from Time Square	Dragnet
9:15				
9:30		The Twenty-First Precinct	I Was a Communist for the FBI	Rocky Fortune
9:45	Edwin D. Canham, news			
10pm	Taylor Grant, news	Louella Parsons, gossip	Frank Edwards, news	Fibber Magee and Molly
10:15	The People Speak	Frankie Carle Orchestra	The Mutual Newsreel	Can You Top This
10:30	Spotlight, New York	Cedric Adams, news	The Cisco Kid	The Stan Freeman Little Revue
10:45		The Irving Fields Trio		

EVENING — FALL, 1953

Wednesday

ABC	CBS	MBS	NBC	
Walter Kiernan, news	Allan Jackson, news	News on the Human Side	Kenneth Banghart, news	6pm
Bobby Sherwood Orchestra	Curt Massey, songs	Dorothy and Dick, talk	Mel Allen, sports	6:15
The Nation's Business	Guest Book	Fred Vandeventer, news	Light Up Time, Jim Coy (6:25pm)	6:30
Bill Stern, sports	Lowell Thomas, news	Stan Lomax, sports	Three Star Extra	6:45
Taylor Grant, news	Family Skelton	Fulton Lewis Jr., news	The Longines Symphonette	7pm
Elmer Davis, news	The Beulah Show	Today's Business		7:15
The Lone Ranger	Junior Miss	Gabriel Heatter, news	Morgan Beatty, news	7:30
	Edward R. Murrow, news	Perry Como, songs	One Man's Family	7:45
Three City By-Line	The FBI in Peace and War	Deadline	Walk a Mile	8pm
Sammy Kaye's Cameo Room				8:15
Hollywood Stairway	Dr. Christian	Bulldog Drummond	The Great Gildersleeve	8:30
Mike Malloy, Detective				8:45
The Philco Radio Playhouse	On Stage	The Man from Time Square	You Bet Your Life	9pm
				9:15
Mystery Theater	Crime Classics	I Was a Communist for the FBI	The Big Story	9:30
				9:45
Taylor Grant, news	Broadway is My Beat	Frank Edwards, news	Fibber Magee and Molly	10pm
The People Speak		The Mutual Newsreel	Can You Top This	10:15
Spotlight, New York	Cedric Adams, news	The Cisco Kid	The Stan Freeman Little Revue	10:30
	The Three Suns			10:45

EVENING — FALL, 1953

Thursday

	ABC	CBS	MBS	NBC
6pm	Walter Kiernan, news	Allan Jackson, news	News on the Human Side	Kenneth Banghart, news
6:15	Bobby Sherwood Orchestra	Curt Massey, songs	Dorothy and Dick, talk	Mel Allen, sports
6:30	The Nation's Business	Guest Book	Fred Vandeventer, news	Light Up Time, Jim Coy (6:25pm)
6:45	Bill Stern, sports	Lowell Thomas, news	Stan Lomax, sports	Three Star Extra
7pm	Taylor Grant, news	Family Skelton	Fulton Lewis Jr., news	The Longines Symphonette
7:15	Elmer Davis, news	The Beulah Show	Today's Business	
7:30	Captain Starr of Space	The Longines Choraliers	Gabriel Heatter, news	Morgan Beatty, news
7:45		Edward R. Murrow, news	Bonnie Lou, songs	One Man's Family
8pm	Three City By-Line	Meet Millie	Official Detective	The Roy Rogers Show
8:15	Sammy Kaye's Cameo Room			
8:30	Hollywood Stairway	Rogers of the Gazette	Nightmare	Father Knows Best
8:45	Mike Malloy, Detective			
9pm	George Jessel Salutes	Meet Mr. McNutley	The Man from Time Square	Truth or Consequences
9:15				
9:30	Horatio Hornblower	Time for Love	I Was a Communist for the FBI	The Eddie Cantor Show
9:45				
10pm	Taylor Grant, news	The Youth Opportunity Program	Frank Edwards, news	Fibber Magee and Molly
10:15	The People Speak		The Mutual Newsreel	Rudolph Halley, news
10:30	Spotlight, New York	Cedric Adams, news	The Cisco Kid	Pickens Party
10:45		The Three Suns		

EVENING — FALL, 1953

Friday

ABC	CBS	MBS	NBC	
Walter Kiernan, news	Allan Jackson, news	News on the Human Side	Kenneth Banghart, news	6pm
Bobby Sherwood Orchestra	Curt Massey, songs	Dorothy and Dick, talk	Mel Allen, sports	6:15
The Nation's Business	Guest Book	Fred Vandeventer, news	Light Up Time, Jim Coy (6:25pm)	6:30
Bill Stern, sports	Lowell Thomas, news	Stan Lomax, sports	Three Star Extra	6:45
Taylor Grant, news	Family Skelton	Fulton Lewis Jr., news	The Longines Symphonette	7pm
Elmer Davis, news	The Beulah Show	Today's Business		7:15
The Lone Ranger	Junior Miss	Gabriel Heatter, news	Morgan Beatty, news	7:30
	Edward R. Murrow, news	Perry Como, songs	One Man's Family	7:45
Three City By-Line	Mr. Keen, Tracer of Lost Persons	Take a Number	Coke Time, Eddie Fisher	8pm
Sammy Kaye's Cameo Room			The Dinah Shore Show	8:15
Hollywood Stairway	Stage Struck	Starlight Theater	The Bob Hope Show	8:30
Mike Malloy, Detective				8:45
The Adventures of Ozzie and Harriet		The Man from Time Square	The Phil Harris - Alice Faye Show	9pm
				9:15
Meet Corliss Archer	The Duke of Paducah and Opry Songs	I Was a Communist for the FBI	The House of Glass	9:30
				9:45
Madison Square Garden Boxing	Capitol Cloak Room	Frank Edwards, news	Fibber Magee and Molly	10pm
		The Mutual Newsreel	Rudolph Halley, news	10:15
	Cedric Adams, news	The Cisco Kid	The Stan Freeman Little Revue	10:30
	The Irving Fields Trio		Pro and Con	10:45

EVENING — FALL, 1953

Saturday

	ABC	CBS	MBS	NBC
6pm	Sam Jones, talk	As We See It	News on the Human Side	Kenneth Banghart, news
6:15	It's Your Business	UN on the Record	Facts Forum	H. V. Kaltenborn, news
6:30	Bob Finnegan, sports	The Saturday Sports Review	Fred Vandeventer, news	NBC Symphony Orchestra
6:45	Una Mae Carlisle, songs	Larry Lesueur, news	Stan Lomax, sports	
7pm	Disaster Strikes	The Johnny Mercer Show	The US Air Force Band	
7:15	The Three Suns		Report from the Pentagon	
7:30	Dinner at the Green Room		Where in the World	The NBC Lecture Hall
7:45				
8pm	ABC Dancing Party	Gunsmoke	Twenty Questions	College Quiz Bowl
8:15				
8:30		Gangbusters	The Family Theater	Know Your NBC's
8:45				
9pm		Two for the Money	The Search That Never Ends	The Baron and the Bee
9:15				
9:30		Saturday Night, Country Style	Lombardoland USA	Grand Ole Opry
9:45				
10pm	Spotlight, New York		The Chicago Theater of the Air	Dude Ranch Jamboree
10:15				
10:30		Dance Orchestra		Pee Wee King Orchestra
10:45				

DAYTIME — FALL, 1953

Sunday

	ABC	CBS	MBS	NBC
9am	Bible Study	The Music Room	News	The Comic Weekly Man
9:15		News	Bing Crosby Records	
9:30	The Voice of Prophecy	From the Organ Loft	The Mutual Radio Chapel	Howdy Doody
9:45				Faith in Action
10am	Message of Israel	The CBS Church of the Air	Henry Gladstone, news	
10:15			Your Hymnal	
10:30	Negro College Choirs		Faith in Our Time	The Horn and Hardart Children's Hour
10:45				
11am	Brunch Time	The Salt Lake Tabernacle Choir	Henry Gladstone, news	
11:15			The Bromfield Farm Report	
11:30	Christian in Action	Invitation to Learning	Mr. and Mrs. Dick Gordon, talk	Peter Roberts, news
11:45				World News Round-Up
12pm	Healing Waters	Let's Find Out	Here's to Vets	Sunday Afternoon Music
12:15			The Men's Corner	
12:30	The Herald of Truth	Howard K. Smith, news	Bill Cunningham, news	The Eternal Light
12:45		Bill Costello, news	Christian Science Monitor	
1pm	Dr. William Ward Ayer, talk	The Twentieth Century Concert Hall	Keep Healthy	For Better Living
1:15			The Canary Pet Shop	Report on America
1:30	National Vespers	Syncopation Piece	Festival of Opera	Citizens Union Searchlight
1:45				

DAYTIME — FALL, 1953

Monday-Friday

ABC	CBS	MBS	NBC	
The Breakfast Club	This is New York, Danny O'Neill	Harry Hennessy, news	Tex and Jinx, talk (8:30am)	9am
		John Gambling's Second Breakfast		9:15
	The Joan Edwards Show	The McCanns at Home	The Jim Coy Show	9:30
				9:45
My True Story	Arthur Godfrey Time	Henry Gladstone, news	Welcome, Travelers	10am
		Martha Deane, talk		10:15
Whispering Streets			The Bob Hope Show	10:30
When a Girl Marries			Break the Bank	10:45
Modern Romances		Ladies Fair	Strike It Rich	11am
Paging the Judge				11:15
Double or Nothing	Make Up Your Mind	Queen for a Day	The Phrase That Pays	11:30
	Rosemary		The Stan Freeman Show	11:45
Turn to a Friend	Wendy Warren and the News	Curt Massey, songs	Faye Emerson, talk	12pm
	Aunt Jenny's True Life Stories	Guest Time		12:15
Martin Agronsky, news	The Romance of Helen Trent	Henry Gladstone, news		12:30
Charlie F. McCarthy, news	Our Gal Sunday	Gabriel Heatter's Mailbag		12:45
Mary Margaret McBride, talk	The Road of Life	The McCanns at Home	The Jim Coy Show	1pm
	Ma Perkins	Pat Barnes and Barbera, talk		1:15
	Young Dr. Malone	Barbara Welles, talk	The Herb Sheldon Show	1:30
	The Guiding Light			1:45

DAYTIME — FALL, 1953

Sunday

	ABC	CBS	MBS	NBC
2pm	The Church in the Home	The Longines Symphonette		The Catholic Hour
2:15				
2:30	Wings of Healing	New York Philharmonic Orchestra		Prescription for Two
2:45				The UN Story
3pm	Dr. James McGinley, talk			Golden Voices
3:15			The Lanny Ross Show	Youth Brings You Music
3:30	The Hour of Decision		Mr. District Attorney	The National Radio Pulpit
3:45				
4pm	The Old Fashioned Revival Hour	Larry Lesueur, news	Under Arrest	Weekend
4:15		The World Today		
4:30		Music for You	Crime Fighters	
4:45				
5pm	The Cinema Music Hall	Arthur Godfrey's Digest	The Shadow	
5:15				
5:30	The Greatest Story Ever Told	The Quiz Kids	True Detective Mysteries	
5:45				

DAYTIME — FALL, 1953

Monday-Friday

ABC	CBS	MBS	NBC	
Maggie McNellis, talk	The Second Mrs. Burton	The Fred Robbins Show		*2pm*
	Perry Mason			*2:15*
The Jack Gregson Variety Show	This is Nora Drake	Wonderful City	Dial Dave Garroway	*2:30*
	The Brighter Day		Pickens Party	*2:45*
	Hilltop House	The Radio City Playhouse	Life Can Be Beautiful	*3pm*
	House Party		The Road of Life	*3:15*
			Pepper Young's Family	*3:30*
	The Wizard of Odds		The Right to Happiness	*3:45*
The Beth Holland Show	The Emily Kimbrough Show		Mary Noble, Backstage Wife	*4pm*
			Stella Dallas	*4:15*
Dean Cameron, talk	Galen Drake, talk		Young Widder Brown	*4:30*
			The Woman in My House	*4:45*
Big Jon and Sparkie	John Henry Faulk, talk	Bobby Benson	Just Plain Bill	*5pm*
John Conte, talk		Sergeant Preston of the Yukon	Front Page Farrell	*5:15*
		Wild Bill Hickok	Lorenzo Jones	*5:30*
		Sky King	It Pays to Be Married	*5:45*

DAYTIME — FALL, 1953

Saturday

	ABC	CBS	MBS	NBC
9am	No School Today	This is New York, Danny O'Neill	Harry Hennessy, news	Top Tunes (8:30am)
9:15			Bing Crosby Records	
9:30		Galen Drake, talk	The McCanns at Home	
9:45				
10am			Henry Gladstone, news	
10:15			Martha Deane, talk	
10:30	Space Patrol	Let's Pretend		Mary Lee Taylor, cooking
10:45				
11am	Platterbrains	Theater of Romance		The Big Preview
11:15			Lorraine Sherwood, talk	
11:30	The All-League Clubhouse	Give and Take	Farm Quiz	
11:45				
12pm	The Home Gardener	The Armstrong Theater of Today	The Man on the Farm	
12:15				
12:30	Martin Agronsky, news	Stars Over Hollywood	Henry Gladstone, news	
12:45	The US Air Force Band		John T. Flynn, news	
1pm	Mary Margaret McBride, talk	Fun For All, Arlene Francis	The State of the Nation	The National Farm and Home Hour
1:15				
1:30		Music with the Hormel Girls	Barbera Welles, talk	Dr. Gino's Musicale
1:45	Sports			

DAYTIME — FALL, 1953

Saturday

	ABC	CBS	MBS	NBC
2pm		Sports	Sports	Music, USA
2:15				
2:30				
2:45				
3pm				
3:15				
3:30				
3:45				
4pm				
4:15				
4:30	Martha Lou Harp, songs		The Sounding Board	
4:45				
5pm	Pan-American Union		The Show Shop	Skitch's Sketchbook
5:15				
5:30	Paulena Carter, piano	Saturday at the Chase		
5:45	The US Army Band			

LISTINGS FOR 1954

EVENING — WINTER, 1954

Sunday

	ABC	CBS	MBS	NBC
6pm	Don Gardiner, news	Gene Autry's Melody Ranch	Bulldog Drummond	NBC Symphony Orchestra
6:15	Paul Harvey, news			
6:30	George Sokolsky, news	Our Miss Brooks	Bob Considine, sports	
6:45	Don Cornell, songs		Harry Wismer, sports	
7pm	This Week Around the World	The Lucky Strike Program, Jack Benny	The Rod and Gun Club	
7:15				
7:30	What's the Name of That Song	Amos 'n' Andy	Serenade in Blue	The Marriage
7:45				
8pm	The American Music Hall	The General Electric Show, Bing Crosby	The Lutheran Hour	The Six Shooter
8:15				
8:30		My Little Margie	The Voice of Prophecy	Sunday at Home, Jan Murray
8:45				
9pm	Walter Winchell, gossip	The Hallmark Hall of Fame	Sammy Kaye's Sunday Serenade	The NBC Star Playhouse
9:15	Taylor Grant, news			
9:30	Call Me Freedom	The Charlie McCarthy Show	Author Meets the Critics	
9:45				
10pm	Paul Harvey, news	The Man of the Week	The Radio Bible Class	Last Man Out
10:15	Elmer Davis, news			
10:30	Revival Time	The UN Report	The Back to God Hour	Meet the Press
10:45		John Derr, sports		

EVENING — WINTER, 1954

Monday

ABC	CBS	MBS	NBC	
Walter Kiernan, news	Allan Jackson, news	News on the Human Side	Kenneth Banghart, news	6pm
Bobby Sherwood Orchestra	Curt Massey, songs	Dorothy and Dick, talk	Mel Allen, sports	6:15
The Nation's Business	Guest Book	Fred Vandeventer, news	Light Up Time, Jim Coy (6:25pm)	6:30
Bill Stern, sports	Lowell Thomas, news	Stan Lomax, sports	Three Star Extra	6:45
John W. Vandercook, news	Family Skelton	Fulton Lewis Jr., news	The Longines Symphonette	7pm
Quincy Howe, news	The Beulah Show	The Answer Man		7:15
The Lone Ranger	The Julius La Rosa Show	Gabriel Heatter, news	Morgan Beatty, news	7:30
	Edward R. Murrow, news	Perry Como, songs	One Man's Family	7:45
Henry J. Taylor, news	Suspense	The Falcon	The Railroad Hour	8pm
Sammy Kaye's Cameo Room				8:15
Hollywood Stairway	Arthur Godfrey's Talent Scouts	Under Arrest	The Voice of Firestone	8:30
Mike Malloy, Detective				8:45
The Metropolitan Opera Auditions	The Lux Radio Theater	The Johnny Olsen Show	The Bell Telephone Hour	9pm
				9:15
Decision		Philo Vance	The Cities Service Band of America	9:30
				9:45
Spotlight, New York	The Camel Caravan, Vaughn Monroe	Frank Edwards, news	Fibber Magee and Molly	10pm
		The Mutual Newsreel	Can You Top This	10:15
	Melody in the Night	The Cisco Kid	The Stan Freeman Little Revue	10:30
				10:45

EVENING — WINTER, 1954

Tuesday

	ABC	CBS	MBS	NBC
6pm	Walter Kiernan, news	Allan Jackson, news	News on the Human Side	Kenneth Banghart, news
6:15	Bobby Sherwood Orchestra	Curt Massey, songs	Dorothy and Dick, talk	Mel Allen, sports
6:30	The Nation's Business	Guest Book	Fred Vandeventer, news	Light Up Time, Jim Coy (6:25pm)
6:45	Bill Stern, sports	Lowell Thomas, news	Stan Lomax, sports	Three Star Extra
7pm	John W. Vandercook, news	Family Skelton	Fulton Lewis Jr., news	The Longines Symphonette
7:15	Quincy Howe, news	The Beulah Show	The Answer Man	
7:30	Captain Starr of Space	The Longines Choraliers	Gabriel Heatter, news	Taylor Grant, news
7:45		Edward R. Murrow, news	Coke Time, Eddie Fisher	One Man's Family
8pm	Three City By-Line	People Are Funny	Mickey Spillane Mystery	The Dinah Shore Show
8:15	Sammy Kaye's Cameo Room			To Be Perfectly Frank
8:30	Hollywood Stairway	Mr. and Mrs. North	High Adventure	Barrie Craig: Confidential Investigator
8:45	Mike Malloy, Detective			
9pm	America's Town Meeting of the Air	Yours Truly, Johnny Dollar	The Johnny Olsen Show	Dragnet
9:15				
9:30		My Friend Irma	Thirty Minutes to Go	Rocky Fortune
9:45	Edwin D. Canham, news			
10pm	Spotlight, New York	Louella Parsons, gossip	Frank Edwards, news	Fibber Magee and Molly
10:15		Dance Orchestra	Wayne E. Richard, talk	Can You Top This
10:30		Melody in the Night	The Cisco Kid	The Stan Freeman Little Revue
10:45				

EVENING — WINTER, 1954

Wednesday

ABC	CBS	MBS	NBC	
Walter Kiernan, news	Allan Jackson, news	News on the Human Side	Kenneth Banghart, news	6pm
Bobby Sherwood Orchestra	Curt Massey, songs	Dorothy and Dick, talk	Mel Allen, sports	6:15
The Nation's Business	Guest Book	Fred Vandeventer, news	Light Up Time, Jim Coy (6:25pm)	6:30
Bill Stern, sports	Lowell Thomas, news	Stan Lomax, sports	Three Star Extra	6:45
John W. Vandercook, news	Family Skelton	Fulton Lewis Jr., news	The Longines Symphonette	7pm
Quincy Howe, news	The Beulah Show	The Answer Man		7:15
The Lone Ranger	The Julius La Rosa Show	Gabriel Heatter, news	Morgan Beatty, news	7:30
	Edward R. Murrow, news	Perry Como, songs	One Man's Family	7:45
Three City By-Line	The FBI in Peace and War	The Squad Room	Walk a Mile	8pm
Sammy Kaye's Cameo Room				8:15
Hollywood Stairway	The Twenty-First Precinct	Nightmare	The Great Gildersleeve	8:30
Mike Malloy, Detective				8:45
The Philco Radio Playhouse	Crime Photographer	The Johnny Olsen Show	You Bet Your Life	9pm
				9:15
Mystery Theater	Crime Classics	Let George Do It	The Big Story	9:30
				9:45
Spotlight, New York	The Wednesday Night Fights	Frank Edwards, news	Fibber Magee and Molly	10pm
		The Mutual Newsreel	Can You Top This	10:15
		The Cisco Kid	The Stan Freeman Little Revue	10:30
				10:45

EVENING — WINTER, 1954

Thursday

	ABC	CBS	MBS	NBC
6pm	Walter Kiernan, news	Allan Jackson, news	News on the Human Side	Kenneth Banghart, news
6:15	Bobby Sherwood Orchestra	Curt Massey, songs	Dorothy and Dick, talk	Mel Allen, sports
6:30	The Nation's Business	Guest Book	Fred Vandeventer, news	Light Up Time, Jim Coy (6:25pm)
6:45	Bill Stern, sports	Lowell Thomas, news	Stan Lomax, sports	Three Star Extra
7pm	John W. Vandercook, news	Family Skelton	Fulton Lewis Jr., news	The Longines Symphonette
7:15	Quincy Howe, news	The Beulah Show	The Answer Man	
7:30	Captain Starr of Space	The Longines Choraliers	Gabriel Heatter, news	Morgan Beatty, news
7:45		Edward R. Murrow, news	Coke Time, Eddie Fisher	One Man's Family
8pm	Three City By-Line	Meet Millie	Official Detective	One Night Stand
8:15	Sammy Kaye's Cameo Room			
8:30	Hollywood Stairway	Junior Miss	Crime Fighters	Meet Me at Kays
8:45	Mike Malloy, Detective			
9pm	Paul Whiteman Varieties	Meet Mr. McNutley	The Johnny Olsen Show	Truth or Consequences
9:15				
9:30		Time for Love	Mystery House	The Eddie Cantor Show
9:45				
10pm	Spotlight, New York	A Minority of One	Frank Edwards, news	Fibber Magee and Molly
10:15		Dance Orchestra	The Mutual Newsreel	Can You Top This
10:30		Melody in the Night	The Cisco Kid	Pickens Party
10:45				

EVENING — WINTER, 1954

Friday

ABC	CBS	MBS	NBC	
Walter Kiernan, news	Allan Jackson, news	News on the Human Side	Kenneth Banghart, news	6pm
Bobby Sherwood Orchestra	Curt Massey, songs	Dorothy and Dick, talk	Mel Allen, sports	6:15
The Nation's Business	Guest Book	Fred Vandeventer, news	Light Up Time, Jim Coy (6:25pm)	6:30
Bill Stern, sports	Lowell Thomas, news	Stan Lomax, sports	Three Star Extra	6:45
John W. Vandercook, news	Family Skelton	Fulton Lewis Jr., news	The Longines Symphonette	7pm
Quincy Howe, news	The Beulah Show	The Answer Man		7:15
The Lone Ranger	The Julius La Rosa Show	Gabriel Heatter, news	Morgan Beatty, news	7:30
	Edward R. Murrow, news	Perry Como, songs	One Man's Family	7:45
Three City By-Line	Mr. Keen, Tracer of Lost Persons	Take a Number	The Dinah Shore Show	8pm
Sammy Kaye's Cameo Room			To Be Perfectly Frank	8:15
Hollywood Stairway	Arthur Godfrey's Digest	Starlight Theater	The Bob Hope Show	8:30
Mike Malloy, Detective				8:45
The Adventures of Ozzie and Harriet	Stage Struck	The Johnny Olsen Show	The Phil Harris - Alice Faye Show	9pm
				9:15
Horatio Hornblower	That's Rich	My Favorite Story	The House of Glass	9:30
				9:45
Madison Square Garden Boxing	Capitol Cloak Room	Frank Edwards, news	Fibber Magee and Molly	10pm
		The Mutual Newsreel	Can You Top This	10:15
	Melody in the Night	The Cisco Kid	The Stan Freeman Little Revue	10:30
				10:45

EVENTING — WINTER, 1954

Saturday

	ABC	CBS	MBS	NBC
6pm	Make Believe Ballroom	Philadelphia Symphony Orchestra	News on the Human Side	Kenneth Banghart, news
6:15			The Facts Forum	H. V. Kaltenborn, news
6:30			Fred Vandeventer, news	People
6:45			Stan Lomax, sports	
7pm		The Johnny Mercer Show	Irene Kuhn, talk	Theater Royal
7:15			Together We Stand	
7:30	Dinner at the Green Room		Have a Heart	The Big Preview
7:45				
8pm	ABC Dancing Party	Gunsmoke	Twenty Questions	
8:15				
8:30		Gangbusters	The Family Theater	
8:45				
9pm		Two for the Money	The Search That Never Ends	
9:15				
9:30	Your Voice of America	Saturday Night, Country Style	Lombardoland USA	Bill's Place
9:45				
10pm	Spotlight, New York		The Chicago Theater of the Air	
10:15				
10:30		The Youth Opportunity Program		
10:45				

DAYTIME — WINTER, 1954

Sunday

	ABC	CBS	MBS	NBC
9am	Bible Study	The Music Room	News	The Comic Weekly Man
9:15		News	Vacation Time	
9:30	The Voice of Prophecy	From the Organ Loft	The Mutual Radio Chapel	Howdy Doody
9:45				
10am	Message of Israel	The CBS Church of the Air	The Men's Corner	
10:15			Your Hymnal	
10:30	Negro College Choirs		Faith in Our Time	The Horn and Hardart Children's Hour
10:45			Bing Crosby Records	
11am	The World of Tomorrow	The Salt Lake Tabernacle Choir	Henry Gladstone, news	
11:15			The American Travel Guide	
11:30	Christian in Action	Invitation to Learning	Rambling with Gambling	Peter Roberts, news
11:45				World News Round-Up
12pm	Milton Cross, news	The Leading Question	Here's to Vets	Sunday Afternoon Music
12:15	Opportunity Limited		The Men's Corner	
12:30	The Herald of Truth	Howard K. Smith, news	Bill Cunningham, news	The Eternal Light
12:45		George Herman, news	Christian Science Monitor	
1pm	Dr. William Ward Ayer, talk	Man's Right to Knowledge	Top Hits	Heritage Over the Land
1:15			The Canary Pet Shop	
1:30	National Vespers	Let's Find Out	Festival of Opera	Citizens Union Spotlight
1:45				

DAYTIME — WINTER, 1954

Monday-Friday

ABC	CBS	MBS	NBC	
The Breakfast Club	This is New York, Danny O'Neill	Robert Hurleigh, news	Tex and Jinx, talk (8:30am)	*9am*
		John Gambling's Second Breakfast		*9:15*
	The Joan Edwards Show	The McCanns at Home	The Jim Coy Show	*9:30*
				9:45
My True Story	Arthur Godfrey Time	Cecil Brown, news	Welcome, Travelers	*10am*
		Martha Deane, talk		*10:15*
Whispering Streets			The Bob Hope Show	*10:30*
When a Girl Marries			Break the Bank	*10:45*
Grand Central Station		Wonderful City	Strike It Rich	*11am*
				11:15
Modern Romances	Make Up Your Mind	Queen for a Day	The Phrase That Pays	*11:30*
Ever Since Eve	Rosemary		Second Chance	*11:45*
George Ansbro Presents	Wendy Warren and the News	Curt Massey, songs	Faye Emerson, talk	*12pm*
	Aunt Jenny's True Life Stories	Tello-Test Quiz		*12:15*
Maggie McNellis, talk	The Romance of Helen Trent	Henry Gladstone, news		*12:30*
Charlie F. McCarthy, news	Our Gal Sunday	Gabriel Heatter's Mailbag		*12:45*
Mary Margaret McBride, talk	The Road of Life	The McCanns at Home	The Jim Coy Show	*1pm*
	Ma Perkins	Pat Barnes and Barbera, talk		*1:15*
	Young Dr. Malone	Barbara Welles, talk	The Herb Sheldon Show	*1:30*
	The Guiding Light			*1:45*

DAYTIME — WINTER, 1954

Sunday

	ABC	CBS	MBS	NBC
2pm	Healing Waters	The Longine Symphonette		The Catholic Hour
2:15	City Hall			
2:30	Wings of Healing	New York Philharmonic Orchestra		The American Forum of the Air
2:45				
3pm	Dr. James McGinley, talk			Golden Voices
3:15				
3:30	The Hour of Decision			The National Radio Pulpit
3:45				
4pm	The Old Fashioned Revival Hour	The Twentieth Century Concert Hall	Counterspy	Weekend
4:15				
4:30		The World Today	Nick Carter, Master Detective	
4:45				
5pm	Evening Comes	Stagestruck	The Shadow	
5:15				
5:30	The Greatest Story Ever Told		True Detective Mysteries	
5:45				

DAYTIME — WINTER, 1954

Monday-Friday

ABC	CBS	MBS	NBC	
Dean Cameron, talk	The Second Mrs. Burton	The Fred Robbins Show		2pm
	Perry Mason			2:15
Make Believe Ballroom	This is Nora Drake	Sloan Simpson, talk	Second Chance	2:30
	The Brighter Day		Pickens Party	2:45
	Hilltop House	The Radio City Playhouse	Life Can Be Beautiful	3pm
	House Party		The Road of Life	3:15
			Pepper Young's Family	3:30
	The Wizard of Odds		The Right to Happiness	3:45
	The Emily Kimbrough Show		Mary Noble, Backstage Wife	4pm
			Stella Dallas	4:15
	Galen Drake, talk		Young Widder Brown	4:30
			The Woman in My House	4:45
	John Henry Faulk, talk	Bobby Benson	Just Plain Bill	5pm
		Sergeant Preston for the Yukon	Front Page Farrell	5:15
		Wild Bill Hickok	Lorenzo Jones	5:30
		Sky King	It Pays to Be Married	5:45

DAYTIME — WINTER, 1954

Saturday

	ABC	CBS	MBS	NBC
9am	No School Today	This is New York, Danny O'Neill	Harry Hennessy, news	Top Tunes (8:30am)
9:15			The Answer Man	
9:30		Galen Drake, talk	The McCanns at Home	
9:45				
10am	Make Believe Ballroom		Martha Deane, talk	
10:15				
10:30		John Henry Faulk, talk		Mary Lee Taylor, cooking
10:45				
11am		The Robert Q. Lewis Show	Prescott Robinson, news	Carnival of Music
11:15			Remember with Tiny Fairbanks	
11:30			Farm Quiz	Woman in Love
11:45				
12pm	Space Patrol	The Armstrong Theater of Today	The Man on the Farm	
12:15				
12:30	No School Today	Stars Over Hollywood	Henry Gladstone, news	
12:45			Lorraine Sherwood, news	
1pm	Mary Margaret McBride, talk	City Hospital	The State of the Nation	The National Farm and Home Hour
1:15				
1:30		Music with the Hormel Girls	Barbara Welles, talk	Dr. Gino's Musicale
1:45				

DAYTIME — WINTER, 1954

Saturday

	ABC	CBS	MBS	NBC
2pm	The Metropolitan Opera	Let's Pretend	The Ruby Mercer Show	The Road Show
2:15				
2:30		Make Way for Youth	The Sounding Board	
2:45				
3pm		Report from Overseas	Bandstand USA	
3:15		Adventures in Science		
3:30		CBS Farm News	Deems Taylor Concert	
3:45		World Assignment		
4pm		UN on the Record	Rambling with Gambling	
4:15				
4:30		Saturday at the Chase		
4:45				
5pm	Tea and Crumpets	Washington, USA	The Show Shop	Skitch's Scratchbook
5:15				
5:30	Marines in Review	The Saturday Sports Review		
5:45		The Port of New York		

EVENING — SPRING, 1954

Sunday

	ABC	CBS	MBS	NBC
6pm	Don Gardiner, news	Gene Autry's Melody Ranch	Bulldog Drummond	The American Forum of the Air
6:15	Paul Harvey, news			
6:30	George Sokolsky, news	Our Miss Brooks	Bob Considine, sports	NBC Spring Symphony
6:45	Don Cornell, songs		Harry Wismer, sports	
7pm	This Week Around the World	The Lucky Strike Program, Jack Benny	The Rod and Gun Club	
7:15				
7:30	What's the Name of That Song	Amos 'n' Andy	Serenade in Blue	Theater Royal
7:45				
8pm	The American Music Hall	The General Electric Show, Bing Crosby	The Lutheran Hour	Sunday with Garroway
8:15				
8:30		My Little Margie	The Voice of Prophecy	
8:45				
9pm	Walter Winchell, gossip	The Hallmark Hall of Fame	Sammy Kaye's Sunday Serenade	
9:15	Taylor Grant, news			
9:30	Answers for Americans	The Charlie McCarthy Show	Author Meets the Critics	
9:45	Don Cornell, songs			
10pm	Paul Harvey, news	The Man of the Week	The Radio Bible Class	Inheritance
10:15	Elmer Davis, news			
10:30	Revival Time	Larry Leseuer, news	The Back to God Hour	Meet the Press
10:45		John Derr, sports		

EVENING — SPRING, 1954

Monday

ABC	CBS	MBS	NBC	
Walter Kiernan, news	Allan Jackson, news	News on the Human Side	Kenneth Banghart, news	6pm
Bobby Sherwood Orchestra	Curt Massey, songs	Dorothy and Dick, talk	Mel Allen, sports	6:15
The Nation's Business	Herman Hickman	Fred Vandeventer, news	Light Up Time, Jim Coy (6:25pm)	6:30
Bill Stern, sports	Lowell Thomas, news	Stan Lomax, sports	Three Star Extra	6:45
John W. Vandercook, news	The Tennessee Ernie Ford Show	Fulton Lewis Jr., news	Alex Dreier, news	7pm
Quincy Howe, news	The Beulah Show	The Answer Man	The Longines Symphonette	7:15
The Lone Ranger	The Julius La Rosa Show	Gabriel Heatter, news	Morgan Beatty, news	7:30
	Edward R. Murrow, news	Norman Brokenshire, news	One Man's Family	7:45
Henry J. Taylor, news	Suspense	The Falcon	The Railroad Hour	8pm
Sammy Kaye's Cameo Room				8:15
Hollywood Stairway	Arthur Godfrey's Talent Scouts	Under Arrest	The Voice of Firestone	8:30
Mike Malloy, Detective				8:45
Music By Camarata	The Lux Radio Theater	The Man from Times Square	The Bell Telephone Hour	9pm
				9:15
Doorway to the Future		Philo Vance	The Cities Service Band of America	9:30
				9:45
Spotlight, New York	The Camel Caravan, Vaughn Monroe	Frank Edwards, news	Fibber Magee and Molly	10pm
		Spotlight Story	The Heart of the News	10:15
	Melody in the Night	The Cisco Kid	Skitch's Scrapbook	10:30
				10:45

EVENING — SPRING, 1954

Tuesday

	ABC	CBS	MBS	NBC
6pm	Walter Kiernan, news	Allan Jackson, news	News on the Human Side	Kenneth Banghart, news
6:15	Bobby Sherwood Orchestra	Curt Massey, songs	Dorothy and Dick, talk	Mel Allen, sports
6:30	The Nation's Business	Herman Hickman	Fred Vandeventer, news	Light Up Time, Jim Coy (6:25pm)
6:45	Bill Stern, sports	Lowell Thomas, news	Stan Lomax, sports	Three Star Extra
7pm	John W. Vandercook, news	The Tennessee Ernie Ford Show	Fulton Lewis Jr., news	Alex Dreier, news
7:15	Quincy Howe, news	The Beulah Show	The Answer Man	The Longines Symphonette
7:30	Captain Starr of Space	The Longines Choraliers	Gabriel Heatter, news	Taylor Grant, news
7:45		Edward R. Murrow, news	Coke Time, Eddie Fisher	One Man's Family
8pm	Three City By-Line	People Are Funny	Mickey Spillane Mystery	The Dinah Shore Show
8:15	Sammy Kaye's Cameo Room			To Be Perfectly Frank
8:30	Hollywood Stairway	Mr. and Mrs. North	High Adventure	Barrie Craig, Confidential Investigator
8:45	Mike Malloy, Detective			
9pm	America's Town Meeting of the Air	Yours Truly, Johnny Dollar	The Man from Times Square	Dragnet
9:15				
9:30		My Friend Irma	Thirty Minutes to Go	Crime and Peter Chambers
9:45	Edwin D. Canham, news			
10pm	Spotlight, New York	Louella Parsons, gossip	Frank Edwards, news	Fibber Magee and Molly
10:15		Dance Orchestra	Spotlight Story	The Heart of the News
10:30		Melody in the Night	The Cisco Kid	Skitch's Scrapbook
10:45				

EVENING — SPRING, 1954

Wednesday

ABC	CBS	MBS	NBC	
Walter Kiernan, news	Allan Jackson, news	News on the Human Side	Kenneth Banghart, news	6pm
Bobby Sherwood Orchestra	Curt Massey, songs	Dorothy and Dick, talk	Mel Allen, sports	6:15
The Nation's Business	Herman Hickman	Fred Vandeventer, news	Light Up Time, Jim Coy (6:25pm)	6:30
Bill Stern, sports	Lowell Thomas, news	Stan Lomax, sports	Three Star Extra	6:45
John W. Vandercook, news	The Tennessee Ernie Ford Show	Fulton Lewis Jr., news	Alex Dreier, news	7pm
Quincy Howe, news	The Beulah Show	The Answer Man	The Longines Symphonette	7:15
The Lone Ranger	The Julius La Rosa Show	Gabriel Heatter, news	Morgan Beatty, news	7:30
	Edward R. Murrow, news	Norman Brokenshire, news	One Man's Family	7:45
Three City By-Line	The FBI in Peace and War	The Squad Room	Walk a Mile	8pm
Sammy Kaye's Cameo Room				8:15
Hollywood Stairway	The Twenty-First Precinct	Nightmare	The Great Gildersleeve	8:30
Mike Malloy, Detective				8:45
Hollywood Airport	Crime Photographer	The Man from Times Square	You Bet Your Life	9pm
				9:15
Mystery Theater	Crime Classics	Let George Do It	The Big Story	9:30
				9:45
Spotlight, New York	On Stage	Frank Edwards, news	Fibber Magee and Molly	10pm
		Spotlight Story	The Heart of the News	10:15
	Melody in the Night	The Cisco Kid	Skitch's Scrapbook	10:30
				10:45

EVENING — SPRING, 1954

Thursday

	ABC	CBS	MBS	NBC
6pm	Walter Kiernan, news	Allan Jackson, news	News on the Human Side	Kenneth Banghart, news
6:15	Bobby Sherwood Orchestra	Curt Massey, songs	Dorothy and Dick, talk	Mel Allen, sports
6:30	The Nation's Business	Herman Hickman	Fred Vandeventer, news	Light Up Time, Jim Coy (6:25pm)
6:45	Bill Stern, sports	Lowell Thomas, news	Stan Lomax, sports	Three Star Extra
7pm	John W. Vandercook, news	The Tennessee Ernie Ford Show	Fulton Lewis Jr., news	Alex Dreier, news
7:15	Quincy Howe, news	The Beulah Show	The Answer Man	The Longines Symphonette
7:30	Captain Starr of Space	The Longines Choraliers	Gabriel Heatter, news	Morgan Beatty, news
7:45		Edward R. Murrow, news	Coke Time, Eddie Fisher	One Man's Family
8pm	Three City By-Line	Meet Millie	Official Detective	The Roy Rogers Show
8:15	Sammy Kaye's Cameo Room			
8:30	Hollywood Stairway	Junior Miss	Crime Fighters	Meet Me at Kays
8:45	Mike Malloy, Detective			
9pm	Paul Whiteman Varieties	Meet Mr. McNutley	The Man from Times Square	
9:15				
9:30		Time for Love	Mystery House	The Eddie Cantor Show
9:45				
10pm	Spotlight, New York	Robert Trout, news	Frank Edwards, news	Fibber Magee and Molly
10:15		Dance Orchestra	Spotlight Story	The Heart of the News
10:30		Melody in the Night	The Cisco Kid	Pickens Party
10:45				

EVENING — SPRING, 1954

Friday

ABC	CBS	MBS	NBC	
Walter Kiernan, news	Allan Jackson, news	News on the Human Side	Kenneth Banghart, news	6pm
Bobby Sherwood Orchestra	Curt Massey, songs	Dorothy and Dick, talk	Mel Allen, sports	6:15
The Nation's Business	Herman Hickman	Fred Vandeventer, news	Light Up Time, Jim Coy (6:25pm)	6:30
Bill Stern, sports	Lowell Thomas, news	Stan Lomax, sports	Three Star Extra	6:45
John W. Vandercook, news	The Tennessee Ernie Ford Show	Fulton Lewis Jr., news	Alex Dreier, news	7pm
Quincy Howe, news	The Beulah Show	The Answer Man	The Longines Symphonette	7:15
The Lone Ranger	The Julius La Rosa Show	Gabriel Heatter, news	Morgan Beatty, news	7:30
	Edward R. Murrow, news	Norman Brokenshire, news	One Man's Family	7:45
Three City By-Line	Mr. Keen, Tracer of Lost Persons	Counterspy	The Dinah Shore Show	8pm
Sammy Kaye's Cameo Room			To Be Perfectly Frank	8:15
Hollywood Stairway	Arthur Godfrey's Digest	Take a Number	The Bob Hope Show	8:30
Mike Malloy, Detective				8:45
The Adventures of Ozzie and Harriet	Stage Struck	The Man from Times Square	The Phil Harris - Alice Faye Show	9pm
				9:15
The World We Live In	That's Rich	My Favorite Story	Can You Top This	9:30
				9:45
Madison Square Garden Boxing	Capitol Cloak Room	Frank Edwards, news	Fibber Magee and Molly	10pm
		Spotlight Story	The Heart of the News	10:15
	Melody in the Night	The Cisco Kid	Skitch's Scrapbook	10:30
				10:45

EVENING — SPRING, 1954

Saturday

	ABC	CBS	MBS	NBC
6pm	Make Believe Ballroom	Allan Jackson, news	News on the Human Side	Kenneth Banghart, news
6:15		UN on the Record	Facts Forum	H. V. Kaltenborn, news
6:30		John Derr, sports	Fred Vandeventer, news	People
6:45			Stan Lomax, sports	
7pm		The Johnny Mercer Show	Keep Healthy	Spotlight on Paris
7:15			Report from Washington	
7:30	Dinner at the Green Room		The US Navy Band	The Big Preview
7:45			The Globetrotters	
8pm	ABC Dancing Party	Gunsmoke	Farm Quiz	
8:15				
8:30		Gangbusters	The Family Theater	
8:45				
9pm		Two for the Money	The Search That Never Ends	
9:15				
9:30	Your Voice of America	Saturday Night, Country Style	Lombardoland USA	Forecast
9:45				
10pm	Spotlight, New York		The Chicago Theater of the Air	Bill's Place
10:15				
10:30		The Youth Opportunity Program		
10:45				

DAYTIME — SPRING, 1954

Sunday

	ABC	CBS	MBS	NBC
9am	Bible Study	News	News	Egbert and Ummly (8:30am)
9:15		The Music Room	Vacation Time	
9:30	The Voice of Prophecy	From the Organ Loft	The Mutual Radio Chapel	Carnival of Books
9:45				Music
10am	Message of Israel	The CBS Church of the Air	Henry Gladstone, news	The Comic Weekly Man
10:15			Public Affairs	
10:30	Negro College Choirs		Faith in Our Time	The Horn and Hardart Children's Hour
10:45			Bing Crosby Records	
11am	The World of Tomorrow	The Salt Lake Tabernacle Choir	Perry Como Records	
11:15				
11:30	Christian in Action	Invitation to Learning	Rambling with Gambling	Peter Roberts, news
11:45				World News Round-Up
12pm	Milton Cross, news	The Leading Question	John T. Flynn, news	Sunday Afternoon Music
12:15	Opportunity Limited		The Men's Corner	
12:30	The Herald of Truth	Howard K. Smith, news	Bill Cunningham, news	They Speak for Man
12:45		George Herman, news	Christian Science Monitor	
1pm	Dr. William Ward Ayer, talk	String Serenade	Sidney Walton, news	Citizens at Work
1:15			The Canary Pet Shop	
1:30	National Vespers	Let's Find Out	Festival of Opera	Citizens Union Spotlight
1:45				

DAYTIME — SPRING, 1954

Monday-Friday

ABC	CBS	MBS	NBC	
The Breakfast Club	This is New York, Danny O'Neill	Robert Hurleigh, news	Tex and Jinx, talk (8:30am)	9am
		John Gambling's Second Breakfast		9:15
	The Joan Edwards Show	The McCanns at Home	The Jim Coy Show	9:30
				9:45
My True Story	Arthur Godfrey Time	Cecil Brown, news	Welcome, Travelers	10am
		Martha Deane, talk		10:15
Whispering Streets			The Bob Hope Show	10:30
When a Girl Marries			Break the Bank	10:45
Modern Romances		The Madeleine Carroll Story	Strike It Rich	11am
Ever Since Eve				11:15
Thy Neighbor's Voice	Make Up Your Mind	Queen for a Day	The Phrase That Pays	11:30
Three City By-Line	Rosemary		Second Chance	11:45
Charles F. McCarthy, news	Wendy Warren and the News	Curt Massey, songs	Faye Emerson, talk	12pm
George Ansbro Presents	Aunt Jenny's True Life Stories	Here's to My Lady		12:15
Maggie McNellis, talk	The Romance of Helen Trent	Henry Gladstone, news		12:30
	Our Gal Sunday	Tello-Test Quiz		12:45
Mary Margaret McBride, talk	The Road of Life	Heatherton House	The Jim Coy Show	1pm
	Ma Perkins			1:15
	Young Dr. Malone			1:30
	The Guiding Light			1:45

DAYTIME — SPRING, 1954

Sunday

	ABC	CBS	MBS	NBC
2pm	Healing Waters	The Longines Symphonette		The Catholic Hour
2:15				
2:30	Wings of Healing	New York Philharmonic Orchestra		Youth Wants to Know
2:45				
3pm	Dr. James McGinley, talk			Anthology - Poetry Series
3:15				
3:30	The Hour of Decision			The National Radio Pulpit
3:45			Music from Britain	
4pm	The Old Fashioned Revival Hour	The Twentieth Century Concert Hall		Weekend
4:15				
4:30		The World Today	Flight in the Blue	
4:45				
5pm	Evening Comes	Stagestruck	The Shadow	
5:15				
5:30	The Greatest Story Ever Told		True Detective Mysteries	
5:45				

DAYTIME — SPRING, 1954

Monday-Friday

ABC	CBS	MBS	NBC	
Dean Cameron, talk	The Second Mrs. Burton	The McCanns at Home	The Herb Sheldon Show	2pm
	Perry Mason	Pat Barnes, talk		2:15
Make Believe Ballroom	This is Nora Drake	Barbara Welles, talk		2:30
	The Brighter Day			2:45
	Hilltop House	The Radio City Playhouse	Life Can Be Beautiful	3pm
	House Party		The Road of Life	3:15
			Pepper Young's Family	3:30
	The Walter O'Keefe Show		The Right to Happiness	3:45
	The Emily Kimbrough Show		Mary Noble, Backstage Wife	4pm
			Stella Dallas	4:15
	Galen Drake, talk		Young Widder Brown	4:30
			The Woman in My House	4:45
	John Henry Faulk, talk	Bobby Benson /	Just Plain Bill	5pm
		Sergeant Preston for the Yukon	Front Page Farrell	5:15
		Wild Bill Hickok /	Lorenzo Jones	5:30
		Sky King	It Pays to Be Married	5:45

DAYTIME — SPRING, 1954

Saturday

	ABC	CBS	MBS	NBC
9am	No School Today	This is New York, Danny O'Neill	The Answer Man	Wake Up Easy (8:30am)
9:15			Bing Crosby Records	
9:30		Galen Drake, talk	The McCanns at Home	Top Tunes
9:45				
10am	Make Believe Ballroom		Martha Deane, talk	
10:15				
10:30		The Robert Q. Lewis Show		Mary Lee Taylor, cooking
10:45				
11am			Prescott Robinson, news	Carnival of Music
11:15			Here's to Vets	
11:30			The Johnny Olsen Show	
11:45				
12pm	Space Patrol	The Armstrong Theater of Today	The Man on the Farm	
12:15				
12:30	No School Today	Stars Over Hollywood	Henry Gladstone, news	
12:45			Lorraine Sherwood, talk	
1pm	Mary Margaret McBride, talk	City Hospital	The State of the Nation	The National Farm and Home Hour
1:15				
1:30		The Peter Lind Hayes Show	Hawaii Calls	Music of America
1:45				

DAYTIME — SPRING, 1954

Saturday

	ABC	CBS	MBS	NBC
2pm	Platterbrains	Let's Pretend	The Ruby Mercer Show	The Road Show
2:15				
2:30	The Art Fleming Show	Make Way for Youth	Barbara Welles, talk	
2:45				
3pm		Report from Overseas	Deems Taylor Concert	
3:15		Adventures in Science		
3:30		CBS Farm News	Sloan Simpson, talk	
3:45		World Assignment		
4pm	Horse Racing	String Serenade	The Show Shop	
4:15	Recorded Music	The Port of New York		
4:30		Saturday at the Chase		
4:45				
5pm		Treasury Bandstand	Teenagers Unlimited	Skitch's Scratchbook
5:15				
5:30		The Saturday Sports Review		The Sixth Burrough
5:45		The Longines Symphonette		

EVENING — SUMMER, 1954

Sunday

	ABC	CBS	MBS	NBC
6pm	Don Gardiner, news	Gene Autry's Melody Ranch	Nick Carter, Master Detective	The American Forum of the Air
6:15	Paul Harvey, news			
6:30	George Sokolsky, news	Summer in St. Louis	Bob Considine, sports	NBC Summer Symphony
6:45	Quincy Howe, news		Harry Wismer, sports	
7pm	Highway Frolics, Jimmy Nelson	Jukebox Jury	The Rod and Gun Club	
7:15				
7:30			John Scott, news	Conversation
7:45			The Globetrotters	
8pm		The Gary Crosby Show	The Lutheran Hour	Sunday with Garroway
8:15				
8:30		My Little Margie	The Voice of Prophecy	
8:45				
9pm	Taylor Grant, news	The Cobbs	The Army Hour	
9:15	Frank Coniff, news			
9:30	Highway Frolics, Jimmy Nelson	Freddy Martin Orchestra	Author Meets the Critics	
9:45				
10pm	Paul Harvey, news	The Man of the Week	The Radio Bible Class	Inheritance
10:15	George Hamilton Combs, news			
10:30	Revival Time	Report from the UN	The Back to God Hour	Meet the Press
10:45		Blair Clark, news		

EVENING — SUMMER, 1954

Monday

ABC	CBS	MBS	NBC	
Walter Kiernan, news	Allan Jackson, news	News on the Human Side	Kenneth Banghart, news	6pm
Bobby Sherwood Orchestra	Curt Massey, songs	Dorothy and Dick, talk	Mel Allen, sports	6:15
The Nation's Business	Herman Hickman	Fred Vandeventer, news	Light Up Time, Jim Coy (6:25pm)	6:30
Frank Frisch, sports	Lowell Thomas, news	Stan Lomax, sports	Three Star Extra	6:45
John W. Vandercook, news	The Tennessee Ernie Ford Show	Fulton Lewis Jr., news	Guy Lombardo Orchestra	7pm
Quincy Howe, news	The Peter Lind Hayes Show	The Answer Man		7:15
The Lone Ranger		Gabriel Heatter, news	Morgan Beatty, news	7:30
	Charles Collingwood, news	Dinner Date	One Man's Family	7:45
Henry J. Taylor, news	My Friend Irma	The Falcon	The Hollywood Bowl	8pm
The American Music Hall				8:15
The Voice of Firestone	Arthur Godfrey's Talent Scouts	Under Arrest		8:30
				8:45
Music By Camarata	Gunsmoke	The Man from Times Square	The Bell Telephone Hour	9pm
				9:15
Sammy Kaye's Serenade	Gangbusters	Philo Vance	The Cities Service Band of America	9:30
				9:45
George Hamilton Combs, news	Mr. Keen, Tracer of Lost Persons	Harry Flannery, news	Fibber Magee and Molly	10pm
The Helen Hall Show	The Milt Herth Trio	Spotlight Story	The Heart of the News	10:15
Spotlight, New York	Melody in the Night	The Cisco Kid	The Stan Freeman Show	10:30
				10:45

EVENING — SUMMER, 1954

Tuesday

	ABC	CBS	MBS	NBC
6pm	Walter Kiernan, news	Allan Jackson, news	News on the Human Side	Kenneth Banghart, news
6:15	Bobby Sherwood Orchestra	Curt Massey, songs	Dorothy and Dick, talk	Mel Allen, sports
6:30	The Nation's Business	Herman Hickman	Fred Vandeventer, news	Light Up Time, Jim Coy (6:25pm)
6:45	Frank Frisch, sports	Lowell Thomas, news	Stan Lomax, sports	Three Star Extra
7pm	John W. Vandercook, news	The Tennessee Ernie Ford Show	Fulton Lewis Jr., news	Guy Lombardo Orchestra
7:15	Quincy Howe, news	The Peter Lind Hayes Show	The Answer Man	
7:30	The Silver Eagle		Gabriel Heatter, news	Morgan Beatty, news
7:45		Edward R. Murrow, news	Dinner Date	One Man's Family
8pm	The Jack Gregson Variety Show	People Are Funny	Mickey Spillane Mystery	It Happens to You
8:15				To Be Perfectly Frank
8:30		Stop the Music	High Adventure	Barrie Craig, Confidential Investigator
8:45				
9pm	America's Town Meeting of the Air	Yours Truly, Johnny Dollar	The Man from Times Square	Dragnet
9:15				
9:30		The Jack Carson Show	Thirty Minutes to Go	Crime and Peter Chambers
9:45	Edwin D. Canham, news			
10pm	George Hamilton Combs, news	Mr. Keen, Tracer of Lost Persons	Harry Flannery, news	Fibber Magee and Molly
10:15	The Helen Hall Show	Dance Orchestra	Spotlight Story	The Heart of the News
10:30	Spotlight, New York	Melody in the Night	The Cisco Kid	The Stan Freeman Show
10:45				

EVENING — SUMMER, 1954

Wednesday

ABC	CBS	MBS	NBC	
Walter Kiernan, news	Allan Jackson, news	News on the Human Side	Kenneth Banghart, news	6pm
Bobby Sherwood Orchestra	Curt Massey, songs	Dorothy and Dick, talk	Mel Allen, sports	6:15
The Nation's Business	Herman Hickman	Fred Vandeventer, news	Light Up Time, Jim Coy (6:25pm)	6:30
Frank Frisch, sports	Lowell Thomas, news	Stan Lomax, sports	Three Star Extra	6:45
John W. Vandercook, news	The Tennessee Ernie Ford Show	Fulton Lewis Jr., news	Guy Lombardo Orchestra	7pm
Quincy Howe, news	The Peter Lind Hayes Show	The Answer Man		7:15
The Lone Ranger		Gabriel Heatter, news	Morgan Beatty, news	7:30
	Edward R. Murrow, news	Dinner Date	One Man's Family	7:45
The Jack Gregson Variety Show	The FBI in Peace and War	The Squad Room	The News Game	8pm
				8:15
	The Twenty-First Precinct	Nightmare	Spend a Million	8:30
				8:45
Sammy Kaye's Serenade	Crime Photographer	The Man from Times Square	You Bet Your Life	9pm
				9:15
Paul Whiteman Varieties	The Jack Carson Show	Let George Do It	Theater Royal	9:30
				9:45
George Hamilton Combs, news	Mr. Keen, Tracer of Lost Persons	Harry Flannery, news	Fibber Magee and Molly	10pm
The Helen Hall Show	Dance Orchestra	Spotlight Story	The Heart of the News	10:15
Spotlight, New York	Melody in the Night	The Cisco Kid	The Stan Freeman Show	10:30
				10:45

EVENING — SUMMER, 1954

Thursday

	ABC	CBS	MBS	NBC
6pm	Walter Kiernan, news	Allan Jackson, news	News on the Human Side	Kenneth Banghart, news
6:15	Bobby Sherwood Orchestra	Curt Massey, songs	Dorothy and Dick, talk	Mel Allen, sports
6:30	The Nation's Business	Herman Hickman	Fred Vandeventer, news	Light Up Time, Jim Coy (6:25pm)
6:45	Frank Frisch, sports	Lowell Thomas, news	Stan Lomax, sports	Three Star Extra
7pm	John W. Vandercook, news	The Tennessee Ernie Ford Show	Fulton Lewis Jr., news	Guy Lombardo Orchestra
7:15	Quincy Howe, news	The Peter Lind Hayes Show	The Answer Man	
7:30	The Silver Eagle		Gabriel Heatter, news	Morgan Beatty, news
7:45		Edward R. Murrow, news	Dinner Date	One Man's Family
8pm	The Jack Gregson Variety Show	Meet Millie	Official Detective	The Roy Rogers Show
8:15				
8:30		That's Rich	Crime Fighters	Meet Me at Kays
8:45				
9pm	Sammy Kaye's Serenade	On Stage	The Man from Times Square	
9:15				
9:30	Paul Whiteman Varieties	The Jack Carson Show	Mystery House	The Eddie Cantor Show
9:45	Bill Stern, sports			
10pm	George Hamilton Combs, news	Mr. Keen, Tracer of Lost Persons	Harry Flannery, news	Fibber Magee and Molly
10:15	The Helen Hall Show	Dance Orchestra	Spotlight Story	The Heart of the News
10:30	Spotlight, New York	Melody in the Night	The Cisco Kid	Pickens Party
10:45				

EVENING — SUMMER, 1954

Friday

ABC	CBS	MBS	NBC	
Walter Kiernan, news	Allan Jackson, news	News on the Human Side	Kenneth Banghart, news	6pm
Bobby Sherwood Orchestra	Curt Massey, songs	Dorothy and Dick, talk	Mel Allen, sports	6:15
The Nation's Business	Herman Hickman	Fred Vandeventer, news	Light Up Time, Jim Coy (6:25pm)	6:30
Frank Frisch, sports	Lowell Thomas, news	Stan Lomax, sports	Three Star Extra	6:45
John W. Vandercook, news	The Tennessee Ernie Ford Show	Fulton Lewis Jr., news	Guy Lombardo Orchestra	7pm
Quincy Howe, news	The Peter Lind Hayes Show	The Answer Man		7:15
The Lone Ranger		Gabriel Heatter, news	Morgan Beatty, news	7:30
	Edward R. Murrow, news	Maggie McNellis, news	One Man's Family	7:45
The Jack Gregson Variety Show	Mr. Keen, Tracer of Lost Persons	Counterspy	Hear America Swingin'	8pm
				8:15
	Arthur Godfrey's Digest	Take a Number		8:30
				8:45
Sammy Kaye's Serenade		The Man from Times Square		9pm
				9:15
The World We Live In	The Jack Carson Show	Strictly Private		9:30
				9:45
Football Forecast	Mr. Keen, Tracer of Lost Persons	Harry Flannery, news	Fibber Magee and Molly	10pm
	Dance Orchestra	Spotlight Story	The Heart of the News	10:15
Spotlight, New York	Melody in the Night	The Cisco Kid	The Stan Freeman Show	10:30
				10:45

EVENING — SUMMER, 1954

Saturday

	ABC	CBS	MBS	NBC
6pm	Make Believe Ballroom	News	News on the Human Side	News
6:15		UN on the Record	Facts Forum	H. V. Kaltenborn, news
6:30			Fred Vandeventer, news	People
6:45		Capitol Cloak Room	Stan Lomax, sports	
7pm		John Derr, sports	Keep Healthy	Spotlight on Paris
7:15			The Globetrotters	
7:30	Dinner at the Green Room	Les Elgart Orchestra	Have a Heart	The Big Preview
7:45				
8pm	ABC Dancing Party	Escape	True or False	
8:15				
8:30		Night Watch	The Family Theater	
8:45				
9pm		Two for the Money	The Search That Never Ends	
9:15				
9:30		Saturday Night, Country Style	Lombardoland USA	Bill's Place
9:45				
10pm	Ozark Jubilee		The Chicago Theater of the Air	
10:15				
10:30	Spotlight, New York	Dance Orchestra		
10:45				

DAYTIME — SUMMER, 1954

Sunday

	ABC	CBS	MBS	NBC
9am	Bible Study	News	News	Egbert and Ummly (8:30am)
9:15		The Music Room	Your Navy Show	
9:30	The Voice of Prophecy	From the Organ Loft	The Mutual Radio Chapel	Carnival of Books
9:45				Children's Music
10am	Message of Israel	The CBS Church of the Air	Henry Gladstone, news	The Comic Weekly Man
10:15			Christian Science Monitor	
10:30	Negro College Choirs		Guest Star	The Horn and Hardart Children's Hour
10:45			Bing Crosby Records	
11am	The World of Tomorrow	The Salt Lake Tabernacle Choir	Henry Gladstone, news	
11:15			Keep Healthy	
11:30	Christian in Action	Invitation to Learning	Rambling with Gambling	News
11:45				
12pm	Pan American Music	The Leading Question	John T. Flynn, news	Sunday Afternoon Music
12:15			The Men's Corner	
12:30	The Herald of Truth	Howard K. Smith, news	Bill Cunningham, news	The Eternal Light
12:45		George Herman, news	The Globetrotters	
1pm	Dr. William Ward Ayer, talk	Your Invitation to Music	Hawaii Calls	Man's Right to Knowledge
1:15				
1:30	Pilgrimage		Festival of Opera	Citizens Union Spotlight
1:45				

DAYTIME — SUMMER, 1954

Monday-Friday

ABC	CBS	MBS	NBC	
The Breakfast Club	This is New York, Danny O'Neill	Robert Hurleigh, news	Tex and Jinx, talk (8:30am)	9am
		John Gambling's Second Breakfast		9:15
	The Joan Edwards Show	The McCanns at Home	The Jim Coy Show	9:30
				9:45
My True Story	Arthur Godfrey Time	Cecil Brown, news	The Bob Smith Show	10am
		Martha Deane, talk		10:15
Whispering Streets				10:30
When a Girl Marries			Break the Bank	10:45
Modern Romances		Florida Calling	Strike It Rich	11am
Ever Since Eve				11:15
Dean Cameron, talk	Make Up Your Mind	Queen for a Day	The Phrase That Pays	11:30
	Rosemary		Second Chance	11:45
Charles F. McCarthy, news	Wendy Warren and the News	Guest Time	Jack Ladelle, talk	12pm
George Ansbro Presents	Aunt Jenny's True Life Stories	Here's to My Lady		12:15
Maggie McNellis, talk	The Romance of Helen Trent	Henry Gladstone, news		12:30
	Our Gal Sunday	The Answer Man		12:45
The Frank Farrell Show	The Road of Life	Heatherton House	The Jim Coy Show	1pm
	Ma Perkins			1:15
Mort Lindsay Orchestra	Young Dr. Malone			1:30
	The Guiding Light			1:45

DAYTIME — SUMMER, 1954

Sunday

	ABC	CBS	MBS	NBC
2pm				The Catholic Hour
2:15				
2:30	Wings of Healing	String Serenade		Youth Wants to Know
2:45				
3pm	Dr. James McGinley, talk	Eddie Gallaher's Music		Anthology - Poetry Series
3:15				
3:30	The Hour of Decision	Musical Hits		The National Radio Pulpit
3:45			Promenade Symphony of Toronto	
4pm	The Old Fashioned Revival Hour	The Terry Allen Trio		Weekend
4:15		Recorded Music		
4:30		Stuart Foster and Louise Carlyle	Flight in the Blue	
4:45				
5pm	Highway Frolics, Jimmy Nelson		The Shadow	
5:15				
5:30		The World Today	True Detective Mysteries	
5:45				

DAYTIME — SUMMER, 1954

Monday-Friday

ABC	CBS	MBS	NBC	
	The Second Mrs. Burton	The McCanns at Home	The Herb Sheldon Show	2pm
	Perry Mason	Tello-Test Quiz		2:15
Make Believe Ballroom	This is Nora Drake	Barbara Welles, talk		2:30
	The Brighter Day			2:45
	Hilltop House	The Radio City Playhouse	Welcome, Travelers	3pm
	House Party			3:15
			Pepper Young's Family	3:30
	Mike's and Buff's Mailbag		The Right to Happiness	3:45
	Galen Drake, talk		Mary Noble, Backstage Wife	4pm
			Stella Dallas	4:15
	The Lanny Ross Show		Young Widder Brown	4:30
			The Woman in My House	4:45
	John Henry Faulk, talk	Bobby Benson	Just Plain Bill	5pm
			Front Page Farrell	5:15
			Lorenzo Jones	5:30
		Cecil Brown, news (5:55pm)	It Pays to Be Married	5:45

DAYTIME — SUMMER, 1954

Saturday

	ABC	CBS	MBS	NBC
9am	The Mort Lindsey Show	The Bob Haymes Show	The Answer Man	Wake Up Easy (8:30am)
9:15		The Robert Q. Lewis Show	Bing Crosby Records	
9:30			Galen Drake, talk	Top Tunes
9:45				
10am	Make Believe Ballroom		Martha Deane, talk	
10:15				
10:30				Mary Lee Taylor, cooking
10:45				
11am			Prescott Robinson, news	John Conte, talk
11:15			Here's to Vets	
11:30			The Johnny Olsen Show	The Jim Coy Show
11:45				
12pm	Space Patrol	The Armstrong Theater of Today	The Man on the Farm	
12:15				
12:30	No School Today	Stars Over Hollywood	Harry Gladstone, news	The Home Gardener
12:45			Lorraine Sherwood, talk	
1pm	The US Navy Band	City Hospital	The State of the Nation	The National Farm and Home Hour
1:15				
1:30	The Art Fleming Show	Let's Pretend	Wonderful City	Home on the Range
1:45				

DAYTIME — SUMMER, 1954

Saturday

	ABC	CBS	MBS	NBC
2pm	Music Festival	Syncopation Piece	The Ruby Mercer Show	The Road Show
2:15				
2:30		Tony Pastor Orchestra	Barbara Welles, talk	
2:45				
3pm		Report from Overseas	Musical Almanac	
3:15		Adventures in Science		
3:30		CBS Farm News	Musical Caravan	
3:45		World Assignment		
4pm	Chatauqua Symphony Orchestra	Operation Music	The Show Shop	
4:15		The Port of New York		
4:30		Johnny Long Orchestra		
4:45				
5pm	Pauline Carter, piano	Washington, USA	Teenagers Unlimited	Skitch's Hi-Fi
5:15	Horse Racing			
5:30	It's Your Business	Saturday at the Chase		
5:45	The AFL-CIO Program			

Bear Manor Media

Classic Cinema.
Timeless TV.
Retro Radio.

WWW.BEARMANORMEDIA.COM

www.ingramcontent.com/pod-product-compliance
Lightning Source LLC
Chambersburg PA
CBHW051332230426
43668CB00010B/1242